More praise for *Barefoot on Holy Ground*

"*Barefoot on Holy Ground* is an invaluable guidebook that will help each of us accomplish the work we have come to Planet Earth to do. This book is packed with insight and wisdom: insight into the joys and challenges, and wisdom into the pitfalls and snags that will confront each of us if we are genuinely pursuing our soul assignments. Gloria Karpinski is a very wise woman. She is an important teacher who articulates the spiritual demands placed upon those of us longing to be of service in our world."

—THE REVEREND DR. LAUREN ARTRESS
Author of *Walking a Sacred Path*:
Rediscovering the Labyrinth as a Spiritual Tool

"All the ground we walk on is always holy; realizing that is another matter. Gloria's wonderful and highly practical book on spiritual craftsmanship goes a long way towards helping us gain and keep that realization."

—DAVID SPANGLER
Author of *Blessing* and *Everyday Miracles*

BAREFOOT ON HOLY GROUND

TWELVE LESSONS IN SPIRITUAL CRAFTSMANSHIP

Gloria D. Karpinski

THE RANDOM HOUSE PUBLISHING GROUP • NEW YORK

A Ballantine Books Trade Paperback Edition

Copyright © 2001 by Gloria Karpinski

All rights reserved.

Published in the United States by Ballantine Books, an imprint of The Random House Publishing Group, a division of Random House, Inc., New York, and distributed in Canada by Random House of Canada Limited, Toronto.

Ballantine and colophon are registered trademarks of Random House, Inc.

www.ballantinebooks.com

Grateful acknowledgment is made to the following for permission to reprint previously published material:

Daniel Ladinsky: excerpts from "All the Hemispheres" by Hafiz, translated by Daniel Ladinsky, from *The Subject Tonight is Love* by Daniel Ladinsky. Copyright © 1996 by Daniel Ladinsky.

Many Rivers Press: "The Opening of Eyes" by David Whyte from *Where Rivers Meet* by David Whyte. Copyright © 1990 by David Whyte. Reprinted by permission of the publisher.

New Directions Publishing Corporation: excerpt from "A Buddha in the Woodpile" by Lawrence Ferlinghetti from *These Are My Rivers.* Copyright © 1993 by Lawrence Ferlinghetti. Reprinted by permission of New Directions Publishing Corp.

Library of Congress Catalog Card Number: 00-193532

ISBN 978-0-345-43509-5

Manufactured in the United States of America

Cover design by Barbara Leff
Cover photo © Jane Vollers/Photonica
Interior design by Ann Gold

First Edition: May 2001

10   9   8

Dedicated with love and gratitude to
my daughter, Dawn, and my son, Carlton,
for the privilege of being your mother, the joy of being your friend,
and the grace of sharing your path

THE OPENING OF EYES

That day I saw beneath dark clouds
the passing light over the water
and I heard the voice of the world speak out.
I knew then, as I had before
life is no passing memory of what has been
nor the remaining pages in a great book
waiting to be read.

It is the opening of eyes long closed.
It is the vision of far off things
seen for the silence they hold.
It is the heart after years
of secret conversing
speaking out loud in the clear air.

It is Moses in the desert
fallen to his knees before the lit bush.
It is the man throwing away his shoes
as if to enter heaven
and finding himself astonished,
opened at last,
fallen in love with solid ground.

—from *Songs for Coming Home*,
   David Whyte

Contents

✤

Contents

Acknowledgments

✤

When I first started teaching and counseling, I made a contract with Spirit that I would not speak of things I didn't know, even though I would certainly quote and continue to learn from wise ones. Fortunately I learned the potency of "I don't know," which creates vacuums that can then be filled.

Little did I know when I started this book all that would come as I lived out that contract with Spirit. The moment I announced my intention to write such a book, I set a powerful magnet in place in my own discipleship. It was as if Spirit said, "You want to write about staying poised in chaos? Well, how about a little practicum?"

So the events in my life heated up on every front, all of which provided an amazing amount of grist for the mill. Sitting with dozens of files that represented years of experience with hundreds of people, I was overwhelmed both by what I know and by what I don't know. I felt I had agreed to write about the world and give examples. When I finally, reluctantly, admitted that the whole thing was actually quite impossible, I surrendered to it. With surrender came grace. And, as it usually does, the grace arrived through people.

I cannot begin to thank my family and close friends enough for their consistent support as month after month they heard my mantra, "After the book." To each and every one, I bow to you from my heart. Your love and loyalty is written into these pages, and I will always be grateful to you.

There are some people whom I must name, as they have provided exceptional support to this project. To my mother, Elizabeth Gilmore; and to my son, Carlton, and his wife, Leslie; to my daughter, Dawn, and her husband, Mitch; thank you for the countless ways you not only have continued to enrich my life, but have communicated to me how much you respected and understood my dedication to this book. To Joshua, Kristen, Patrick, Kevin, and Alex, not only does your presence in my life bring me joy, but you make the vision of a more balanced world immediate, personal, and imperative.

Judith Alexander has truly been my book angel. From the origin of the idea to the last draft, she has never faltered in her enthusiasm and encouragement, reading the manuscript many times and always sharing from her wise-woman well of wisdom. For her friendship and her uncompromised faith in me and this project, I am deeply grateful.

Faye Collett has been another book blessing. Working as my assistant through much of the book's pregnancy, she was a good labor coach at its birthing, preparing the final manuscript with careful and loving dedication.

Early in the book's development, Robin Blair Harmon, with her sharp mind and creative insight, provided a clear mirror for my ideas while she also kept the office running.

The universe has blessed me with two other personal assistants through the years, Meredith Holladay-Adler and Julie Flack. Each of these women—Faye, Robin, Meredith, and Julie—is a talented, accomplished professional, and I am appreciative of them for more reasons than could possibly be enumerated.

One test of true discipleship is the willingness to support another disciple's work. My deepest gratitude goes to Catherine

Jourdan, who added to her already busy professional schedule as a therapist by providing assistance to me several hours a week when I was between assistants and pushing tight deadlines.

Stephanie Bartis, Kathy Clark, and Gay Baynes were always there for me from the first moment I exclaimed, "What *have* I agreed to do?" Through all the rewrites, the dramas, and the traumas, to the end, their encouragement has never wavered. They always believed in my intention with this book and supported it in both spiritual and practical ways.

My life and this project have been richly blessed by friends who are also dedicated disciples. I salute their commitment and thank them for all the ways they renew my faith in my own path and the One Path we are walking. Reluctantly, I can only list the following, but I truly wish I could write a testimony to each of them, for they were, like divine grace, there when I really needed them: Susan Peterson, Vaughn Boone, Jan Adams, Lauren Artress, Linda Beatrice Brown, Stephanie Cole, Dave Boyer, Andy Silver, Ginny Wright, Ellis Pearce, Bob and Carol Wells, Eugene and Gail LeBauer, Travis and Linda Jackson, Rikki Rhoten, Nancy Prescott, Florence Bacchetta, Gabrielle Beard, Cass Cattlett, May Fleihan, Andre and Theres Studer, Susan and Roger Kennedy, Michelle Powers, Donna and Dave Gulick, Lynn Hill.

I am grateful to all the workshop participants, sponsors, and clients who have given me the privilege of sharing with them. They have been and continue to be my teachers and inspirations.

I am also indebted to the 125 busy disciples who shared their precious time and wisdom with me in the Discipleship Forums. Their energy, wisdom, and experience are an inseparable part of this book.

There is probably no way to fully thank an editor who believes in a book. Cheryl Woodruff is herself a disciple of the spiritual path. While protecting the manuscript as it endured the delays brought on by everything from family surgeries to publishing mergers, she never gave up on it or compromised its intention.

This book has benefited enormously from her editorial skills. I am grateful to her, as I am to the two editors who assisted her: Barbara Shorr, who before her death guided the first major and necessary cuts, and Gary Brozak, who not only assisted Cheryl in the editing, but brought to it many helpful perspectives. As the book entered its last phase, another grace arrived in the person of Joelle Delbourgo, an agent, whose acceptance of this project was an encouragement now and for the future.

Above all I thank the Mother-Father-God for the privilege of making this offering, and for the grace that was, is, and always shall be present.

Namaste.

> *The Twelfth Number leadeth the dance.*
> *All whose nature is to dance doth dance*
> *Who danceth not, knows not what is being done.*
> —From the Hymn of Jesus,
>   Acts of John, Gnostic Gospel

BAREFOOT ON
HOLY GROUND

**Twelve Lessons in
Spiritual Craftsmanship**

BOOK ONE

CHOOSING TO LIVE ON PURPOSE

The New Disciples

All the way to heaven is heaven.
—Catherine of Sienna, fourteenth century

As we move into the twenty-first century, spiritual inquiry has entered a phase of ripening maturity. Today a large number of seekers have abandoned the glitz and glamour of so-called spiritual trappings. They are more sober and realistic about the quest, better educated, less naive about quick weekend fixes, and generally less argumentative and resistant.

Over the last three decades, more and more of us have become aware of the interconnectedness of mind, body, and spirit. We've been rebirthed, reparented, Rolfed, and realigned with acupuncture, chiropractic, homeopathy, therapeutic massages, and energy work. We've been recovered and 12-stepped, cleared and cleansed with everything from colonics to sage, sweats to primal screams. We've learned to find shadows, codependent patterns, past lives, and lost inner children. We've given up cigarettes, hard liquor, and red meat and taken up veggies, flower essences, and herbs. We know our cholesterol levels and our heart rates. We know where the sun and moon are on our astrological charts, the number personal year we're in, our enneagram and Myers/Briggs acronyms.

We've gone to workshops for our souls, our sex lives, our aura, and our finances. We've filled countless notebooks from more lectures than anyone can name and spent weeks in ashrams, convents, monasteries, and retreat centers. We've meditated, recycled, networked, drummed, danced, inner-journeyed, and chanted in a dozen languages. We've listened to gurus, shamans, channelers, visiting lecturers, and a multitude of teachers who act as escorts through our passages.

And now are we all saints and masters? Probably not. Are we more awake? I think so. Are we more prepared to carry out our missions? Probably. For all the flaws and missteps, the dabbling and psychobabbling, and in spite of the ever-present potential for narcissism and inflation, through the process many of us have been made ready for our assignments in the world.

A new breed of spiritual seekers has emerged in the last several decades. I call them disciples—awake, aware, committed, and global in worldview. They have been identified by many names, among them Transitionists (journalist Marilyn Ferguson), Enzymes (futurist William Irwin), socially transcendent (author and business consultant Marsha Sinetar), preservers, promoters, and prophets (minister and author Louis Richard Batzler), new world servers (the Tibetan channeled through Alice Bailey). They come in many forms and from many backgrounds, and these new disciples are all rolling up their sleeves to do the work they came to do.

At first I hesitated to use the word *disciple* in this book. Perhaps what seemed most risky about the word is that it has usually meant devotion to one particular spiritual or religious tradition, but it also holds creative, active energy of consciousness. A disciple is one who recognizes, commits to, and is obedient to the promptings of his or her inner spiritual imperative and chooses to bring that consciousness into every aspect of life.

Disciples are responsible for themselves, knowing they are always in the process of growing and choosing to shape their personalities to serve their spiritual intentions. Disciples tend to be open, flexible, and teachable, inclusive in their worldview and dedicated to participating in the healing of planetary challenges. In the movie *City of Joy*, one of the characters says there are three ways to go through life: run, observe, or commit. Disciples commit.

Disciples are found everywhere and are identified by their *being*, not necessarily by their *doing*. Disciples tend to call forth the positive and the good in every circumstance. One by one they discipline their resources—body, mind, emotions, money, careers—and these resources become their servants, not their masters.

Disciples struggle under the weight of rules imposed by external authorities but gradually grow freer by their obedience to inner guidance. So whenever you see the word *disciple* in this book, put in parentheses in your mind *freeman* or *freewoman*.

Disciples have matured in consciousness from "saving the world" into serving the world. Some are true visionaries, often appearing hundreds of years ahead of their time. They bring the first hints of changes to come. Today they are sometimes just minutes ahead of the rest of us because the lag time is closing between those who sound the call and those who respond. Dr. Martin Luther King Jr. is an example of a true visionary who saw and spoke the dream for those who would follow.

Next come the rebels. Their job is to disturb the status quo, and they usually do. They push against boundaries wherever they focus their attention, challenging systems, exploring, even demanding new possibilities. Whether they question health care or education, a scientific assumption or a local environmental problem, they challenge our conceptions of reality at the nuts-and-bolts level. They are innovative, creative, and sometimes downright outrageous. Suffragettes and their sisters who followed are examples of rebels who challenged accepted societal myths.

Some disciples are here on assignments of preservation. The job of the conservationist disciple is to hold on to the accrued good we have already learned and attained. When they do their job well, they keep us from enacting changes too quickly during a transition. Those who defend the Constitution, especially the Bill of Rights, are an example. Even as we have to adapt and redefine our understanding of those documents so that all people benefit from guaranteed rights, we have to maintain the stability of the document in the first place.

Some people are <u>bridges</u> who grasp the new vision and figure out pragmatic ways to make it work in the material world. They may come up with practical new ideas for elder care or offer new plans for integrating non-English-speaking students into a public school. An example of bridge building is reflected in the new forms of mediation, for example, in settling differences between industrialists and environmentalists.

Whether we are here to dream, preserve, disturb, heal, implement, or model, modern disciples learn that the dreams in our hearts have to be matched by our craftsmanship in the world. No matter what role we are chosen to play, the important thing is to realize that we are neither the role we are playing nor the play itself. We are the playwright, the creator behind all the drama. The more clearly we know that, the better we play our part.

Even so, each disciple faces the challenge of how best to play the part he or she is assigned. A letter from a friend who accepted a major new appointment in her profession characterizes the initial difficulty. "Oh, Gloria," she wrote, "how does one wear the purple?" She meant, how do any of us step into our roles with authority and humility?

Spiritual Craftsmanship

We don't automatically know how to live our truths. It takes careful craftsmanship to bring truth into the material world.

Individuals in all traditions demonstrate the possibility of spiritual craftsmanship through the peace and clarity with which they craft their lives. Like a master cabinetmaker or a fine jeweler, they can teach us skills and techniques, be our models, mentors, and guides as we move from apprenticeship to journeyman status and finally into the position of master craftsman. Still, no amount of reading about them or observing them will cut the diamond or turn a graceful leg on a lathe. Dabbling, momentary inspiration, or admiration won't make us masters. We must dedicate ourselves to finding the synergy between method, motivation, and material in our own lives.

Spiritual masters have taught ways and means of spiritual craftsmanship universally. They have taught that spiritual craftsmanship is a way of life, an ongoing process of self-responsibility. Whether we are in training to be a shaman, sitting at the feet of a guru, following a devotional path in a convent or monastery or studying eclectically on our own, if we are serious, we will find ourselves experiencing similar initiatory passages no matter what road we follow. These passages are described in the sacred stories of traditions throughout the world.

We can gather priceless pearls from modern disciples as well as from those who left us their treasures. We are indeed blessed to have such a legacy and to live in a time that allows us to have so many choices about powerful techniques and practices.

It has been my privilege to work with hundreds of disciples over the past two decades. These people have a great deal to share about the traps and privileges of the path. I have watched many of them flower into spectacular lights and a few of them give it up when the temptations or demands were too great.

Throughout this book I will be sharing with you observations, inspirations, and techniques that come from a variety of universal traditions. Because this book is not about religion or comparative religion, I have no interest in arguing the case for any one way of walking the path. I am interested in the spiritual essence that is present in all of life.

I will also be sharing with you stories of people who have made commitments to live their deepest spiritual intentions in the world, identifying the struggles they have encountered and mastered and how they did it, revealing the wisdom they uncovered and describing the practices they do.

Our lives are our stories. Ultimately it is the state of our total being that affects the world. I was impressed by a comment made by someone who was part of a party invited to dialogue with the Dalai Lama. While this person was certainly interested in what His Holiness had to say, he admitted that he mainly wanted to see how the Dalai Lama tied his shoes. That's what eventually affects us most of all, isn't it? Not the eloquence of words, nor books and concepts, but the way the truth is being lived in the world.

My Personal Walk

My own discipleship accelerated on what started out as an ordinary day in March 1975. Before charging into my busy schedule, I settled down to meditate, said a prayer, and took a few deep breaths, and within minutes the course of my life was redirected as surely as if I had been lifted off one highway and placed on another.

With no warning I felt a rush of concentrated energy, a sensation of compressed wind that started in my feet and moved quickly to my head. It was intense, undeniable, and very physical. I felt no fear, but my left brain was scrambling unsuccessfully to understand what was happening. I had been a spiritual student for many years and had been clairvoyant in varying degrees since childhood. I'd also had a typical Western left-brain education and put a high priority, as I still do, on being grounded and making things work in this world. As this unexpected and unidentified door opened, a wiser part of myself took over with the simple directive "Be still."

As if in a vivid dream, I saw the spine of someone I knew. I could see exactly what was wrong with it, and my hands seemed to know how to "fix" it. The disharmonies deep in the person's psyche that had manifested in this spinal problem were equally clear to me.

Just as suddenly, the image was gone, the energy was apparently gone, and I was lying on the floor thinking that I must have been doing way too much deep breathing.

Well, the person's spine was indeed "fixed" and the information confirmed. Many similar experiences followed over the next months, and I was mercifully led to Vaughn Boone, a brilliant and dedicated healer who understood what was happening to me and guided me through the early phrases of the unfolding work. He not only modeled for me a method of healing that operates outside space and time as we know it, but he helped me embrace with my heart this new commitment while encouraging me to soberly face the realities it would bring. I am forever grateful to him. He was a firm hand when I stepped away from known realities and into the mystery.

Gradually my path led me into counseling, which in turn led to teaching, lecturing, and writing. I never said that was what I was going to do when I grew up. But when I woke up I knew it was exactly what I had planned in my soul. I know now that every single road and footpath that I have taken up to this point, even the detours, have been necessary to get here.

The journey that began that day has taken me all over America and Europe as a spiritual teacher and counselor. I have been blessed to work in new-consciousness conferences, large cathedrals, churches, centers, universities, and intimate gatherings in people's homes—even a couple of castles. I have shared with people from all walks of life and all races, young and old. I have worked with CEOs and schoolteachers, psychotherapists and actors, the very famous and the unknown saints quietly changing their corners of the world. I have been invited into seekers' personal hells as a counselor and friend and into their ecstasies in shared meditations and insights. I've studied, danced, sang, cried, and dreamed with many new visionaries.

Part of my task has been to use inner seeing and intuition to perceive psychospiritual patterns in people and their manifestations in the material realm. The intuitive ability has been present since childhood but took a quantum leap that day in March, moving from being a random ability to being present on demand.

Walking the Universal Path

My life walk has been about gathering insights from many paths of truth, and I am boundlessly grateful for the gifts I received from each. There are many tools that I've worked with over the years as I continue to seek to fulfill that universal and primary directive: Know thyself. I knew that I would be helpful as a counselor and teacher only to the degree I was willing to explore my own lights and shadows.

Since childhood I have been a passionate student of the ways we grow: world religions, mysticism, symbologies, psychology, mythologies, and metaphysics. Yet it was only when I turned the search inward that my personal synthesis began—and, of course, continues in this ever-unfolding process.

What I haven't done is to follow any one path to the exclusion of all others. I have not sat at the feet of any one guru, yet I have learned from gurus. I have felt equally at home spiritually at a Hindu blessing in Bali and a Buddhist monastery in Hawaii. Tibetan chants take me deeply into worship, as does the "Ave Maria." I hear the Divine speak through nature, the tales of a shaman, the song of a Christian mystic, or the scholarship of a dedicated philosopher. I have felt the Light equally present during a Mahakari healing treatment, at a storefront charismatic church, and in an American Indian sweat lodge.

I celebrate and honor this diversity, for I seek to find the common ground, not the territorial boundaries.

This search has not come without a price tag. Learning to trust the inner teacher against the protests of self-doubt, familiar forms, and outer convention was no small task. Before a truly universal path emerged, I often wished for one system or one teacher, even though I was finding inner resonance in just about every system I studied. During the first seven years of my work I was keenly aware of a teacher in Spirit who didn't so much disappear later as stand back, much like a wise parent who is constantly attentive in the beginning and gradually teaches independence.

I was raised as a Christian, and my love of the Christ was awakened early and has never left me. My questions about dogma, however, also arrived early and never left. When I was very young I stood up in Sunday school, pointed to a painting of a blond, blue-eyed man on the wall, and announced, "That is not what Jesus looks like." My questioning attitude wasn't always welcomed, to say the least. When I perceived that a particular system was attempting to capture the Christ in a narrow, exclusive container, I began to seriously question the container, but not the contents.

"Good Christians don't question" carried a definite subtext: "Good little Christian *girls* especially don't question." Fortunately, there were notable exceptions to that rule, starting with my mother. She grew up in a very conservative environment with her own doubts and questions and didn't discourage mine. An important figure in my early quest was an uncle who was a minister. No doubt puzzled by my insistent questions, he sent me home with thick philosophy books. At thirteen I understood none of them; however, he took my questioning seriously—a great gift for which I will always be grateful.

The challenge for me was to build a bridge between the Jesus I loved as a child without the theological trappings and the Christ that my deepest intuition knew was universal. As I followed my own quest to repair this split, I discovered the same wound in many people who had felt that the price of their spiritual freedom was the abandonment of their childhood religion. Through the years I have heard many spiritual histories filled with stories of shame, anger, guilt, longing, and confusion. Too often a theology of love is hammered in with fear. Little wonder the psyche, not to mention the intellect, rebels.

Sometimes I felt stuck in a psychic purgatory, attempting to listen to both my inner guidance and outer voices. I learned that ambivalence cannot be avoided or simply intellectualized. I had to plunge head and heart into the quest and trust that the truth I sought could be found. It often turned me upside down before it set me right side up.

Today I relate to Gandhi's response to a query about his religion: "I am Christian, Buddhist, Hindu, Moslem." Through Eastern meditation techniques I have learned that the kingdom of heaven is as close as my next heartbeat. Through the study of psychology and a variety of spiritual sciences I have grown in my understanding of the power of mind and belief. "Seek and you will find" became a living reality as I learned from enlightened minds in all traditions. I bow to all of them in respect and gratitude. Ultimately the true teacher is inside, but as we are all works in process, we need our elder brothers and sisters to guide and reassure us. So while my queries often took me further away from any one formal religion, they took me deeper and deeper into spirituality and a reverence for all Ways to God/Goddess.

I am not sharing any of my personal experiences in the spirit of "show and tell." If through this book you are giving me the privilege of sharing some part of your own walk, you need to know where I am in mine. When our personal paths cross (as in this book) there can be the delight of recognition, support, and reassurance. And when and if we part or differ, I honor that choice as well. I have never lost my child's knowing that there are many roads to God, and as the poet Rumi said, "there are hundreds of ways to kneel and kiss the ground."

Conscious Evolution

❧

> *God is an intelligent sphere whose center is everywhere*
> *and whose circumference is nowhere.*
> —Book of the Twenty-four Philosophers

The longing for reunion with our Godselves is coded into our cells. Inevitably we will all return to the Source after the long circuitous route of trial and error that eventually erodes the illusion of separation. Fortunately we can take a more direct route. It is the Way of conscious evolution.

At any point in space and time we can say, "Enough, I want to go home"—home to reunion with God/Goddess, home to the sweet peace of surrender to the eternal dance of light and shadow, home to the Self that flows like a river toward the sea. Home is *shanti* and *shalom*, so be it, amen, and allelujah. And home is here, now, in this holy, holy place.

Until we choose to seek our own Way home and dedicate ourselves to it, we are, as Buddha put it, "like a cowherd counting someone else's cattle."

We can't avoid any lessons on the direct path into self-knowledge. In fact, when we consciously set foot on our path, the lessons come with even more speed, heat, and challenge. They also bring a quickened spirit, passion, creativity, and the liberating keys of the kingdom.

The Tao Te Ching calls the Way the "path of all wonders; the gate to the ecstatic nature of everything," a Way that we first long for, then walk and eventually become.

Buddha called it the "Middle Way," Jesus the "narrow way through a straight gate." Isaiah called it the "Way of Holiness"; the Moslems call it "Mazhah"; the Rishis in the East spoke of the "Great Passage"; the Koran named it the "Straight Path"; it's the "Sanatana" of Sanskrit, the "Middle Path" of the Kabbalistic Tree of Life, the "Royal Road" of yoga, the "razor's edge" of Gandhi.

The process of walking the Way is also called by many names: the Perennial Philosophy or Timeless Wisdom, the Search for the Holy Grail, the Hopi Road of Life.

The Way is often described as a means of bringing ourselves into alignment with the natural order of the universe. Natural order does not split heaven and earth into two sciences. It sees true science as the study of the essential nature of *all* things, what the ancients called *physis*, that mysterious essence that fills all life and all forms, not just the material but the philosophical, economic, governmental, and cultural systems that together encompass the full range of human expression.

The Way of wisdom frequently says, "Look to Nature as the ultimate teacher." And Nature replies: "You are all from One and are therefore one family, and each of you carries the cosmic DNA within you."

We look up to the heavens and see in macrocosm the spiraling of our own molecules, or down into the microcosm of the sub-atomic world and see the same activities as the galaxies. The stars and the atoms and ourselves are all from one unbroken web of life, and yet all is as unique and wondrous as a single wildflower blooming in a wilderness, a wildflower whose pattern reflects the same mathematical precision found in the heavens and in our bodies. How could we ever think such a mystery could be definitively captured and named?

If I can hear the mystery, does it mean you can't? Is the symbolic language of my belief system an expression of superstition because it differs from yours? If we find it strange that someone blows through a conch shell to invoke the Divine, offers tobacco to the Great Spirit, or walks repetitive circles around a sacred stone, imagine how strange it might sound to some to say one worships by eating the body and drinking the blood of a god resurrected from the dead. Ultimately there is much more that unites us than separates us.

Challenges and major turnings on the path are universal, and these turnings are carefully marked for the seeker. The big turnings are major initiations. We can spend many lifetimes working on any one of those as we walk through the twisting detours and dangers, gradually confronting all illusions and seeking, however slowly, to release our inner radiance. During times of major evolutionary change, such as now, everything accelerates, including the lessons and opportunities for spiritual growth.

Recognizable stages along the Way are typically symbolized by spirals, wheels, paths, stages, or turnings in a labyrinth. As one masters various stages, they are integrated into our total life. These central points of synthesis are often symbolized by a mandala, wheel, lotus, or rose.

The Way of conscious evolution moves us gradually away from fear-based relationships to the Divine, in which an entity or an outer force has to be appeased, and into morality-based religions, which tell us how we should behave, what we should believe. Both of these forms require authorities outside ourselves. Eventually we grow into unitive states of consciousness in which we seek union with the Beloved, knowing that the Mother, Father, and ourselves are One. We might choose to stay within a familiar form for many reasons, but at the point of unitive consciousness we don't confuse the rituals, rules, and practices with the essence. We are all aware of different aspects of the journey, and wherever we enter the path is the right place for us.

In the Gnostic manuscript *Dialogue of the Savior* (one of the lost documents about the life and teachings of Jesus discovered in this century), it is written that the disciples asked Jesus, "What is the Way? What is the place to which we shall go?" And he answered, "The place you can reach, stand there."

The parables taught by the outer forms of religions often carry secret codes. Unlock the codes and you enter a secret garden. And if we do not know the codes, we need only ask with an open, teachable mind and a longing heart, and we will be given the keys that are right for us. The gates will swing wide and welcome us into that garden of all delights. We just can't go into the garden with the same illusions that worked outside the garden.

Jesus was once quoted as saying that he gave his disciples the keys to the kingdom (the sciences of the Way); however, since there are those "who, seeing, do not see and, hearing, do not hear," He taught in the time-honored way of great teachers, with parable and metaphor. To avoid throwing pearls before swine or giving meat to babes is loving, not exclusive.

Yet there comes a time when we are ready to see and hear, a time when we're ready to move beyond secondhand knowledge to seek our own Way. Sometimes this happens when the path we have walked for a while simply dries up. It's taken us as far as it can. That doesn't mean it wasn't worthy, any more than a local road that leads to the superhighway is less significant in our travels. As Jewish wisdom puts it, each of us has to at some time "re-create Sinai for ourselves." The path of synthesis often seems new to us because we are accustomed to hearing it expressed in the language and symbolism of various cultures. Just as water poured into a vessel takes on that vessel's shape, the universal story of transformation has conformed to a multitude of cultural descriptions. But synthesis is an ancient path of transcendence that recognizes the common threads that weave life into a unified whole.

It doesn't seek to homogenize all Ways to God/Goddess, any more than a gardener would decree that all flowers should be roses. Rather, it seeks to understand the one Power that makes all life grow even as it celebrates the diversity born of that one Power. Grace is as mysterious as the force that makes the flowers bloom. While we can neither cause it nor make it happen, we can tend our own gardens.

Many of us have tasted the fruits of many wisdoms from many traditions. Now we are asking ourselves, what will actually nurture us on our paths? Must we pick one from the many in order to ground our spiritual longings? If not, how do we synthesize the many truths we have discovered without being overwhelmed by choices?

The path of synthesis is the path of conscious evolution. We are all in evolutionary process, whether we are aware of it or not. Disciples choose to become awake and aware of the journey, therein accelerating and serving it. They deliberately set their feet on a path that has been described in sacred stories around the world. Sacred stories provide maps to mastership, spiritual alternatives to the endlessly winding roads of human trial and error.

Sacred Stories

Sacred stories are the illuminated narratives that tell us *how* to walk the Way. Stories become sacred because of their ability to teach us the lessons of Spirit at whatever level we are ready to hear them. They are the ego's way of relating to God/Goddess and of finding our place in the cosmos. They usually start at the point when the soul is ready to begin a serious quest; thus they often open symbolically with the birth of a special child, which represents the awakening of the Light.

Sacred stories can be read as (1) what happened to one enlight-ened individual; (2) a portrait of the path of return, therefore an inner drama of transformation; (3) an archetypal pattern of evolu-tion; (4) a cosmic drama of the renewal of the sun after the long winter, the cyclic rebirth of light and life; and (5) all of the above, for the macrocosm is always reflected in the microcosm.

The genius of a sacred story, however, is its application to our lives no matter where we are on our path. Imagine a spiral that brings us back to the same landscape over and over. With each turn of the spiral we gain more knowledge and insight. Therefore our perspective on the landscape of our life changes. The same sa-cred story takes on deeper meaning with each turn of the spiral, becoming more and more inclusive.

A deeper understanding of a sacred story no more negates the understanding that preceded it than one level of a ladder makes the previous level unnecessary. Each level of understanding em-braces the one before it, making it unnecessary for any one of us to be wrong about our interpretations.

The most powerful sacred story can rivet the attention of ten people sitting side by side in a service listening to the same words. Even though they're all being spiritually fed at different levels, each according to understanding and need, each one can be in harmony with all others.

As the Sufis say, the great stories of the Way teach us to go be-yond understanding that one and one makes two and become aware of the meaning of *and*. They teach us how to stand poised in paradoxes, how to blend our shadows and light, how to inte-grate grace with hard work—in short, how to be in the world but not of it.

The great stories are also cosmic dramas that are beyond any one soul's journey but describe the nature of the universe and the process of evolution. Their brilliance lies in their truth at every level, from the macrocosm of the universe to the microcosm of one life. One learns to understand a sacred story first physically as a material drama, then psychologically, intellectually, spiritually, and finally cosmically. Sacred stories chronicle the cosmic drama of evolution, all the cycles we undergo in our journey toward the promised land of enlightenment. They tell us the Way of every-man, everywoman.

If all we can integrate at any one time is a literal interpretation of a legend, then its value will lie in teaching moral principles and ethics as well as providing heroes and heroines as models. If we are ready for more than that, we see that the dynamics of the legend are being played out over and over in the human soul as it seeks reunion with the Godself. We are the characters in the dramas and all the story lines. We are the hero and the villain, the betrayer and the master. We experience the desert and the mountaintop.

From the fall/separation of Adam and Eve to the resurrection/reunion symbolized by Jesus, the Bible lays out the journey each soul makes. The hero, the villain, the bride, the king, and the beggar all exist inside each of us. Events such as marriages, wars, births, and deaths represent passages each soul makes in its journey home to the promised land (cosmic consciousness). Everyone wanders lost in a dry desert, climbs a mountain of higher awareness, feels the despair of exile, celebrates the reunion through the marriage of the inner hero and heroine. Geography, animals, plants, numbers—all are part of the colorful, symbolic clues for reconciling humanness with Godness.

Sacred stories are less about treating symptoms than getting to the cause of our illness—our illusion of separation from God/Goddess. They tell us that a battle to the death between illusion and truth is sure to happen as soon as the desire for truth is announced in the inner kingdom. The stories lay out the stages of the process and the Way of victory. And while mastery is ultimately inevitable, the stories make it clear that the path can be very challenging. So we should be very tolerant with ourselves and each other if we don't always find the process easy.

Gradually surrendering rulership of the inner kingdom to the

Highest Self takes us through a number of universal passages recognized as initiations. We are always in the process of being initiated into our next level of understanding. We're not always willing to cooperate with the process. But whether it takes us one life or ten, whether we come to it easily or reluctantly, when we are ready for a lesson we will continue to attract to ourselves the perfect classroom, teachers, and experiences until we learn that particular lesson. Anything one learns so thoroughly that it becomes an integrated, working reality is initiation. As we progress through our initiations, we gradually master the blindness and fears that have kept us endlessly whirling around on the wheel of karma.

If we stay clear and remain persistent in our intention, no matter what pathway we use, we will arrive at universally recognized gateways in consciousness. Then the whole process of mind-body-spirit integration and personal mastership accelerates. At each gateway we leave behind more and more unconsciousness, addictions, appetites, and attachments, and we surrender more consciously to the Highest Self. In time we acquire complete mastership of the mind, emotions, and body. Sacred stories describe this journey through universal portals, prepare us for the challenges and responsibilities at each level, and offer us accumulated wisdom of our spiritual elders.

Golden threads weave through our many sacred stories like sunlight through a forest. The Light calls forth life equally from the oak, the flower, and the mossy bank by the stream. A few of these golden threads shared around the world are:

- Enlightenment is possible; there are ways to prepare for it.
- Deep desire, meditation, and discipline are important.
- Self-knowledge is fundamental. The Divine is within.
- Death of the old self, the lower consciousness, is necessary.
- All things born are on a return path to bliss.
- Duality is an illusion; the return is to wholeness.
- Temptations to serve the ego will be met along the path.

- Multiple realities exist simultaneously, and we can become aware of them.
- Mastership of the emotions, body, and mind is essential.
- *Gnosis* (knowing) and *pistis* (faith) characterize discipleship.
- The universe's essential nature is love.
- The greater the master, the greater the servant.

The Universal Christ

The voice of the universal Christ, affirming "I Am" originates in the heart of the universe to be everywhere present and powerful.

Known by a thousand names, the universal Christ is the bridge that arches between our humanness and Godness. It is the ultimate potential in everyone to balance all duality, stand poised within polarities, and synthesize heaven and earth. In all languages, it speaks with the authority of the logos, the Word, using the power of I Am.

The same Light that brought enlightenment to the Buddha is the Light that shimmers through the pages of the Tao Te Ching, the Bhagavad Gita, the Holy Bible, and the Koran.

Many enlightened ones lived and taught so brilliantly, it is impossible to separate history from the myths that gathered around them. Among the giants of the sixth century B.C. alone there were several whose teachings birthed religions: Zoroaster, the Buddha, Mahavira, Lao Tzu, Confucius, and Pythagoras. Through popular myths, rituals, and holidays the universal Christ story wove its message into acceptable cultural packages.

Many of these illuminated beings were considered sun gods. The sun was worshiped as a symbol for divinity throughout the world. The cult of the sun god was quite common, and some of their legends were similar to the Christian story but predated it by centuries.

We know from legends that the idea of the sun as savior was strong in rites and worship in the Middle East. It was Helio to the

Greeks, Horus to the Egyptians, Shamash to the Babylonians, Sol to the Romans, the Goddess Amaterasu to the Japanese. Mithras was considered a sun god. So were Apollonius, Bacchus, and Zoroaster, who was said to be conceived by a ray of divine reason from the sun. Adonis (sometimes known as Tammuz), who was born on December 24, was murdered, and rose from the tomb in late March, was also a sun god. There were many others.

Without the sun, life on earth couldn't exist. The sun became a symbol in legends for sustaining life, a mythic symbol for a creator. Many of the ancient cyclic rituals we celebrate even today grew out of observations of and awareness of dependence on the various positions of the sun. Major religious holidays have their roots in the winter and summer solstices and spring and fall equinoxes. In the dark winter, when life seems barren, hope is born, and in the spring we celebrate the green renewal made possible by the sun.

Teachings from many sources say that the universal Christ appears whenever It is the most needed. When we are ready to choose heaven over hell and truth over mere illusion, grace gives us a perfect model, a way to get there. Out of our collective self a deep cry arises that invokes from the universe a response so great that an Illuminated One will leave the realms of Light to bring us another embodiment of the Way. We can then see, touch, and hear spirit made manifest and see our own potential.

In the Mahabharata, a Hindu scripture, Krishna says:

When goodness grows weak
When Evil waxes mighty
I make for myself a vehicle.
In every age I return
To deliver the Holy
To destroy the fault of the evildoer
To establish true goodness.

Beyond Chaos

Every tree in the backyard is potentially a Bodhi tree and a cross.
—Jay Williams, *Yeshua/Buddha*

Out of the East and West, from tribes and ashrams, esoteric studies and popular religions, we are bringing all of our known Ways to God/Goddess to the banquet table in an unprecedented cornucopia of spiritual delights.

So many choices. That's where our challenge lies.

Many of us are asking ourselves, "Now what? Now that I've tasted the fruits of wisdom from many traditions, what will actually nurture and sustain me on my path? Must I pick one from the many in order to ground my spiritual longings? If not, how do I synthesize the many truths I have discovered without being overwhelmed?"

It is universally taught that in the beginning was the Word. That Word is still resounding through the universe. It echoes through all languages, lives within all metaphors, enlivens all truths. It lives in every new generation. We could no more capture it than we could catch sunlight in a net.

The Word was not spoken five thousand or two thousand years ago and never uttered again. Nor has it whispered revelations to a chosen handful, leaving the rest praying to a silent universe. The Word is the eternal sound in which we all live and from which infinite patterns are born. It calls us to evolution's dance through the muezzin chanting from the minaret, through the digeridoo, the drum, and the hymn. Where is there a culture that has not sounded the Word?

In spite of all of the horrors and deep wounding of dualism in our world, leading to wars, inquisitions, and dehumanization of all kinds, there have always been disciples in every religion on earth who have listened deeply to their inner guidance and challenged the lies of ignorance and bigotry. They have often paid with their lives to do so.

Illuminated beings have emerged from all paths, and they have left us legacies of immeasurable value. Their wisdom forms an unbroken trail of stepping-stones from the ancient past to this very moment. Without them we would be stumbling around in the dark. They demonstrate the flowering of the potential in all of us. Through them we see that enlightenment is not an impossible goal.

Religion is a container; spirituality is the living essence that is everywhere, always alive, ever renewing, ever revealing itself. The container builds a form around the mystical teachings of an enlightened person who embodies the essence of the teaching. The enlightened masters in every culture teach the ways to discover and accept the grace of our birthright as sons and daughters of the Divine. Their followers are very real human beings who become the architects of the structures we call religion.

We have a multitude of treasure maps that transcend differences in culture. And when we arrive at the treasure itself, we recognize that we are beloved, eternal expressions of the Divine, and so is everyone else. The only difference is who knows it and who hasn't remembered it yet. The trip to the treasure, and the packaging of it, may be as different as the rose is from the passion flower, or the

oak from the weeping willow—and just as delightful if we celebrate its unique expression.

Regardless of accent and emphasis, messengers of the Word
agree on many points:

- Look inside Self for the truth.
- Breathe with awareness.
- Pay attention.
- Be still and listen.
- Have faith.
- Accept grace.
- Be grateful.
- Walk without harm.
- Love all life unconditionally.
- Forgive everybody everything.
- Serve.

A transcendent path has been modeled for us in the symbology
of sacred stories around the world because the pattern of fusing
the Godself with the human self is universal. Stories of gods
walking among us issue invitations over and over for us to follow
their steps. Their words, stories, miracles, and indeed their whole
lives provide how-to manuals on living the sacred in the mundane.
This spiritual wisdom is *our* legacy. When we discover this, we
move beyond comparative religion into a true harvesting of what
we have learned.

Before our times, a path made up of stepping-stones from different religions was not as viable an option. Now, thanks to our
diverse forms of communication, the concepts, language, rituals,
and messages that were once considered esoteric have been woven
into our lives. We're gradually becoming comfortable with everything from Native American vision quests to Eastern mantras.
References to past lives, karma, or a multitude of international

healing techniques show up in the soaps, in popular magazines, and in suburban grocery store conversations.

Meantime, the messages from the edge of biology and physics, psychoneuroimmunology, increasingly reveal the truths that have already been represented in the symbolism and teachings of the world's mystics. We're building bridges between all our ways of knowing.

We are now seeking to understand the *anima mundi*, the world soul. Millions are no longer willing to accept any one priesthood or any one dogma as the final authority for the sacred on earth.

There is always a risk in taking material out of its cultural context. In the beginning, our motives for exploring other traditions might be curiosity rather than quest. There is always the danger of trivializing, oversimplifying, or distorting. *And* there is the possibility of wondrous discoveries, recognition of universality, shifting perceptions, and reexamination of conditioning and personal myths, all leading to probing our own path more deeply.

I saw a cartoon recently that showed two signposts. One pointed to answered questions; the other pointed to unquestioned answers. It is the unquestioned answers that are dangerous, as is any atmosphere that tacitly or openly prohibits questioning.

We pay a high price for submission to an outer authority, and the risk of indoctrination and the abuse of power is great. In many systems of training, students are asked to hold their questions until they have learned enough to even understand the questions, let alone the answers. However, there does come a time when questions are welcomed and encouraged. That is very different from a system that demands lifetime obedience with no questions asked.

The children today who are zipping around the world on their computers, faxes, TVs, and cell phones are going to ask a lot of questions. They are not likely to accept provincialism easily or stay confined to borders and boundaries very well.

One-world awareness is here—not yet integrated, but definitely here. Clearly, we don't know what to do with it yet. Large numbers of us are still resisting the reality of a unified world. And certainly there are distortions in the translations of symbols from one culture into another. Resistance is predictable in the cycle of change. Facilitating change with stability, imagination, clarity, and compassion is the work of modern disciples, who are here to build bridges during this transitional time. Such bridges must first be built from within.

From Pisces to Aquarius

First we have to build through the last of what the Hindus call the Kali Yuga, the great time of purification that we have been experiencing for so long.

We are all family members of a home planet that is shifting under our very feet. It is as though we are loosening from one orbit or way of understanding reality and being irresistibly drawn into another. The much-anticipated new orbit is still mysterious, and interpretation of the process varies. Some see the force of evolution propelling us toward major new insights into the universe and our place in it. Some see signs of the return of Jesus the Christ as planetary ruler and expect a thousand years of peace and harmony. Others interpret the return of the Christ as a metaphor for a collective leap in consciousness. They, too, believe we are at the edge of a wondrous new age, a time in which some say that those who have endured purification in mind, body, and spirit will transcend the limitations of physical reality and live in light bodies of higher frequency.

However we frame it, it's clear we are in the midst of serious change, and the unhooking from the old is a chaotic process, unrelenting in its intensity. In the dying gasps of the Age of Pisces, assumptions about reality are collapsing around us like trees falling in a storm. We are all sharing the purification of denied and despised personal material boiling to the surface in all our outer forms for us to see and transform.

Here's a quick reminder of where we are now as we cycle through our part of the cosmic drama. Our Earth, balanced on its axis, dances a circular path through the skies that takes approximately twenty-six thousand years. The dance is called the precession of the equinoxes. Within the total program our Earth moves through succeeding cycles or ages that last approximately two thousand years. There are twelve great ages related to the houses of the celestial zodiac. As the Earth spins backward through the zodiac, humans have experienced the Age of Aries, and now we are leaving the Age of Pisces to enter the Age of Aquarius.

Imagine a huge spiral along which we are constantly moving from one age to another. My guidance tells me that we started around the bend of this particular shift in the evolutionary spiral around the time of the Industrial Revolution. We revved up around World War II and have been picking up speed exponentially ever since. Time itself seems to be collapsing. In this century we have endured more changes and have had to integrate more versions of reality faster than at any time previous in the Earth's history.

The universe is fluid, not rigid. The flowing energy of the universe will fill whatever container we bring to it, here and now equally as much as thousands of years ago. In one sense, time is nonexistent and a matter of perception. The past, present, and future are not neatly lined up. Rather, we are living all of it in the creative now. Power is in the present moment. And what we create now instantly affects time in all directions.

Age changes typically bring both upheavals and innovations as evolution offers us another chance to expand consciousness. Souls clamor to get born in such times, for they offer unusually extensive opportunities and high energies for running off past karma, for learning, and for service.

Many of the children who are being born during the intensity of this shift truly hear a different drummer, one that marks an Aquarian rhythm and carries the themes of a new myth for our species. A major challenge we face in parenting and educating these young Aquarian prototypes, often identified as Indigo Children after the book of the same name, is that many of our systems and our myths are built on an understanding of reality created prior to and during Piscean consciousness. Consequently, perceptions vary widely.

It is clear that we are not living through an unfortunate little string of crises after which all will return to an imagined state of normalcy. All around us we are seeing desperate attempts to empower the old myths. But no amount of financing, legislation, or control of any kind will stop the new from manifesting. Our DNA is programmed to respond to evolution's urge. We are pulled toward our goodness, toward our Godness.

Of course, the dying and the birthing overlap. We may be two or three hundred years into Aquarius before the new insights and values become working reality. We've already been challenging the old paradigms for several hundred years, most especially during the last century. It is precisely the period we live in that is the most intense battle zone of the two paradigms.

We're being shown not only the possibilities, but the internal and external messes that we have to clean up before we can proceed. Inequities of all kinds are being grotesquely acted out. We can't fail to see them. Who on this planet of abundance is going hungry at the banquet table? Who is falling through the cracks? Who is responsible for these inequities?

Prophecy: Projected Possibilities

Evolution has been inviting us to its party for quite a while. Now it is pretty insistent that we show up. The invitation may be expressed through the revival of ancient prophecies from the Hopis to the Tibetans, from the Egyptian pyramids or Mayan calendars. Others are interpreting events as indications of the end times as prophesied in the Bible, and anticipate the coming of the Messiah.

The market has been flooded with books on impending disasters. If we are not being assured that God has proclaimed the end of the world through prophets, then we are being told that the poles might shift or whole land masses will fall into the sea.

Prophecy is about projected possibilities. We all use it to one extent or another. If we observe a person consistently behaving in a certain way, we can accurately predict what is going to happen. But prophecy is *not* fixed reality. Prophecy allows us to look ahead and say, "Pay attention, wrong way, back up, redo it."

Those who use psychic sensitivity know that within a person's pattern you can see deeply held self-images that will manifest unless the person makes a radical change. So one can prophesy a probable result and very likely be right unless that person wakes up. We can all change our future by changing our consciousness. People do it all the time. And what is true for the microcosm of one life is true for the macrocosm of our collective life. If an individual can challenge a prophecy through creative change, so can we as a society and as a species.

Like all sensitives, I prophetically "see" what might possibly happen if we don't clean up the environment; I can "see" the awesome assault on our planetary nervous system because of the age change. And I maintain that during the shift we can hold those prophecies in a very detached, observant manner while simultaneously choosing to use our creative energy to hold the vision of stability. We can observe the symptoms and energize the new vision. But we can't split our intention, and there is no way to fake it. We are vibrating, resonating instruments, so if we are holding fear around the shift, we will resonate with the fear peddlers. If we examine and release our fears, anything is possible.

Even though we don't know *what* will happen, we know from experience that as we pass through various cosmic cycles, something will happen. The first few times that I received the number 2012 in a meditation as a significant date, I took it with a big dose of cosmic salt. Like the contents of Pandora's box, the prophecy pot has been overturned, and the contents have poured out into the collective for anybody to pick up and interpret. I asked myself: Is this a truth I have been shown, or have I simply picked up on an arbitrary date because so many people have energized it that it is accepted as truth? But I realized that this date had begun showing up in my meditations before I knew that anyone else was getting it. Then as I read various prophecies, learned the unusual astrological lineups of that year, and talked to others around the world who had received the same information, I realized that if I was off, then lots of us were off at the same time.

It is important to be clear about that date. I don't for a minute think the world will stop. Nor do I think Pisces will come to a screeching halt and Aquarius will be ushered in with fanfare. I do suspect that we have been given this date from so many quarters as a kind of grace period. We still need time and space to shape our realities, and knowing about 2012 gives us a bit of a deadline, telling us how long it's going to take us to get through the intensity of this turning. It helps us put the purification time in perspective.

In the beginning of the 1990s I was asked to give a lecture on prophecy for the decade. As I prepared to meditate on this, I anticipated a recital of the scientific breakthroughs, along with a smattering of earthquakes and such—the kind of predictions that have become part of our psychic landscape. Instead what I perceived were two images. The first was of pure Light pouring into everything throughout the planet. I saw great awakenings everywhere. No matter what words were assigned to it, there was definitely a quickening response of people's hearts and spirits to evolution's call to make a better world. The leaps were enormous and profound. This image gladdened my heart.

Then, before my inner eye, the image shifted to a darkness as great as a black hole that eats light. This was not the darkness of balance, as in yin and yang. No, this was the darkness of fear, ignorance, and despair. That, too, it seemed, would be the 1990s. And so it was—great waves of Light pouring in to lift us into awareness of unity, and great resistances of fear pulling us into separation.

The tension between these two creative forces lies deep within our individual and collective psyche. As physical beings, we naturally want to order universal energy into organized, physical patterns. And just as naturally the cosmos pulls us out of one pattern into itself. For a while chaos reigns, and out of the chaos another pattern emerges.

Out of Chaos, New Order

Before old patterns die and new ones are fully formed, a period of disorder reigns. We are living through this part of the growth cycle right now. The old myths are breaking down and the new ones are not yet clearly defined—or trusted—by a critical mass. Much of life *seems* to be in a state of chaos.

Chaos appears more directionless than it actually is. We can learn a lot from physics about this dynamic in the growth cycle. Chaos theory tells us that any system (and that would include you and me as well as societal institutions and systems in nature) is considered chaotic when its path becomes totally unpredictable. But it only appears to be unpredictable, for behind the confusion of the chaos a new order is emerging. We just have to be patient and trusting. This developing order will in time organize itself into a new pattern.

An amazing dynamic starts to happen in the midst of the chaos, a phenomenon called "the strange attractor." It sets the boundaries beyond which the chaos will not go. The term came from scientists Dr. David Ruelle and Dr. Floris Takens. Physicists John Briggs and F. David Peat observed the "strange attractor" by tracking systems on computers and following them through the chaos. They report that chaos appears as thousands of lines moving in an apparently random fashion. Although it seems initially that the system in question is completely without order, over time the lines begin to form a pattern and a new order starts to emerge. The shape the chaos begins to take is known as a "strange attractor."

Briggs and Peat write in *Turbulent Mirror: An Illustrated Guide to Chaos Theory and the Science of Wholeness*, "Eventually familiar order and chaotic order are laminated like bands of intermittency. Wandering into certain bands, a system is extruded and bent back on itself as it is dragged toward disintegration, transformation and chaos. Inside other bands, systems cycle, dynamically maintaining their shapes for long periods of time. But eventually all orderly systems will feel the wild seductive pull of the strange chaotic attractor."

They also say, "Wholeness is what rushes in under the guise of chaos whenever scientists try to separate and measure dynamical systems as if they were composed of parts. *The whole shape of things depends upon the minutest part* [My italics]. The part is the whole in this respect for through the action of any part, the whole in the form of chaos or transformative change may manifest."

Whatever is happening in any system is related to all the other energies that are inseparable in a deep order that weaves the universe together. The seed of chaos is at the heart of every new order. So it has been taught in spiritual sciences and the ancient teachings. So now it is being revealed through our physical sciences.

It would seem that evolution's "strange attractor" first speaks to mystics, visionaries, and responsive disciples willing to believe in a new order they cannot yet see but definitely sense coming out of the chaos.

Beyond Chaos

Chaos is not the enemy. Granted, it causes discomfort. But while it may blow up our theories of reality, it also blows out our minds, clearing pathways for new ideas.

In many cultures one of the faces of the Divine is the destroyer, the purifier who prepares the way for a higher stage of consciousness. In Hinduism, for example, Kali holds that energy. As a destroyer of illusion, She is ultimately a welcomed presence for the spiritual seeker, since She embodies all that rips away nontruths and makes way for the new growth. Nevertheless, She is portrayed in horrific images—usually shown with tusks, wearing a necklace of skulls, and dancing on the bodies of humans. She symbolizes the way we often experience the destructive aspects of the growth cycle.

Many religions use swords as the symbolic instrument of cutting away illusions. They are often seen in Tibetan icons. St. George slew the dragon with a sword. St. Michael is sometimes depicted with a sword. Jesus says, "I come with a sword." The more the Christ consciousness permeates consciousness, the more it destroys illusion.

Everything on the path is accelerated when we say yes to our Spirit. The dying that all holy scriptures, oral or written, speak of is the death of illusions, and for most of us, such a death is not easy. We're usually kicking and screaming all through the process. This toxicity in our consciousness is being brought to outer awareness so that we may transform it, and it frequently brings a healing crisis that precedes a major breakthrough.

We seem reluctant in the West to pass on this wisdom to each other. We suffer more than necessary when we fail to acknowledge the destructive aspect of sacred cycles, their purposes, and the chaos they temporarily bring. To deny this aspect of existence is to deny Nature, which clearly gets rid of whatever it no longer needs, often with little ceremony.

At turning points life brings us the dissolving force that will eventually free us from the past. In the doing it often destroys all that is familiar and reassuring, pushing us into the unknown. If we use our wisdom and practices to become quiet, centered, trusting, enduring, observing, and as nonreactive as possible during the chaos, we can expect our own "strange attractor" to emerge. And it will. The task then is to align with its call. In the midst of the chaos the attractor brings new insights, new longings, and the realization that the illusion we dreaded losing was simply a garment that no longer fits.

We are being given the greatest opportunity in human history to collectively shift our perceptions of who we are and what is possible for us individually and as a species. It is happening so rapidly, our interpretations haven't caught up yet with the actualities.

It already seems normal to a great number of us to be in touch in a flash with anyone anywhere on the globe. We go to war or peace nightly on TV. Our heroes and our villains in this drama are in our face daily. We can't hide out in ignorance of other people's needs, religions, and selfhood any longer. Denial is possible but a more difficult state to maintain; the facts are there, bombarding us, persuading us, making us aware. We're taking inventory, tracking our successes and failures—resisting, of course, but also challenging assumptions in every field.

Even as we are struggling with what to keep and what to claim, there are common ideals of the new myth emerging. Some of these are balancing the feminine and masculine at all levels; rechanneling warrior energy away from conquest and conquering into creative activities; protecting all sentient life on earth; sharing knowledge between physical and spiritual sciences; cross-pollinating ideas from the world's disciplines, religions, and cultures; reevaluating, redistributing, and managing the world's resources; providing educational and health support for all of the world's children; increasing awareness of mind-body-spirit integration; and creating a new vocabulary of connectedness.

We are changing, even though our inherited myths maintain some dangerous assumptions that influence our actions: "War is inevitable," "All is fair in love and war," "Boys will be boys," and that all-purpose standby "It's just human nature to [fill in the blank]."

We all choose which myths we will honor and serve. Choice is the Divine's greatest gift. Our fears are front and center at this stage of evolution, and there's never been a better time to own, claim, and then transform them. Of course, we can simply shrink and collapse in powerlessness before the fears. Whatever we choose, it will be highly energized because of the power that is present on the Earth at this time, a power that will propel us around the next great spiral of our collective journey.

Many of us have been intuiting for a long time the new undercurrents in our collective consciousness. Like a great wave deep at sea, the longing for a new, more whole, and healthier world has been building energy. It will break on the shores of the physical world to the degree that we respond and commit ourselves to its urging. Each of us is only one drop in the forming of that wave, but there isn't going to be a cohesive, powerful wave at all unless we come together in response to the current. It is our intention and commitment to a higher vision that adheres to the intentions and commitments of others of like mind and forms the wave.

According to wave theory, if the frequencies of several waves coincide, the waves strengthen; if the frequencies are opposed, the waves weaken; and if there are gaps, which are called points of neutralization, they cancel one another out.

We are invited, even compelled, from the soul essence of ourselves to respond. Yet we are not forced to do so. We are self-actualizing creators every step of the way, and that privilege, with all the power and responsibility that word implies, is never taken away from us. However, that comes with a significant corollary:

We will experience the full repercussions of whatever we choose, individually and collectively.

The call of the current to be part of the wave is enormous. So is the undertow. Those who sense the shifts and wish to serve the emerging new patterns will have to face their own dualities and their own shadows. It is the prerequisite for committed discipleship.

Healing the Divided Self

❧

> *Beyond this place there do be dragons.*
> —Marking on a medieval map of the Atlantic Ocean

Soon after we discover the Light, we learn that not all parts of self are standing in it. Out of fear and denial we have relegated many aspects to the shadow lands of unconsciousness. The task of a disciple is to identify, embrace, and eventually integrate all parts of the divided self.

Our shadows are filled with anything we have rejected, denied, dismissed, or disowned about ourselves. They are locked in the subconscious by guilt and shame, self-judgment, and lack of self-love. They are actually phantoms because they are untruths about who we are. Yet they are alive, and therefore active dynamics, as long as we don't recognize them.

Wherever we fail to recognize the omnipresence of the sacred throughout all life in the unbroken continuum from Spirit into the physical, there denial, dismissal, and dishonoring dwell.

We all live in varying degrees of maturity, understanding, and cooperation between parts of self. Some aspects of self may be very developed, responsible, and ready for full service, while others are still rebelling like adolescents, hiding in shame, raging in anger, or whimpering in fear.

If we don't honor the aspects of ourselves that are less skilled, cooperative, ready, or attractive, we spend a vast amount of energy trying to hide them. And, of course, they are always there, nipping at our heels, creating chaos with other people, compromising our joy with shame, and asserting themselves at all the worst possible moments. Our shadows are only one manifestation of the divided self.

One of the most dangerous divisions we make is between the ego and the Divine. Spiritual literature can even be confusing on the subject, leading one to believe the ego is the one thing that stands between us and enlightenment. Perhaps "personality self" is a better phrase, because the ego is so often understood merely as vanity. The ego is our unique incarnating unit for human life. Spiritual practices are meant to fuse the ego, or personality self, with the eternal Self, not deny it. If we haven't developed a healthy personality self, we have no effective vehicle for functioning on this plane. "Thy Will and mine be one" is the goal and the resolution for the split. "Thy Will" *is* the Will of the essential Self, which never experienced a split in the first place. The ego has to be trained to remember that truth.

All traditions recognize that any life is a chiaroscuro of shifting lights and shadows. Light and dark sisters, Cains and Abels, Jekylls and Hydes appear in stories around the world. In Hinduism and Buddhism as well as the great sagas and myths from Greece, Iceland, and many other cultures, we find personifications of the various hues of light and dark. Some of the characters in these dramas are so powerful, we perceive them as acting upon human affairs rather than being psychospiritual symbols of our inner personal worlds.

Mastership requires that we understand human duality and eventually integrate all our feared parts into Self. Otherwise we blame all that we deny or hate in ourselves on someone or something outside of self, often a devil or demon. This demon has been called by a multitude of names, among them Lucifer, a fallen angel; Satan, who was Jesus' persecutor; the dark Ahriman, opposing the Persian Light-bearer Ahura-Mazda; Mara, Buddha's tempter; Iblis, who tormented Mohammed; and Osiris, who experienced death and dismemberment at the hands of his dark brother Seth.

Tales of the struggles of duality exist in all mythologies. Methods of mastering the darker parts of self vary. Images of slaying the dragon evoke a different inner response than taming the dragon. Slaying wants to destroy that part of self that we perceive as evil, bad, unattractive, or less than, images of ourselves that perpetuate dualistic self-concepts.

But to tame the dragon is to transform it by first embracing it.

The duality trap decrees certain qualities bad, while proclaiming others saintly. It's symptomatic of the crippling disease of either/or. As we explore qualities of discipleship, we soon realize that *any* one quality can become the subject of obsession. For example, the ability to create orderly systems on the material plane helps us organize and teach all that we've learned. Yet if that same ability is not integrated and balanced with other qualities, it can be used to concretize rigid rules and dogmas that disallow the ongoing revelation of the Divine. Most of us are not 100 percent orderly or 100 percent rigid. We are always in process, with degrees of clarity.

The objective is to pay attention, looking for checks and balances in our clarity on any subject, gradually owning all of the content in our psyches, seeing both light and shadow, and learning to accept all of it. The degree to which I can see—and accept—all of who you are depends to a large degree on my willingness to see—and accept—all of me.

We must be very gentle with ourselves and others as we recover lost parts of ourselves. We have all suffered from the "should syndromes" imposed on us by family, religion, education, peers, the media. Rights and wrongs reverberate in our minds, reminding us of where we have failed to meet others' criteria.

The systems through which we are socialized have thousands of ways of letting us know what will be accepted or not. Right and wrong get further complicated by the fact that my culture might have a different set of "sins" than yours. With their relentless list of rules, the outer forms of formal religions have often caused us to doubt our own instincts.

Many times children are taught that not only should they not express certain taboo feelings ("Maybe there isn't a hell," "What if Jesus wasn't the *only* way?" "What if girls could be priests?"), but they should not even have the feelings that gave rise to those questions. This attitude only adds more repressed material to the psyche.

Some religious manuals from the eighteenth and nineteenth centuries give terrifying descriptions of the tortures hell has for disobedient or doubting children. And while they may seem extreme, it makes an interesting exercise to list the tortures, both spoken or tacit, that threatened your world as a child. The challenge is to remember how you felt as a child, not the careful, intellectual way you might now frame the experiences. For example, what were the family labels assigned to you? Were you the black sheep, just like your father, smart as a whip, the pretty one? And what part of yourself did you have to give up to play the part? Were you "special," designated to prove family or racial worth or to make up for Mama's unhappiness or Daddy's frustrations? Who was the scapegoat for family or racial problems? Who were the outsiders? What put love or approval at risk?

Many ancient cultures had traditions that allowed people to act out that culture's feared shadow. The Aztecs chose a young man and woman to carry the shadow and then sacrificed them to a deity in a ritual. In India communities chose a man to act out the role of bogey, which included all their dark feelings and fears. He was scheduled to die at the end of a year during which he could do anything he wanted because he took the sins of the group to his death. That's how we got the term *bogeyman*, with which we still threaten little children.

Whenever, as children, we painted outside the accepted lines and were criticized, ridiculed, or punished for it, whenever love was withdrawn or security was threatened, we often created an unconscious cellar in which we could hide the unacceptable impulses that had brought on the disapproving body language, the harsh words, or the spankings. All children want to be loved, and equally important, they need to be accepted into the tribe. How many of us could psychologically withstand being excluded from the circle? So we learn to adapt and hide our true selves as surely as an insect hides itself amidst a sea of green leaves for protection.

In *The Little Book of the Human Shadow* poet Robert Bly writes of our arrival as infants. He says we come here "with 360 degree radiance and offer this gift to our parents. They didn't want it. They wanted a nice girl or a nice boy. That's the first act of the drama."

We must be very loving in recovering the lost feelings of the inner child who often felt forced to bury his or her radiance along with many feelings and talents. It was, as someone has said, "shadow as survival." If any of us had been unable to create a cellar, we might not have survived psychically. But we must also be firm and honest with ourselves. Denied aspects of self don't disappear, in an individual, family, or society. They are just driven underground and then passed on to the next generation, which struggles again over the same unresolved issues.

The Dangerous Divide: Heaven from Earth

During a walkabout with an Aboriginal family in Australia, a friend asked an elder what he should tell the young people in America. "Tell them that it is just an idea of Western man that we were exiled from the Garden. The Garden is here."

Historically, the more "civilized" the West became, the more we forgot that truth and divided the world into the sacred and the profane. Often the sky gods "up there" were put at odds with the earthly ones down here. The lush fertility and sensuality of a Mother Earth, calling us to enjoy and explore our senses in this paradise, became suspect in the worship of a pristine, powerful Father God from the heavens.

When we were conscious of our dependence on the earth, we paid homage to the Great Mother of us all. However, when we began to perceive ourselves as conquerors of the world, we devalued the qualities of our yin-ness that are symbolized by the concept of the Divine Mother. Among these qualities are connectedness, sexuality, wisdom, and caretaking of all parts of the whole, including other species and the earth itself.

We increasingly valued the extremes of yang-ness—specificity, knowledge, hierarchy, dominance, and possession, extremes that led to separations from each other and the earth. This was but an outer dramatization of the collective inner drama, a drama that is neither male nor female but human. We are whole beings, needing the constant balance of yin and yang. So where did all the yin-ness go? Much of it went into the shadows, and we set up social, cultural, political, and economic systems to keep it suppressed. And when the fears of yin-ness erupted, psychic poisons were released into the world.

One reflection of this fear of yin-ness was the holocaust that occurred between the fourteenth and sixteenth centuries in which millions of women (the most conservative scholars place the figure at three million, others up to nine million) were put to death, largely as witches. There are, of course, religious, political, and economic explanations for such wholesale slaughter. Still, the energy that fueled such mindless madness arose in part from centuries of denying, and thus fearing, yin-ness. Finally the fear erupted from the collective like a monster rising from the sea. Indeed, are not all holocausts, inquisitions, and "holy wars" (an oxymoron if

wars are

there ever was one) the volcanic outbursts of shadow material that society can no longer contain? So are our personal wars as well.

When nature isn't honored in a religious system, it usually follows that the body isn't, either. In such systems the body is seen as a trap for Spirit, so naturally all of its insistent demands are perceived as anti-Spirit, especially sexuality. For centuries we've maintained a deep ambivalence about our bodies, caught between longing and shame, defiance and penitence. The deep ambivalence about sexuality that has existed in the American shadow from its beginnings is being acted out now on the outer stage.

Matthew Fox, rebel Catholic priest, visionary leader, and originator of Creation Spirituality, captured our ambivalence well in a lecture he gave a few years ago at a Common Boundary conference. He spoke about two groups—in the same state, during the same time period—that opposed the teaching of relaxation and breathing techniques in the schools—one because it might take the children out of their bodies, and the other because it would make them have too much body consciousness. Fox commented, "This really is a narrow path; you can't be in your body or out of it!"

Unprocessed sexual ambivalence is present in many religious systems. While most spiritual leaders have done their own shadow homework, it is nevertheless not unusual to hear of a guru, priest, monk, or teacher who professes celibacy or monogamy while having sexual relations with students, devotees, and, in the worst cases, children.

One such guru I knew was a brilliant teacher. He also courted scandal through his sexual involvement with students. Fortunately, he finally confronted himself and got his act together. He later reported that he had been taught to transcend his sexual energy but had not been taught to first embrace and understand it. Whatever is left unattended in the psyche will eventually come out.

When someone we respect, such as a guru, falls from a pedestal, it allows all of us great opportunities to process our own shadow projections instead of avoiding them by judging.

A woman who was for years the lover of the great teacher Krishnamurti ended up thanking him for teaching her "to be free from the desperate seeking and searching for respectability and security, from gurus and masters and ideologies." This was reported by her daughter Radha Rajagopal Sloss in a book entitled *Lives in the Shadow with J. Krishnamurti*, a tale that covers abortions and battles over money between the great teacher and his lover.

As long as we are dominated by a dualistic consciousness, we live in a maze of contradictions and ambivalence, caught between spiritual longings and the immediacy of physical needs and challenges. That split allows us to run our businesses, our relationships, and the rest of our world as if they had nothing to do with our spirits.

There is no real split, only illusory ones we've imaged into place through a fear that constricts the natural flow of universal energy into the physical as surely as a dam inhibits a river. It is our choice to constrict; the universe never withholds the flow.

Poised in Paradox

Once the soul's wake-up call has been heeded, the dilemmas of paradox present themselves. What seems to be true at one level seems contradictory at another. How many truths can one hold at the same time? For example, the Dalai Lama has acknowledged that in the midst of the holocaust brought on Tibet by the Chinese, there has been good as well. Tibetan wisdom has been dispersed worldwide, and the religion itself has been revitalized by its interaction with other cultures. Does the latter insight make the horrors of destruction and exile less real? Obviously not.

Can we work hard at social reform *and* at the same time embrace things as they are right now? Can we remember that the universe eventually brings all things to justice and balance even as we see injustice and imbalance all around us? Are we willing to be scientific mystics and pragmatic visionaries?

It is very liberating to accept that we are always living in multiple realities simultaneously. For example, it is certainly tragic that a young man loses his life in war. He may also have sacrificed himself for others in the process. Laying down one's life for another is a major step in spiritual evolution. His death might have triggered responses in his family and friends that led to reevaluating their lives. Perhaps a young person in the family chooses to work for peace as a response to the soldier's death.

The goal is to keep affirming the truth of wholeness in a world still selling divisiveness, to keep remembering the infinite truths of Spirit while honoring the finite truths of humanness. If one person is right, then does another person have to be wrong? Is our only choice either/or? What is being cast out in that duality? How can we ever experience heaven on earth as long as we believe they are totally separate realities?

It is important to ask: Do I believe in a God/Goddess out there, a transcendent state to be reached? Or do I believe that the Divine is immanent and moving through our every molecule, as inseparable from ourselves as music from the flute?

I once saw a cartoon that showed two men with banners. The first held a sign that said JESUS IS COMING, JESUS IS COMING. The second, walking right behind him, said BUDDHA HERE NOW. What about a third that says BUDDHA/CHRIST HERE AND THERE, NOW, TO-MORROW, AND ALWAYS?

Nature, as always, reveals the Divine Plan. For example, current scientific theory states that energy is both waves and particles. It is not one or the other. It can express itself in specific locations in space as particles or be dispersed as waves over a finite volume. If we want to get a fix on the particle aspect, we can measure position. If we want to study momentum, we watch the wave. The potential to become one or the other depends on the observation, for as we now know, the act of observing affects the observed. The truth of any situation depends on the way we observe it.

Paradox shows us that we are living in a circling mystery that will reveal itself to us according to where we enter the circle. Change the entry point ever so slightly, and the view of the circle changes.

The challenge for committed disciples is to stand well poised in the center of the circle, the eternal Self, so that they can move awareness up and down the continuum from the spiritual into the physical and not be pulled into duality. Duality divides; paradox stretches the mind to hold relative truths and *seeming* opposites in wholeness.

Rebels in Shadow

There is no high quite like waking up to one's spirit. Inner resistance starts to give up. Dams break, and the living waters rush throughout all parts of the psyche, ending droughts. Or so it seems until a less cooperative element shows up in the flow. Then you can find yourself face-to-face with rebel parts of self.

The more challenging rebels usually don't show up until we have made a certain level of commitment. These are the ones that we have reinforced so powerfully that they have become assumptions about outer reality. We have woven them into our self-images even if they are uncomfortable. These are the deep cellular beliefs, the real down-and-dirty street fighters. We have to build a certain amount of inner security to take them on.

I've seen many committed disciples judge themselves harshly because they encountered the attitudes represented by rebellious characters within themselves: "How could this be when I have worked on myself so hard and I am so committed?" It has come up precisely *because* one is committed. Until we say we want to get conscious, our undeveloped, rebellious, or downright nasty little "demon" selves just rest in the shadows. As long as we run the illusions—and that includes the self-righteous ones that insist we should have no darkness in the first place—we don't get a lot of hassle from these aspects of self, to some extent because we project them onto other people. These rebels get in an uproar when we choose to become aware of where they really reside—in us!

Most of us have been carefully taught to mask the "undesirables." For hundreds and hundreds of years life and death depended on the skill of blocking natural feelings and talents. If you were a peasant in ancient Japan, India, or medieval Europe, a slave anywhere, a member of any minority or a woman in many cultures, you needed to be able to hide feelings, or your life was worth nothing.

Mask-making is a great art form, but when we mask aspects of our own personalities and our true feelings, it is divisive and self-destructive. Ripping off our masks is not wise, but it is important to know that they exist and when we are wearing them. Then we learn to gently remove them as we feel safe with our own authenticity in any situation. We do that to the degree that we take back authority from the outside.

Freeing the Gold

Dr. Carl Jung once said that psychology had not gotten out of the first three chakras: security, sex, and power. We certainly know the potential shadows they carry. Just turn on the TV or go to the movies, both of which constantly report our current myths to us. Although more and more people are in process of opening to their heart centers—the fourth chakra—that doesn't mean we won't still have unresolved issues of light and dark around the first three.

Fear and avoidance of the powerful drives of the security, sexual, and power centers can be a big trap for spiritual students. Mastership means taking full responsibility for all the contents of the psyche, both the impulses that linger in the cellar and the ones that soar in the heavens. We can't master anything we don't first acknowledge we have.

Sir Laurens van der Post, the great anthropologist who taught us so much about the world of those he identifies as Bushmen, said in an interview in the August 1994 issue of *New Dimensions* magazine, "Every human being has a two-million-year-old man within himself and if he loses contact with that two-million-year-old self, he loses his real roots."

Jung also said that most of what was in our shadow was gold. He taught his students that it would be this gold, more than the skeletons, that would be difficult to dig out of our depths. I have seen this confirmed in my work over and over. People are often afraid of their power and creativity and their potential for greatness, nobility, even mastership.

It is unimaginable, the paradises we could create if we fully accepted all that we are. Imagine what would happen in one generation if we really honored the creativity of all children and taught them that they were literally made in the image of God/Goddess and could therefore create in a multitude of ways. What if we told them that their thoughts, words, intentions, and actions could be pooled to create paradises? What if we told them the truth, that reality is a blend of Light and shadow?

Many children are carefully taught to be self-doubting, to question both their inner authority and their right to help create the world. Every time we were told that the sky isn't green, as we painted it, or that people don't fly or talk with animals, a bit of self-confidence in our own imagination fled to the cellar. Often the most terrible legacy of self-doubt is that we may learn not to trust our perceptions of reality. And if someone accuses us of lying when we said that Uncle Joe, who died last year, was standing in the corner, then we might well have distrusted our own seeing ever after.

We do give children and each other double messages about talents. I had the usual assortment of those programs as a child. But

as a young woman, I began to cognitively understand the ambivalence we carry about talents. My explorations into my own inner
conflicts and the projections of others were triggered by an experience I had in the '70s within a women's group I'd been part of
for a year or so. It was facilitated by a very intuitive and strong
therapist who created a safe place for exploration. Dedicated to
self-awareness and consciousness-raising, we were totally supportive and honest with each other.

One day a woman in the group had a major explosion around a
deep issue with herself. I reached out to comfort her, and she
whirled around and screamed at me, "I don't want any of your
goddamn words!" She immediately looked shocked, as did the
others, and put her arms around me. "I don't know why I said
that, Gloria. You've never said anything to hurt me." After she
calmed down, the therapist went around to the other seven
women in the group, asking them one at a time, "Do you admire
Gloria's abilities with words?" Yes, they did, and they said many
nice things about how they perceived that I could give language
to feelings. That was very affirming.

Then she went back to each of the seven. "Have you ever
heard her misuse that ability?" No, they had not, not a one. And
that was very affirming. Then she went back a third time. "Are
you a little bit afraid of her abilities with words?" And to a woman
they said yes, the reason being succinctly expressed by one of
them: "I know she could rip me to pieces with words if she ever
wanted to."

For me this brought up old anger and frustration. Clearly I
didn't use words to hurt—everyone knew this—and yet here was
this fear that the therapist clearly identified as being in their own
shadows. For me it was also an opportunity to go into another dimension of my own shadow. I realized I had always been fed a
double message about talents, and I was carrying deep ambivalence.

Even then I was grateful, for I knew it was important that I face the anger I held in my own shadow around mixed messages. I still experience it now and then, just as one has scar tissue from a wound. Now I know where it lives, and I take responsibility for it.

Ambivalence About Power

We humans carry a great history of ambivalence about power and women, sensitivity and men. As evolution is inviting us to our own healing, which is to say our own balance, we are challenging some of the most persistent and powerful archetypal images and symbols we've created over several thousand years. The symbols are exploding into the outer world for us to see almost faster than we can assimilate them.

Powerful women often carry huge projections from others that have nothing to do with the truth of their being. Strong, self-actualized women are emerging in our time, and they are providing role models for younger women, for male and female children, and, blessedly, new models of partnership with men. Meantime, they are catching the heat of collective projections, not only from those men who may be less than together about their own feminine selves, but equally from other women who have not yet claimed their inner authority. So the shadow predictably provides the backlash.

The reverse is true with men. We project onto them the archetypal yang hero images. Even as women often insist their men come into relationships with more openness and sensitivity, less emphasis on conquering and more on relating, so do we also want them to be strong heroes who, incidentally, have made a pile of money. It's a mixed message all the way.

Jungian language speaks of the animus, or masculine, in a woman, and the anima, or feminine, within a man. When a woman has rejected her animus and driven it to the cellar, she ignores her ideal inner spiritual guide, for that is one of the functions of her animus. In the midst of expanded thinking and emotions, "he" creates specific stepping-stones for her. Denying this within herself, she can project that need outwardly, expecting the men in her life to be the strong guides. An angry animus in a woman isn't fun. She can be very opinionated, critical, and driven, ridden also by what one woman called her "duty demon."

When a man is out of touch with his inner feminine, his anima, he can be moody and emotionally unavailable. One of the purposes of his anima is to lead him to his soul, the way Beatrice led Dante into heaven after he had encountered his hell, his shadows. A man who denies his inner woman goes dry with too much sun and not enough moisture and coolness. Most of all, he forgets the reasons behind all the drive for accomplishment.

When either men or women refuse to accept and then integrate the "other" within themselves, they seek it outside themselves. A man might seek a goddess (however he might fantasize such a creature). Of course, real women aren't goddesses, so they might have to be replaced with new goddesses now and then. Men who don't live up to a woman's projections of a god invariably fall off their pedestals, and disenchantment follows.

The biggest setup for failure and disappointment is when we expect another to complete us. Our need for wholeness is our need for the Self (Godness) and the personality self (ego) to be one. Lovers can do many things for us, and they are our teachers always, but no one on the outside can make us whole. There's an old saying around therapy circles that if we don't develop it, we'll marry it. If we've denied our rages and abuses, we often repeat them in partners. If we've denied our talents and powers, we often expect our partners to express them for us . . . in the way we want to have them expressed, of course.

Recognizing the Shadow

So let's look at some indicators that we might be acting out of un-examined shadow material. These are certainly not absolutes, as the psyche is complex and there can be many explanations for feelings and behavior. Consider the following clues as warning signs that unexamined dynamics *may* be present:

1. You tend to place people on a pedestal (not just admire or respect them). Pedestals dehumanize, and people fall off. Disappointment and disillusionment often follow.
2. You criticize another with generalized summaries: "He's no good," "Her only problem is . . ."
3. You find it hard to laugh at or accept your own mistakes.
4. You find it hard to accept your own power and talents.
5. You find it hard to accept compliments from others.
6. You feel envious or jealous of another's resources or talents.
7. You have strong physical reactions to people or circumstances: stomach tense, throat tight, palms sweaty.
8. You get a rush of glee from a put-down or gossip that undermines someone you don't like. If it's someone you *do* like, it may present you with a shadow within a shadow.
9. You feel passionately indignant. Cleaning up the world's abuses first requires ruthless examination of those same things in ourselves.
10. You feel victimized by the inability to find time and energy for yourself because you are so busy with others' needs.
11. Your tongue or your behavior "slips"—"I don't know why I did or said that."
12. You have a well-defined list of pet peeves.
13. You are excessively for or against something without careful examination of the opposite or options.
14. You need to ridicule anything.

15. You feel guilty about spending resources on your needs.
16. You are excessively attracted to a person or idea.
17. You are excessively repelled by a person or idea.
18. Inner dialogues sound like authority figures from your culture or family.
19. You are obsessed with anything: work, money, sex, status.
20. You are sick with unreleased anger or frustration.
21. Look to the shadow-at-work signals of depression, a run of accidents, and psychosomatic illnesses, knowing there can be many reasons for them. They can sometimes point to shadow material you need to explore.

SUGGESTIONS FOR BALANCING
LIGHT AND SHADOW

The integration of light and shadow is a goal we can achieve if we commit to it. After we accept that we have a mix of both inside, the next step is to create balance. The middle way is always the way of wisdom. Throughout our discussion of the twelve aspects of spiritual craftsmanship, we will be looking at ways to integrate light and shadow.

• In your mind create an altar of Light and give everything to the Divine—all the shame, blame, self-judgment, and so on. To sacrifice means to make holy. An altar is an archetype, and the subconscious knows what it means: Give it up to the highest vibration, which is light. Mentally create your altar in an environment that is empowering to you (a fantasy place, a chapel, a setting in nature).

• Ask for help. Ask a therapist, ask your spiritual director. Ask the angels, your guides, and your teachers. A loving but objective ally reduces the confusion and fear of being alone in unknown territory.

⊙ Find nonharmful ways to give expression to the shadow. I know a doctor who occasionally dresses down and goes out on the town to clubs she wouldn't normally frequent. She isn't looking for "action" or trouble, but she doesn't appear to be the responsible physician that she is most of the time. Somehow for a few hours the ambiance harmlessly feeds the shadow that she accepts is there. As another example, a well-known spiritual teacher says that after he has prepared a very thoughtful lecture or article, he'll write a blood-and-thunder low-grade short story just to release his shadow.

⊙ Balance high experiences in spirit with ordinary mundane tasks such as taking out garbage or cleaning the bathroom.

⊙ Own the impulse but refuse revenge. The impulse simply tells you that the karma or understanding is not complete. Revenge, no matter how small or justified, will perpetuate the karma. Gandhi once reminded us that if you follow the old code of justice, an eye for an eye and a tooth for a tooth, you end up with a blind and toothless world.

⊙ Personify your fears or rejected parts (the Dark Queen, the Critic, the Macho Man, and so on). No matter how scary they may seem, naming them clarifies them in your mind, gives them humanity, and decreases the terror of the unknown.

⊙ Grant permission for both the light and dark sides of an issue to exist within you, and then learn to wait. There can be powerful, creative tension in waiting, simply holding all possibilities, denying no voice in yourself. Allow debate and listen to both sides. Notice how both the light and shadow attract people and experiences to you.

⊙ Use creative imagination to give expression and insight into the darker contents of the psyche. Try drawing, rituals, dance dramatization, clay modeling, and dialoguing.

Make a list of all those things that disgust you and push your buttons. Some of them might be rejected bits of your psyche.

Use prayer and meditation for guidance and insight. If you seek insight through prayer, be prepared to have it mirrored to you in hundreds of ways. In meditation we expand by shining the Light of awareness into all the corners of our soul, and in time we will see anything that we have rejected.

Take time alone to know all parts of your psyche better. Paying attention to personal reactions to people and events on a daily or weekly basis by using practices such as journaling or nightly reviews of the day keep us in touch and honest with ourselves.

• An oldie but goodie: Use plastic bats or a pillow to beat out anger and frustration.

Learn to appreciate the strength of vulnerability, of confessions, of saying "oops" and "I don't know." This process is empowering, not demeaning. Winston Churchill once said: "I have had to eat many of my own words, and I found the diet very nourishing."

• Do an honest inventory of all of your own "them" and "us" biases, owning any chauvinism about lesbians, gays, blacks, whites, singles, the wealthy, the poor, members of other religions and political parties, immigrants, or inhabitants of the third world.

• Try this simple but very powerful test to recognize the duality you are empowering through fear. In fear we feel separate from God/Goddess, so observe any part of your life that is dominated by fear and say to yourself, "This is where I have an illusion that God/Goddess is not present." Then breathe into this and affirm the truth that the Divine is present in everything you are and everything you do, regardless of outer appearances.

We find the pearls when we dive deep into self-knowledge. As most of us will not live in a monastery, forest, or ashram, the venue for self-knowledge is in the rough-and-tumble world of jobs and relationships and dailiness.

Acceptance of ourselves without judgment brings to all wounds the tincture of self-love, which widens the channel for receiving the healing power of grace. So welcome your shadows and celebrate them. They are primary characters in your own sacred story, an ancient tale of transformation written in your soul and the Way home to wholeness.

BOOK TWO

TWELVE LESSONS
IN SPIRITUAL
CRAFTSMANSHIP

Barefoot on Holy Ground

*"Take off your shoes; the place where you stand is holy ground,"
said God to Moses. It is now being said to you and me. Let go of the
past, let go of limitations and pretensions. Stand barefoot wherever
you are, and you will see that every space and every moment is sacred. You can no more separate the sacred from where you are sitting
at this moment than you could separate the instrument from the music or the moon from moonlight.*

*To walk in reverence and humility is to walk barefoot on holy
ground. Our feet represent our understanding, our foundation, and
our groundedness in this dimension.*

*There is no greater point of power than the one within yourself.
There is no more sacred ground than where you are standing today,
no more significant face in evolution than the one you are looking
into, whether it's the one in the mirror, the one across the breakfast or
conference table, or the one you pass in the street.*

*I now invite you to take off your shoes and walk with me barefoot
on holy ground.*

The whole universe is an intricately woven tapestry. The same
proportions that make a sunflower beautiful show up in great architecture, musical octaves, conch shells, even the way roses grow.
This connectedness is reflected in the tiny replication of the galaxies we carry in our bodies. We are our own little universes revolv-
ing around energized intention.

Geometric patterns through which raw energy is collected,
shaped, and directed seem to provide nature with vibrational tun-
ing forks, creating mathematical patterns that align with the har-
monics of the universe. When these mathematical equations are
manifested into the physical world, the beauty that comes forth is
no less astounding than springtime erupting from winter ground.

The Greek philosopher and mathematician Pythagoras, who

once said that "God geometrizes," also observed that all the laws of the universe were latent within us, and wisdom was the process of bringing that knowledge out of us.

The spiritual sciences also have grammars that speak the languages of connectedness. When people are introduced for the first time to a symbolic system that indicates their connectedness to the cosmos, such as numerology or astrology, they are usually staggered by the accuracy with which such symbols can describe a single life or the life of a civilization. These symbols form archetypal patterns that are constantly influencing us. When we understand these patterns, we can apply them consciously.

The Universal Dozen

The number 12 is one of the most powerful and universal of archetypal patterns. We can look up to the heavens or down into a microscope at certain tiny bacteria and see perfect geometric combinations of twelve. Numerologically 12 is $1 + 2$, and that forms the triad—we know it as both the sacred trinity and the creative stability of the triangle. We are encoded with the magical 12 right down to our physical bodies. We start with twelve DNA strands. We average twelve breaths a minute and have twelve thoracic vertebrae, twelve muscles in our eyes, and twelve cranial nerves.

The wisdom of the ages has been collected in systems of twelve containers. Buddha was said to have written the Wheel of Life on the ground, drawing a circle of twelve interconnecting causes that fuel the life cycle. In the middle of the wheel Buddha put the three poisons of misknowledge, greed, and hate. On the outside edge of the wheel are twelve scenes that symbolize the twelve links of dependent origination.

According to the Christian sacred story, it was at twelve that Jesus first spoke in the temple and announced to his parents that he was to be about his Father's business. This code in the story tells us that as we take responsibility for the twelve aspects of consciousness, we are then ready to be about Divine business, fulfilling our part in a larger Plan.

The sacred story says that Jesus called the twelve disciples to him. Confucius and other great teachers also called twelve to themselves, just as we, too, must call into service our inner disciples. We are also told that Jesus prophesied a race of men who would sit on twelve thrones judging the twelve tribes of Israel.

In the Hebrew tradition twelves appear in abundance: patriarchs, prophets, tribes, even paths to the Red Sea. Joseph and his brothers numbered twelve. It is the age that marks entrance into manhood and womanhood through the rituals of bar mitzvah and bat mitzvah that take place at thirteen.

The early Gnostic religions speak of time moving through twelve great eons. The Great Period in Babylon was 12 times 1,200 days. And, of course, we live our lives by a calendar of twelve months, dividing the clock into two twelve-hour periods.

Our modern mystics, no less than the ancients, have found that truth pours through the power of 12. Many channelers today speak of twelve realms and twelve dimensions of reality. People who work in subtle realms tend to receive similar information. Increasingly healers and psychics refer to twelve chakras instead of the traditional seven, the additional five being the means through which we build higher light bodies.

Charles Fillmore in his book *The Twelve Powers of Man* interpreted the twelve disciples of Jesus as archetypes that live within us. Speaking of the transition in consciousness that happens to an individual when he or she wakes up the inner twelve, he wrote: "The first coming is the receiving of the truth into the conscious mind, and the second coming is the awakening and the regeneration of the subconscious mind through the super conscious or Christ mind."

The Twelve Lessons of Spiritual Craftsmanship

As I sought out the strong containers necessary to hold the powerful energies discipleship evokes, I did not find it surprising that the material repeatedly gathered itself in units of twelve. I have chosen the twelve aspects of consciousness that I consider to be fundamental to the disciple's path. This is my way of giving order and meaning to the essential lessons disciples must master through observation, experience, meditation, and contemplation.

My spiritual guidance refers to these as the Twelve Lessons in Spiritual Craftsmanship. The number 12 represents psychological wholeness. In the process of the disciple's awakening, all of these qualities will be trained, tried, and tested. I offer these lessons for your consideration as a way of giving some shape and direction to your own quest.

The Twelve Lessons are not fixed realities. They are dynamics in the river of life through which our spiritual intentions are brought into the physical plane. They are constantly moving on a continuum of awareness from unconscious to conscious. As the potential for enlightenment or for personal sabotage exists in all of them, we will examine both the Light and shadow dimensions of each lesson.

Part one of the Twelve Lessons is called "Knowing the Way" and explores the ways we recognize, study, and understand our discipleship through knowledge, revelation, discernment, and body wisdom.

Part two of the Twelve Lessons, "Becoming the Way," includes the fundamental building principles of strong discipleship: love, will, faith, and power.

Part three of the Twelve Lessons is "Fulfilling the Way," the practical process through which we bring the *way* to life: creating, transforming, enduring, and serving.

It is important to remember that all Twelve Lessons of your discipleship are present simultaneously. You are the awakening Self poised in the middle of your energy field. The task is to infuse each of these qualities with the Christ energy. That is not done linearly or one step at a time. We don't master love, check off endurance, and then move on to discernment.

Throughout the book I am using the word *Christ* in the universal sense, meaning the full manifestation of the god/human. The Christ is the full flowering of the potential in all of us, the crowning peak of mastership recognized in all religions and spiritual traditions.

The Christ consciousness is found in the center of a circle, not at the top of a ladder. It is a state of awakeness that gradually permeates every aspect of our lives, from our intellect to our sexuality. Training in spiritual craftsmanship allows us to gradually bring all aspects of consciousness, light and shadow, into alignment with the intention of the inner Christ.

While there are recognizable stages in this ongoing process, we always take all of ourselves to each gateway. Focus, intention, concentration, and intensity shift as the circumstances of one's karma and place in the dharma unfold.

All of the questions addressed in the Twelve Lessons transcend any one religion, and all disciples on their journey, regardless of the Way they choose to walk, will face them. Our task is to make these twelve energies conscious: first identifying, then naming, owning, and understanding them, and finally choosing which we will serve. We'll look at both the shadow and the light of each of the twelve aspects.

Each lesson offers:

- Opportunity
- Choice
- Privilege
- Power
- Challenge

We can offer any one of these twelve energies to the Highest Self, and we can offer these same powers to the lower self, which will usurp any one for its own agendas. So our work is to understand and claim all twelve powers and bring them under the tutelage and mastery of the inner Christ.

Conscious Discipleship: Are You Ready?

Disciples are works in progress. They don't present themselves as saints, finished products, or masters. They share the following twelve characteristics:

1. A refusal to take truth secondhand
2. An insistent longing to participate in creating a better world
3. A willingness to face and purify illusions and self-deceptions
4. A willingness to accept and integrate shadows and dualities
5. A knowing that money and status are resources, not identity
6. A retirement of attitudes of exclusivity
7. An honoring of both knowledge and the mystery
8. An intuitive sense of purpose
9. A commitment to a discipline that shapes talents for service
10. A concern for all children, other species, and the earth itself
11. A desire to bring yin-ness in full balance with yang-ness
12. A collaborative attitude in working with other world servers

Discipleship Forums

As we look to the lives of the great spiritual giants of history, sometimes we feel their achievements are beyond our possibilities. One of my desires for this book has been to see what real-life disciples look like, without the projections or interpretations of history. So I began a series of gatherings I called Discipleship Forums.

In these sessions I set up dialogues for groups of four people committed to spiritual growth, and asked all the tough questions: How did you first consciously set foot on your path? What tools really helped? What didn't? How did you handle this temptation, that struggle? What did you read? What practices kept you on center? What did you do about sex, money, fame, dark nights of the soul, loneliness? What do you recommend to those just setting out on their paths?

Disciples are busy, involved people, but these groups generously gave a day or an evening. They represented a cross section from around the United States and Europe. They included Christians and Sufis, Jews and Hindus, Buddhists, shamans, and those who follow other eclectic paths.

One of the special by-products of the Discipleship Forum sessions was the value that participants said they gained from sitting down and discussing their paths with other committed individuals.

Their stories and insights are presented throughout the book, and you will see for yourself the wisdom, humor, intelligence, and profound dedication that guide their lives.

Because we are in this evolutionary maelstrom together, we need to tell each other our personal tales of transformation. We need the support and guidance of our real-life how-to stories for getting beyond all the limitations of the old myths. We need recovery stories from the shadow side of the Piscean Age we are now leaving, particularly the woundings that drove shadows underground and perpetuated guilt, elitism, and shame, erupting periodically in racial, religious, sexual, and political wars all over the planet. We need to hear the new revelations along with those we treasure from our past. We need to consider the costs and the benefits of choosing to stay awake, aware, and committed.

The Twelve Foundations of
Spiritual Craftsmanship

1. Knowing you are Spirit is the first step, and the awareness of this may come suddenly. It takes practice to bring that into full flower in the material world. Pay attention to the lessons and feedback life offers you. Seek out and practice the techniques that support integration of spiritual awareness in daily life.

2. Spiritual craftsmanship is an ongoing process during which we gradually free our inner radiance by confronting and transforming illusions. This work is both universal and highly personal. Tools that work at one point on your journey might be set aside later when you concentrate on another skill.

3. Trust the process that brought you to this point of inquiry. You are in the right place at exactly the right time, no matter what is going on. The shortest route to enlightenment is from exactly where you are. You brought into this life much that is already well developed. You are not starting at ground zero.

4. "I don't know" is not only an okay answer to any question, it is often the beginning of wisdom. Remember that quoting is not knowing. Whatever you believe must be put into practice before it becomes your own. Our egos have been reading the same books we have.

5. Pay attention to everything—your breath, your body, your emotional reactions, your mental gymnastics. You are constantly giving yourself clues to your inner world through your responses to the outer, including a book you are reading. Periodically stop in the reading, breathe deeply, and ask: "What is going on inside me right now? What am I feeling?"

6. Develop an observer who just watches, doesn't make judgments, but reminds you that things are not what they

seem—and also that things are what they are. Can you hold both of those insights?

7. Retire any purely linear point of view. The way we perceive anything depends on where we entered the circle, not where we are on some imaginary ladder going up to heaven. Keep in mind that your left brain researches, reasons, and organizes, while your right brain attempts to see the whole picture and synthesize all usable material.

8. Ask for additional information. The law of magnetic attraction works, and it is no more sentimental than the law of gravity. Whatever you seek you will find. The trick is to know yourself well enough to know what you are seeking. Sometimes the ego just wants to seek justification for its biases. Place your question on an altar of Light and let it go.

9. Give your ego a break. Don't translate the word *ego* immediately into vanity. The ego is the unit of incarnation, our sense of personality and selfhood. Like a body, you use it here on this earth as long as you need it. The goal is to surrender the will of the ego to the highest. "Thy Will" and "my will" become one.

10. Be willing to look at everything you've been taught. Don't settle for predigested nourishment. You may very well conclude that the beliefs you inherited are the ones you chose to keep, but upon examination they will be yours. You may also discover that learning about other ways enhances understanding of your own.

11. You must perform a delicate balancing act between pushing your edges and staying poised within what you know, being open-minded and not gullible. Be aware of where your personal growing edges are and how much information you can integrate. The truth has a way of stretching our perceptions.

12. Pay attention to your reaction to specific words. Words such as *surrender* and *sacrifice*, *obedience* and *service*, are heavy with

old and distorted meanings. Yet the essences of these concepts are alive and vital. We are constantly redefining what they might mean as we synergize the local into the global, the exclusive into the inclusive. At best, words are little containers to catch a bit of meaning. We will in time create a new set of transcendent, universal words and symbols.

One of the most practical lessons I have learned and which may help you as you move through the twelve lessons came to me during a frustrating cycle of working on this book. When I was about halfway through and keenly aware of deadlines and pressures, suddenly the following words popped in my mind, and I have kept them around as a reminder ever since: "Process, not product. Privilege, not pressure." I have found that if we stay in process, the learning and energy in the present moment will sustain us, and product will evolve and complete in its own time. Further, if we remember that it is a privilege to make a positive contribution, we can transform the pressure we are feeling into positive energy. Integration, balance, and wisdom are the ripened fruits of the Twelve Lessons of Spiritual Craftsmanship, the treasured syntheses of yin and yang, Light and shadow, heaven and earth.

Remember, it is always a privilege to serve life.

KNOWING THE WAY

❧

Knowledge: The Pointing Finger

Revelation: In the Twinkling of an Eye

Discernment: Clear Seeing, Clear Choices

Body: Temple, Archive, and Laboratory

Knowledge:
The Pointing Finger

❧

An uneducated mind is as dangerous as a high-speed automobile with weak brakes.

—Guredev Chitrabandhu, Jain master teacher

As I laughed my way through a little book called *Children's Letters to God*, it occurred to me that the essential questions don't change, no matter how old we are.

We can all hear the doubting Thomas in the child that writes "Dear God, are you really invisible . . . or is that just a trick?" Or the promising little scientist who says, "Dear God, how did you *know* you were God?"

Many people seem content to leave all those questions up to religion and science. But disciples seek insights into the Way that will effectively unite Spirit with the physical.

When we first step away from the pack and the packaged to seek our own Way, we are like eager young adults leaving home for the very first time who soon discover the cosmos is a big place with lots of choices. Most of us need guidance.

Fortunately, there are excellent maps available in all languages and persuasions to guide us along the Way. But we have to learn to read them, otherwise we explore the unknown by trial and error. The challenge for the disciple is to not confuse the pointing finger with what it is pointing toward.

Spiritual Sciences

The maps form a collective body of spiritual science, an overflowing cornucopia of knowledge from spiritual disciplines all over the world, complete with guidelines, practices, and a multitude of applications. In order to protect the integrity of the maps, the keys for reading them were buried in myths, language, and symbols that would appear baffling, naive, or merely curious to the uninitiated.

Passed down from master to chela, rabbi to student, initiate to aspirant, initiatory instruction was provided for the step-by-step training of mind, body, and spirit. Such training paralleled the outer religions, which provided dogmas, rituals, and a community structure. Jesus was reported to have said to his inner circle of students that although he taught by parable in the outer world, he offered them the "keys to the kingdom," the sciences of Spirit.

It has always been accepted practice to teach to the degree people are able to absorb and use the teachings. If I am learning to spell c-a-t, not only would it not be loving to put Shakespeare's plays in my first-grade primer, it would be pointless.

It is clear that the psyche can receive valuable information at random. But revelation without intelligent management can be like water without a container—inherently good, but unusable and quickly dissipated.

One of the first things one studies in a spiritual science is how to decode myths. While emphasis may vary, basically all systems will teach several things: the science of the breath and of the subtle bodies and chakras (without which one can be prey to superstition as surely as if one didn't understand the way the physical body works); methods for clearing and cleansing old memory patterns, thus unblocking pathways for Spirit; techniques for harnessing the mind as an instrument; purification processes for the body; insights into how energy works; understanding of and preparation for various stages of initiation into higher awareness and the responsibilities that go with each stage.

Most systems will include the study of basic universal principles that bring one in sync with the higher frequencies (such as "All life is one," "As above, so below," the Law of Return, and so forth). It is clearly beyond the scope of this chapter to explore those principles, but they are present throughout this whole book. The objective of any science of Spirit is to prepare the mind, body, and emotions to express the soul's intention.

Any one of the maps can prepare us for and direct us through recognizable gateways that lead to enlightenment. These portals are often referred to as initiations, indicating degrees of integration of mind, body, and spirit. Through those portals the many paths converge into the universal Way that leads to the heart of the Christ and the mind of the Buddha. Devotees from all traditions who have pursued their paths with commitment and passion now pass through the same initiatory portals. The words and outer forms of the practices may be very different, but as in mathematics, physics, or biology, the underlying principles are the same. A loving heart, clear mind, and dedicated longing take us through the first gate of initiation, regardless of the symbols we use to get there.

Workshop participants often report unknown archetypes or arcane symbols appearing in an exercise or meditation. The relaxed mind promotes easy exchange between the right brain and left brain. As the right brain is capable of accessing universal knowledge, it can, like a precocious computer techie, break into knowledge that may seem unintelligible out of its context. We may find we know too much to go back to religion-by-rote and yet feel overwhelmed by intuited fragments of insights.

Invariably when a symbol is explained, it becomes, as with a dream, completely clear as to why it appeared as a teaching. Eyes light up with recognition when the spiritual principle hidden in a story or symbology is illuminated. Without knowledge we can sometimes feel alone in our quest, unsure of our footing, even afraid of the next steps. Knowledge illuminates the path, showing us that it is well trodden and that we are safe and not alone.

We have a great need to give order to our experiences, and religion is one way we attempt to understand the great mystery of our beingness. Perceived by nonbelievers as a matter of opinion and by believers as the final word, religion works well unless in our eagerness to ground spirit in the material realm and interpret it we stop the ever-new, ever-revealing flow of revelation that inspired the religion in the first place.

We can choose a religion or not, but it is impossible not to be a spiritual being, for Spirit is essence of life. One can ignore or deny Spirit, or opt to express it in or out of a religion. It is possible to adhere successfully to an outer religion that includes fear, materialism, racism, sexism and other ugly isms that squeeze Spirit out, leaving only empty forms.

Yet is not possible to walk the Way, either in or out of a religion, and hold on to those prejudices. For the Way is an inner quest and not an outer form. And as it is a state of being, it can't be faked.

Being made in the image of God, we are all creators, and we are creating in many dimensions simultaneously. Spiritual sciences teach us how to consciously create with our intentions, thoughts, and energies at causal levels in mind and spirit. Physical manifestation naturally follows.

For thousands of years the spiritual sciences have studied the principles that govern consciousness and the means through which higher frequencies that operate in the universe are brought into manifestation. These sciences of the spirit have been refined in ways very similar to other sciences—through observation, repetition, and the proof of millions of transformed lives. All science is God/Goddess revealed.

In *Beyond the Post-Modern Mind*, Huston Smith, dean of religious historians, suggests that just as science has to have instruments and experiments, so mysticism requires a prepared instrument to detect the love that permeates the universe. Noting that Aldous Huxley once said, "It is a fact confirmed and reconfirmed by two or three thousand years of religious history that Ultimate Reality is not clearly and immediately apprehended except by those who had made themselves loving, pure in heart and poor in spirit," Smith comments that "perhaps such purity of heart is the indispensable instrument for disclosing the key perceptions on which religion's incredible assumption is grounded." That assumption is that love permeates the universal, and within each of us is the natural longing to grow in knowledge of that love.

"Poor in spirit" does not mean self-effacing. It means true humility, which is teachable. Most of us have to work through issues of the personality self, including ego arrogance, before we are ready to say to the universe, "Teach me." There are many frequencies of energy in this universe that simply cannot be tapped until the mind and nervous system are prepared. The mind would be literally blown apart if one's spiritual greed exceeded a willingness to clean up and clean out first. Preparation is keyed to right motive, sincere longing, love, and a willingness to face and master (meaning to know and be responsible for) all the contents of one's psyche.

Smith also reminds us that most of the great discoveries about our universe could not be seen with the naked eye. Andromeda, our second-closest neighbor, is two million light-years away and barely visible. Who could see that the number of molecules in approximately half an ounce of water is a hundred thousand billion? How can we see or weigh love or peace?

As Smith puts it, "From the vantage of our ordinary sense the vision is incredible—utterly, absolutely, completely incredible. Only, of course, it's true."

The Eyes to See

In the sacred story of Jesus, disciples need to intellectually understand that which was symbolized by the disciple Thomas, who wanted to see the nail marks on Jesus' hands before he believed in the risen Christ.

Spirit once said to me, "The desire to understand is coded into your drive toward reunion. Follow its call courageously, for it will lead you through the debris of fallen idols and undeciphered mysteries into freedom."

Certainly we cannot prove enlightenment, but neither is the enlightened mind careless or indifferent to knowledge. An unenlightened mind can acquire a lot of knowledge. But the enlightened mind has wisdom to integrate knowledge with awareness and love.

In both the classical mystery schools and those of today, knowledge of the material sciences is understood as necessary for a complete education. Down through the ages, mathematics, social sciences, medicine, architecture, archeology, languages, philosophy, diplomacy, law, astronomy, history, literature, music, politics, mythology, and more have been included in curricula for spiritual students. In our age, we are blessed with communications of all kinds that make all these areas of knowledge easily available.

Some of the most committed disciples I know personally are very informed in both spiritual and material sciences. They might, for example, be dedicated to meditation practices while they earn a living in computer science, practice yoga and teach biology, or speak of "sacred" mathematics (the esoteric language of math) as matter-of-factly as they would equations to engineer a highway.

One of the best teachers I know can deliver a lecture on quantum physics that gives the brain a workout. But if he senses that students are using knowledge to puff themselves up, he will give a basic, simple lecture on loving yourself and your neighbor.

Buddha was a serious student of existing spiritual knowledge before he received direct revelation. In esoteric traditions it is taught that Jesus was as well. According to unproven but persistent legends scattered around several countries, Jesus studied the great teachings of spirituality with masters in Egypt, Persia, India, and Tibet before he began his own ministry in Galilee.

In the 1880s Russian writer Nicolas Notovitch traveled throughout Afghanistan, India, and Tibet and wrote of a manuscript that exists in a monastery near Lhasa that tells the story of Issa, the equivalent name in Buddhism of Jesus. Paralleling much of the Bible story, it also tells of his travels between the ages of twelve and thirty, the unreported or "lost" years. The book, published in 1890, begins, "The earth trembled and the heavens wept because of the great crime committed in the land of Israel. For there was tortured and murdered the great and just Issa, in whom was manifest the soul of the universe."

A few decades later it was said that an Indian swami researched the manuscript and wrote about it, but since the Chinese have taken over Tibet and destroyed so many monasteries, it is doubtful that full investigation of the manuscript, including radiocarbon analysis to determine dates, can now take place. It is interesting that the legend reported in the Tibetan manuscript echoes much that appeared in a book that showed up in 1911, called the *Aquarian Gospel*. This book, still regularly reprinted, tells of the many travels of Jesus in the East.

Prophet and world-famous psychic Edgar Cayce, much to his own surprise, found many references coming from his channelings that indicated Jesus learned and taught in many lands. So if we believe these stories, it would seem that even Jesus, who was carrying the mission of the Christ, prepared himself with refresher courses!

Today there is a wide variety of programs that train students in spiritual sciences. Most anyone who is sincere in the pursuit of understanding can go on a supervised vision quest, learn hatha yoga or tai chi, and attend lectures and workshops on everything from Zen practices to shamanism. The treasure trove is wide open, rightfully bearing some warning labels, but nonetheless pouring out proven maps for seekers. And of course there is an even stronger backlash. The degree of resistance is testimony to the prevalence and effectiveness of the knowledge now available.

Seeking a System of Study

The following considerations may be helpful as you explore and evaluate the spiritual sciences.

1. Relax and remember that your longing and desire will attract possibilities to you. You then must exercise good judgment in what you choose to follow.
2. Above all, seek a system, teacher, or class that speaks to your heart. Study and practice will no doubt be required, but unless the object is to help you realize your true identity, it might be stimulating and not necessarily transformative. Release all expectations for instant results.
3. Include Nature (and her science) in your studies. The yield is far more than the charm of metaphor. Knowledge of nature is a gateway into deeper knowledge. The same principles that govern the heavens apply to all of life. Spiritual science teaches, "As above, so below."
4. Be willing to explore: read, talk to students and the teachers, ask lots of questions. Beware of any system that discourages or doesn't allow questions.
5. Be willing to listen with an open, receptive mind. Listening is not committing. In the beginning of a study we often don't know enough to ask the relevant questions.

6. Be patient. It takes a while to grasp a new vocabulary, new principles, and new symbols. Every discipline has a core curriculum that must be mastered in order to comprehend the teachings.

7. Don't be intimidated by senior students who seem facile with the system. Glib is not necessarily wise. We are all beginners, and we are all wise.

8. Knowledge is not a religion. You no more choose between a system of study and a religion that is important to you than you would choose between college or going to church. The study of a spiritual science will deepen your understanding of your religion.

9. Don't confuse the messenger and the message. Ashrams and spiritual centers are populated with real human beings seeking enlightenment while they work out unresolved jealousies, pettiness, power issues, greed, sexual projections, and the full range of their shadows.

10. Ask yourself a few basic questions in considering a group.

- Is this group suggesting they have the *one* Way? Are they suggesting they are the chosen elect? If so, maybe you should reconsider joining.

- Are you being asked to give up your will, money, family, or friends? If so, run the other way as fast as you can. Along the Way you may choose to move into a community, change your profession, or donate money, but those are inner-directed decisions, not externally compelled ones.

- Are the teachings you're being offered built around a personality? If so, you have to evaluate: Is that just what the students are projecting onto a beloved teacher, or is the teacher requiring this? It is natural to be grateful to a good teacher. Yet in time the personality of the teacher will pass; the teachings do not.

- Do you feel empowered? Do you feel you are honored and

respected? Will this help you play your role in the world better?

- Can you integrate what you are learning in this system? Do you have the inner and outer resources to support new openings in your psyche? If your answer is no, then slow down. Take a step back and integrate before you move on.

11. Seek out resources in your area. If you're just beginning to seek out a formal structure for study in your community, a few of the places you might begin your search include health food stores and vegetarian restaurants, which often post announcements of local workshops. Other sources are meditation classes and healing groups, holistic healers, energy healers, chiropractors, naturopaths, homeopaths, acupuncturists, massage therapists, and teachers—those at wellness centers as well as those who stress the fusion of mind and body, such as teachers of yoga and conscious Eastern body disciplines including tai chi or chi gong. Employees in metaphysical bookstores usually know everything going on in town, but even scanning the spiritual section of a regular bookstore can sometimes help guide your search.

    The religion, psychology, and sometimes art departments in local colleges and universities often have interesting lectures on consciousness and may post announcements of workshops.

    Magazines on consciousness advertise conferences and introduce teachers and systems through their articles. Find writers you like and write them through their publisher, asking to be put on a mailing list for newsletters and workshops. Take leads from the bibliographies in books that you like.

12. Explore the possibilities of correspondence courses and local chapters of national organizations. Many systems of

training offer courses by mail or have local chapters, such as the Rosicrucians, the Anthroposophical Society (originated by Rudolf Steiner), the Arcane School from the Lucis Trust (based on the Alice Bailey material), the Theosophical Society, the Agni Yoga Society, the Course in Miracles, Transcendental Meditation Society, the Fellowship for Self-Realization (based on the teachings of Paramahansa Yogananda), and others. Training programs that last a year or more, such as the Jean Houston Mystery School, based in Oregon, or the New Seminary, in New York, are popping up everywhere, renewing the concept of the mystery schools. There are literally thousands of centers, ashrams, and communities all over the world. Give yourself permission to research what's available before you choose.

Mind Is Knowledge in Process

We cannot talk about knowledge without considering the mechanisms of consciousness. Naturally we think first of our brains, but we hold knowledge everywhere. Mind is in every cell, every aggregate of cells, every tissue and organ. Each of these has intelligence in it, and thus we can contact it.

Mind is far vaster than the physical brain and what we normally call thinking. Mind is integrated awareness of the self (the personality) as it operates within the Self (the Godself), from the knowing held in any one chakra to the deepest soul memories.

What we hold in the brain is but a small boat on a vast sea. Through meditation and a dedicated search for the truth, mind can dive into the sea and bring treasures from the depths into the brain and consequently into outer consciousness. As we expand mind, lo and behold, the brain expands to hold our new discoveries.

Our whole consciousness, expressed through the body, emotions, and mind, is in constant process with our many environments—the immediate ones, the remembered ones, and the ones we fantasize.

From physics to biology to social systems, there is more and more evidence that the whole universe is moving energy in process. Process applies to even the smallest single cell that is without a brain or higher nervous system but is nevertheless seeking survival and self-expression. And process is at work within the most complex organism. The dynamic energy behind brain activity is mind itself, the *process* of being that includes the brain as its vehicle but is not confined by it.

As physicist Fritz Capra once put it, "The fact that mind is a noun is really a hindrance." Mind is an active process, ever moving, ever changing, always interacting, always evolving.

The very term *mind/brain* has only recently entered our vocabulary, but its wide acceptance acknowledges that there is a consciousness using the brain and creates a possible meeting ground for both spiritual and material scientists.

Even one of Lily Tomlin's characters (created by Jane Wagner) in *The Search for Signs of Intelligent Life in the Universe* had a suggestion: "Reality is just a collective hunch." Would that mean we go to war, live, or get sick based on our agreed-upon "hunches"? Maybe virtual reality, which completely challenges objective reality, will in time be harnessed and used to imprint ideas of health and peace into the brain.

In our insistence on reason, we have often placed a lower value on what writer Daniel Goleman calls "emotional literacy." In his book *Emotional Intelligence*, he presents the case for whole-brain education, "schooling the emotions" with our children, and not treating the brain as a high-tech computer, emotionless and without heart.

The emotional component of the brain is always feeding us intuitive and emotional information. Sometimes we try to reason ourselves away from the very truth this part of our brain gives us.

And then again, sometimes the haste of our emotional brain needs the analytical function to sort out the prejudiced and reactive from the actual. Whole-brain functioning calls for both perceptions.

The reasoning parts of our brain are always in a dance with the emotional parts of our brain. The dance can be a graceful waltz or maybe a sexy tango. Split apart, each part seems either coolly detached or in a self-absorbed frenzy, trying to find the beat when half the notes are missing.

The Cells Remember

Memory doesn't reside neatly in one corner of the brain. Rather, it is a constant process in the lobes and synapses and chemicals throughout the brain. We've known for some time that we deal with various kinds of memory, both long-term and short-term.

Research is showing that the same parts of the brain that play a role in recording visual memories are also the parts we use in dreaming and fantasizing. It seems that once again our ancient Greek relatives were very aware. The Goddess Mnemosyne was both in charge of memory and the mother of the Muses, who served the arts—poetry, music, dance, drama.

For years I cherished a childhood memory of a magical day with Uncle Mark on his farm, when, astride a magnificent steed, we had carried a picnic into a sylvan grove beside rushing waters. Twenty years later I asked if he remembered that day. "Of course," he said. "I still got that old mule Nellie; she's on her last legs now."

Mule? Well, it seems that the sylvan glade was a bunch of scrubby bushes, and the roaring water was a trickle of a stream. I was actually sad that my adult perception had destroyed my childhood memory, but the experience stimulated a reflection on the subjective nature of memories.

Flashbacks are another challenge in the memory maze. Years ago I received a request for healing from an architect who was having flashbacks from drugs he had taken many years before. As I worked with him I was shown that the brain rather impersonally records visual images. It doesn't ask if they are true or not.

While he was stoned he would be particularly fascinated by the way lights and shadows fell on buildings in a variety of angles and patterns. Of course, in that hyperstate of mind, they didn't exactly look the way they do with normal sight. Yet his brain impersonally recorded the image, and years later, when he observed light falling on a building in a similar way, maybe all but unnoticed consciously, his brain would fire into the memory clusters, kicking out the associative image, and suddenly he was experiencing a flashback of the image he had had while stoned.

I perceived that "treatment" would involve finding a way to erase this route in his brain. Perhaps that was *my* fantasy, but after treatment he didn't have the flashbacks anymore. Maybe more healing would take place if both the patient and the healer agreed on a fantasy that could be fed to the brain to replace the discarded patterns.

In meditation I once experienced merging with a meditating monk in Tibet, finding myself looking over the Himalayas through his eyes. For days I was not sure if I had dreamed him in my mind or if this life I now experience is his dream. The image was so vivid, it took a while for my brain to find a proper place for it within the reality of being Gloria. (It came to rest in a we'll-see file, one I wouldn't be without.)

I do know that brain patterning can be changed, but it takes real dedication to do so deliberately. However, sometimes it happens spontaneously, with insights so profound that they, in effect, shake loose the pattern. I know a case in which infant imprinting set up the following pattern: "I'm crying, but help doesn't come, therefore I am powerless; now I am waiting, tense but expectant; when help arrives, I am grateful." Powerlessness followed by waiting followed by gratitude—that was the cluster. That triangular pattern repeated itself in relationships and career settings until the person recognized it and chose to change it. Biofeedback can be a good tool for replacing programs. Affirmations, mantras, and visualizations can help, especially if they are done in conjunction with bodywork or energy healing.

Memory clusters can be triggered in a nanosecond through sound or smell. How long does it take the solar plexus to react when you hear the beginning notes of a song shared with a first love? The heart quickens, the tears gather, and the whole body is enveloped with emotion, all before the second line of the song.

Among the Australian Aborigines, it is assumed that a child will be born with "the memory," possessing knowledge that the group has spent eons of time mastering. What if we do actually pass on our accumulated knowledge of Spirit to our children, just as we do with material knowledge? What if we taught all our children that they are spiritual beings (infinite and unlimited), literally made in the image of God/Goddess (yang and yin), having a human (finite and limited) experience together in an indivisible whole? What kind of paradise might our children create with that legacy?

Whether we are perching at the edge of the mystery wearing a lab coat or a meditation shawl, we are all seeking knowledge.

Miraculously, today it is scientists across the full spectrum of human experience who are jointly midwifing our new birth. There's a kinetic energy leaping from experimental lab to philosophy salon with the speed of excited neurons firing around the whole brain. And even if *all* the material scientists are not sitting down with *all* the spiritual scientists, enough of them who walk the exploding edges of their own disciplines are daring to build bridges to other fields of inquiry. These meetings of the minds in the outer world are powerful symbols of the inner work we are all doing to heal the divided self.

❦ Journaling Seeds

Note: Suggestions for journaling will be offered throughout the lessons. They are to provide focus for your inner explorations.

1. What questions did you have as a child? Were they honored? Answered? Dismissed?

2. Review the people, books, lectures, and other sources of knowledge that have inspired and stimulated you.

Exercise: Memory Clusters and the Thousand-Petaled Lotus

All of us have cluster patterns—learned assumptions that are grouped in the mind. For example, if we grew up in a family that dishonored originality, the cluster might come up as: "It's dangerous to express myself; safety comes from appeasing and conforming; asserting my creativity will lead to abuse or ridicule."

Examine as many of your own clusters as possible. What patterns do you now see repeating over and over in your life? You may have researched these patterns in various therapies. Now see if you can track the history of assumptions about reality that have hooked up in your psyche.

Sometimes we can get to our clusters through an exercise. The thousand-petaled lotus is an ancient exercise from the East that can research our hidden patterns by gradually revealing our links to memory clusters. If we followed it closely enough, it would eventually lead us to our links with everything.

1. You begin by picking a seed word for something you want to understand more deeply. Draw a circle and write this word in the circle, as the center of a lotus blossom. For ex-

ample, you might want to place the word *love* in the center of your lotus.

2. Next, focus on your breathing. Relax, close your eyes, and wait. Soon a word association will come to mind. You then draw a lotus petal and write the associated word in it. Don't resist or be concerned about whether you understand it at this point.

3. Then release the association and bring your attention back to the center, to the word *love*, and wait. Soon another association will come. You draw another petal, write in the word, release it, and return to the center of the lotus.

4. Continue this process for as long as you like. *But be certain to always return to the seed word in the center of the lotus.* There is no right or wrong way to do it. In time this little exercise can reveal clusters and provide real insight into hidden associations you might be carrying.

You might discover that the first associations are obvious—or perhaps they are so fragmented that they make no sense. Just stay with it, even when you hit a block. That may be the point at which you are peeling away to some deep issue or vulnerability you need to encounter.

5. When your mind is slow to give a new association, pay close attention, as your defenses are starting to show up and say, "That's far enough." Then take the last word association and make it the center of a new lotus.

Knowledge in Shadow

Knowledge's shadow doesn't just say, "I think, therefore I am." It declares, "I think, therefore that's all that is." The shadow fears losing control: "What if I don't know? Will I be vulnerable?" Not knowing makes us feel vulnerable. It is at that point that we are ready to seek out knowledge.

Problems start when we want our answers to be exclusive and conclusive. Periodically, it seems, our technicians and pundits assure us with great authority that we now have defined the boundaries of reality, and sometimes they even pronounce what is good and bad.

Once we accept that we live in a maze in the middle of a mystery, we are teachable. The quickest way to prohibit new knowledge is to think we already know it all. Then we can become like a prisoner bragging about the size of his or her cell.

We might have read voraciously and accumulated facts, but that doesn't mean we *know*. We can't dance, make love, or know God by reading about it. And yet there's probably not a one of us who didn't fill our bookshelves, our notebooks, and our minds with secondhand information about the spiritual path before we opted for direct experience. Most of us have been profoundly influenced by others' descriptions of the spiritual path, but at some point we realize that the most powerful testimonies are the ones that provide guidance for discovering our own truth.

The story is told of a woman who was very surprised when she walked into a new shop in the mall and discovered the Goddess behind the counter. Of course she wanted to know what in the world was being sold. Goddess assured her that *everything* she could possibly want was there. So the woman laid out a list of desires: wisdom, peace of mind, happiness, and love, not just for herself but for all the world.

"I'm afraid you don't really understand, my dear," said the Goddess. "Fruits are not sold here, only seeds."

"I Don't Know" Leads to Knowing

"I don't know" unlocks the door to myriad possibilities. For one thing, it releases arrogance and empties a too-full mind. This in turn creates a vacuum that can be filled with a new awareness that takes us back to innocence. We become children again in the best sense of the word. It is this "beginner's mind" that the Zen Buddhists encourage in their devotees—the teachable mind, empty of opinions and sureties and therefore empty of limitations. Just as death signifies birth and endings announce new beginnings, so does emptiness precede fullness.

After one of the Dalai Lama's brilliant lectures at a conference, he opened the microphone for questions. The well-educated members of the audience posed complex questions that seemed designed to reveal their erudition rather than seek insights from His Holiness. After a question was finally formed, a silence would follow, and then the Dalai Lama would say, "I don't know." Another complex question, another "I don't know." The most amazing quality of the exchanges was that there was no put-down of anyone, but the point was well made.

In *The Aladdin Factor* writers Jack Canfield and Mark Victor Hansen suggest that there are five major reasons we don't ask enough questions. The first is ignorance, followed by limiting and inaccurate beliefs, fears, low self-esteem, and pride.

I would add to that list the "doubting Thomas syndrome." We all have an inner disciple who says, "Show me," and we need to honor him. But we must not make him the executive director of our consciousness. Each new doorway that opens in our understanding of the way the universe works simultaneously introduces new mysteries. There's an old German saying that translates as "Few know how much one must know to know how little one knows."

Unless we keep our Thomas in proper perspective, we might be like the persistent student who kept asking her teacher, Thai

Buddhist master Achaan Chah, to elaborate on the subtleties of
the eighty-nine classes of consciousness in the Buddhist *abhi-
dharma* psychology texts. The teacher finally said to her that she
was like one who has hens in her yard but picks up chicken drop-
pings instead of eggs.

It's said that Aristotle told his students they should give up
everything close to them in their quest for truth. One devotee
pronounced he was ready to give up everything, wealth, friends,
family, country, life itself, so what else was left?

To which the master teacher calmly replied, "One's beliefs
about God."

The disciple went away saddened, for he feared ignorance even
more than death, just as the rich young man walked away from Jesus when he was told he must give up everything. Perhaps such
stories exist in the legends of all great teachers because the concept of giving up is less about things than it is about ideas, images
of ourselves, and our attachments.

Knowledge is a stepping-stone toward enlightenment. It is not
enlightenment itself. Ideally we live in a balance of knowing and
not knowing. Not one, not the other: both.

One of Us Has to Be Right, Right? Wrong!

A potential shadow of knowledge is polarization, the need to
make anything different wrong. That's when we get stuck in one-
of-us-has-to-be-right. It follows, of course, that one of us is going to be wrong. In truth, wisdom stretches to embrace both.

Art, science, and spirituality all contribute parts of the whole,
often simultaneously. In the West we have raised specialization of
knowledge to a religion. The good news is that we have multi-
plied knowledge in every field of inquiry. The bad news is that
sometimes we have brilliant but isolated fragments.

Not only do we not have all the answers, but the people who
influenced us when we were growing up didn't, either. We all

have to work our way through centuries of distortion that have been handed down as truth.

✤ Journaling Seeds ✗

1. How do you feel when your versions of reality are challenged?

2. Do you say, "I don't believe that!" before you listen carefully?

3. What does it mean to you to have an open mind?

4. When do you feel the need to defend your point of view?

5. Have you questioned the beliefs you were taught as a child?

Displaced and Dangerous

The shadow will grab information meant to illuminate other levels of reality and instead concretize it on the physical level. Parables, myths, and symbols lose their dynamic power when they are forced into three-dimensional patterns. Stories meant to point to eternal truths are told as the truth itself, and guidelines are hardened into rules and dogmas. Then come the enforcers who declare what is acceptable and what is not.

Not only can knowledge be distorted out of its vibrational context, it can be seriously twisted when symbols and practices are taken out of their cultural context. It can even, in extremes, be dangerous.

For example, I know a teenager who was deeply attracted to the rituals of American Indian culture. During a very difficult time in her life, she performed a cleansing ceremony that she had read about that involved cutting herself as an act of purification. Such a ritual is part of a much larger context, but she had no spiritual foundation for the ceremony, no guidance before, during, or after, and no follow-up support. She had to be hospitalized, having only added to her original problem.

We can acquire the facts about something and still be very naive about the possible effects of practicing it. I once counseled a young man who had gotten in over his head when he started excessively doing chants from a Japanese tradition in which he had no teacher, no parameters to determine effectiveness or danger, and no real understanding of the power of chant. It did indeed shake some things loose in his psyche, but then he had no resources to handle those shifts. I encouraged him to see a therapist. He did, and in time acquired some skills to sift through the unconscious material that had surfaced during the chanting.

Practices from any tradition exist within a larger structure that has an underpinning of beliefs, preparation, supporting rituals, and guidance. Certainly the current availability of the world's knowledge is a veritable banquet, but it requires increased discrimination if we don't want severe indigestion or worse.

Before taking up practices from another culture, ask yourself:

• Are you really prepared?
• Do you understand the intent and the expected result of the practices?
• Do you have the resources for integration?
• Do you have outside guidance you can call on?

Just as the shadow can glamorize whatever seems exotic, it can also dismiss the sacred stories and myths of another Way. We smile as if listening to children when we hear myths from other cultures. Yet we still keep one variation of a creation myth lurking around the edges in the Judeo-Christian religion, the one in which one woman, Eve, started all the problems of the world in the Garden.

This myth, which seems purely symbolic to an educated mind,

has for thousands of years shaped religious rationales for the suppression of women, and even now Eve's rebellion is occasionally dragged out to legitimize terrifying and bloody backlashes against women. Myths are strong affirmations of belief and have the power to shape social, political, and religious choices. They are not harmless.

Power: Handle with Care

Knowledge is power. It is not sentimental. One can learn how to manipulate energy in the astral and lower mental planes just as on the physical plane. That is a major reason esoteric knowledge was protected for centuries and taught only to those who were emotionally, intellectually, and spiritually prepared to use it in service and for the highest good. But in all times and places that knowledge has been usurped and employed by leaders, including Hitler, to help them plot the domination of others.

It is not so surprising that many people have mixed feelings about those who know how to work in the unseen. Often we lump them together in our minds, barely distinguishing, if at all, between witches as devotees of a religion and the stereotypes from fairy tales, for example, or between shamans as spiritual leaders and healers and the "witch doctors" from grade-C Hollywood movies. While we may admire those with "the sight" and "the power," we are equally afraid of the power of those who we believe can "cast spells." We can even declare that those of our religion have "gifts of the Spirit," while those of other religions are at the very least suspect and at worst demonic.

Knowledge is neither inherently good or bad. It simply is. As we acquire more knowledge about the unseen, we will retire a lot of these old superstitions and fears. Both exaggerated admiration and fear are often grounded in lack of knowledge. When knowledge is available to all, it soon loses its ability to intimidate.

Knowledge can be put in service to the highest intentions or the lowest. For example, let's look at a couple of principles that are equally effective for good or harm.

1. The Heisenberg uncertainty principle, discovered early in this century, says that the consciousness and intentions of the observer affect whoever or whatever is being observed.

Many of the phenomena that seem supernatural are actually this principle in practice. Spiritual science has always taught initiatory candidates in mystery schools, alchemists, priests and priestesses, healers, and shamans how to use their minds to alter the wave motions of energy and imprint the connecting field that permeates all things, thus charging any substance or object with their intention.

This knowledge empowers many sacraments. When water, food, or even the air is blessed by the intention of conscious people, everything in the environment changes positively.

By the same principle, poisonous thoughts and intentions can be impregnated into a substance. Those who practice black magic make use of this knowledge.

Using this principle requires intense and controlled concentration, which is why most people are unable to use it consciously. Nevertheless, unconsciously we are always affecting everything in the environment—cars, computers, refrigerators, and our pets and gardens, not to mention people. Imagine what we're doing to our energy fields when we focus on negative and limiting thoughts about ourselves and the world day in and day out.

2. Science now reports that time and space are not immutable constants but rather are relative. Spiritual science has taught this for a very long time. In the Upanishads it is written: "That is far, and the same is near; that is within all this, and this is also outside all this."

Any clairvoyant, healer, or mystic knows that you don't need to spend time and cross space in order to be with anyone, anytime, anywhere. Most people experience that awareness now and then at random. People who understand the principle use it on command. You only need to think of a person or a place, and presto—you're both there and here simultaneously. There are those who choose to use this principle harmfully, through psychic attacks, destructive thoughts, and psychic spying. However, neither of these is to be feared by conscious people. An environment filled with Light is never in danger from such attacks because they come from lower frequencies that cannot penetrate the higher frequencies of the Light.

"Seek ye first the kingdom of heaven" is the first directive in spiritual science. Right motive is essential. Any misuse of resources—and knowledge is a resource—carries heavy karma. Any harm we do to another is done to ourselves in the same moment, even if it takes a long time to manifest.

❧ Twelve Considerations on Knowledge

Note: It is recommended that you use the considerations that follow each of the Twelve Lessons as discussion, journaling, or meditation seeds.

1. Knowledge obeys the spiritual law "Seek and you shall find."

2. Knowledge provides the maps; we must make the journey.

3. Knowledge illuminates the blindness of superstition.

4. Myths and symbols depict dynamics, not fixed realities.

5. A beginner's mind is unbiased and therefore teachable.

6. Intelligence exists in every atom of life and can be contacted.

7. Mind is a process, always interacting with other processes.

8. Wisdom synthesizes the knowledge of mind, body, and spirit.

9. One who knows is free to say "I don't know" and learn more.

10. Knowledge solves and creates mysteries simultaneously.

11. Science is God/Goddess revealed. All seekers are true scientists.

12. Knowledge prepares the vessels that revelation fills.

Exercise: Shaman and Scientist

Build your own bridges to consciousness by starting a notebook in which you take a principle from spiritual science and research what material science is learning about it. Here are a couple of examples:

At one time NASA made a film called *The Power of Ten*. Cameras recorded the dynamics in a skin cell, and then the cameras were turned out toward space to capture the same principles at work on a much larger scale. Spiritual science long ago came to the same conclusion: "As above, so below." In other words, if you want to understand the outer universe, understand the inner one, and vice versa.

Another example: The beauty and mystery of nature unfold in the mathematical equation of the golden mean, which expresses itself in everything from the sunflower to the perfect acoustics of an ancient Greek theater.

Other examples of principles you could start with are "Light is essence," "All life is connected," "We create our realities."

The next step is to explore how these principles could be used for either good or evil.

This is an exercise that is good for a group to do, with everyone researching and reporting different principles. Don't limit your inquiries to physics, but include math, biology, astronomy, sacred geometry, psychology, and the social sciences.

Exercise: Fantasy or Fact?
Whose Fantasy, Whose Fact?

Naturally, our understanding of reality changes as we open our minds and are teachable. However, the ego mind often prefers to believe in the information it already has. The following is a simple exercise that can demonstrate three ways we can deal with new information. We can reject it because we haven't experienced it; we can consider it because we have partial information; or we can fully open our minds to new possibilities.

1. First, describe skiing downhill to one who has never actually seen snow or a skier and doesn't believe they exist.

2. Describe the same thing to one who has seen snow, but has never seen skiing and is skeptical that it can be done.

3. Finally, describe the same thing to one who has not ever actually seen snow or a skier but has had a brief encounter (perhaps in a dream, in a vision, or through the testimony of another in a book, poem, or conversation) and wants to know.

Notice how explanations can shape themselves into intelligent presentations once one considers that (1) snow is a reality; (2) it is possible to descend the mountain gracefully and with joy; (3) many have done it; (4) it can be demonstrated and taught.

Prayer

I will turn the power of thought into a searchlight whose brightness will reveal the face of Omnipresence. Teach me to think of thee until thou does become my only thought.

—Paramahansa Yogananda

Affirmation

I am a receptive vessel for universal mind. I accept truth and truth only.

Quotes

We are what we think. All that we are arises with our thoughts. With our thoughts we make the world.

—The Buddha

As a man thinketh within himself, so is he.

—Proverbs 23:7

The search for answers is a canoe trip into the wilderness. Every time the canoe rounds a bend in the river, the landscape changes.

—Dr. Patricia Churchland,
professor, University of California

Revelation:
In the Twinkling of an Eye

❧

Unconscious people read the scripture. Like parrots saying "Ram, Ram" in their cages. It's all pretend knowledge. Read rather with me, every living moment as prophecy.

—Lalla, fourteenth-century Sufi mystic

Revelation is one of evolution's little perks. While knowledge requires study, revelation arrives, more often than not, like a sudden, unexpected gift.

I use the term *revelation* to embrace all the nonlinear forms of learning about ourselves and the universe: dreams, visions, intuitions, epiphanies, prophecies, near-death and out-of-body experiences, the sudden *aha*, and the full range of extrasensory perceptions that gestalt whole realities and operate outside the known boundaries of time and space.

Fortunately, we are equipped with a brain capable of processing both existing knowledge and sudden knowing. We have our own custom-designed computer brains, and we are connected to each other through the morphogenetic field, so that whatever one learns potentially becomes available to all of us. In addition, we have the capability both to access the universal mind and to cut like a laser through confusion to the essence of anything.

As in most aspects of discipleship, the ideal is balance: the focused mind seeking knowledge and the receptive mind accepting knowledge, happily coupled and working in a flow back and forth.

Revelations catapult us out of orderly learning patterns. A window flies open in consciousness, and suddenly the light pours in. It doesn't trickle in one molecule at a time. It floods the mind with new awareness. Confusion is dispersed in a sudden insight, like the moment a code is broken or the letters in a crossword puzzle magically become words. Even as it answers questions, it often poses entirely new ones.

At the beginning of my work I perceived all kinds of specialists in Spirit—angels, doctors, teachers, guides, and the like. As I became more accustomed to the work, I saw fewer and fewer individualized entities, and more and more pure Light. My intellect constantly questioned: "Have I made up Spirit specialists to satisfy my left brain? Or is it all indeed pure Light?" I was never concerned about negative spirits, as I was clear from the outset in my prayers, intentions, and declarations that I would receive only that which served the universal Christ.

As I prayed over this puzzle I received the following explanation. In my inner sight I first saw bright, undifferentiated Light. Gradually within the field of Light, molecules gathered to form a golden oval denser than the bright, diffuse Light. Within that oval the molecules began to form a still denser, loosely outlined figure. Within that outline, an even denser image of a "doctor" appeared. And within that, in the most dense collection of molecules of all, I sat in the physical body. The message became clear: The Christ can manifest at whatever level is necessary to get the work done. I then more clearly understood that there are nonvisible intelligences that serve healing in all frequencies. The need calls forth the level of response.

We all exist in many bodies simultaneously. Each "body" expresses a different range of frequencies, not unlike different octaves on a piano, all of which exist on one keyboard. *We can receive revelation from any one of those levels. Intelligence exists in all of them.* All of us are capable of becoming sensitive to the presence of subtle energies, but we interpret what we perceive according to our understanding.

The universe is constantly revealing itself. If we are bound by the revelations of the past, as true as they may have been, we will be unable to hear today's messages. Revelation is a catalyst that leapfrogs us to our next level. Like the monolith in the movie *2001*, it can appear as a guide on the edge of our reality, pointing a way through unmarked territory.

Epiphany: The Unexpected Gift

With no warning, in a deep, dreaming sleep or a waking vision, any one of us can know with certainty something that we didn't know seconds before. We don't always have the evidence to prove such knowing; all we have are thousands of similar reports.

For example, mystics throughout time speak of becoming aware during meditation of a great void, a peaceful emptiness.

When I was a young woman I began to daydream in class one day and suddenly found myself pulling the sky apart with my fingers. Beyond the tear was unbroken emptiness. It somehow thrilled me. I had no idea why, but I intuitively knew it was an important awareness, even though I had no knowledge of the concept of nothingness. The teacher's explanation was that I had a "terrific imagination."

Many years later, in a meditation, I found myself again in this void, and it held great meaning for me. This time I was aware that just as nothing was there, so was everything. Perhaps the peace comes from the sweet dissolving of the ego back into remembrance of Oneness. Once we experience it, we never forget it, even when the personality self asserts its demands.

Knowing is a mysterious synthesis that happens in consciousness. To know is to comprehend in every cell of your beingness even when you can't explain it. A British writer calls it "Faculty X."

The Huna teachings of Hawaii say that such experiences provide a short circuit between the Highest Self (the Godself) and consciousness, without passing through the filter of ego.

Here are excerpts from a letter I received from a workshop participant in England that demonstrates this point. Her experience is universal. At the same time it is also completely fresh, just as it is every time it happens to any one of us, as it can at any moment. She wrote:

> *I woke up and found a new world. Everything was illuminated from within as well as without. . . . Every member of the group was absolutely perfect and new. I was stunned by the beauty of the sound and the shape of sentences. I went to sleep to attempt to return to what I was used to perceiving—the old, comfortable imperfection. When I awoke again, every single leaf of the trees was outlined by white light. I could re-create this light at will. It has left me now, as it is time, I think, for action. It's enough to know the other exists in parallel. I believe now that what I saw was the perfection of reality without the lies of my ego's perceptions. I always knew it existed, but to consciously experience it in this life is very precious.*

This kind of instant knowing is often described to me by clients, students, colleagues, and friends: "All of a sudden the world opened up," "I knew it was absolutely true," "I was overwhelmed by love," "Suddenly I knew I was not alone."

People speak of these phenomena differently, but the common denominator is the lasting quality of the insight. Whether it happened to us as a child or as a teenager, during a crisis or on an ordinary day, the effect is the same. It creates an instant shift in perception, and the memory remains acute throughout our lives.

Theoretical argument cannot explain away direct experience.

One can't always articulate a revelation, teach it, or repeat it. Until we reach a full integration of mind, body, and spirit, our nervous system can no more handle direct revelation all the time than it can sustain orgasm indefinitely. Yet even a little bit of revelation can last for a lifetime.

I've seen knowing on the faces of people who have had near-death experiences, and I hear the knowing in their voices. It hardly matters what their common sense, their previous beliefs, or their family, friends, preachers, priests, and counselors say. They are immovable in their knowing, even if they choose to be quiet about their experiences. They know that they know.

Revelations alter our perceptions. As long as we don't know about a thing, we can be blind to it, ignore it, be prejudiced against it, even actively fight it, as Paul did before he was struck with Light on the road to Damascus. Once a truth has been revealed to us, we can never again pretend it doesn't exist.

Revelation puts us in touch with our inner intuitive authority. Carl Jung in his last interview was asked, "Do you believe in life after death?" And he answered, "Believe? I know. There is no mental question."

None of us can force revelations into happening, but we can prepare a receptive consciousness for them. As the sage answered the frustrated student who questioned why he should practice disciplines if they wouldn't make him enlightened, "So you will be awake when enlightenment comes."

Channeled Insight

Knowledge can be transmitted from nonphysical intelligence to human intelligence. *Channeling* is a term that has more than one level of meaning. Any one of us can suddenly possess great wisdom or say the perfect thing to another person. In those moments we may actually be "channeling" our own highest inner knowing, which is connected to all knowledge. Typically we don't sustain that level of channeling day in and day out unless the information is fully integrated at all levels.

Information that is transmitted from Spirit intelligence to a receptive mind maintains clarity and authority, even when the information is as yet unproved or untested.

Many of our most treasured sacred writings have been received through a channel. In the early years of his emergence, Mohammed's disciples wrote down what he said on palm leaves because he couldn't read or write. Later he learned to do both. People would have to speak the questions they wanted interpreted by Hui-Neng, a sixth-century Chinese Buddhist sage, because he also didn't read, nor, it is said, did the great mystic Ramakrishna. Manley P. Hall, who wrote profound books on many subjects, never went to school beyond the eighth grade.

Most religions and movements grew out of someone's personal revelation. Islam began with one man of profound integrity, Mohammed, and a small band of followers who believed his revelation. Joseph Smith's revelation was the foundation of the Mormon faith. John the Beloved sat on Patmos in a trance and received revelation. Buddha sat under the bodhi tree. St. Ignatius sat by a stream and watched running water. And medieval theologian/philosopher Jacob Boehme sat staring at a pewter dish.

Tribal people will eagerly await the revelation of the shaman who fasts and goes into solitude for days in order to receive a guiding truth for the tribe. Aborigines enter the Dreamtime together for the same purpose.

Great channeled works that have influenced millions were revelations, not philosophical constructions. The many books that form the great body of work by Alice Bailey were revealed to her in Spirit by the Tibetan Djwhal Khul. *A Course in Miracles,* channeled by a nonbelieving New York psychologist named Dr. Helen Schueman, was reportedly dictated to her by Jesus. People all over the world receive information from sources that are perceived as spirit teachers, angels, guides, and extraterrestrials. Some of the information is filled with prophecy, and some, such as the voice of Emmanuel speaking through Pat Rodegast, carry a wisdom that rings so true, thousands turn to them for daily guidance.

Certainly not all channeled material seems revelatory, and one is wise to use discrimination in evaluating it. We shall look at this issue more closely in the chapter on discernment; nevertheless, the phenomenon is too universal to be dismissed.

Symbols: The Universal Language

Revelations often come to us in mystical language, and we usually don't give the same credibility to the colorful, poetic language of subjective experience that we do to objective knowledge. Can you imagine the reaction to a visionary in the first century insisting the world was round? Imagine how Leonardo da Vinci's contemporaries responded to some of his ideas: "Can you believe the man is now drawing people flying in machines?"

We have to report all revelations from the language and symbols stored in our brains. Sometimes, with words alone, it feels like trying to capture the wind with a net. With symbols we seem to ride the winds above our differences. The privileges and problems of being Spirit embodied in a human experience are universal, and the language we use to express them is symbolic.

Whether I do a counseling session for someone in Europe, Latin America, or downtown Des Moines, the language of symbols overrides cultural differences. A desert, a cave, or the sun; animals and seasons; stages of life, geometry, and colors are all part of the archetypal language of symbols everywhere.

Actually all of the created objects in the world are symbolic. A table is a table because we all agree to perceive it as such. It's really just a collection of molecules adhering to each other in predictable and repeatable patterns. The table is simply a symbol for someone's idea. All the things that we have created around us are stand-ins for our beliefs and understanding.

Very often revelation runs ahead of existing knowledge, and we don't know if the information we intuit is literal or symbolic. Early in my work I saw "wormholes" in space in my meditations when I was asking questions about the mechanics of traveling between parallel worlds. It was many years later that I saw identical drawings in books on theoretical physics. To this day I can't explain the scientific theory, and certainly not the math. Nor am I an inventor or an engineer, yet I saw technologies in my meditations that I knew would exist on the material plane years before they actually did (such as sound waves used to bombard and break up kidney stones). Many people have such visions, including science fiction writers, who often excel in describing technologies that emerge years later.

Many practicing scientists dream of equipment and technologies because they rationally know the possibilities are probable. People who are not scientists often see similar inventions and have no context in which to put them. It's as though knowledge that has not yet manifested floats freely in the ethers and is occasionally picked up by a mind that is receptive, not unlike a radio receiver picking up a signal from a distant place. Then, like the biblical prophet Ezekiel, we have to describe our visions with the symbols we have in our mind and culture.

Here is a sampling of Ezekiel's vision from the Old Testament. Many surmise it was a vision of a spacecraft.

> *When the living creatures went, the wheels went, and when the creatures stood, they stood also, and when they were lifted up from the earth, the wheels were lifted up with them, for there was a living spirit in the wheels. (1:21)*

> *And when they went, I heard the noise of their wings like the noise of great waters, like the voice of God, like the sound of speech in a host, and when they stopped, they let down their wings. (1:24)*

Perhaps because he was so attuned to spiritual wavelengths, Ezekiel picked up signals that presaged something that only in the last hundred years has been manifested in the physical realm.

Journaling Seeds

1. If you look at your home as if it were in a dream, how would you analyze the symbolic content of each room?
2. Are the things you live with beautiful to you? Empowering? Were they inherited? Is there clutter and disorder?
3. What do the symbols tell you about your inner life?

A Child's Garden: Seeds of Truth

Many people remain secretive about their revelations because they can't explain them and they fear ridicule. For example, it's not uncommon for people to wait years before they reveal visions that occurred during near-death experiences. Children are frequently aware of energies around people, see entities from other kingdoms and relatives who have passed over, and refer matter-of-factly to past lives. But they pick up the taboos and fear of the adult world very quickly.

When a direct revelation is debunked, that negative message cripples the spiritual flowering of a child. It teaches children that the truth is outside themselves. It limits personal revelation by assigning it a lower value, and one of the most insidious ill effects is that it teaches self-doubt.

Antoine de Saint-Exupéry, author of *The Little Prince*, tells the story of a six-year-old boy who drew a picture of an elephant that had been swallowed by a boa constrictor. The adults didn't get it, and as the boy grew up he occasionally showed the drawing to adults, who invariably thought it was a hat. "Then I would never talk to that person about boa constrictors or primeval forests, or stars. I would bring myself down to his level. I would talk to him about bridge, and golf, and politics, and neckties. And the grownup would be greatly pleased to have met such a sensible man." The "little prince" consciousness was probably in most of us when we were children.

Tony told me that he certainly didn't know a thing about quantum mechanics when he came upon this truth as a child: "I remember thinking that I was like a speck in the center of this puzzle, and as every little piece moved, it affected my movement, and every movement I made affected every little piece of the puzzle."

Over and over I've heard things like "I knew the adults wouldn't understand," "It was obvious to me as a child that God was a God of love and forgiveness," "I wrote things when I was a child like 'God is the reed, God is the stream' and so forth," "I saw that people didn't believe what they said."

A young child recently told me he sees pictures of geometric shapes in his head. Pointing to his forehead, he said, "All I have to do is ask and the answer pops in right here. And if I want to see a different angle, it will turn and even change colors. Isn't that cool?"

This child, who already has a predisposition toward science, is actually following a pattern of many scientists, many of whom report they first received the answer to an important question intuitively or through a dream or meditation/contemplation symbol. James Watson and Francis Crick discovered the double helix structure of the DNA strand. Watson saw it first in a vision. Elmer Gate, an inventor with hundreds of patents, would go into his lab, turn off the lights, and concentrate on a seed thought that would then bloom into ideas.

❧ Journaling Seeds

1. Did you have experiences with the unseen worlds as a child?

2. Were your experiences respected or dismissed?

3. Did your religion conflict with or support your knowing?

4. How can you nurture your inner child's knowing?

Vision as Prophet and Guide

During a visualization exercise to project oneself into the future, Maria was amazed to see a new little dark-haired child in her family, especially since she'd had a tubal ligation and had no plans for more children. She dreamed and thought about the baby a lot.

Months later Maria attended a funeral in another town. At the funeral home she saw a small child, seemingly withdrawn and distrustful, and her heart began to beat rapidly. "My behavior was unusual," she reported. "I didn't do what you are supposed to do at funeral homes. I was fixated on this little girl. I *had* to have a picture of her, so I borrowed a camera and took a rather poor-quality picture, but it was a picture nonetheless."

Maria learned that the child was living in very difficult circumstances and often had to forage for food. She arranged for the child and her parents to visit her and her family. At first the child was guarded. But later, as visits extended for longer periods, she relaxed and captured everyone's heart. Within a few months the birth parents agreed to an adoption. Maria's prophecy in her vision was fulfilled.

We rarely understand the full implications of our prophetic visions at the time they occur. They often have to be put on a wait-and-see shelf. But occasionally they are very clear.

Anna received a comforting vision shortly before her favorite sister died. In her vision she saw her sister in bed with a medicine bottle on a bedside table. Suddenly the bottle dissolved into a white dove. She intuitively knew that the long illness her sister had endured, symbolized by the medicine, was soon to be transformed by death into peace, the white dove.

I am often asked to "prophesy" for another. And I am very cautious about that. However, on occasion the message between my soul and another's will be as clear as reading a book. (Even then I'm always aware that it is my mind "reading the book"; therefore I must always be as aware of my own filters as possible.) In the case of Sam and Barbara and a new baby, prophecy was a help.

Sam and Barbara are a delightful couple, both professionals in their fields and both deeply committed to their paths, which included living in the country close to Nature. At the time of this story they lived about thirty minutes from the nearest hospital, a fact that was important because Barbara was pregnant.

Normally, instead of presuming to tell people what to do, I will discuss patterns and possibilities as I see them. Yet when I learned that Barbara planned to have natural childbirth at home, I found myself emphatically saying, "No, you can't do this." I had psychically seen that there would be difficulty with the birth. Fortunately, they listened, for there were indeed problems during the birth.

Knowing in an altered state resembles the knowing one has in dreams. I was aware that the baby was a girl and terrified. I saw images of a Jewish child during the Holocaust. I "knew" that Sam and Barbara's daughter, Molly, would need time to overcome her fears. However, I also knew she would do so within a few years with the help of her conscious parents, with whom she had made a soul contract. Barbara told me years later that she might have gone crazy those first few months if she hadn't had that information. The baby screamed constantly and clung to her like a monkey. She was terrified of strangers, especially men.

However, the parents said that Molly's reaction was very strange every time she heard my name. As she got older, she would dance in circles and repeat it. All of us assumed it was because she somehow picked up on their regard for me. Molly was three years old before I was able to accept their invitation for a visit. They warned me that she was shy. When I drove up I was in a car with four other women. This "shy" child, who had never seen me, dashed down the steps, ignored the other four women, grabbed my hand, pulled me to her room, and proceeded to show me all her treasures.

I think that Molly's soul contacted me before she was born to help her through the transition into earth life once again, and while I seriously doubt that Molly has any conscious awareness of that, I think she had intuitive recognition of the brief but important dance we had shared.

Dreaming Answers

The left brain is so busy plotting and planning, there's often no empty space for revelation to enter. So it waits until we go to sleep. Remembered or not, dream revelations can show up in the next few days in hunches and resolutions to problems. Dreams can capture psychic fragments and weave them into a pattern, monitor and report on the health of the mind, body, and emotions, remind us of soul intentions, run off excess energy, and resolve struggles.

Dreams are often the venue for meetings between those who are in the body and those we love who have passed into another realm. They can also be the venue for meeting teachers.

Sean, a therapist and businessman, said, "In the dream I met somebody, and he checked me out. Actually he looked at my fingernails. I found out years later that in the Jewish tradition, the base of the fingernails has some indication of the evolution of the soul. In the dream the guy looked at me and said, 'You are not yet born.' I wonder if he is coming back."

Because dreams bridge a multitude of unconscious aspects of self and the outer mind, we must be careful not to oversimplify

their interpretation. Certainly not all dreams are equally important. Nevertheless, big dreams are kin to parables that can all be
understood at many levels.

Obtaining a list of dream symbols might be useful as a starting
point. Certainly there are archetypes that we all share. Remember,
however, that while a black dog might be a negative in a dream
book, it wouldn't be negative if you loved a black dog as a child. It
might be a symbolic stand-in for acceptance, love, or even advice
to examine the period associated with the dog.

Always consider a simple free association with the dream image
or key word as a beginning step in your dream work, trusting in
the emotional content, dismissing nothing, no matter how illogi-
cal. When stuck, just ask yourself, "And what else?" Also, it's
sometimes helpful to put a key word from the dream in the middle of a circle, and then enter the circle in your mind from different places on the circumference. When you exhaust one line of
inquiry, pull back and enter at another point. The perspective
changes as you move around the circle.

The more attention we give dreams, the more this bridge between the conscious and unconscious is strengthened. Many disciples plant dream seeds, asking in writing for input on a question
while they sleep, carefully recording the dream when they awake.
We can train our minds to dream solutions, and we can learn to
actively participate with awareness in the dream drama. There are
books listed in the bibliography that teach the how-tos of lucid
dreaming, that is, knowing consciously within the dream state that
you are dreaming.

Refining Our Intuition

Intuitive knowing is encouraged by attention that honors it as a
legitimate and powerful way to know yourself and the world.
Since intuition has often been relegated as an illegitimate, irrational category of knowing, we have to train ourselves to trust it.

No one way of receiving intuitive information is better than any other. The three "clairs," for instance—clairvoyance (clear inner seeing), clairaudience (clear inner hearing), and clairsentience (clear inner sensing or knowing)—are equally valid ways of knowing. When energy comes into the auric field, the stimulus races to the brain for instant identification. How it translates that information into recognizable information depends on the way the brain is "wired." This involves a complex amalgam of genetics, conditioning, and soul intention. You might admire the way another receives information, but you will increase your own capacities if you honor the unique way your mind works and let go of comparisons.

Many outstanding leaders attest to the power of their intuition. Periodically magazines such as *Fortune* conduct surveys among CEOs about their methods of making decisions. The great majority admit that after all the data is analyzed, they make decisions "by instinct," "by the seat of my pants," by "gut feeling." They trust their intuition.

Honoring Your Intuition

- Trust yourself. You are a beloved child of the universe. Only a tiny part of your vastness is expressed in this finite world of time and space. You are a link in an unbroken chain of consciousness. You carry memories of all that you have learned. You were there at First Light, and that knowing, living deep in your memory, will never leave you.

- Dedicate your intuition to the Highest Good, and it will be accelerated. Before going into any situation, pray for right action and right speech. An old Hebrew prayer is simple and clear: "May the words of my mouth and the meditations of my heart be pleasing unto You, my Beloved."

- Know yourself. Go deeper, wider. Be more honest with yourself. Embrace it all. Anything rejected may be projected. Projection distorts the understanding of our revelations. For example, unresolved childhood needs for power and attention can usurp revelations and use them to support self-aggrandizement. A fear of persecution can block acceptance of spiritual gifts.

- Learn to recognize your personal symbology. Your life experiences have created a host of symbols that are uniquely yours. What symbols are charged with energy?

- Study the language of symbols, myths, and metaphors. Archetypal images capture complex dynamics quickly. Your intuition can reach into the collective sea of consciousness and teach you through universal symbols.

- Pay attention to the body as provider of feedback. Do you get chills, rushes of heat, or prickles as confirmation? A sinking in the belly? Sudden tears? Learn to interpret and then trust these messages. Intelligence exists in every cell and is constantly communicating. We have to learn to listen.

- Clearly distinguish your own feelings from those of others, and develop healthy methods of both releasing energy that is not yours, and drawing clear boundaries. Whose feelings are you feeling? Whose feelings did you feel as a child?

- Learn to read the environment: What is going on around you? Practice in nonpersonal settings: Is the energy in a given place flowing, or is it congested? No matter where you are, a department store, downtown traffic, or your own backyard, you will gradually become attuned to flows of energy.

- Keep meditation and dream journals. Especially note the impressions that come in sudden flashes and slip by the intellectual controls. Periodically review your notes, and then fully acknowledge the wisdom of your intuition as time reveals its meaning. Gratitude increases the flow.

- Break the tyranny of your intellect, which tends to rerun the same answers to a problem. Stream-of-consciousness writing, unstructured painting, playing in clay or sand, free-form dancing—all may possibly produce a fresh insight.

- Relax, be playful, and don't force. Intuition cannot be bullied. Just as a dream can turn into smoke when we try to grab it, so will intuition if we try to force it to happen. Relaxed expectation encourages the intuitive process.
- Don't judge or defend wrong guesses or inaccurate interpretations. Sometimes we feel "in the zone" and can't miss. Other times we're off. Keep a light touch, let go, and try tomorrow. It's part of learning, so don't criticize yourself and feed a shadow of self-devaluation.
- Practice. If the phone rings, ask yourself, "Who is on the line?" If you are watching a mystery on TV, who did it? Don't figure it out; just ask yourself.
- Learn to love the questions and the quest itself, not just the comfort of answers. Don't try to force answers. The question you pose will bring additional information to you because the law of magnetism works. If you empty yourself of sureties, answers will come.

Dancing with All of Life

Because we are in a dance with all of life, any aspect of it can offer us an insight. The Native Americans remind us that the four-legged creatures, the winged and finned ones, the green growing ones, even the creepy crawlers are all our relatives. Most of us are not able to live up to the strictness of certain orders of Buddhist monks who sweep the ground before them as they walk lest they kill tiny life-forms by stepping on them. Still, it is not such a stretch to pray to walk without harm and to give thanks to the life-forms that are sacrificed that we might live.

So what does reverence for life have to do with revelation? A great deal. If we pay *attention*, the mystery of life will reveal itself through interaction with other species. I've talked to horses, swans, hawks, pigs, dogs, cows, and once a group of ants that I convinced to leave my house. I've also failed to make contact as often as I've succeeded, so I don't know an infallible formula. I do know that contact starts with respect for the presence of life and a deep honoring of the form it has taken, plus a withdrawing of human projections. I wouldn't expect a wild hawk to live by my rules or knowledge, and I don't imagine that I have its eyesight or swiftness.

Contacts with other life-forms can very quickly reveal the mysterious interconnections between us. I once dreamed that hundreds of goldfinches landed on my roof. The next night there were two feathers in my bed, one white, one black, the colors of a goldfinch's tail feathers. Can we explain such a phenomenon today? No, it is part of the mystery we share with all of life, and now and then Nature reminds us of the interconnectedness of all things.

During a workshop exercise I asked each participant to write down all his or her fears on rocks. We carried them to a nearby lake, and as part of a ritual, we threw the rocks into the water. When we declare we are going to release something, we usually get more of it for a while. Carol's story is a wonderful illustration of this point.

Carol had chosen to release her fear of spiders. After throwing the rocks in the water, twenty-six of us were sitting in a big circle when suddenly a big spider appeared and walked right over to Carol. Of course, we noticed the synchronicity. Nature is thorough when she's in a teaching mode, and she wasn't through. That night Carol lay in bed talking to her roommate. They looked up to see a spider slowly descending on one delicate filament over Carol's bed.

The point was unequivocally made the next morning when she was washing her hair in the tub, looked down, and saw between her feet a spider. She was laughing by then, and now she is sure that her spider "karma" is over. No other person had even noticed spiders during that intensive, let alone had intimate experiences with them.

Amy reported the following incident that took place when she was living in Findhorn, Scotland: "We were all in the ballroom dancing a special dance that had been created to celebrate the lake and the swans on the lake. And as we danced, a swan feather floated down from the ceiling. There wasn't any way it could have gotten in there. It arrived. They were so used to such things happening; someone just picked it up and said, 'Oh, it is a swan feather,' and handed it to somebody, and we carried on. And it's like this extraordinary relationship, something beautiful that is just outside our daily common experience. And it became ordinary reality, but was still very precious nonetheless."

Awareness that is both precious and ordinary—that seems highly desirable, doesn't it? It also seems to sum up the gift of revelation—the cosmic plan revealing itself through all of its players: Nature, you and me, here and now, wonderfully, magically, preciously ordinary.

Exercise: Museum of Significant Symbols
In this exercise you will use both visualization and symbology.

- As in all exercises, use your breath consciously to help you relax.
- Use a release technique to cope with distracting thoughts— exhaling them, sending them in smoke clouds or bubbles, putting them on an altar of light, and so forth.
- Imagine that you are entering an inner museum that contains all of your significant symbols. Be sure to notice everything, since major clues can be in the smallest details. A museum houses valuable treasures, so respect everything that is shown to you. Symbols might appear as sculpture, art, photographs, film, furniture, murals, or anything else.
- As you walk through the museum, accept what it shows you in response to your questions:

1. What is a symbol of personal empowerment for you?
2. What is a symbol for your spiritual quest?
3. What is an effective symbol for receiving from Spirit?
4. What is an effective symbol for giving to others?
5. What is a strong symbol of protection?

Other symbols might spontaneously appear, or there may be other questions you want to ask. Feel free to linger as long as you like.

- When you are ready, leave the museum. No matter what you saw, it is useful information even if you don't understand it at the moment. Express gratitude.
- Use your breath to return to alert consciousness, affirming your balance in mind, body, and spirit.
- In your journal write down all the symbols that appeared to you. Over the next few days allow yourself to concentrate on one at a time, using techniques you prefer for processing (free association, sketching, journaling, etc.).

Shadows in Revelation: When It's More like "Oh, No" than "Aha"

Revelations gone awry are like birds flying through a window unexpectedly opened and then quickly shut. Trapped, they frantically dash around the boundaries of the rational mind. With no logic on which to perch, panic sets in.

Depending on the interpreter, the revelation might be pronounced a messenger from the divine, a demon, a figment of the imagination, or a sickness. Some "experts" will set up an experiment to test the revelation, and if a similar revelation does not appear on command, then, according to them, the whole thing never happened.

Like the unconscious processes that restore the body after traumatic shock, in a healthy human the psyche can usually absorb radical new information, finding ways to weave it into known reality. This protects us from falling over psychic edges.

Wisdom will always steer us away from lusting after insights we can't integrate. Occasionally a revelation is so intense that our system can't assimilate it quickly enough. Then a person can be overwhelmed and appear excessive, irrational, even mad.

In India, Indonesia, and certain African cultures, such a person might be said to be "drunk with God." Often villages accept such people, even feel blessed by them. The fourteenth-century mystical poet Lalla is to this day deeply revered in the Indian province where she frequently danced without clothes through the streets in spiritual ecstasy.

Spiritual breakthroughs aren't always predictable, and sometimes we can feel momentarily as if we don't have the inner containers to handle them. The mind can race as if on speed, the emotions can feel explosive, and the body can shimmer with reactions from *kriyas* (spontaneous body movements), even going into states of bliss frequently described as whole-body orgasms.

If a culture denies revelation as a legitimate way of knowing, then what happens to those who don't integrate their experiences quickly or well, or who haven't learned to hide them sufficiently? If they are not *too* noisy with their insights, they might be mildly tagged flaky, in the ozone, weird, or eccentric. If they are too insistent, others may feel they need to be sedated.

Certainly professional help is required when health is threatened. Still, I wonder how many conditions considered pathological are forms of soul despair or what the Sufi poet Rumi once called "astounding lucid confusion." How many health professionals even acknowledge either soul despair or ecstasy? How might healing models change if they did?

What happens in cultures where there is little ritual that acknowledges and celebrates mystery, when soul intention is not treated as the primary business of incarnation, when spiritual ecstasy is questionable if not downright embarrassing? Too often going through wilderness experiences that feel spiritually lonely and dry are treated about as seriously as having a tough weekend in the country.

It takes a great deal of psychospiritual strength to survive and then thrive in settings that deny spiritual passages. Others survive by using their addiction of choice: alcohol, drugs, relationships, even work. But for some the inner defenses won't hold. The psyche overflows, with few containers to hold its insights. Sometimes people who can't integrate revelation well have gotten caught in the cul-de-sacs of their spiritual journeys.

In *Myths to Live By* Joseph Campbell speaks of the schizophrenic patient who may be floundering in the same mystic ocean the yogi and saint are swimming in. As the poet Stevie Smith wrote, he or she is "not waving but drowning."

I fully agree with the many health professionals who are now recognizing that alcoholism and drug addictions are at their roots a misguided search for the Divine. Perhaps any addiction—sex, cigarettes, work, drugs, or food—is an attempt to feed a hunger that has psychological and physiological manifestations but is ultimately a longing for reunion with the spiritual self.

I keep a reminder on my refrigerator of the link between feeding ourselves and sustenance at all levels: "What you want is not in here. Drink water and talk to God."

✖ Journaling Seeds

1. How do you integrate new information and revelations?

2. Has fear been part of your spiritual history? Explore this.

3. Review past insights through dreams or intuitive knowing. How have they influenced your life?

4. If you have any addictions, do you know what is driving them? How can you redirect them toward your well-being?

Fact or Fantasy?

A man wants to go into a shop in a bazaar, but it is crowded. So he creates a distraction by yelling, "Hey, did you know there is a big sale going on down the road?"

Well, of course everyone immediately leaves the shop and heads down the road in pursuit of the big sale. As he watches this, he starts into the shop, stops, looks down the road, and thinks, "Maybe I'd better go see; there really could be a sale going on."

Fantasies can lurk in the shadows and masquerade as revelation. Our minds are infinitely rich and creative. If you have ever embroidered a story just to make it a tad better, you know that after a few repetitions, the embellishments seem part of the original fabric of the story.

However, sometimes revelations can appear to be mere fantasies to those who don't understand them, because the truths are taught in parables. A really good parable grows in richness and depth as we grow. Yet myths and parables, created as teaching metaphors, are too often taught as the truth itself. If this can happen to the teachings of masters, just imagine the temptations we have with our own metaphors.

Separating fantasies and wishful thinking from inner guidance requires unblinking honesty, attention, and a deep desire to know your truth. In this, as in all things, we are reminded once again that there's a straight path but no shortcuts. Learn to know yourself. Know your shadows. Know your filters.

Never be afraid to test what seems like a revelation. If it's real, it will survive your questions. If you can't make it compute, neither accept nor dismiss it. Put it aside with "we'll see," and ask your Spirit for clarity.

Discerning guidelines also need to be applied to people's revelations about you or your life. Intuitive insight in the hands of an unconscious ego can be quite manipulative. I once knew a psychically skilled individual who could accurately pick up on the fears of others. She then encouraged those fears, which in turn made others dependent on her. I knew another clairvoyant whose brilliance was compromised because he would not face his own biases. For example, he didn't personally believe in divorce, so when he correctly "saw" another marriage partner in someone's future, he simply said the first partner would die. He left a lot of upset people in his psychic wake.

There are times when we feel the need for confirmation and support of our revelations from others. Choose carefully. Buddhist tradition suggests that one not meditate on a crooked Buddha, and that's also good advice in selecting advisors, models, and mentors. If you look in a distorted spiritual mirror, you will get distorted images as surely as if you were looking in a funhouse mirror. If you seek reflection of your revelations from someone who is competitive, then the message might be something like this:

"*I* have a revelation; *you* are self-deceived; *he* is of the devil."
"*I* am anointed; *you* are on an ego trip; *he* is possessed."
"*My* God is the true God; *your* God is less; *His* doesn't exist."

Ask yourself if the person from whom you seek confirmation seems relatively balanced and integrated. Do you feel respected? Does the person seem relatively free of prejudice, comparisons, and competition? While duality is our shared problem, how well does this person seem to hold opposites?

We must be especially cautious about accepting information from disincarnates. Just because an entity is disembodied does not mean it is enlightened. There are earthbound spirits who seek hosts to vicariously enjoy physical senses and sensations. Seances, Ouija boards, and psychic parlor games can draw in mischievous, even harmful, entities from nonvisible worlds who (1) are not a source of true revelation, (2) are not capable of spiritual guidance,

(3) can deceive with astral razzle-dazzle, and (4) can attach to another's auric field. It is good judgment, not fear, that teaches us to avoid such games.

Gifts of the Spirit: Handle with Care

Traditions all over the world acknowledge what the Christians call "gifts of the Spirit" and the yogic teachings call *siddhas*—healing, prophecy, psychic sight, scriptural insight, channeling—while warning about the pursuit of those very powers. If these "gifts" are so treasured, why all the warnings?

The warnings are just that: yellow lights, not red ones. They don't say stop; they say slow down and pay a lot of attention. Investigate your motives. We don't want to become mentally imbalanced by visions we can't integrate, or be deceived by lower energies, distracted from the real quest, or so enchanted by other dimensions that we won't be present in this one.

Manifestations of Spirit are often glamorized in the earth dimension. Disciples have to be very clear not to get caught in that very seductive trap. If the world is not decrying your spiritual gifts, it may well be applauding them. And, as we all know, the ego likes applause and can create instant rationalizations for believing its own press. Satisfaction and joy in the process of fulfilling your intention doesn't require others' constant approval.

To Fear No Evil

We are often both fascinated by and fearful of the vastness we encompass beyond our senses. Fear squeezes shut the pathways between aspects of self. We've all learned to rely on our senses and our ability, imagined or not, to control reality. We've learned to believe in the "I" that is physical, and that perception assures us that the Earth is flat, the sky is up, and our current knowledge about reality is absolutely correct. As we open our minds we realize how limited our perceptions have been, and hidden fears may rise to the surface.

While our fears seem real enough, many of them exist only in our minds. I once had a frightening psychic image of myself falling down on jagged mountains. They looked real, but as I "landed" on them, I fell through them as easily as through a cloud. They were ghost mountains, creations of my own mind.

What are your ghost mountains? Maggie feared persecution. Charles was afraid he would misuse his abilities. Kelly was sure his revelations would be ridiculed. Joanne feared that if she tapped her psychic ability, she wouldn't have an "off switch." They all discovered that the way through their fears was, as Joanne summed up, "simply by asking that my gift be used for the good of myself and other people."

It's important for disciples to research their most secret fears about darkness and evil. Otherwise a dive into the oceanic universal mind for its pearls can be tyrannized by the sudden appearance of a monster from the unconscious, often a childhood fear of the "devil" that has been lying in wait until one dares to claim the authority of the truth.

Living without fear does not mean living without caution, common sense, and attention. Those that serve the Light and dark exist in all dimensions. Intelligence can live anywhere along the continuum from density to pure light.

"Seek ye first the kingdom of heaven" is universally taught as the best guide through the unknown. The ultimate objective of any spiritual practice is not to have psychic experiences, but to remember who we are. Along the way the process brings us revelations—some personal, some universal, some seemingly paradoxical, all according to our understanding. In time, as we are ready, all will be revealed.

Exercise: Spiraling Revelations

Often we can become frustrated with our problems because we have explored the same territory over and over. In this exercise we seek deeper insight without negating what we've already learned.

1. Take a journal with you throughout this exercise.

2. Begin by writing down what you have learned about your problem so far ("I smoke to cover anger," "I'm having trouble with my boss because he's like my dad," etc.). After you have written all you currently understand, turn to a fresh page.

3. Imagine that you are standing at the top of a spiral staircase. Follow the curving steps down to the next floor. There you will see a place to rest. Take a seat and turn your palms up in your lap; breathe naturally and with awareness. Then say to yourself:

"I accept that universal mind expresses through me, and I am now open to receive guidance about [name the problem or challenge]. I will receive information only from that which serves the universal Christ. I give thanks for the revelation that I know is already seeking me."

4. Now wait with expectancy but without expectation. Expectancy is heightened receptivity. Expectation already has results in mind. Breathe and wait.

5. Write down any impressions you have—symbols, memories, messages, and so on. If none comes, stay relaxed and breathe away any disappointed feelings. Sometimes information arrives later.

6. As soon as you are ready, proceed to follow the spiraling steps down to the next level, and repeat the process. Do this a total of three times—sitting, breathing, affirming, waiting, writing, and releasing at each turning.

7. Walk the spiral back to the top floor where you began, noting anything along the way that is different than before.

❧ Twelve Considerations on Revelation

1. Insight can arrive suddenly; integration takes time and effort.

2. Wisdom fuses pragmatic knowledge and intuitive knowing.

3. Truth, like flowing water, cannot be captured in a net.

4. The universe reveals itself through each of its living parts.

5. The heart can know a truth that the brain merely theorizes.

6. Angels, teachers, and guides empower; they don't dictate.

7. Insight can be a sudden gift or the fruit of daily practice.

8. Pride in the known, and fear of the unknown, block revelation.

9. Messages are everywhere; pay attention and be grateful.

10. Be aware truth speaks universally; be aware of exclusive words.

11. Knowledge carefully builds; revelation suddenly reveals.

12. Snowflakes and sunsets are unique; so are revelations.

Prayer
From the unreal lead me to the real
From darkness lead me to light.

—Upanishads

Affirmation

I become empty that I may be filled.
I accept the revelations of my soul with gratitude.

Quote

Penetrating so many secrets, we cease to believe in the unknowable.
But there it sits, nevertheless, calmly licking its chops.

—H. L. Mencken

3 Discernment: Clear Seeing, Clear Choices

❧

First of all I believed nothing was impossible and at the same time I questioned everything.

—Sri Aurobindo

The Queen of Sheba wanted to test the fabled wisdom of King Solomon, so she brought him two beautiful lilies that looked exactly the same, even smelled the same, but one was real and one was not. No one could tell the difference, including Solomon, but he sent a slave to bring him a beehive. Of course the bees flew to the real plant. The artificial lily, beautiful as it was, could never provide nourishment.

Would that we had such a quick and clear-cut test for knowing the difference between the real and the unreal. While we are gradually learning to trust the inner voice that warns or confirms, we can be confused, overwhelmed by conflicting values and propaganda from every direction.

When we try to make peace between the "truth" we inherited and the truths we are discovering, we sometimes feel caught between progress and paralysis.

The quest for truth is, of course, worth any price and at every stage offers magnificent gifts. It also has traps. However, with well-developed discernment a disciple can avoid them. We learn how to be wary without fear, courageous without carelessness. We can learn to avoid the glitter of fool's gold and go for the real thing. As always, it requires paying attention.

The opportunity to practice discernment is at the heart of the gift of free will. No one is going to force us to become conscious. With discernment we learn to observe without energizing, to notice all things, then choose what we will empower. We learn to question without negating, to choose without excluding.

Distinguishing a part of the whole does not negate the whole. Shadow and light, illusion and truth all coexist. We learn to hold friend and enemy in the same unconditional love, but we learn to see and then energize what we perceive to be serving the good of the whole.

Questions Attract Answers

One of the most dangerous things we can do is give up the right to question.

In *The Guru Papers*, a book that poses all the right questions for someone working on discrimination, authors Joel Kramer and Diana Alstad point out that "once people do not trust themselves, they are subject to easy manipulation, especially at pivotal points in history when the foundations of social cohesion break down because what has made them successful in the past becomes dysfunctional."

The authors write that any system of values that places tradition above the experience and questions of the present is destined to become limiting. Yellow warning lights should go off when anyone dismisses, disregards, or insults legitimate questioning.

Intelligent seekers know that the introduction to a new system of thought takes a lot of learning and listening before we can even begin to ask the right questions. Otherwise we just ask questions about the things we already know. Sometimes new information challenges our assumptions so powerfully that our defenses come up and all our rationalizations kick in. Our first impulse can be to dismiss the threat to familiarity without further probing.

On the other hand, it's also easy to romanticize whatever is new and perhaps a bit exotic. Never forget that Light and shadow exist in all traditions. Any system of study, no matter how ancient, is vulnerable to human egotism.

Certainly there can be teachings that are totally appropriate for us because of temperament, karma, and points of growth that particular practices can encourage. Part of discernment is recognizing appropriateness. I have studied many practices that I knew wouldn't work in my present lifewalk but which I admired nonetheless.

Any ritual or practice is impregnated with the subtleties of the culture that birthed it and may not be fully understood by someone outside that culture. Certainly we don't have to live within a particular culture in order to find practices from that culture that are valuable and that we can assimilate with care and discernment. But we can never afford to be casual about the practices we adopt. With a good guide, the risk of distortion in crossing cultures is reduced. If there isn't a guide, then we need to practice a lot of common sense.

Many techniques are effective because of their supporting environment or lineage. There are, for example, mantras from many cultures that are designed to stimulate certain chakras, and others that are deliberately trance-inducing. This is great if you know what to do when it works. In their rightful context such openings are supported by meditative practices and daily disciplines. However, when we open centers within ourselves without this level of support, we run the risk of losing our groundedness and integration.

In many spiritual sciences, students have to pass initiatory tests that prove their understanding and mastery of skills before more powerful techniques are given to them. For example, shamans cannot theorize, speculate, or philosophize about nonvisible worlds. They must be able to demonstrate abilities to enter and interact with those worlds on command. If they cannot, they can't be shamans or medicine persons. Such an undertaking has long been recognized as dangerous, even for those who are well trained and supervised. To pull unrelated skills out of that context is potentially as irresponsible as going into a wilderness without survival training.

Perhaps the more balanced perspective is first to listen and observe. For example, it was from the Balinese culture that I really learned the value of making daily offerings. Every single morning, offerings to the Divine are found everywhere, from the smallest rice cake on a palm leaf in front of a restaurant to multilayered fruit and flower displays presented to a temple.

I really got the full impact of this ritual when I watched a woman make a charming little animal figure out of palm leaves, which she then tucked into a hidden part of the offering. I asked her who was going to see it. She smiled and said, "The gods." It wouldn't work in my lifestyle to spend large amounts of time making material objects for offerings. Yet I was inspired deeply to remember that offering one's life and talents is a daily practice. Often simply placing a flower in front of a holy picture in the morning reminds me of that.

We need to seek a balance between being receptive to new information and being assertive in questioning any parts of it that we don't fully understand. We won't grow unless we're willing to challenge our limits. But we'll get in serious trouble if we buy into everything outside of them.

I would be very cautious about groups or individuals who attempt to push you faster than you want to go into practices for which you don't feel ready or that don't feel right. If a system is authentic and its members are living its truth, such discernment will be respected.

It's wise not to give your allegiance too quickly. And it is unwise to turn over your personal authority at all. The Buddha was always quick to tell his disciples to test everything he said. He said to examine words like a goldsmith testing the purity of the metal. Once someone challenged the Buddha that some teaching he offered was not in the scriptures. "Well, then," said the Buddha, "the scriptures are wrong."

Jesus, too, corrected this letter-of-the-law mentality after he had been challenged for working on the Sabbath. "The Sabbath was made for humans, not humans for the Sabbath," was His reply. Both Buddha and Jesus were accused along the way of dealing in black magic. Questioning the status quo often elicits accusations.

Anyone who has ever tried to challenge the sexist or racist language of sacred texts knows how rigidly the human psyche holds to the familiar, even when it is clear that the information and/or language sprang out of a distinct cultural context that is no longer applicable or relevant. It's also helpful to remember that the individuals who wrote ancient scriptures were influenced by their times as well as by their revelation.

Containers: Vessels or Traps?

Our natural impulse is to give nonphysical realities shape and structure in our familiar three dimensions. We have a great need to order things, to make them usable, repeatable, and teachable. (In this discussion, the word *order* is used to indicate any of our systems that shape spiritual knowledge in the physical world.)

Because *we* can give order to information, we can organize and pass on our accrued wisdoms through disciplines, scriptures, stories, ritual, art, architecture, music, and symbol.

The twists and turns of the path, predictable obstacles, and travel tips for the spiritual journey have been described and pre-scribed for centuries. Otherwise, every one of us would have to reinvent the cosmic wheel every time we longed for enlighten-ment. There is great good in order; there are also deadly traps. It takes discernment to know the difference.

The danger is in getting more attached to a truth's container than to the contents. Great truths are born in the flow of revela-tion and inspiration and then are brought into the material world to be manifested. When that flow is frozen, then we cannot per-ceive new insight. *The mastership comes in using order, not being used by it.*

Any formal spiritual or religious order that has lasted for a long time magnetizes enormous power. If a living truth still thrives within the established order, it is a life-giving vessel. If, on the other hand, the form itself has become the law, not only is it empty, but it can be quite toxic. Jews, women, homosexuals, Asians, and Gypsies, as well as people of various other races and nationalities, have been tortured and killed by the followers of well-established religious systems.

If one takes away from any people their scribes and historians, their preservers and skilled observers, then their truths can be completely distorted and nontruths paraded before the rest of the world as fact. This regularly happens in racial, gender, and reli-gious prejudices. For example, over the past few decades we have been reviewing our past to recover "herstory," not just history. We have also been uncovering the dominant U.S. culture's corruption of African-American history, not only to correct inaccuracies, but to acknowledge to the whole population previously unreported contributions.

In the catacombs in Jerusalem early Christians who were hiding there made drawings. One original drawing clearly showed men and women as celebrants of the Eucharist. As this part of the cata-combs was very fragile, it was closed, and the drawings were du-plicated in a safer place for tourists. But in the transfer, there was one little exception in the reproduction: All the celebrants were drawn as men.

Men *and* women were healers, teachers, priests, and prophets in the young Christian church. When any systematic passing on of information leaves out such critically important information, it builds a distortion into the system from the outset. After a while few challenge the lie; it has simply become part of the accepted order.

The story is told of the guru who had a cat that usually sat on his lap. One day the guru didn't want him in his lap, so he tied the cat to the chair to keep him from running away. Shortly after that the guru died. In respect to his memory and the guru's fondness for his cat, the disciples tied the cat to the empty chair. Time went by, and new disciples joined the order. Down through the centuries, they always tied a cat to the guru's chair. No one knew why, but it was assumed that it was a necessary part of sacred practice to tie a cat to the guru's chair.

Esoteric principles are the basis for most rituals. Often the original principle is no longer taught, and the outer rituals can seem irrelevant. Thus many intelligent people simply dismiss the ritual as pointless. I have seen many skeptical eyes light up when the esoteric teachings behind an outer ritual are explained. Often these skeptics can then return to their own traditions relieved and ready to enjoy the richness of continuity, community, and ritual because they now have greater understanding.

Someday we may be able to pass on whole libraries of knowledge instantaneously, simply by being in each other's presence. In the meantime, discernment helps us sort through all that has been handed down in order to know which parts are a great inheritance and which parts are unexamined Legacies.

Knowing When to Speak,
When to Act, When to Choose

Discernment helps us choose appropriate ways to walk and talk our deepest intentions in the world. During the first flush of spiritual highs, we tend to want to run out and enlighten everyone we know. We soon learn that the world is not always receptive to our new perspectives.

Even if we have discovered the Light within, it doesn't naturally follow that we yet know how to manage it. It takes a refinement of our discernment to know when to speak out or be quiet, or how much energy to apply to any situation.

In traditions around the world initiates are warned not to "throw pearls before swine," as it was put in the Christian teachings. Hinduism makes a similar point in the story of the master who would accept some students for his training and not others. "Don't attempt to teach a pig to sing. It wastes your time and irritates the pig," he explained. There is no judgment in these stories. Everyone is exactly in the right place and the right time for their perfect lessons. The stories teach discernment. Imposing our quest onto others who are not ready or interested is usually less about meeting their needs than our own.

We also come to learn that it is pointless to argue with extreme prejudice, fanatical passion, and ignorance. And it's also humbling to admit that we may have some of those traits. The degree to which I need to react to another's biases is probably the degree to which they are lurking unidentified in my shadow.

Sometimes prejudice can be very challenging for a committed disciple. Marcia is a doctor who teaches classes on consciousness at a community center. She is attempting to create a safe place for dialogues between all points of view. Fundamentalists sometimes attend the classes and heckle her to take a stand on abortion. No dialogue is possible with highly polarized positions. She has reluctantly accepted that.

A word of warning here: *Conservative* doesn't translate as "closed." Discernment teaches us to avoid stereotyping. I was reminded of that when I was asked by a colleague who had an emergency to teach his class at a retirement center the following evening. He wanted me to show my slides on the feminine aspect of God, which include some eighty images of the Divine Mother from traditions all over the world. I had no time to adapt anything, and I questioned how this particular group might relate to the material. He insisted, and I wanted to help.

This audience of retired men and women, who probably averaged seventy-five years of age, were totally receptive, asked great questions, nodded, and paid full attention. If I'd just had a casual conversation with them, I might have assumed they were ultra-conservative. One more time I was reminded that in order to be truly discerning, we have to recognize and set aside cultural prejudices such as ageism, being aware that these blind spots are often very subtle, hiding out behind our niceties. Someone asked me what I would have done if that group had reacted negatively. I suspect I would have confined my remarks to Mary, mother of Jesus, and the Jewish concept of Sophia, perhaps discussing other influential women in those two traditions.

Discernment teaches us to look behind labels such as "conservative" or "liberal" for authenticity of energy. Often we are seeking the same truth, just approaching it from a different perspective and speaking a different language. In either case, the Presence is always authentic, regardless of the form it takes.

🌺 Journaling Seeds

1. What did you question as a child and as a youth?

2. How do you balance listening and questioning?

3. How do you typically evaluate new information, new teachers, new groups, new practices?

4. How do you recognize warnings from your inner guidance? How are those warnings different from fear?

Discernment Teaches Perspective

Einstein once said, "Two sides disagree because they are both wrong and both right." He noted that to solve a problem on one level, we must approach it from a higher level.

Standing toe to toe with a problem can make it hard to discern anything more than the problem. At eye level with a passing train I may be able to see only one car at a time. If I'm standing above the train, I can see the many cars that make up the whole. Moreover, I can see where the train has been and where it is going. Writer Alice Walker once put it this way: "Your balloon strings might have been cut, but what a view!"

Discernment teaches us to take another look at our world with new eyes. The same ground of reality that creates a chalice also creates a paper cup. One is considered holy and another ordinary. An interesting shift in perspective is possible if you walk through your own world with awareness, noting the symbols in your life that have been declared special, sacred, untouchable, or profane. A question to ask in any setting is: "What do I perceive here to be sacred or profane?"

It requires effort to discern realities different from our inner pictures. Have you ever suddenly looked in a shop window or mirror and been startled to realize that the stranger reflected was you? Once seen, though, the mind will quickly arrange the reflection to mirror your image of yourself. The mind likes a recognizable perception. However, when it is perceiving one way, it's not seeing something else. It selectively eliminates in order to perceive.

I have a set of slides on perception that I use with groups, asking them to identify and interpret what they see. In close-up photography, the inside of a rock can look much like a shot of the planet taken from space; moss on a rock can look like a mystical forest. Until there is a recognizable reference point (grass near the moss, for example) the reports reflect the projections of the observer, which are, more times than not, as varied as the participants.

There is a perceptual phenomenon called "early blur" that used to result in hunters in the forests accidentally killing each other, thinking that they saw a game animal instead of a person. The problem was corrected with the introduction of fluorescent orange clothing, which prevents the brain from making images of deer where none exist.

We can learn to monitor our thoughts without engaging or energizing. The difference between engaging and observing is the difference between wrestling with the tiger and watching the tiger walk by.

Discern New Possibilities

The world is filled with people who have defied the collective thought forms of their culture to create their own standards of what is possible. There is a Chinese proverb that says the greatest pleasure is in doing what people say you cannot do.

Some of the most amazing people are the Japanese marathon-running monks of the sacred peaks of Mt. Hei, near Kyoto. Similar to the monk marathoners of ancient Tibet, these monks will train for a thousand days and then run fifty-two miles a day for a hundred days, all of which is perceived as a way of unifying mind and body. Clearly that seems impossible by any standard we have for endurance, but they do it.

Deaf musicians and dancers do what may seem impossible; so do blind people who complete medical school. I saw a television report on the nature of happiness that featured a quadriplegic who paints. In his spare time he teaches people to read.

As our population ages, perhaps we'll create new models for

aging, such as the people I saw interviewed on a program called *Life Begins at Ninety*. One ninety-four-year-old retired doctor runs several miles a day and sings in a barbershop quartet—in competitions. A ninety-six-year-old blues singer performs nightly in a club in New Orleans. A ninety-eight-year-old therapist sees clients, has a personal body trainer, and has just started voice lessons.

Beatrice Wood, who died at 102, was still a potter at 98 (and still selling her pottery). She said her personal secret was "younger men and chocolate." Someone told me recently that this amazing woman celebrated her 101st birthday with a showing of erotic art!

Emile Coue, whose simple affirmation "Every day in every way I'm getting better and better" has been quoted thousands of times, once said that "no idea presented to the mind can realize itself unless the mind accepts it."

Guidelines for Increasing Discernment

1. Don't accept any of these suggestions unless you feel they're right for you at this moment. This is your first exercise in applying discernment.

2. Teachers, books, and techniques can assist you, but be wary of any teaching that doesn't send you inside yourself for the truth. If information is true, it will stand up under time and testing and your examination.

3. Keep querying yourself about the relevance of new information. Does it help you expand your understanding? Does it help you to cope creatively with the issues and people in your life and times? Can you integrate it into what you currently believe or think?

4. Angels and spirit guides are with us for support, not to take away our choices. If you often say, "*They* told me to do this or that," ask yourself if you have self-doubt or fear of owning your own power and wisdom.

5. Psychic impressions from yourself or another can be correct or off. Create a "we'll-see" place in your mind and seek more information. Then pay attention. The universe is a whole; any part of the whole can speak a truth for any other part.

6. Stay grounded. Go to Nature for renewal. Feel yourself rooted into the earth like a tree. Breathe and affirm, "I am fully present in my mind, body, and spirit."

7. Examine carefully any message from a group that suggests it has been singled out by the universe as *the* voice of truth. All our missions are interconnected in the vast web of life.

8. Discernment teaches integration. Ask yourself, "Can I stay balanced with this new practice?" If so, you'll remain stable. If not, perhaps you want to slow down and reevaluate.

9. Pray for discernment, but understand it often brings disenchantment. Bubbles can pop; illusions may shatter. The soul rejoices; the ego can suffer.

10. "By their fruits you shall know them" is still a very reliable guideline. Look for congruence between words and actions, attitudes and actual teachings.

11. Learn to recognize your own inner signals of discernment: "I felt the truth of it in my bones [or heart, or solar plexus]," "Everything in me said yes [or no]," "My guard went up," "I already knew it somewhere inside."

12. Not all nonphysical intelligence is enlightened. Each of us has the divine right to decree what we will or will not accept as influence. If we are willing to learn, we can ask to be taught by the highest masters. Just keep in mind they are not likely to be hanging around Ouija boards.

Last, accept the fact that you will probably miss the point now and then. Like the mullah Nasruddin, we can be so close we can't see the obvious.

[handwritten margin note: reference has come up several times. I think this place holder could be good for me.]

Nasruddin earned his living selling eggs. One day someone came into his shop and said, "Guess what I've got behind my back."

Nasruddin asked for a clue.

"Well, it is in a shell . . . it's yellow and white inside, and it is liquid before it is cooked."

Upon being told that it was laid by a hen, Nasruddin shouted, "I got it, I got it. It's some sort of cake."

Exercise: Discerning the Self

This exercise is based on a Sanskrit mantra designed to open your heart center, the entrance into your love nature, which is the essence of who you are. The more we know who we are, the less we are deceived by appearances and illusions.

1. Gently keep asking yourself the following question (you can use the Sanskrit, the English, or both): "*Kohum?* Who am I?" As you take the question into your meditation, notice whatever your mind sends up. Don't wrestle with it; simply and gently go to the second step.

2. "*Nahum,* I am not that." Allow your mind to run through all the images that respond to "Who am I?" As you affirm the second step, "I am not that," support your affirmation by releasing the images, seeing them dissolve into nothingness.

3. Now affirm who you are: "*Sohum,* I am that." In your mind imagine pure Light. You will want to be careful what you image, as you are affirming it for yourself. If you need a specific image, think of a holy being, such as Jesus, Buddha, Kuan Yin, or Mary. If you feel your mind drifting during this, stop, breathe, and then return to it.

Judgment:
The Mask of Discernment

One of the shadows lurking around discernment is its negative form, judgment. The person we judge the most harshly is likely to be ourselves. The language of self-judgment is filled with *should* and *ought*, regrets, comparisons, and unhealthy competition, such as the idea that winning equals self-worth.

What we don't accept in ourselves is likely to be projected onto others and then, of course, judged. Naturally, there are times when we both as individuals and as a society, have to walk away, protect ourselves, or discipline and even jail some people in order to establish clear boundaries of what we will or will not allow. Still, we don't ever have to throw anyone out of our hearts. "There but for the grace of God go I" is always a handy reminder.

By embracing the "other," whether we agree with it or not, we create a container big enough for understanding and integrating differing points of view. Whatever we exclude sooner or later erupts with anger in the collective.

Researching one's judgments requires a lot of skill. There is a delicate line between discerning (seeing things as they are) and judging (seeing things as they should be).

Are you aware of the early warning signals telling you that you are moving from discernment into judgment? Does your voice or your language change? Can you feel it in your body? Does it pop out as gossiping, criticizing, or complaining?

Finding the Right Teacher

We were programmed to believe that authority resides outside ourselves. When we start to question the voices of those we have perceived as experts, we can be surprised by the amount of resistance that bubbles up from our shadows. "What if everything spins into chaos?" "Isn't somebody in charge?"

The unknown can feel scary. This is why so many of us need assurance that God, by some name, is in heaven and all will be right with the world. This attitude can open the doors wide for control outside oneself, whether that is the control given to an authority figure, a theology, or the newest channeled spirit.

There are guidelines we can use to help pry loose lingering childhood projections of spiritual authority. "By their fruits you shall know them" is still the best guideline. The next question is: What does the fruit look like to you? Do you require your "authorities" to look, talk, or be a certain way? Do they have to be vegetarians? Celibate? Nonsmokers, nondrinkers, and so on? What are your criteria?

Once you have examined what Dr. Charles Tart named your "observer bias," then there are some standards worth your consideration:

1. Does the teacher create bridges between people?
2. Do you see the manifestations of compassion?
3. Does the teacher have an attitude of "my way or no way"?
4. Do you feel empowered to be yourself?
5. Does the teacher walk his or her talk?
6. Does your intuition tell you to trust this teacher?
7. Is she or he teaching love of the Divine in self and others?

An incredible bond exists between the student who yearns for freedom and a clear teacher. Such a relationship is far more than the exchange of facts or psychospiritual processing. It is a contract of love made at the soul level, often one that is continuing from other lifetimes.

Through a clear teacher, a student might experience for the first time unconditional love, harmony, nonjudgment, and so forth. The student might surrender to the care and guidance of such a teacher, who is an embodiment of the qualities being sought, and the heart is rightfully respectful, sometimes even ecstatic. In a

healthy relationship surrender to a teacher is a place of deep gratitude, not worship. The objective will always be clear: the liberation of the student, not the adoration of the teacher.

To Deny Is to Delay

In the past few decades we have been learning that denial is a
major block to self-awareness, and without awareness, discernment is not possible. The only way to assess anything is to see it in
all its glories and glitches, successes and shames.

We can run away from our disowned parts for lifetimes, but
they run with us. The soul is patient. Out of sight is not out of
mind. It is intact and in denial.

For denial to be positive, it must be deliberate. To deny the
power of a negative affirms choice. One can refuse to give authority to a disease or a seemingly tragic circumstance. In such a
case, the power of the negative is denied, but not the fact that it
exists. As a result, it is the healing potential within the experience
that is energized, not the outer appearance.

I remember sitting by the bed of a young woman who was
dying because she had denied the fact that she had cancer and refused medical help until it was too late. It takes a lot of discernment to know if one is denying with full awareness or just
denying out of a refusal to face fears.

What Causes You to Close Your Eyes?

How can we make discerning choices unless we open our eyes
completely? How can we vote intelligently, assess options, and
participate in our families and in our neighborhood with fairness
and compassion if we have our eyes shut? And how can any of us
possibly face the cruelties of the world if we are not willing to
face the ones lurking in our own shadows?

Always Weigh Psychic Information

Psychic abilities are neither good nor bad. Their worth depends on the consciousness that uses them. We all have psychic abilities to different degrees. As yet we don't have a reliable set of objective measures to provide credentials for such abilities.

Because psychic gifts are wrapped in so much mystery, we have a fascination, and sometimes a fear, of those who clearly have the abilities. That can breed gullibility and wishful thinking.

Having used these skills for many years, I have a great respect for the insights, affirmations, and new perspectives they can bring. In my experience, when psychic abilities are used by Spirit rather than ego, information is more about soul patterns, options, and potentials and less about what might happen.

I would be wary of being told this or that is "definitely what will happen" or what you "should" do. These are warning flags. The highest guidance from Spirit doesn't dictate. It is true that one can sometimes pick up on karmic contracts made for this life before they unfold. And one can certainly see probable outcomes if certain energy patterns continue. Nevertheless, I always make it clear to clients that these are *my* interpretations for *their* consideration.

Your own self-knowledge and intuition are your best tools for evaluating psychic material from others. When in doubt ask yourself the following:

Actually, I leave feeling "too good."

1. Is this guidance without harm to you or another?
2. Did this session help you define some of your growing edges?
3. Did you leave this session feeling encouraged? Empowered?
4. Did you receive insights into your deeper purposes?

If you are asked to do anything against your will or better judgment or are asked to give money beyond paying for services rendered, run to the nearest exit. If you are tempted to stay, re-double your efforts to be clear and discerning.

The Shadow Side of Visualization

"That which we hold in mind we become" is a basic wisdom teaching around the world. Thoughts consistently held will mani-fest. This is a fact, no more romantic than the probable outcome of eating badly for fifty years. So pick your models carefully be-fore you hold them in your mind as an ideal.

The very fact that visualization is highly recommended in everything from sports training to treatment of disease speaks to its power. And so does the fact that there are serious warnings against careless use of it. It is not a harmless toy of the mind, and the principles by which it functions are no more sentimental than the laws of physics.

Our deepest beliefs about reality make up our unconscious vi-sualizations. Random thoughts skirting across the top of the mind now and then are no more going to change a pattern than wrap-ping up a box of trash in fancy paper and ribbons will magically change the contents. A new and healthy image has to be consis-tently held, and when all that energy is used to fuel a positive view, magic happens. Natural magic.

> *A wise sculptor told the king that he could cure his son of a dis-ease that had left the boy's body ravaged, even though the best heal-ers in the land had tried to heal him but failed. The sculptor made a perfect image of the boy and stood him in front of the statue every day. In two years the boy was cured and his body looked like the statue's.*

In a *Quest* magazine article (summer 1995) Dr. Georg Feuer-stein, a practicing Buddhist, warned about the irresponsible use of visualizations. He labeled them "laser beams that can have a constructive or a destructive effect." He said, "Just as laser beams can remove cataracts or cut through armored cars, visualizations can literally call things into existence on the subtle planes. These creations may be benign or malevolent in their impact in which case they can cause severe harm to oneself in this and future lives."

A famous example of the power of thought was Alexandra David-Neel, a nineteenth-century French woman who traveled and studied with lamas in Tibet. She allegedly became so good in her visualizations that she created a guardian spirit that manifested in the physical world. Then she found him hard to get rid of. He had a life and opinions of his own.

In Kabbalistic literature it is said that a devout rabbi can bring a golem into being to help the people when no earthly help is available. It is returned to the dust once the task has been accomplished by erasing the holy name that was inscribed on its forehead or heart chakra when it was first formed from clay and animated.

While most of us don't have the mental concentration or the desire to manifest such creations, the extremes remind us of the possibilities and alert our discernment. Thoughts are indeed real things. They have real consequences. When visualizations call upon the Light and are employed to lift awareness, integrate, and encourage the body to heal and perform, they are positive. However, just playing around with visualization, not examining the implications of concentrated, targeted thought or using it to invite other intelligence into your space, is highly questionable and potentially harmful.

Three Lessons in Discernment

Because pitfalls in discernment are so often linked with so-called spiritual seduction, which is directly or indirectly played out through sexual energy, I am sharing three stories from three different traditions. I have italicized key words or phrases because they offer us clues for understanding how discernment can get lost in shadow and how it can be reclaimed.

The important thing is to first discern vulnerability within ourselves. As a friend once said, "Without a womb, there isn't going to be a pregnancy."

1. *Personal power lost and found.* Jon met Jim Jones of the People's Temple in San Francisco when he was a *deeply troubled* twenty-two-year-old college senior. This was years before Jones lost touch with reality and led hundreds to their death in a jungle in Guyana. In the early years the Temple appeared to be a thriving, dynamic institution in the community.

"He *seemed to me to be the safest* person that I had ever met. I shared with him a lot of the anguish I had been feeling." *Bathed in the attention and approval* of this charismatic man, Jon gradually *gave his personal authority* over to Jones without realizing it was happening until it was almost too late.

As the months went by, Jon took responsibility within the Temple. He was also increasingly aware that Jones was becoming tyrannical, that he was having sex with both men and women in the church, and that drugs were all around.

It was a time of great *confusion* for Jon. He was *lacking self-confidence* and had *not acquired discernment* growing up. He had *projected spiritual needs* onto Jones, including a need for fathering. His only *friends were in* the Temple. For the first time in his life he had a *place and a purpose.* But his world was falling apart, and he had *no skills* for interpreting the situation.

However, his tale was not to end in the jungle, as it did for many of his friends and colleagues. When others moved to Guyana, he stayed in San Francisco to take care of Temple business. After the massacre occurred, Jon was devastated. He fled to Europe for two years.

It took Jon years to even be able to talk about his experience. He has *had to work through* horror, shame, self-criticism, and a multitude of other feelings. Using many *therapies*, he gradually began to heal.

"In the obvious sense it was like the worst thing I could have done," said Jon. "I don't think we ever really lose. It may look like we have made the wrong choice. *But it taught me things about myself, about giving away personal power, about recognizing people who are giving away their power, and those who will take it, and how dangerous disempowerment is.*"

Today Jon is a successful businessman, husband, father, grandfather, and seriously committed disciple who deeply values the discernment he earned the hard way.

2. *Not-so-mindful monk.* Allison was twenty-one and pregnant when she and her husband moved into one room in a Buddhist temple. They both *wanted to learn* Eastern philosophy while Steve finished college. They became friends with the monks. It seemed like a *safe place.*

Allison's first inner alarm went off when she had a run-in with a monk who told her to ignore her crying three-month-old baby in order to practice her yoga. At first she *thought he knew best* and she *should* "detach," but her mother wisdom won out. When she tended to the baby, she was dismissed from the class.

"I had long hair, which he said that I had to wear up because it was too distracting to the monks when it was hanging down."

At this point she still *assumed that the monk was more knowledgeable* than herself. But soon he made sexual advances, telling her he could give her more pleasure than her husband.

"*I had a lot of fear and a lot of excitement.* I was young and very *vulnerable*, and I had *trusted* this man, but I didn't like *secrets*. I was very disappointed. When he said that I didn't need to tell my husband, I really *listened to my feelings*. This wasn't right. So I told Steve, and together we decided to leave.

"We got out, and that is what I think about when I think about discernment, *knowing when it is time to leave.*"

3. *Magic and manipulation.* Celia and Mary are two African-American professionals, serious spiritual students, who were understandably attracted to teachings that appeared to be from the Egyptian mystery schools with an Afrocentric twist.

The group was led by a powerful, charismatic man. At first the community seemed to be a *safe and nurturing place* made up of like-minded seekers. Both women felt a strong sense of familiarity with the material and admitted they felt *playful*, even titillated *by the magic*; it was part of the *sense of adventure*.

What they hadn't anticipated was the *submission* of the women to the men, the *manipulation* of the women's sexual energy, and the encouragement of polygamy.

"There was an automaton-like quality to the women," Mary recalled. "These really talented, intelligent women not only *subordinated themselves* to these men, which is not that unusual in society, but they were enervated. They all went into trance the minute they were in that setting.

"There was this whole element of magic. The leader would walk by and blow in your ear, and you would instantly go into trance. It was the *perfect seduction and temptation*."

Both women have subsequently researched the experience for the hooks within themselves as well as for the lessons learned.

Celia says that part of the setup for her was *loneliness*. "One of my places of *frustration* is that I work in an environment that doesn't racially mirror me back to me. In this group there was familiarity and a community, a tribe, one in which I didn't have to define myself. It was based on Egyptian teachings, which I am drawn to, and one of the male priests was a friend from many lifetimes. Also, there was an element of magic that I hadn't been exposed to before, and I *didn't realize that magic wasn't play*. The leader represented for me things that *hadn't been explored*. It was the perfect shadow experience."

Mary said, "I think there were lessons to be learned in terms of the *little girls in us that never grew up*. I think we felt *safe* with each other being kids, playing. Because of this we went into a situation people might think is not that dangerous, but it can be. Then there was the whole question of *going back* and doing things the African way. This taught us that we couldn't go back.

"But I don't think we were ever off the path," she continued. "We always prayed. *We always watched out for each other.*"

Celia added, "*We constantly tested our perception of reality against each other.* Part of what always happens in that kind of setting is the attempt to separate. The leader would talk to one of us and tell us not to tell the other."

Their joint advice is to be cautious about exploring in spiritual groups alone.

Discernment is a moment-by-moment choice for clarity. The very things that serve one stage of the journey may become counterproductive in another. Discernment teaches us where the essentials and nonessentials are in our lives at this moment. What is enough, and when must we let go? What is the spirit of the law, not just its letters?

The ancient teachings tell us that there are three things that have to be overcome for us to become fully conscious: mental illusions, glamorous delusions, and *maya*, the world of appearances. All require that we walk with discernment.

Twelve Considerations on Discernment

1. Unflinching self-honesty is the basis for discernment.

2. Wait to speak, believe, and act. Breathe. Wait a minute.

3. Unquestioned assumptions are potentially lethal.

4. Discerning disciples ask: "Do I choose to energize this?"

5. Discernment fuses intuition, experience, and knowledge.

6. Listen. Question. Evaluate. Choose. Then trust yourself.

7. Noncritical laughter restores perspective.

8. Wisdom never judges, but is always discriminating.

9. Seek inside, not outside, to discern your truth.

10. Discernment reveals the lies behind prejudices.

11. Disciples seek mentors that "walk their talk."

12. Self-judgments are projected onto others.

Exercise: Breaking the "Should" Syndrome

1. Add to your journaling seeds an investigation into the origins of your *shoulds*. Parents? School? Media?

2. Invite your inner critic to sit with you and talk. Interview it without judgment. Where was it created? Whose voice does it sound like? If lovingly listened to, the critic that now judges can be transformed into a discerning ally.

3. Make yourself a "should bank." Use a box or bottle. Every time you hear yourself, in your mind or in your speech, reinforce an I-should message, pay yourself a dollar. (It has to be enough to get your attention!) At the end of the month, spend the money on a special treat.

Prayer/Affirmation

I seek truth behind appearances.
I seek order in chaos.
I seek new life in death.
I seek Oneness in division.

Quotes

I realized it is not so important how much we see of things as how much we can see into them.

— Judy Taylor (whose blindness was corrected), *As I See It*

> *Believing everything she read*
> *In the daily news,*
> *(No in-between to choose)*
> *She thought that only one side won,*
> *Not that both might lose.*

— Langston Hughes

4 *Body: Temple, Archive, and Laboratory*

❧

What you cannot find in your own body, you will not find elsewhere.
—Upanishads

The imagined split between body and soul is the great-great-grandparent of most of the duality we experience on earth. Throughout the centuries of spiritual questing we've pronounced the body originally sinful, a temptation, and a distraction that seduces us to explore our senses at the risk of our souls. Periodically we've decreed that it must be mortified, shamed, punished, denied, or at the very least overcome. Even if we defiantly chanted, "Eat, drink, and be merry," afterward we often felt guilty and ran to our prayers and confessions for forgiveness. Maybe it's not okay to feel this good or have this much fun?

Whether we celebrate it or deny it, the body is with us as vehicle, focus, and record of our earth experiences. The goal is to synthesize spiritual mindfulness with an awareness Father David Steindl-Rast calls "bodifulness—full deep-rootedness in our bodies."

As spiritual beings, we carry heaven inside of us—forgotten, perhaps, or dimly recalled. But heaven is here, not out there.

Heaven is right here on this precious spinning thought of God we call Earth.

The elements of the earth are in our bones; the rivers and oceans run in our bloodstreams; the wind tides of life fill our lungs; fire energizes our minds and bodies. Our heart pulses with the beat of the earth. In order to live, we need the sun, just as we need the great forest. From the sacrificed animal and the abundant harvest, our cells carry the life force of all that we take in. We cycle to them; they cycle to us in an interdependent, circular dance of life.

Whenever we don't listen to the body, we don't listen to the earth. If we don't regard Nature, can we respect our own nature, that of all others, and the life force that universally we call Mother Nature? If we don't, doesn't rape, conquest, or at least indifference follow? And if we don't regard the Mother, how can we regard Her daughters or the feminine energies in Her sons?

Once during a visionary journey with a spirit teacher, I saw an eagle carrying nuts and fruits land on the teacher's shoulders. The teacher gave me the food, saying: "Never forget that nothing flies so high but that it must be fed from the earth."

The Body Remembers

Our body is a library of everything that has happened to us, to our ancestors, and even to our species. Buried in the folds of the more primitive parts of our brains are memories of the swamp, the jungle, and the treetops. Every joy and trauma has left an imprint.

The body catalogues what is still painful, unforgiven, and blocked, just as it does well-being, joy, and pleasure. Whether free or fettered, it unfailingly reports our emotional responses to the world, leaving tracks that reveal our thinking patterns and the intentions of our soul. As a friend quipped, "My body sends faxes to my mind."

We might forget, but the body doesn't. It consistently files data in the cells. I read about a woman who started longing for beer and french fries after a heart transplant, even though she had never liked either one before the surgery. She learned that the heart donor had loved them. The cells remembered.

In my practice I find myself frequently saying to students, reflecting body messages back, "Did you notice that you started rubbing your throat when you talked about so-and-so . . . that you crossed your legs when you mentioned this or that, dropped your voice when this subject came up?" My intention is to help them increase awareness of the tight connection between memory, emotions, and the body.

I know a psychiatrist who specializes in using biofeedback in a stress-reduction process he calls self-regulation. He told me that in every female patient he has ever tested, the inner thigh muscles were the last group to let go of tension. Little girls are warned to keep their legs together, and they often wrestle their way through adolescence protecting themselves from unwanted invasion, and learning quickly, if rather unconsciously, to watch out for "attack." The body records all that.

When I was very young I was on my own with a baby and a toddler. My children were never anything but a blessing, my delights and joys, and they still are, but survival in those days was a challenge. I was determined that my children would have a good life, so I worked very hard, and by the time I remarried I was self-employed and was buying a home in a nice neighborhood. In order to do it all, I had repressed the darker fears of the dissolving first marriage and the lack of support. But my body remembered.

Ten years later I dreamed that I walked into a train depot like Grand Central Station and saw an East Indian woman about eight months pregnant lying on a bench. A fifteen-month-old baby crawled on her. She had her mouth open as if in a scream, but nothing was coming out. "Why don't you scream?" I asked her in the dream. "I'm trying, but I can't," she told me.

Two days later I woke up with a vicious headache that continued for three days. This was unusual, since I don't usually have headaches. No treatment would touch my severe pain, and no cause ever showed up in spite of many tests. The headache simply left one morning, just the way it had arrived. Later I realized that the headache was the scream of repressed feelings that I couldn't get out of me.

As there is no time and space in the subconscious, memories can travel with us from lifetime to lifetime until we are ready to face and transform them. For example, Carl, a medical doctor, told me: "As long as I can remember I've been very reluctant to be open with some of my interests, such as Buddhism and meditation.

"In 1983 you [Gloria] asked me if I was going to share with my colleagues what I was studying. I said, 'Oh, no, I don't want to be crucified.' I said it as a joke, but it may have been unconscious material coming out, in the way Freud says that it does in jokes.

"In 1991 I was doing some holotropic breath work and suddenly remembered being part of an unorthodox religious group in the Middle Ages, a group that was considered heretical. I enthusiastically preached on occasion. I was arrested and felt guilt that I had let the group down. The main issues had to do with guilt and responsibility.

"Several years after this memory I was having problems with my calves cramping at night, always in the same place. Doing the breath work I felt pain and tightness in that area—also in my hands, with my elbows and wrists and fingers all being flexed to some extreme.

"In October 1994 I was doing another breath-work session, and my hands spontaneously rose above my head and crossed. I flashed upon that earlier memory. I was being crucified against the side of a building with both of my hands above my head, my feet crossed one over the other, and my face to the wall. The nails went through the calves in exactly the same places that had been hurting me for quite some time. When I came home from that breathing session, I felt much more open about discussing where I had been and what I had been doing, I would elaborate on it instead of avoiding it."

This doctor is now teaching holistic workshops, something he believes he wouldn't be doing had he not had this release.

How and where the cells record memory depends on our perception of the experience. Not every traumatic experience is recorded and held as negative in memory. If, for example, Carl had perceived his crucifixion as true martyrdom on behalf of truth, he might have internalized the memory in his body in a more positive way, rather than feeling guilty for getting arrested and killed.

❧ Journaling Seeds

1. How many really good times *in the body* do you associate with your spiritual self? How much laughter, dance, or sheer joy of being alive?

2. Do you experience Spirit present in your sexuality?

3. Are you critical or approving of your body?

4. Do you view aging as an enemy rather than as part of a cycle?

Hiding Our Emotions in the Body

Since we were in the womb, we've all been recording memories in our bodies of a world perceived as safe or not. We learn early on where the power is, who can be trusted, whether our needs will be met or not. We learn about yes and no from the set of a jaw, a look in the eye, a tone in the voice.

Children raised in abusive households learn that even physical safety depends on correctly reading the energetic climate. They learn to use their bodies as detectors. They don't always have accurate interpretative skills, and sometimes they believe their bad thoughts or behavior caused the abuse, or even a death or divorce in the family.

In ancient diplomatic training in Asia, one learned not to move a muscle during a negotiation, lest one's position be revealed. Lots of children learn that ancient skill from growing up in emotional or physically dangerous environments. If their separation of feelings from the body becomes severe, they dissociate, bury the feelings deep in the cells, and then repeat the inner script over and over in the world. The body has to be reeducated in such circumstances, and that is best done by a spiritually aware therapist.

We can stash great pain behind intellectual armor. Many bright children learn to hide in the mental body. Doing so hurts less than feeling. The pattern then carries over, and they can become an overly intellectualized adult who is afraid of feelings and vulnerability. But we really can't fake out our deepest feelings, no matter how much we intellectualize. The cells in our bodies know what we really believe reality to be. And usually we have quite a collection of paradoxical beliefs. We're holding energy that is both old and wise, young and foolish, believing and doubting. Embracing all of it, we grow, gradually reeducating all the cells toward self-love, which in turn opens us to the flow of Spirit.

The full drama gets taken into muscle groups that relax or tense, and into breathing patterns that are shallow or deep. If we feel safe, we express that freely in our body postures, our voices, and our movements. If we've been taught that our bodies and many of our natural feelings are not acceptable, we set up complex distortions, subterfuges, and illusions. Feeling unsafe, we create masks that we hope will protect us or be accepted by the outside world.

Eric came for counseling primarily because he couldn't perform sexually with any woman he loved. When I entered his energy field I saw him as an infant being lovingly bathed by his mother. He was floating in joy in a sea of unconditional love—until his mother cleaned his genitals, an act she did with great distaste. His body recorded this as abandonment, and the fear was set up that when his genitals were involved, love would be withdrawn. Eric felt the truth of this because his mother had always been very prudish. He had never discussed sex or body functions with her as a child or as an adult because he knew these were unpleasant subjects to her. He had forgotten, but his body had not. His task then was to reeducate the cells.

Mind to Matter—Instantly

Think about your thumb and nothing else for a minute. Within seconds your thumb will become hot or cool, maybe prickly. Your inner visual sense of the thumb grows proportionally larger than it actually is because you are focusing your attention on it.

It takes less than a microsecond for body chemistry to alter in the face of changing circumstances. And it has nothing to do with an objective outer reality. It has everything to do with what we *believe* reality to be at the moment. Our chemistry prepares our bodies to fulfill beliefs. All emotions *and thoughts* translate immediately into biochemical combinations—messages of love, safety, fear, the full range that kicks off the neurotransmitters—and within seconds the body tenses, relaxes, feels safe, or runs for cover.

I know a woman whose oncologist had been very discouraging to her prior to a bone marrow transplant. Depressed, she talked to another oncologist, who was encouraging and offered to take over her treatment. Her white blood cell count doubled overnight, and she sailed through the transplant. She believed in the possibility of positive outcome, and her body responded positively.

We report perceptions and beliefs to the whole body through a system of messengers called peptides. Deepak Chopra calls them "messengers from inner space." As we learn more about peptides, we are also learning more about the web of interconnections in the emotions, mind, and body. Systems that biologists used to think were separate—namely, the endocrine, immune, and nervous systems—are now understood to be in a close relationship, linked by these chemical messengers. Biologist Candace Pert has called the immune cells and T cells "bits of brain floating around in the body."

We are learning that information is widely distributed and not limited to particular neuron sites. Rather, it is more like patterns of electrical activity. Information is stored in a network of relationships among neurons, so that even if a section of the brain is harmed, the information isn't necessarily lost, as other areas will have that material in some form.

Psychoneuroimmunology studies links between the brain and the immune system. Researchers have discovered that nerve fibers in the thymus gland (the gland that produces the immune cells known as T cells, which work within the bloodstream to protect the body from foreign agents) have cells that receive signals from the nervous system, which is, of course, connected to the brain. These nerve fibers have been traced to all areas within the immune system. The implication is that we can mentally hold healing thoughts and images that will be transmitted to the immune system.

Cellular Releases

Through various therapies, many of us already know who did what to whom and why in our lives, who had the power, and who was the threat. The work now is to release the *energy of the emotional responses* being held in the cells. Reinforced negatives and unreleased traumas are imprinted into tissue as surely as if they were stamped in clay. But the body can be remolded. That starts with paying close attention to the patterns in the body and where energy is repeatedly stuck.

When we have lost communication with our bodies, it is hard

to find a free-flowing joy. Feelings frozen into cellular memory block the flow of pain *and* pleasure. Defrosting the feelings often first brings pain, but later it becomes the portal to joy.

Our bodies are phenomenal managers of stress and can compensate for all kinds of toxicity. The problems come when the immune system is overloaded. A major part of psychospiritual training is to rout out distorted cellular memories and replace them with healthy, conscious choices.

Reeducating the Body

Here are a few specific suggestions for getting in touch with the body:

- Begin with gratitude. Regardless of how you got here, now is the time to flourish, not just survive. Gratitude empowers.
- Bless your body in meditations. Mentally direct Light to all parts, seeing healing pouring through your body like rain falling on thirsty ground.
- Forgive everyone everything and gain your freedom at a cellular level. Rage and grief must first be confronted and then embraced. Inherent in your divine birthright is the power to release all people, acts, and lies from this life or any other.
- Talk to any body part that is hurt. Ask, "Why are you hurting?" Then listen. Insights might come instantaneously, or they might arrive in a dream, a reverie, a conversation, or a book.
- Touch the hurting body part with deep compassion. Self-pity and self-compassion are no more alike than pity and compassion are for another. It is important to respect with love our own suffering.
- Free-associate with the affected body part through words or drawings, beginning with a phrase such as "A sore throat is . . ." Do this long enough to get beyond the obvious into the subtle, and it will provide insights into the disharmony.

• Breathe into body disharmony. Inhale energy in deep breaths that expand the abdomen. Direct the breath into the hurting body part. Next, exhale all the toxins and send them back to the Source.

• Symbolize body pain and discomfort: How big is it? What shape? What color is it? Is it an animal? Through symbols the brain can creatively offer supports, such as injecting soothing blue into red pain.

• Visualize health. See any affected part as glowing with light. See yourself doing desired activities. Feel the emotions that go with healthy functioning. (Warning: Watch out for getting caught in dualism on this one. You can embrace the reality of the disturbance without fighting the fact that it happened in the first place.)

• Consider using the services of a trained bodyworker or bioenergetic therapist. They know physiology, offer safe therapeutic techniques, and can support your body through healing crises and releases.

• Consider natural supports such as chiropractic, naturopathy, and acupuncture, not as alternatives, but as complements. They maximize the body's inherent capacities to heal itself.

• Remember that the operating room can be as healing as the health food store. Release any feelings of failure in not healing the problem "naturally." Blessings, not censure, facilitate healing.

• Find a support group that can help with acceptance, integration, and emotional support as you process health issues. Such groups also provide fresh viewpoints, current information, and the pooling of good ideas.

• Strengthen the link between mind, body, and spirit with a body movement meditation such as yoga, tai chi, and chi gong. In time the postures and forms open the body and calm the mind.

• Put on music and let the body move. Dance to liberate

tightness in muscles and emotions. From sacred group circles to free-form, dance can be profoundly healing.

- Fast to rest the body, clean out toxins, restore balance, and directly involve the body in a spiritual process while it heals. Experiment with methods until you find the one best for you.
- Be wary of the I-shouldn't-need-any-medication and I-should-be-able-to-heal-myself syndromes. If you need anti-depressants or insulin or a painkiller or anything else to restore balance, be grateful for the medication. Bless it.
- Take your body to Nature. She is the mother of the body, and She is the great healer. Walk the earth barefooted. Sit on it. Rest your back against a tree. Inhale. Receive balance and beauty.
- Become food-conscious. If the life force is abused (as with hormones and chemicals), then Nature is compromised. Lighter diets typically help integration. But listen to *your* body.
- Test responses to food and discover dietary culprits and allies by recording everything you eat for thirty days. During this time, record energy levels, moods, and your general sense of well-being. After thirty days assess and evaluate; look for healthful patterns and connections.

Subtle Energy Systems of the Body

It is not my intention to explore the subtle bodies and the chakra system in depth in this book, though necessary information is provided wherever appropriate. For those interested in exploring this subject more fully, I've listed several books on the subject in the bibliography. Keep in mind that students of holistic healing need to have a working knowledge of the subtle bodies. To not know them would be like a medical student refusing to learn the physiological systems in the physical body.

Most spiritual sciences have substantial foundations. While one has to allow for cultural and therefore language and symbolic differences, along with some variation from teaching to teaching, the basics are pretty universal. Centuries of careful observations have noted the typical characteristics of the subtle bodies and the chakras.

Basically we experience life through at least seven different frequencies, often called bodies. The sum total of these bodies and the life force moving through them make up our aura. These bodies, from the most dense to the most subtle, are:

1. *The physical body.* It has the slowest rate of vibration and acts as the focused vehicle for our intentions in our familiar three dimensions.

2. *The etheric body.* This "double" or health body holds a blueprint of every cell in the physical body. Illnesses can often be picked up psychically at this level before they manifest.

3. *The astral body.* Desires, emotions, and attachments reside here. Two distinct frequencies make up the astral. The higher vibrations are those feelings that motivate and guide our incarnation, like the deep currents move the oceans. The lower vibrations are made of those feelings that are constantly changing as we interact with stimuli, like the top part of the ocean, which is calm or stormy depending on outer passing conditions. Don't get confused by the word *astral.* In some systems it is used to cover some or all of the nonphysical frequencies.

4. *The mental body.* This is also represented by two frequencies: higher (abstract) thinking and lower (ordinary) thinking processes.

5. *The first spiritual body.* This level of spiritual consciousness holds memories of past lives. It is at this level that we have knowledge of the evolving self.

6. *The second spiritual body.* The Bible describes this frequency

as the body "not made by human hands." Here we experience the awareness of I Am, the transcendent Spirit Self
beyond karma.

7. *The third spiritual body.* This is the unitive state of consciousness, in which the Mother-Father-God and I are One. It is
pure Spirit, One with all.

Consciousness resides on this continuum of energy, from the
rapidly vibrating spiritual levels to the relatively denser physical
one. All of these function in all of us all of the time, but we might
be unaware of them. The fully awakened individual is conscious
of all of the subtle bodies.

All of our vibrations, from the spiritual into the physical, are in
a constant dance of color and sound in the aura. *Everything* in
consciousness is reflected in our aura: self-image, emotional states,
thinking patterns, wellness or sickness. How we interpret what is
there depends on the symbols we know. Because disharmonies
usually start not at the physical level but in more subtle levels, such
as emotional suffering or chronic negative thinking, the disharmony often shows up in the more subtle ranges before it does in
the body.

Similarly, the chakra system is like a vast network of energy sta-
tions, large and small, that gather and disperse energy throughout
our aura, linking the subtle bodies to the physical. The major
chakras are the junctures where energy from the universe enters,
changes frequencies to match the physical, makes connections,
and finds directional lines of energy to feed the whole body. Access to memories (ancient or current) can come through the major chakras, as energy often clusters in and around the major nerve
centers and glands that are linked to the chakras.

Anakaranah is a Sanskrit term for the bridge of energy that builds
awareness between all our parts of the energy continuum, so that
the highest spiritual intentions can be brought down through all

the vibrational levels into the physical. There they can manifest. The process is like a cascade of water pouring unobstructed down a mountain, through the valley, and to the sea. The more successful we are in building the bridge through which Spirit can pour Light and wisdom into the physical, the more we build what the Tibetans call the Rainbow Body, the Chinese Taoists call the Diamond Body, and the Holy Bible calls the Light Body.

One day we will have instruments that can monitor the shifting processes of the auras and chakras, as clairvoyants now do. These instruments will be able to translate the aura into colors that will eventually be charted onto scales of wellness or impending sickness.

Then we will begin whole new explorations into out-of-body and near-death experiences, find new ways of perceiving basic predisposition in infants and young children, and obtain even more comprehensive insight into post-traumatic stress syndrome, phantom pains, and a multitude of other bodily mysteries. As research into the aura grows, we will also open up a vast new level of investigation into the manner in which we attract and hold material from the collective, from ancestral memory, and from past life memories.

We will also be able to detect the ways negativity held in the energy field stagnates and becomes toxic. Then our doctors will stress positive thoughts and forgiveness, based on knowledge of energetic consequences.

Breath of Life

Breath is life. Breath is blessing, revitalization, and anointing. Breath and spirit are inseparable: the Greek *pneuma*, the Sanskrit *vagu*, the *ruach* of the Hebrews. Aristotle believed *pneuma* connected the physical body parts to the psyche. *New Dimensions* magazine called the breath "a portable altar."

Many disciplines encourage breathing through the nostrils, as there are nerve pathways in the nose that lead to and stimulate the pineal gland or third eye. As sensitivity grows, one becomes aware of the breath entering various organs and traveling subtle pathways in the body. The breath can be used to anchor intention, to clear out stale energy, to balance yin and yang, and to build bridges between Spirit and the body. It heals, cleanses, and steadies the emotions as it fuels the body. You can store the breath for power, direct it like a sword, and, with training, use it to break bricks and boards.

Gay Hendricks, who wrote *Conscious Breathing*, suggests we take an "oxygen cocktail." He writes, "On a purely physiological level, if you learn how to breathe deeper and more powerfully with exercise, for example, you actually grow more capillary space in your body. There are about sixty thousand miles of capillaries in your body. But if you're a regular exerciser, you have a lot more than that. You may have another ten or twenty thousand miles of capillary space in your body, so you've literally got more space for feeling in your body. Good breathing enhances your ability to grow a larger version of yourself on a purely physiological level."

Several therapeutic breathing systems have been created over the past few decades, notably holotropic breathing, rebirthing, vivation, and transformational breath. They use the breath in specific ways to recover memories, to clear emotional and physical blocks, to facilitate the flow between mind, body, and spirit, and to reeducate unhealthy and fearful breathing patterns. As with all things, it takes practice to achieve balance between inhalation and exhalation, expanding the abdomen while not raising the shoulders.

In his book *The Blooming of a Lotus*, Buddhist master teacher and social reformer Thich Nhat Hanh offers many meditations that focus on the breath as one and the same with awareness. He recommends that we smile as we breathe, an act that relaxes the whole body.

The New Body

Prophecies of a superhuman have existed for centuries. The mastery of pain, disease, and aging has seemed impossible. But as we are finishing up the purification rites of the Kali Yuga, our attention is once again drawn to the possibility that each of us can create a stronger, more illuminated, healthier body, one that embodies the Light of heaven while walking on this holy ground.

Throughout history there have been individuals who have challenged our assumptions of aging. Count Germain, known today as the Ascended Master Saint Germain, was reportedly ageless. The story is told that the Countess de Georgy told Count Germain that she had known his father in 1710. He told her that it was he whom she had known fifty years earlier, when he had been forty-five years old.

I once visited a well-known mystic deep in the wilderness in Iceland. This man was in his late eighties and looked to be in his fifties. When I asked him his secret, he calmly said, "I have fairy blood in me." Oh, well, that might not be an option for most of us!

We may well be on the way to discovering our own fountains of youth. Dr. Deepak Chopra says we can reverse all the biological markers of aging. While acknowledging that genetics certainly affects longevity, he says that "thinking and self-perception change your life by 30 to 50 years.

"I think growing old will soon be considered synonymous with becoming glamorous because we shall see a new era emerging where the elderly will become the springboard for a new kind of renewal and rejuvenation and creativity that civilization has never had."

Charles Fillmore, cofounder of the Unity School of Christianity, once said: "Through mental energy or the dynamic power of the mind, man can release the life of the electrons stored in the atoms that compose the cells of his body. Physical science says that if the electronic energy stored in a single drop of water were suddenly released, its power would demolish a six-story building."

It is universally recognized that there is a powerful force that is released through deep meditation that can generate healing in humans and animals and accelerate the growth of plants. This force can be constructive, when used unselfishly, or very destructive, when used negatively. If our prayers and meditations are compromised by distraction and lack of intention, by unwillingness to love ourselves and others, then we're like substations removed from a power plant. We get some juice, but nothing like the full power we get when we are fully plugged in to the main supply, loving and intentional.

Ascension is a term often used today to describe the process in which every cell of the body is transmuted into a higher, lighter frequency. One wonders if the ascension of Jesus from the tomb was indeed more than a metaphor for spiritual transformation, perhaps a precursor of the superman to come one day. Legends abound of individuals who "translated," meaning they were reported to have ascended into their light bodies without having died. In esoteric terms such a person is an adept, one who has achieved the fifth initiation (the Resurrection, in Christian terminology). An adept can preserve a body or create whatever he or she prefers. In Sanskrit this is called a *mayavirupa*, a body of one's own making.

One of the more famous stories of ascension in our century was told by witnesses of the translation of Analee Skaron, a devoted elderly Mormon who was excommunicated for the teachings that she put in a book called *Ye Are Gods*. One night her housemate saw a bright light under Analee's door but chose not to disturb her. The next morning Analee Skaron was gone. That evening she appeared to her family in a robe of light, and then disappeared in front of them.

The body of Paramahansa Yogananda lay in state for three weeks in 1951 and did not deteriorate. Similar phenomena involving saints and enlightened beings have been reported in all religions. St. Francis Xavier's body remained uncorrupted for a long time, as have those of other Christian saints.

The Indian mystic and scholar Sri Aurobindo and his spiritual partner, known to thousands as the Mother, taught that the fusion of the spiritual into the physical would create what they called a "supermental" being, one who would have a body capable of perfect physiological balance, manifesting at will all that it needed. Aurobindo wrote: "If a total transformation of the being is our aim, a transformation of the body must be an indispensable part of it; without that no full divine life on earth is possible." And the Mother said it this way: "It is not a crucified body which will save the world, but a glorified body."

Exercise: Body Appreciation

Think of your hands and all their wondrous skills. Contemplate their many functions and services to others.

Hold your palms up to receive energy from the universe; hold your palms down to bless the earth. Place them over your heart. Feel love for your own body. Sit quietly and allow thoughts and feelings to surface. Use your breath consciously to exhale, release, and forgive abusive hands.

Select another part of your body, and then another, until you have done this process with all parts of your physical self. Concentrate on any traumatized organs with great love.

Exercise: Breath of Harmony

1. Inhale slowly through the nose into the lower abdomen, filling it up and pushing it out. Watch the breath.

2. Exhale slowly through the nose, watching your lower abdomen pull back in as the breath ascends through the upper abdomen, chest, and throat and out the nose.

3. Do this several times, bringing your mind back to attention as it becomes distracted. With practice you will build up the number of times you can comfortably do this.

4. After you have done this a few times, your inbreath and outbreath will become more balanced. You can encourage that by counting on the inhale "one thousand and one, one thousand and two," and so on, pausing between the inhale and exhale.

Exercise: Cleansing Breath

A cleansing breath starts by inhaling through the nose and exhaling through the mouth, as if whistling, with a series of energized, quick breaths. You'll feel the action in your solar plexus.

Another form of cleansing is to inhale through the nose and exhale with a huge sighing *ah-h-h*, rolling up the exhale from the lower abdomen to the upper chest, throat, and nose until you feel empty of the breath.

Body in Shadow: Illness, Disease, and Suffering

Mama vs Biamama

As disciples choosing to live aware through *all* of life, we have to make peace with impermanence, disease, death, and suffering. In spite of the limits of the rational mind, we can find peace. The soul knows what the brain can't grasp.

When the body is running smoothly and is full of energy and pleasant sensations, we are enchanted with it, especially in its youthful vigor and beauty. Then we celebrate our physicality.

Then comes a malfunction that darkens our delight like a cloud covering a meadow. Poignancy often haunts our most delicious times, as we know that they are exquisitely temporary.

Our attempts to understand suffering wind around a cosmic maze. How can we reconcile an omnipotent God/Goddess with the pain we experience and see around us? Why does He/She "allow" it? Is it punishment? Testing? Did we create this pain?

Yes, of course there's karma. We're all in exactly the right place at the right time. Understanding that helps, but karma can also be used too quickly as a glib, dismissive answer to a complex puzzle. Whose karma? Mine? Family? Race? Species?

What we can't understand or control, historically we have called an "act of God." Plagues have been named God's punishment for everything from heresy to sexual choices. Even the pain of childbirth was said to be penance for Eve's disobedience.

So we rage and resist, get depressed, feel guilty, turn stoic, or go numb. Sometimes we just pass along the clichés because it seems too scary to consider that nobody, not even the wisest among us, really knows why we suffer.

Coming to terms with pain is simply not easy. Cynicism misses the mark entirely, and, for all its posturing, so does intellectualizing. Once we accept that there are no easy answers, then insights do start to emerge from our deepest knowing.

Pain exacts excruciating dues and grinding endurance. It is a great equalizer, completely indifferent to the bribery of money or intelligence. Pain is the material of initiation—personal, group, and planetary. Mass suffering, as in war, acts of terrorism, violent storms and earthquakes, epidemics, and plagues, scathes us to our souls. But even as these events plunge us into unspeakable hells, so do they set the stage for heroism, self-sacrifice, reprioritizing, new perspectives, courage, endurance, transformations that reposition our lives, and a multitude of opportunities for growth. In the fires we become new beings.

If we don't learn compassion from such experiences, then it all has to be done again and again until we realize that we are in this together. The suffering of others screams at us to identify, understand, and change the conditions that contribute to all suffering on this planet.

Pain Without Suffering

There is a difference between pain and suffering. Pain is an experience or condition; suffering is a response to the pain. It is not its inevitable twin.

The degree of emotional, mental, and even physical suffering is strongly influenced by the degree of resistance to the pain. What we resist we energize. "It is what it is" is a sober reality, and there is enormous power in accepting it. Then no energy is wasted in fighting the fact of its existence. Acceptance prepares the ground for surrender, an even deeper level of release in which the gifts of the experience are more likely to be revealed.

One mother reported the gift of new perspective that she received from her teenage daughter's bout with cancer. "We can say now that it was the best thing that ever happened to us as a family. In an instant, reality collapsed, and my ground of being was entirely altered. Driving home from the hospital the first day, I passed a grocery store. I saw that the ability to go in and buy groceries and bring them home to my family and cook dinner was a sacred, divine gift."

Acceptance of a physical challenge is not to be confused with the despair of "I quit," which withholds acceptance. An inner battle usually precedes surrender to the Highest Self. In surrender we let go of the ego's interpretations and prayers, which are understandably variations of "make it go away." The Highest Self knows the truth that is being born through the labor of the pain.

Angela said that it was through surrender to the events after her child's premature birth that she truly grew. Her baby was in a neonatal intensive care unit for several months. First she bargained with God; then she surrendered to "Thy will be done," and it became the mantra she used through rounds of surgeries, tubes, and procedures.

"Until him," she said, "I had stayed aloof, the interested observer of life. Birthing a child was not an experience that allowed me to stay apart. Staying present was not optional. Being aware of my thoughts was as important as giving him his medication on time. I consciously gave him back to God at the outset. Now he's a loving and sweet child. I know that even under our care now, he is a unique being with his own path."

There is great creativity within surrender. In resistance we can block our capacity for creative problem solving. We get burdened by expectations, protesting ("This isn't happening—I hate it"), reviewing the past with hindsight and regret ("If only . . . I wish"), and rehearsing the future ("What if this or that happens?").

Surrender is in the present moment, and therein lies its power. The river of life is incessantly flowing. We cannot see around the next bend. Sometimes all we can do is survive the white water. Fighting it increases the chances of going under. Surrendering to it, we can either be carried through it or more clearly see how to negotiate the passage.

Priest and psychotherapist John E. Fortunato writes in *AIDS: The Spiritual Dilemma* that after anger and tears comes release and yielding, "a rush of energy and almost, strangely, joy. Just at the moment when it seems there is nothing to be done, that all is hopeless, at that very moment I become charged with vitality and the will to do everything that needs to be done."

"Thy will, not mine" was the prayer of surrender during Jesus' dark night in Gethsemane, as it is so often in our most painful passages. In that moment, our humanness and Godness fuse.

Acceptance Includes Tears and Anger

Sometimes spiritual students become perplexed that crisis often follows commitment. As soon as the desire to become more conscious is telegraphed to all the cells in the body, the detox process begins. As one disciple put it: "What happened? I dedicated myself to my path, and all hell broke loose in my body!"

What happened was that God/Goddess took her seriously, and the process of cleaning out began. An anonymous poet in Egypt once said, "And what is hell but a dam I did put in my own flow." Decide to become more conscious, and the dams start breaking.

This is a beautiful and often difficult process, and if we have the eyes to see, it is truly one that indicates quite clearly the inseparable intimacy of the mind–body–spirit relationship.

There is no spiritual shame in responding to the onset of pain with anger, dread, or tears. We beg, "Please let this cup pass." If we add guilt or blame to the pain, we magnify the condition. God/Goddess is patient and can deal with a lover's quarrel with the Beloved. The point is not to avoid the protests of our egos, but to accept them as part of the journey and not get trapped in them. As one disciple told me, "Weep and press on."

It's said that St. Teresa of Avila, while on a difficult journey to do God/Goddess's business, was unceremoniously pitched off the back of her donkey into a freezing mountain stream. She shook her fist at heaven and yelled, "No wonder you have so few friends; look how you treat them!" Most of us have had such a moment.

Illness as Opportunity

Many traditions teach that sickness reflects inhibited soul expression. Ultimately that's probably true. Yet a dreaded illness often catalyzes a life into transformation; the athlete stopped in mid-career by a crippling accident becomes an inspiration to the young; a tumor becomes a wake-up call.

Mama vs. big mama

The purposes of illnesses are complex, and we must be careful not to be simplistic. To say "sick equals wrong" only adds guilt to a challenge and probably reflects more fear than comprehension. Understanding comes with asking, "What are we learning?"

The body prints out precise metaphors. Generalizations can be destructive. We're enough alike that causation charts can start us on our inner research, but we are different enough to have unique ways of imprinting our cells. For example, eye problems *might* indeed be a metaphor for what we don't want to see. And they might not be. Lower back problems *might* mean one is feeling lack of support—but not every time. Not every neck pain means there is a "pain in the neck" in our lives.

Nothing replaces self-knowledge. For example, if we grew up in a family where self-assertion was a no-no, we might have problems in parts of the body that strike out, such as feet or hands. If we played sports, we might have worked out some of the energy around striking back. If we didn't, the energy might be held in a tight jaw.

In her excellent book *Alchemy of Illness*, psychotherapist Kat Duff writes about her extended bout with chronic fatigue syndrome. Her perception of her illness shifted when she heard of a woman who had been thinking she had bad karma due to illness. A Zen Buddhist friend told the woman, "Good karma, huh? Brings you close to the Way."

Duff points out that among the many opportunities that illness brings is the surfacing of all the parts of ourselves we don't like: "nag, crybaby, martyr, addict." She points out that we also get to work through the things we find offensive, including sores, bad breath, disfigurement, and so forth. "The longer I am sick, the more I realize that illness is to health what dreams are to waking life, the reminder of what is forgotten, the bigger picture working toward resolution."

At one point Duff speaks of offering her pain to the earth. This is a healing exercise any of us could adapt to our surroundings.

When I'm so upset, wound up and knotted with rage and sorrow or regret that I cannot rest, I walk down into the pasture in front of our house, find a place where the cows have trampled a path, making a soft bed of dirt and lie down, face flat on the Earth. I go down slowly, first to my knees, as if in prayer, then on all fours, like an animal and finally stretch myself out like a snake until my stomach rests on the belly of the Earth. Lying there, with my face and fingers in the dirt, I empty myself into the Earth with whispers and tears until I finally come to rest and my breathing returns to normal. Then and only then do I become aware of my surroundings.

Yours, Mine, and Ours

If we mastered all of our karma, individually and as a species; *if* we lived on a pollution-free planet; *if* the lamb and the lion were lying down together; *if* there was no conflict of interest between viruses and us, then we would all be well.

In the meantime, we are participants in the body of the entire race. It only *seems* as though it is *my* pain, *my* disease, *my* immune system. As we progress in awareness we realize it is *the* pain, *the* disease, *the* immune system. Our one body can only sustain so much toxicity before *our* immune system becomes overloaded and has to release it through some of its parts.

As long as we collectively pollute our environment, chemicalize our foods, and constantly live under the threat of war and violence and intolerable stress, disciples will probably have the same or similar body responses as anyone else. There are enlightened souls who have outlived everyone, eaten poisons, and subsisted on air. Remember, though, even enlightened beings have pain, and many of them die around the same ages we all do. They just approach the experience differently.

Certainly the more conscious we become, the more we can counter toxicity. We know that thoughts and emotions trigger instantaneous physiological responses in individuals. So do collective national and planetary thoughts and emotions.

The pain from the Holocaust, Vietnam, Bosnia, the Middle East, Ireland, and Africa has fallen as impersonally as rain into everybody's world. So has the threat of nuclear war, which sits like a panther at the edge of the jungle; maybe it's quiet today, but we never forget it's there. Assuming we are not affected by those thought forms is like saying, "I'm a good person who will not breathe air that is polluted."

Inherited and Shared Shadows

Many cultures have understood that individuals act out group problems. In old Hawaii, when someone in the village had done something wrong, they would bring all the members of the extended family together to research what was happening that caused the disharmony to erupt. We know that in family patterns someone frequently is designated to act out the group pathology. We just do this on a larger scale in society.

We are personally being led toward reunion with the One, and at the same time we are participating in the transpersonal work of evolution, which needs millions of beings to fulfill the next stage of growth. It's as though the universe is saying to us, "Nothing personal, but we need some checks and balances . . . need to bring about a bit of justice here . . . clear up this ignorance or that prejudice . . . and we'll have to use quite a lot of souls to get this done." So we sign on to share the price of transformation for all of us.

I was once told in Spirit, "Nothing is ever lost. The mastery of any illusion, the release of any fear or limitation, is not only a liberation to the individual, but is, in essence, a gift to every generation that follows."

Familial and national guilt, prejudices, negative deeds, and injustices can all be passed on in the family gene pool, handing down, as the Bible puts it, "the sins of the fathers." Recognizing this, the American Indians advise us to consider everything we do with an awareness of the implications for the next seven generations.

I read for a woman whose place in the dharma has largely been to complete generational patterns. She shares this task with her grandmother and mother, the three of them spiritual collaborators spanning a hundred years, each one dedicated to purifying family patterns that went back countless generations.

 In preparation for the incoming age, many families like this one are completing patterns. Some individuals, in the spirit of "the buck stops here," are even choosing from a soul level not to have children rather than perpetuate the negative inheritances.

All things do work together, and there is an exacting precision in the manner in which we run our personal karma *and* participate in the collective karma at the same time. For example, a woman might be helping to change societal attitudes toward the feminine while at the same time she works on her personal karmic fears about being in a female body; or a man might be using his racial heritage to combat prejudice for everyone while he works on a personal initiation of sacrifice.

Regardless of its roots, if we are experiencing a disharmony, then we are responsible for restoring it to harmony. The healing formula is the same for individuals, families, or societies: nonresistance, inner research, commitment to change, forgiveness of everyone, and gratitude for the privilege of healing.

We can rise from any burning crisis as new creatures: more in touch with our own spirits, more compassionate; ready to make a contribution, change a law, or call attention to a neglect; prepared to teach or inspire others.

"After great pain," poet Emily Dickinson said, "a formal feeling comes." The familiar mind-sets have been exposed for weakness and strengths, and, in a sense, one is newborn. Therein lies new power and peace.

❉ Body Tyrannies: Twelve Ways to *Never* Find Peace in Your Body

1. Meet the CCC standards (current criteria for correctness).

2. Avoid the A word (Aging) and refuse to accept cycles of life.

3. Look to the media to teach you the one standard for beauty.

4. Compare yourself to others. It will keep you sharp.

5. Don't eat; thin is better than well.

6. Never accept yourself just as you are. Remodel for perfection.

7. Define your self-image by your sex appeal.

8. Ignore stress signals; push the limits.

9. Evaluate others by CCC. It will keep the myths alive.

10. Feel guilty about illness. It's pointless but familiar.

11. Give your body a diet of negative thoughts and feelings.

12. Deny your own death. Maybe it won't happen.

Exercise: Antidote for the Body Tyrannies

1. Stand nude in front of a mirror. Begin with the top of your head and work your way down to your toes, giving thanks for every single function of this miraculous instrument. Appreciate the design and unique beauty of each part. Bathe it in approval. If you have trouble doing this with any part, breathe and remind yourself that you have been programmed to deny or criticize. Claim your power to choose and approve. Do it again and again until you feel as a loving parent toward your body.

2. Anoint each part of your body, evoking a holy name. Holy names carry power. Each part of yourself that you touch in love and compassion will light up with the Presence. "In the name of the Christ [Kuan Yin, your guru, whoever] I bless my eyes, my heart," and so on. You can do this for another as well.

✖ Twelve Considerations on the Body

1. Mind exists in each cell and can be contacted.

2. Breathe. Say yes to this day. Breathe and release yesterday.

3. The body is of the earth. Both require respect and loving care.

4. A healing for any one of us is ultimately a gift for all of us.

5. Physical purification often accelerates with spiritual dedication.

6. Surrender expands possibilities; quitting eliminates them.

7. Remember the Infinite Self; celebrate the finite self.

8. The Mother/Father God has no hands and feet but ours.

9. Embraced with compassion, pain can be transformational.

10. Soul intention is fulfilled through the body, not in spite of it.

11. Gratitude empowers and enhances the immune system.

12. Pain is an experience; suffering is a response.

Prayer and Affirmation

Inhale, palms up to receive the gifts of heaven: "I gratefully receive the blessings of the universe." Exhale, palms down to bless the earth: "I gratefully offer blessings to the earth."

& talk about my hands experience at NH.

Quotes

When you pray, move your feet.

—African proverb

There are 90,000 sense receptors per square inch of the human fingertip. When I just mention it, my fingertips are trembling. That is what connects us to God.

—Paulus Berensohn, artist, teacher

BECOMING THE WAY

❧

Love: The Master Key

Will: The Divine Birthright

Faith: Cornerstone of the Cathedral

Power: Focus for the Flow

5 *Love: The Master Key*

❦

Tell me whom you love and I'll tell you who you are.

—Creole proverb

With every step on the Path, we are invited deeper into a love that is both mysterious and so practical it transforms everything it touches. Love continually corrects our meandering and brings us back to center. It realigns us with our purpose and breathes through us into the world. It stretches us until we know no strangers to our love. Love takes us into the fiery death of lies and resurrects us to truths.

Seek love above all. When words and theories fail, when the violent upheaval of change horrifies you and even your favorite dreams are passing, close your eyes, breathe, and ask: "How do I bring love into this?"

Unconditional Love

Many of us grew up in families and systems where love was very conditional. Good little girls and boys got it; the ones who stepped outside the lines got less; and often a deity (out there, of course), was the designated judge who rewarded or punished with love. Many spiritual seekers struggle to untangle subconscious misperceptions that they're loved when things are going well in their lives and are not so loved when things are not.

We all like the harmonious times when the world is just right and we win the moment. We feel great; people around us are not ill, unhappy, or unusually demanding; we glow with love. And then life brings challenges. The goal of the disciple is to enjoy the easy passages, let them go as their time passes, and seek the love that is present in all circumstances. That constant love will sustain us during the dark nights, wilderness experiences, and awesome assignments that commitment brings. It takes practice to stay aware that love is always with us. As Kim, a counselor and teacher, put it, "We're all learning unconditional love in the trenches. Isn't that the best way?"

As unconditional love is the essence we seek to channel into the world, it seems important that we grasp exactly what that means. What is this love that mystics and martyrs, masters and devotees around the world celebrate?

Unconditional love exempts nothing and no one. It is not attached to anything or anybody at the personal, national, racial, sexual, or religious levels. It's not dependent on sensation, and it neither flows or shuts down based on momentary feelings. Love moves through, above, around, and in between all seasons of change. Like Light, it is a constant in the universe.

Love will rush in wherever there is the slightest vacuum to fill. That alone makes a good case for the disciple to walk moment by moment in love. We never know when there is an opportunity, perhaps imperceptible, to receive the tincture of love.

Agape: The Essence of Divine Love

In the English language the word *love* carries a lot of light and shadow, and a lot of ambiguity. Love is the theme of pimps and preachers, pop songs, advertising jingles, chants, and arias. We unselfishly serve or self-serve in "love." "I *love* my dog; I *love* choco-late; I *love* God." That's a lot of duty for one small word.

In Sanskrit there are over ninety words for love, offering a wide range of nuances. In ancient Persia there were more than eighty words for love. The Inuit have a subtle phrase that says, "I love you but I won't go seal hunting with you."

From the Greeks we inherited three powerful words for love. *Eros,* from which we get *erotic,* means a love filled with passion. When we are in touch with eros we can experience both our hu-man desire to merge with another and our deep longing for con-nection with the ultimate Beloved.

Philos communicates the need for friendship and community. The name of Philadelphia, the city of brotherly love, comes from *philos.* Sacred texts remind us that it is easy for us to love our friends. But if people are different or difficult, can we love them? If so, then we begin to understand *agape.*

Agape is unconditional love. It is a steady force moving through us as impersonally, and as intimately, as the air we breathe. It doesn't pardon or bless our definitions of worthiness. It flows freely to everyone and everything. We can be unaware of its pres-ence, but it is always with us.

Agape will not allow us to divide the world into pieces: this in-ner, this outer; this one worthy, this one not; this profane, the other sacred. Division leads to fear, and fear constricts the flow of energy. "Perfect love casts out all fear" is more than wishful think-ing. It's a statement of the way energy works.

In our souls we long to be absorbed in the sea of agape, just as in the story of the salt boy, who had been seeking his true home. He found it when he came to the sea, stepped in, and slowly dis-solved, losing his life but gaining everything.

Once we have ever been consciously aware of being in that ocean of love, we long for it thereafter, no matter how much the ego pulls us back into the illusion of separation. However, until we have cleaned up all our stuff, our nervous system simply can't handle undiluted bliss all the time, any more than it could sustain an orgasm for hours. Yet in time we will be aware of unceasing cosmic love flooding our beingness.

Until then, we practice loving one person at a time. No one needs love more than the next person we meet. If we pray to do really significant work with our love, but at the same time we are impatient with the people in front of us, we will be presented with similar people over and over. Real love is not about ego preference.

Years ago I had a reminder of this when I was walking behind a bag lady in New York who suddenly fell. Several of us rushed to help. Someone called an ambulance. Another recognized her from the neighborhood. I put my hands on her and spoke softly to calm her, as her head was cut and bleeding. She was old, layered in dirty rags, and smelled overripe.

I looked into her eyes and felt as though I were spiraling down into an abyss. Suddenly I saw myself in her. I was not a nice lady helping a troubled one. She was an experience of myself, and I knew it. I loved her from that place that knows no separation. After the ambulance left, I sat in a nearby cafe, allowing awareness of this small crossing to sink in. I hoped I had helped a bit, but mainly I felt gratitude to her for the piece of our darkness she is carrying. I felt compassion for her lifewalk.

I have thought of her often. It seems like a small moment; still, I suspect that our deepest wisdom is a necklace strung with tiny insights. Even as I write this, I see a stream of love energy surrounding her.

We recognize when we are with someone who embodies agape. It enfolds us but doesn't grasp. There is a peace and harmony emitted by such a person even when discipline or "tough love" is necessary.

When you were a child and asked, "Who is God?" the usual answer was, "God is love." If you were fortunate, the person who said this really believed it. Often it is spoken with very little energy, just a grown-up's easy response to a child's probing question. As we grew, we heard the same answer repeatedly from pulpits and gravesides, at weddings or sickbeds. By the time many of us grew up, we were quoting the party line ourselves without much examination. "Oh, yes," we said with a yawn, glancing at our watch, "God is love."

And then one magical day we encounter someone who *is* love. And that person says: "God is love." Smoke comes out of your ears; your head spins. And you're never the same. The very energy of such a person kindles the embers of love in others to full flame. It can be done with a touch, a look, a word. How often do we call someone from whom we feel love and say, "I just needed to hear your voice"?

We are constantly held in the mind of enlightened ones from all traditions who embody agape. They do not make adjustments in their love because we as Hindus or Christians or any other religion ask the question "Who is God?" Their effectiveness and influence in our evolution are beyond measure. We can only express our gratitude for their love by receiving it and then becoming bearers of that love to others.

Love as Service

Service is the natural expression of agape. When we serve another, we serve ourselves and all others, for life is an unbroken whole. Unconditional love goes far beyond the dualism of noblesse oblige: "I am the blessed good person; you are the great unwashed that I will help."

Service is the path of the Bodhisattva. The term *Bodhisattvas* indicates those who have integrated everything in this dimension and no longer have karmic reasons to incarnate; instead they choose to stay in our evolution so that we may benefit from their love and radiance. Kuan Yin from the Far East is often called the Bodhisattva of compassion, as is Avalokitesvara of Tibet. While Christians might not use the term, Jesus could be called a Bodhisattva. A Bodhisattva vows to serve until the last of us has awakened. I have done readings for people who set themselves on the path of the Bodhisattva eons ago, vowing to take as many incarnations as necessary to free themselves in order to help free others. They choose incarnations that will teach them unconditional love.

Sometimes I hear people say, in effect, "I just want to finish my karma and get out of here, and I'm never coming back." Well the fallacy of that is that when we have mastered all that is here, we will be so full of love and awareness of wholeness, we won't want to leave any other unenlightened or unloved, not even the most aggressive among us, as this story from ancient Japan teaches.

There was once a powerful and much-feared samurai master of the martial arts. One day he sought out a great sage, demanding that the old man tell him the difference between heaven and hell.

The old sage looked at him, then waved his hand, saying, "Go away. You are disgusting with your warlike ways and your posturing. I don't want anything to do with you."

The samurai could hardly believe his ears. No one dared to speak to him that way. He immediately reacted with his usual response to insult and raised his sword to strike the old sage.

"That is hell," the sage calmly said, looking him in the eye.

The samurai dropped his sword, awed by the courage and love that was so great it would risk life itself to teach him. He began to cry with humility.

"And that," said the sage, "is heaven."

Love Without Judgment

When we come into contact with another, our subtle fields respond and translate the quality and intensity of the person's energy. If we are unconscious, we might decide that anyone who is different is the "other," maybe even the enemy. We might see difference as wrongness—the wrong color, the wrong religion, the wrong nationality.

That may seem like a very low level of consciousness, but we all need to pay attention, for as we grow, the ego learns to be more subtle, even more soft-spoken, and definitely more insidious. It may not scream with bigotry. It is more inclined to be reasonable, practical, and realistic in its prejudices.

Karla teaches antiracist workshops for religious leaders of different denominations. She often finds they are in states of denial and become highly defensive about their own racisms that emerge during the workshop. They had images of themselves as being free of prejudice.

Many times I have heard teachers, gurus, and systems of spiritual training minimized, dismissed, and criticized by supposedly conscious people. I have found for myself a "rule" with two parts: first, don't criticize, and second, take a good look inside self. Why would I need to say anything about another's path? Love calls us to attention every step of the Way.

An awakened person knows that in the course of our development through time and space we have all been sinners and saints. Catching a person on a difficult incarnation—or in a difficult cycle within one incarnation—can be like taking a snapshot. Yes, it is one picture, but only one. I haven't met an "ordinary" soul yet. I've seen a lot of fear, repression, denial, and other distortions, but they are just the self-created "demons" we must meet and master in the quest.

me → Clare

everyone → me

❧ Journaling Seeds

1. Where do you draw the line on love? Is it a rapist? An abusive parent? A mass murderer? From whom would you withdraw your love?

2. How do you know the difference between disliking a person's behavior and withdrawing love?

3. Review your family messages, your experiences, and your attitudes about other races, ages, social status, religions, nationalities, and the other sex.

Compassion with No Agenda

"Detached compassion" is a phrase we soon meet on the spiritual path. None of the higher vibrations in discipleship is won cheaply, least of all this one. How can I both be with you in your passion (compassion) and unhooked (detached) from results or personal agendas? That's the goal.

Detached compassion certainly doesn't mean avoidance. Avoidance is a kind of it's-your-karma-I'm-not-getting-involved attitude. Detachment without compassion can lead to indifference; indifference can swiftly become frigidity and callousness. However, detachment with compassion leads to clear, insightful choices about the appropriateness and methods of helping.

Then comes the discipline to make that attitude our practice in the world. Detached compassion encourages us to explore our own motives for serving others. Is the love effortless even though the work may be hard? Am I expecting to acquire cosmic brownie points? Do I basically just feel sorry for someone (and thank God it isn't me)? How much of my own fears are being mirrored in this person, and do I want to embrace him or her or run? Do I secretly believe the suffering means that the person has done something wrong? Do I think, "I know best"?

Detached compassion helps us perceive when it is not appropriate for us to intervene. A person birthing a new consciousness may indeed be temporarily suffering, but we don't want to stop the process. In the early years of my work, I often wanted to jump in and soothe heartaches, wipe away tears, redirect anger. Of course, a lot of that was about my own need not to witness the suffering. Now I've learned more about waiting, listening, watching, and holding loving spaces while people work the pain to the level they can handle. With good intentions we can do more harm than good if we prematurely cut off another's process by intervening with instant and too often packaged consoling and coaching.

If we saw a building being razed and had no idea what was happening, we might conclude this was mindless destruction. Yet if we knew it was being destroyed so that a better building could be constructed on the site, we would understand. Destruction is often the first step in creation, and while we might not always be comfortable with that principle, it is useful to contemplate what it looks like in personal development.

In the West we seldom speak of the destructive quality of the Divine. In Hinduism, for example, Shiva, the destroyer, is part of the trinity (Brahma, the creator, and Vishnu, the preserver, being the other two). Hinduism also gives us Kali, the face of the Mother that will destroy illusions. Perhaps we should examine more carefully the statement attributed to Jesus: "I come with a sword." The sword is an archetypal symbol for that which cuts through illusions, thus destroying them.

Compassion allows us to see the Light in others no matter how wild and woolly their outer behavior is. And what we see we energize. Detached compassion sees through the eyes of the Highest Self and honors all cycles of the soul's progression. Mere sympathy looks through the eyes of the ego and divides human experiences into good and bad.

I have never experienced a single guide, angelic presence, or teacher in Spirit who holds an edge of judgment, even when giving a student a sharp correction in the path. They support us, but they do not rob us of the ways we can grow through our illusions in order to earn our own wings. We are supported by the wise counsel of detached compassion, not by the temporary relief of sympathy.

Any one of us can become a stand-in for the grace of God for others, even when they are in situations that seem intolerable or hopeless. There are innumerable stories from the Far East of Kuan Yin, Goddess of compassion and mercy, appearing in the jail cells of hardened criminals to comfort and inspire, but not to remove them from prison.

We don't have to be a Goddess to demonstrate that level of compassion. For example, Evelyn runs an alternative sentencing program. She had been working with one young man who had been doing drugs, but he kept getting back into trouble and then finally into jail. "He was really surprised that I came to see him in jail. It is easy in this culture to write people off, close the door and lock it. But we have to try to keep connecting."

The young man later testified, "I just about gave up on myself, but she never gave up on me." She didn't remove him from jail . . . or from her heart.

Today Do Nothing to Disturb the Harmony of the Universe

Love teaches us that every single thing we say, think, and do has far-reaching consequences. It requires a great deal of mindfulness to choose our thoughts and words as well as actions so that they do no harm. That starts with making harmlessness a goal that can be reached with attention and the steady reprogramming of careless habits.

There are things we can get away with temporarily earlier on the path. Yet as we progress, they simply have to be given up if we

intend to proceed any further. A child's tantrum may be disturbing, but it will not have the wide range of effects as someone who
has acquired a certain amount of power and then unleashes it to
fuel revenge, rage, or harm of any kind. Whenever those feelings
are uncovered, it is wise to find a safe environment, such as
therapy or spiritual counseling, in which such imbalances can be
faced squarely and released.

To be harmless, first to self and then to others, takes a lot of
discipline, and we don't get there through self-judgment, which
actually slows down the whole process. We get no mileage awards
for beating up on ourselves. That's the first piece of harmfulness
that has to go.

Encouraging Harmlessness

• Become keenly aware of the way harmfulness toward yourself
recycles until it is made conscious. Re-creating dysfunctional
family patterns over and over, mistreatment of the body through
neglect and addictions, and accepting emotional abuse from others
are a few ways we perpetuate harm to ourselves.

• Ask yourself: "Am I willing to love myself enough to give up
anything that is harming me?" If the answer is yes, then the world
is full of assistance no matter how much time and effort it takes. If
the answer is no or not yet, don't judge yourself, but realize that
the harm may continue.

• Without judging, carefully observe the ways in which you
use words about yourself and other people, including public figures. Ask yourself: "Do I really want to add these words to a world
brimming over with negativity?" Commit to doing no harm with
words.

• Develop the habit of reviewing your day at bedtime, check-
ing out your responses to people and events: "Was the harm

avoidable? How could I have done that differently? Who or what do I not accept in the situation?"

• Be for something instead of against. How can you use your resources to build bridges in understanding, solicit cooperation, suggest win-win solutions?

• Harmlessness can be assertive. Sometimes *harmless* is wrongly used as a synonym for *ineffective*. Real harmlessness is quite the opposite. It calls for strength and courage. Think of Gandhi or Martin Luther King Jr. leading people in nonviolence, or the suffragettes flying in the face of centuries of restrictive laws and attitudes.

• Release the negative thoughts and feelings that are acting as magnets and drawing harm into your pattern. As negativity surfaces, explore it for self-knowledge and then exercise your right to choose. Simply affirm your intention to let the negativity go: "I release this thought or feeling to the Light." See it rise and dissolve as easily as a puff of smoke disappears into the air.

Harmless, Not Foolish

At every frequency of energy in the mind-body-spirit continuum there are connecting cords between people who have had intimacy. The more energy in a relationship, the thicker the cord. These cords are made up of subtle ether and can be seen psychically. They are not imaginary or sentimental. We send messages through these cords regularly, if unconsciously. Think of someone and she calls. Wake from a deep sleep at three in the morning and discover later that someone you love had an accident at that moment.

When cords from toxic relationships have not been dissolved, the poisons can continue to be telegraphed through those cords, even if there has been no physical contact for years. We then need to break those cords in the subtle dimensions even if the other person has no interest in resolution. Here is a possible technique.

Cutting the Cords

Step one: Get totally straight about the contents in your own psyche. Are you still holding guilt, shame, resentment, anger? These feelings strengthen the cords and act as magnets. Removing yourself physically from a difficult relationship or situation might have been the right move on the material plane. Yet you may not have budged energetically.

Step two: Remember who you are, a daughter or son of the Mother-Father-God. In that remembrance is your best protection. It sends immediate empowerment throughout all of your bodies; an invisible strong shield is formed. Highly conscious people may be warm; nevertheless, they always seem centered in a quiet zone. Such a person walks protected in the world by the power of truth, not fear.

Step three: Total forgiveness is necessary if you want final unbinding to take place. Birth and death are not enough to destroy the heavy bonds of attachment. There is no time and space in the subconscious. All unforgiven acts and people are brought back into our drama through many lifetimes. Forgiveness is the release, the alchemy that breaks the cycle. It releases attachments and frees everyone involved. Eventually one has to forgive everybody everything, not because we are blindly obedient to this law, but rather because we understand it, and even the worst offenses are perceived less as evil than as ignorance.

A word of caution: While there is a short, intense path for the disciple, there are no shortcuts. If you are still not finished with the anger (and the grief that is frequently just under the anger), you'll need to confront and release those feelings. Good therapies can teach you how to access and release those feelings in safe and lasting ways. Unreleased anger and grief might be serving as the guards to your own prison, refusing to allow you full forgiveness, therefore depriving you of full freedom.

Step four: Pray for the person. Prayer comes from your remembrance of the truth behind appearances. In praying for the other's well-being, you entrain that person's Godness and call it forth.

I was barely started in my work before Spirit was teaching me the effectiveness of prayer. During that first year a friend and I were called in to counsel some young people who were coming off heroin and wanted some guidance.

When we arrived there was also a middle-aged man present called John. The young people obviously feared John. He knew how to use subtle energies and could direct energies with his mind. The teenagers had seen him make tires go flat on command, start fires, and create "accidents" with his thoughts.

John saw himself as the instrument of punishment for a patriarchal god. I was naive enough to think I could change his mind. So we debated. He would quote the Old Testament; I would quote the New Testament or some other source of love. He talked about punishing; I talked about forgiving. Every time I bested him on a point, his energy field would flare red with anger. I ignored it. Put that in the category of going where angels fear to tread. Still, I have to be grateful for the crash course that followed.

Within twenty-four hours I began to get sick. And people began to notice what several people called a "black inky thing" in my house. (Such an apparition is a negative thought form projected by the mind to a person or location.) Then my friend, wondering if this had anything to do with John, suggested I see a healer who is very gifted psychically.

He "looked" and announced that we had better turn this one over to higher powers. And then he said, "This isn't your responsibility." In a split second I heard a clear voice in my head: "Oh, yes, it is. Now you must pray for him." So I launched a prayer campaign. I daily prayed for John's health, his well-being, and his soul.

One of the young women who was cleaning herself up from heroin had a job at a cafe in a rather dingy part of town. She called to tell me that she had nearly dropped a tray when one of the neighborhood kids came in and asked her if she knew Gloria. Startled, she asked the boy how he knew about me. "Oh, John says she comes to visit him every day, and he thinks she's pretty cool." He was psychically aware of the prayers.

I don't know what happened to John. I never saw or heard anything about him again. I quickly got well, and there were no more inky manifestations in my house again, not then, not since. When we are guided in spiritual training to "pray for our enemies," there are multiple reasons for the advice, and one is surely that it is our greatest protection.

As Spirit has taught me, who or what you don't love says nothing about the other person. It only defines the boundaries of your understanding.

Love is surely the most important vibration we can consciously activate for our walk as committed disciples of the Way. All other aspects of discipleship are empowered by love, and no matter how skilled or knowledgeable we become, all our actions are sterile without it.

Exercise: Agape

Note: If you find yourself losing awareness, stop, pull back, contract a bit. Breathe to the edge at which you can maintain awareness. This exercise is not about getting out of your body. It is about mastering your ability to expand and contract your beingness at will and send love consciously anywhere in the world.

1. Sitting quietly, breathe naturally. Become very aware of your breath, watching as it makes its cycle from the universe into your lungs. You are alive because of the breath of life. Feel gratitude to the trees that inhale the carbon dioxide we exhale, and put out the oxygen we need in return. Watch your breath for twenty or so times.

2. Now take your breathing awareness into your heart, the center for agape. Begin breathing through your heart, a breath that sends your love into the world and equally receives the love back into your beingness, a great balancing cycle of unconditional love.

3. The mind is the director of energy. In your mind direct the energy out of you in waves of love that expand beyond where you are sitting. Expand it into your home, your community, your state, and your country. Expand the breath of love with your mind, sending it across the seas, to every continent, from pole to pole, until the whole planet is covered. The mind and love are not bound by time and space. Everything that lives and breathes and has its being on this earth is now held in your love. Feel the power, the grace, and the privilege.

4. Gradually begin directing your breathing and mind into a pattern of contraction, first from the whole planet to the various continents to the oceans, your country, your community, and then into your immediate surroundings, and into your heart. Now breathe normally.

Your capacity to love is without limits.

Counterfeits and Challenges of Love

Unconditional love will turn you inside out. It will take your controls and snap them like matchsticks. It roots out all bigotry, bias, and comfort. Little wonder that even as we long for it, we sometimes fear the changes it might bring.

Love does ask us to give up a great deal: self-punishment, limitation, poverty of spirit, and guilt, just to mention a few. If we have based our concepts of reality around these lies about self, the personality is seriously threatened when love enters with the truth.

Love will catch us out in all our games. If we love humanity but can't stand people, love will point that out. If we are doing duty out of a sense of obligation to someone, that will be brought to our attention. Of course, we all do have obligations and commitments in the world, so the question is how to bring them out of mere duty into love.

I have a colleague who suddenly found her free lifestyle totally compromised when her aging mother moved in with her. She told me she was alternately loving, resentful, angry, and ashamed. She took her ambivalence into prayer to the Divine Mother, asking for guidance. She was told, "See My face in your mother's face and serve Me." She did and has been at peace since then. Her peace came after she acknowledged all her feelings.

All of the counterfeits of love will come bubbling up from the subconscious for review when we choose to live consciously. For example, women are often conditioned to put up with anything and call it love. Men are conditioned to fix anything, or at least pay for it, and call that love. In the South when I was growing up, females who drew clear boundaries of self-love were often seen as selfish, usually with another word or so added to the description. On the other hand, women who kept doing for others and abandoning their own needs were often admired.

Love prods us to question all these old identities and values. We circulate through many worlds with our families, partners, institutions, careers, and interests. And even when we know our interactions are askew spiritually and not really making us happy, they are still familiar, and we know all the rules. Sick and miserable though our illusions might be, they are nevertheless ours.

Unconditional love upsets all that. The rules change, and that can be temporarily disquieting: "Maybe I won't even know who I am. *How* will I know who I am? What will I have to give up?

Will this love consume me? What if my tiny drop of consciousness really does disappear into a sea of nothingness? Will I still
be me?"

Love will go after all addictions. That can range from the obvious to the very subtle: numbing substances, compulsive busyness,
sexual addiction, and a multitude of self-punishing habits. That
includes those sticky attachments that hold us in a parody of love.
"I can't live without you" may simply mean "I haven't finished
this karma with you." Love releases; it doesn't bind. Connections
are then made by choice, not out of addiction. That can be pretty
scary for the personality, because even though it will eventually be
freeing to everyone concerned, in the meantime it has to give up
manipulations, possessiveness, and other binding games. That can
even include retiring one's place in the family myth, such as being
the "smart one" or the "rebel" or the "black sheep."

Our inner child might still be clinging to the belief that there
are entities somewhere out there keeping track of every naughty
thought and deed. The corollary to that belief is to be good by
the accepted standard and hide any bad stuff. Imagine how threat-
ening that is when we start dragging everything out of the closet.
Always remember the inner child shares the transformational journey every step of the way. We must be loving parents to our child
selves, especially if terror, lies, or even subtle distortions of truth
were the daily diet of childhood.

Light is painful to the eyes when we have been in darkness for a
long time. And the Light of love can be decidedly disturbing.
"The Light comes into the darkness, and the darkness likes it not,"
said Jesus. Anyone who has ever challenged inner feelings of
shame or self-hatred or pointed out a destructive fallacy in a
family myth or a rigid doctrine knows very well how swiftly and
viciously the darkness resists. The status quo has predictable, and
thus manageable, discomforts.

It takes tremendous self-knowledge, courage, and patience to
love the truth so much that we will seek it no matter how many

skeletons it exposes. Before love brings peace it detonates every-thing in sight that is illusory. And we can be very resistant to our own liberation.

I recall a young woman running away in great emotional pain from a celebration circle I was conducting, because, as she told me, "I couldn't take all that love from everyone." She later said she intended to repeat that course until she could receive that love. Happily, she did learn to receive, and it changed her life.

We can become overwhelmed by the power and force of love and its unconditional acceptance of us, especially if we have dreamed up images of being unworthy, and most of us have. Love asks us to give up all that and simply allow it in. We don't have to do "time" or penance or prove anything. There's no way to earn it, as it has never been withheld. But we do have to allow our-selves to receive, and sometimes that feels like the hard part. No matter what we've done, if we go to the universe begging for-giveness, it will say, "For what?" It is ourselves who hold to self-punishment, not the Divine.

Past Life Attachments

I have found that many times people are still punishing themselves for something held from a past life experience. In cellular memory there is no then and now; it's all just now, which explains why we can meet someone from the past and have feelings that are strong and immediate. However, it is not necessary to recall an exact ex-perience in order to release it. Whether we are remembering our own unique past or tapping into racial and ancestral patterns, we can release all energy that holds the memories in place.

The grace of unconditional love transcends time and is pouring its healing tinctures on the past, present, and future right now, this minute, even as I write and you read. Our only job is to accept it. We don't have to worry about balancing out misdeeds and mis-perceptions; our souls will see that the balance comes about.

Meantime, the greatest challenge is to stand naked before love, offering absolutely everything to it.

Sounds good, but beware. Impatience is a henchman sitting in the shadows saying, "Well, I tried to receive love for these lousy feelings yesterday, and here they are back today, so it doesn't work; I quit." Once the contract with love is made, it's like jumping into the sea. You don't know where it's going to take you or how long it will take to get there. You arrive only by surrendering to the current moment by moment.

An art therapist once showed me a series of paintings done by a little girl who had been seriously traumatized and was overwhelmed by her fears. The first drawings showed a monster bigger than a house. As the weeks went by and the therapy progressed, the monster grew smaller and smaller. It didn't go away, but it was whittled down to a size the child could handle. And then she began to make quantum leaps until the monster had no more authority over her. Time, attention, and persistence were the requirements of her humanness. Grace did the rest.

Without compassion for all that we have experienced individually or collectively, we drive self-disgust deeper and deeper into the shadows. Any unforgiven "sins" that we imagine we have committed, or that we think others have committed that hurt us, are toxic in all of our bodies. The body will often show us exactly where we are holding such material. As always, the key is to pay attention. When I feel guilt, fear, shame, and so on, where does that feeling live in the body?

Buddhist teacher Thich Nhat Hanh teaches a simple but effective technique. Place a hand with compassion over the place in the body that is holding the energy of shame or fear. Breathe and use the mind to direct a soothing blessing of peace there: "Be still and receive love."

Unconditional love is the perfect antidote to fear. It feeds every cell. Notice how people who practice unconditional love have an unusual glow about them. Paul is ninety years old and still has an active healing practice. He has a vitality that keeps moving his prime time to the decade he is currently in. His face often seems lit from within. People automatically assume you are in love when you have that glow. And, of course, you are—with life.

Fear Blocks Creativity, Love Releases It

Love calls us, whispering at first, eventually shouting, to come out of the trance of illusions and be the creators we really are. We each bend the Light that comes through us in a unique way, and we are happiest when we can express that individuality. As we do so, it can bring up the critics we have stashed away in the shadows. Memories of every threat, every bit of ridicule, dismissal, and criticism surface in order to be met and mastered.

I realized how pervasive this fear is when I first taught a workshop on creativity. It's not unusual for people to be a bit edgy entering any new experience in transformational work, but the subject of creativity brings up an unusual amount of buried material: fears of not being good enough, of being less than another, of looking foolish, of attracting criticisms or ridicule, and the like. So in this workshop we address those fears immediately, and everyone sees how universal they are and how much they block our self-fulfillment, both in personal satisfaction and the actualizing of our assignments in the larger plan.

I recall a young man in Europe who attended the workshop on creativity. The opening night Ethan was quiet. I could see the intelligence flashing in his eyes, but he was verbally unresponsive. As I totally trust the unseen forces that bring people together, I let it be. On the opening evening I gave everyone their stash of supplies. Included among them was a mystery packet holding bits and pieces of "things," all of which they had to use somewhere in their projects over the next few days. Each packet was completely unique. Ethan didn't open his the first evening.

The next day Ethan came to me with tears in his eyes as he told me about a synchronicity that had happened since he arrived. He said that he usually liked to show off intellectually wherever he was. His own creativity had been sacrificed as a child in order to become the smart son his family wanted. As time went by he'd bought into that image of himself. Friends had suggested that if he would try listening in this workshop, he might learn something. So he came prepared to try a new way.

During the first night of the workshop, he had dreamed that a newborn insect was emerging out of a shell with its antennae probing the air. He recognized this as a symbol for the birthing of his own fragile creativity. When he came to class he opened his mystery packet for the first time, and one of the things in it was a golden walnut shell. He was filled with gratitude for the affirmation mysteriously given to his true creative self,

If we love ourselves enough to dismantle false identities, the universe will support our emerging true identities.

Empathy for the World

A heart that is in love with life feels the full range of human experience. That includes grief. I have wept for my sisters in Bosnia, for my brothers in Tibet, for untouched old folks and bewildered children everywhere.

The tears wash away the imaginary divisions between us, and I thank them for their sacrifices. I may not understand why we, as the one life, still allow and create abuses. However, if I stay in clear mind, I can support those who are suffering, knowing that the physical is but one way to reach them. My role in life may not put me physically near them, but I can touch them in many other ways: through supportive thoughts and prayers, through my vote, my money, my freedom of speech, and any access I have to influence others. I can refuse to rationalize, deny, or pretend that their suffering has nothing to do with the rest of us. If I bring my own fears of what others are enduring out of the shadows and own them, I participate in hastening the day when we no longer allow the suffering anywhere.

Agape requires honesty. It asks us to take an unblinking inventory of ourselves, asking hard questions such as: "What am I pushing away? What form of suffering scares me so much I won't even look at it?"

Sensitive people sometimes say they cannot watch the news or observe the pain in our world. While I know the feeling well, I believe love insists that we be present with all of life, its joys and its pains. We must watch, listen, pray, and serve where and how we can. As we accelerate around this evolutionary spiral, Light is pouring into the world, and darkness fears it and fights to retain its hold on human consciousness. This is likely to become increasingly more intense over the next couple of decades. If we want to help bridge the ages, we have to stand poised in both the Light and the dark. When we challenge our own duality we are striking at the very chains of our own prison.

Imagine that someone you love dearly is going through a terrible passage. Would you look away? No, you would find the place inside yourself that is strong and could hold a force field for the beloved. Love says we must do that for anyone, no matter who they are, where they live, or what unspeakable hell they are enduring. We don't look away hoping it will just disappear.

Unconditional love is a practice, a day-by-day, minute-by-minute choice to return to essence. Our challenge is to keep the valves open so that love has channels through us into the world.

Describing love is like describing great beauty. It eventually takes you into silence. A few years ago friends and I were sharing the exquisite beauty of the Caribbean. After less than a day on the island we were laughing about the futility of language, words such as *beautiful, fabulous, charming, peaceful.* Soon we moved into a mutual silence and just occasionally waved a hand or smiled toward the beauty that is incapable of being translated into words.

So for whatever I haven't said about love, consider this a wave and a smile from my heart to yours.

Twelve Considerations on Love

1. Love is constant, undisturbed by shifting circumstances.
2. Love accepts our "crazy" places, warts, foibles, and secrets.
3. Love embraces light and shadow as the original dynamic duo.
4. Love's compassion serves others, but it doesn't bind them.
5. Love is authentic; all feelings, pain as well as joy, are real.
6. Love is a healing mist penetrating every molecule of life.
7. Love aspires to be harmless in thought, word, or action.
8. Love has reverence for life no matter what form it takes.
9. Love assists, but it doesn't rescue or steal lessons from us.
10. Love is grateful for all experiences no matter what they bring.
11. Love forgives even when it must discipline or say good-bye.
12. Love is poised in chaos, centered, peaceful, remembering.

Prayer/Affirmation

The love of the universe flows through me into the world. For this privilege and remembrance I give thanks.

Exercise: Merging with Divine Being

Begin as always by slowing down your breathing (counting slowly, if necessary, for a few breaths), gradually pulling your attention away from all distractions. Be in this moment. Gently and lovingly keep pulling your attention back from any distractions, saying "Not that. This."

Visualize before you a Divine Being who embodies love. It may be Jesus, Buddha, Tara, Kuan Yin, your guru, or another. Look into the Being's eyes. Feel the unqualified acceptance, the unconditional love that radiates to you. Here is one who sees everything there is about you, the light and the shadow, and loves all of it without judgment. Open your heart like a chalice to receive this blessing of unconditional love.

The arms of the Being reach out to enfold you. You feel yourself dissolving into this wondrous Being. Arms, torso, and legs are both yours and the Being's. You begin to realize that you have merged with this exquisite expression of love. You are now looking at the world through those eyes, feeling the love pouring through the Being's heart, which is now also your heart.

Now imagine members of your family in front of you. You are seeing them through the eyes of love, blessing through the hands of love, seeing their dark and Light, loving all of it. Feel the cells in your body accept this awareness. See through these eyes your friends and coworkers, neighbors and strangers. A ceaseless flow of love pours through you to them.

Now release all the people. Become aware of stepping out of the energy of the Sacred Being and into your individual sense of self. Look into those eyes of love and express your gratitude. Notice the glow that is now with you as surely as if you had been soaked in living Light. You are an expression of love in this world. For this remembrance and privilege, give thanks.

Quotes

Someday, after we have mastered the winds, the waves, the tides and gravity, we shall harness for God the energies of love. Then, for the second time in the history of the world, man will have discovered fire.

—Teilhard de Chardin

It makes no difference how deeply seated may be the trouble, how hopeless the outlook, how muddled the tangle, how great the mistake, a sufficient realization of love will dissolve it all. If only you could love enough you would be the happiest and most powerful being in the world.

—Emmet Fox

6 Will: The Divine Birthright

✤

I always wanted to be somebody, but I see now
I should have been more specific.

—Lily Tomlin in
The Search for Signs of Intelligent Life in the Universe,
by Jane Wagner

Imagine that we were there (and we were) at the big bang, the great exploding of Light. Out of the One we were blasted into a journey of expansion through time and space. We carried within us the Holy Light out of which we were born, a Light that can no more be apart from its Source than the wave is from the water.

Ever since "Let there be Light" was pronounced, we've been in the glorious process of seeking both individuation, that is, our unique sense of selfhood, and reunion with a paradise we once experienced, lost, mourned, and now seek again.

In self-realization we achieve both of these goals, which were never really separate goals at all. We only dreamed that they were. Thy Light *is* my light. Thy will *is* my will. Understanding this, we return to paradise not as unconscious drops in a primordial soup, but as fully self-actualized beings.

Had we not "lost" paradise in the first place, would we be able to appreciate its value? Were we, in fact, aware of anything when we were in that first primordial, slumbering state? How different it seems to contemplate paradise by choice, to return to it fully aware. To be *aware* in paradise—surely that is the stuff of ecstasy.

The very fact that we could dream illusions and live them for as long as we liked and as often as we chose is testimony to the unconditional gift of the will. We return to paradise by choice, not coercion.

The story is told of a shepherd who would go out looking for lost sheep every night. Yet he would not repair the hole in his fence. No force in the universe, no master, no angel, no avatar will choose for us. However, once we say yes to the highest will, the universe rushes in with support, like water filling every twist and turn in an empty bottle.

The Will in the Heart of True Identity

The Will is the "I am" behind all the roles that we play. Roles come and go. Through our evolution we play many roles: hero/heroine or antagonist, saint/villain, rich/poor, famous/infamous, some clear, many muddled. As long as we remain unaware, no matter how brilliantly the part is written and how well it's played, the role will come to an end, and we'll perform another.

However, perspective will shift greatly when we realize that not only did we create the role, we designed the stage, made a contract with the other players, and then sat in the front row and critiqued the whole thing. A big *aha* comes with the awareness that I Am is the playwright, not the finite I that is wearing a different costume and attitude for each new part. I Am is the affirmation of the Will that picked the perfect part, the Self that is still present when all of the plays are over.

The more we know who we are, the better we play all our parts. If I believe I am my role, then everything in my world is riding on the success and failure of the play. If I know who I Am, then I can play a role at full stretch, risking and experimenting, holding nothing back. If it goes well, then I've gained experience. If it doesn't go well, then I've gained experience.

As one disciple, a psychiatrist, said, "If I say, 'God takes care of me,' then everything that happens can be defined in terms of God taking care of me, so it is not a matter of everything is going to go well; everything is going to go."

Gradually, and sometimes in sudden epiphanies we remember: I Am. Under the disguises of all our roles, I Am. Lost in a wilderness of forgetfulness, still I Am. When we close our eyes and listen to our heartbeats, we hear: "I Am, I Am, I Am."

I Am calls us out of the depths of despair and darkness. It drives us to create possibilities where there are none. It inspires, prods, and holds us to the intention of our incarnation when everything in our world conspires to make us forget. I Am carries us across the threshold between life and death.

When avatars and masters speak from their place of Godness, they use the authority of the sacred I Am. It is not used to indicate the authority of personality.

Jesus was quoted in the New Testament as saying, "I am the way, the truth, and the light. No one comes into the Father but by me." Krishna was quoted in the Vedas, the holy scriptures of India, as saying, "I am the beginning, the middle, and the end of all existing things," and "I am the embodiment of the Supreme Rule and of the incorruptible, of the unifying and of the eternal law and eternal bliss."

In the Egyptian Book of the Dead, we find: "I am thy son, Osiris. I am thy love." Also, the god of ancient Egypt is quoted as saying, "I am Osiris. I enter and reappear through you, I decay in you, I grow in you."

The Old Testament gets right to the point with "I am that I am," a mirror reflection of the Hindu Upanishads' "*Tat tvam asi*, Thou are that."

These are certainly not the words of warring deities. They are the universal affirmation of the enlightened state. I Am is the mantra of the Will that is free to live its truth.

When you and I use I Am, we are taking our divine birthright, the Will, and decreeing realities. Think of I Am as one of the most powerful tools for building realities. We don't want to use it to empower negativities within ourselves, or to further pollute the common psychic environment.

It's very sobering to monitor one's use of the phrase "I am" for a week, not judging, but listening to the times "I am" is used to drive home a self-deprecating or limiting remark: "I am too fat," "I am not good at doing this or that," "I am afraid of . . ." Even the casual or negative use of "I am" is not harmless. When the subconscious hears "I'm afraid," it doesn't say, "Oh, he is just kidding around," or "She doesn't *really* mean that." It files that away as a request to be filled.

Intention: Focus for the Will

When the archer shoots for nothing, he has all his skill.
When he shoots for a brass buckle he is already nervous.
When he shoots for a price of gold, he goes blind.
　　　　　　　　　　　　　　—Ancient Chinese saying

Will is the driving force behind intention. Intention focuses Will. Everything begins with the intention of the soul, which pours down from Spirit through the mental and emotional aspects of self into the physical with all the directed force of a waterfall destined to follow a predictable course. If intention is compromised or foggy, then its manifestation will also be unclear.

A good affirmation to remind you of the role of Will and intention in your life would be, "With clear intention I am choosing to act rather than react to the world around me. I choose . . .

everything." You might put that statement in your wallet or on a mirror or on your desk for a week or so to increase your awareness of the power of choice.

Because we are living the consequences of choices made a long time ago, in this lifetime or another, and because we are also living with the consequences of collective choice, it can be very hard to fully accept the power of choice in any one moment. No, we can't choose to undo a civil war, alter the national economy, even lay aside a handicapped body. We *can* choose, every moment, what we will do with any circumstance, and those choices will ultimately influence all of the larger collective issues. The same situation that offers possibilities for enlightenment can perpetuate vengeance or depression. Whatever happens, happens. What we do with it is our choice.

All of us arrive with an assortment of potentials in our karmic package, talents we've "stored in heaven." I see heaven as a state of consciousness. Good deeds and developed talents don't die, but energy spent serving the ego does; it rusts and decays.

What we have access to in this life is governed by the intention of our soul. We can't let the ego's attachments override the soul's intention. The soul's limits are not punishments; they are containers for learning through precise experience. We always get to choose how we will live within the limits. I recall hearing an interview with a quadriplegic who had been an athlete. Asked if the accident hadn't colored his life, he answered, "Yes, and I picked the colors."

In Dominique Lapierre's book *Beyond Love*, he reports on the early days of the search for the AIDS virus, telling the intertwining stories of several key people. In the midst of the drama involving egos and laboratories around the world, I was most intrigued with the play within a play that brought people's very divergent life streams together.

The story begins with a young girl born into the lowest caste in India. Then there was a young American anthropologist who had

an accident that left him paralyzed. In the "normal" scheme of
life, one wouldn't imagine their paths crossing. But through the
introduction of another young man, a priest who was a friend of
the injured anthropologist, their patterns intersected. The young
girl joined Mother Teresa's Sisters of Mercy and was assigned to
an AIDS team. The anthropologist became her prayer partner.
She worked sixteen to eighteen hours a day on her feet; he
matched her from his frozen body with his mind, sending love and
support to their joint mission.

Why Am I Here Now?

Behind any chaos in our personal lives there is order, just as there
is an emerging order for us collectively. We probably don't see the
order while we're surviving the chaos; nevertheless, we can see
significant patterns in retrospect, even in this one lifetime. And
most of us will admit that even though we went through our
transformational fires kicking and screaming, it was in those very
fires that our illusions were burned away and the intentions of our
Will for this lifetime were made clearer.

All of the theology in the world falls short if we haven't addressed the fundamental question: "Why am I in this particular
incarnation?" Once we accept that our Will (our Highest Will,
not our ego will) chooses the lifetime that will maximize our
lessons and our contributions, then many things fall into place
rapidly. Lingering traces of the victim mentality can be retired,
along with a bullying god that must be appeased and cajoled into
creating better circumstances. Our perception of the other players
in the drama shifts. Self-responsibility and gratitude even for the
hardest parts come easier to us.

Our Highest Will made many choices before we incarnated,
including the race, sex, culture, and timing that will best carry out
our highest purpose. The "right" ancestry sets up the necessary

physiological, mythic, and psychic genetics, imprinting us with the textbooks for our classroom.

The Will views incarnations from the highest perspective: How will this help us along our journey into self-realization? "You cannot do anything that has not already been decided by God," Jesus said as he stood poised before Pilate. This is the acknowledgment that from the deepest self we have chosen all of our initiations. Surrendering to Thy Will is not about reluctantly obeying a will outside of self, but rather accepting the Highest Will of Self.

If we try to argue the case of human justice for any one lifetime, we are going to fail. We could become bitter and cynical, or at least maintain a running argument with imagined deities who dole out—or withhold—grace like benevolent dictators. While we literally live in the mind of those who are enlightened and are constantly showered by their grace, they are not going to take away our opportunity to learn, and sometimes our classrooms don't seem fair to the personality. However, *seems* is the operative word. All things come to balance in time.

None of us can really evaluate the intention of another soul, as is evident in this story of an event that happened a few years ago. The newspapers reported the suffering of a young child who had been routinely abused by her father, an educated man, and her mother, who had a serious drug problem. The child's abuse had been reported to several different agencies, but nothing had been done to remove her from her tormentors. She finally died as a result of their abuses.

I was deeply moved by this child, as we all are by abused children. The day after I read this in the newspaper I brought the child into my prayers. This child appeared to psychic sight like a star burst, radiant and angelic. I was told in Spirit that she had sacrificed her life in order that other children could be helped. She was experiencing a major initiation in her soul's journey. She had accomplished exactly what she came to do. Of course, she was filled with joy.

As a result of her sacrifice, I saw that new systems would be put in place that cross-checked abuse reports from schools, agencies, neighbors, and doctors. This is indeed what developed over the next few months. Many children are being saved from a life of torment by her gift.

In our quest to live beyond duality, we can hold several awarenesses simultaneously as we think about cases such as this. There is, of course, never any spiritual justification for child abuse (or spousal abuse, or any abuse), and we are often called upon at the physical level to stop its perpetrators. Yet we can choose to do whatever is necessary without judgment and hate.

Second, abuse doesn't happen because God/Goddess "allows" it and withholds support. If all our injustices and imbalances were corrected for us, we would remain forever spiritually infantilized. All of us, liberated and lost, are in this together, and we are all using our free wills to create joint as well as personal realities in this dimension. That fact alone makes a good case for doing anything we can to positively influence consciousness.

Last, we have to honor the souls that choose to sacrifice that we might all benefit. Sacrifice is a principle of the universe. Life in one form surrenders its life force that another form might live and prosper. As life is continuous, and to sacrifice means "to make holy," sacrifice ultimately means gain, not loss. The Highest Will chooses when and how we are given the opportunity to learn that great lesson of Oneness.

Remember the little boy named Nicholas Green who was shot apparently at random while in Italy with his parents? The family donated several of his organs for transplants, triggering out of his death a cycle of love and growth that grew in widening circles like a pebble thrown in a pond. No doubt it will take a lot of sacrifices of one kind or another for us to finally and unequivocally get it that all life is one. Transplants are a poignant metaphor.

Joseph was a brilliant musician and president of a music academy. He was in his thirties when he died. We talked freely about death, and once he said to me. "When you start looking at mortality, as all of us eventually do, things start speeding up all around you. Mortality puts an edge on the sense of mission; it focuses it. It put me back on track. When you are contributing at your best is when you are the happiest. But if you are not doing something that is contributory, you are not going to be happy ultimately."

Sometimes we get instant prioritizing through what seems like tragedy. A flood, an earthquake, a serious disease, or the sudden death of a loved one finds us redoing our priority list. Invariably after natural disasters people report that all that matters is love and life. Loss tosses our social schedules, our investments, and all our pretty possessions into a pile of debris after the storm. At that point we stop and remember.

Choosing to lead life purposefully and not reactively requires that we remember this in the good weather as well as the bad. Up or down, I Will to remember. Rich or poor, a success or a failure, no matter what, I Will to remember. I heard of one community that kept a banner flying that simply said REMEMBER. That's another one of those good words to put on altars, wallets, desks, and mirrors.

✖ Journaling Seeds

1. What would you be willing to die for?

2. If you had only one year left to live, what would you do? How would your priorities change? Who and what would you forgive and release?

3. What would you want said in your obituary?

Resistance Versus Acceptance

Acceptance is not passivity, but rather it is an energy of nonresistance that brings power to the moment. Acceptance means that we don't invest energy in resisting what has manifested so far. Once we assess what has materialized, we might indeed choose to create something new. But we can begin to work with any situation only when we see it clearly and don't fight the fact that it exists in the first place.

Paying attention to resistances as they surface will point out what (and who) we don't want to accept as is. If we don't accept a situation, our options become very narrow. We might dress up the denial into something it really isn't ("He didn't really mean to do that") or pretend it never happened ("Maybe I just made it up"). We can rationalize, fantasize, excuse, ignore, and try a hundred other avoidance tactics. If we want to make any situation conscious, one of the first things we have to do is to remove as many filters as possible and see things as they are. Then we have to accept them. We don't have to like, endorse, or plan to keep them, but we do have to accept them.

In his book *Sacred Hoops* basketball coach Phil Jackson reminds us that Zen teachings tell us that the gap between accepting things the way that they are and wishing them to be another way is "the tenth of an inch between heaven and hell." He adds, "If we can accept whatever hand we've been dealt, no matter how unwelcome, the way to proceed eventually becomes clear."

I have found that serious spiritual students understand this principle, and most are very realistic about the world. They have to be. They are willing to go into darkness everywhere in the world, roll up their sleeves, and work with conditions *as they are*. They can't be effective unless they accept that this person is dying *right now*, that one is hungry *right now*, this is what's happening in the educational system, that is what needs help here or there. Disciples bring the vision of what can be, and they start with what is.

Sometimes people simply know what is right for them regardless of what anyone says or how unlikely the circumstances. Marion is a psychotherapist who says, "I was a therapist before I was even born. My grandmother was in a mental institution, having tried to commit suicide, and the thing that got her out of there was telling her I was on the way. I was named for her. I've been doing the work my whole life—finally I'm getting paid for it!

"When I decided to get my Ph.D., I had no money to pay for it, and nothing else about my choice made any sense either. Everybody thought I was crazy. It turned out to be the most empowering experience of my life up to that time. There was absolutely nothing that deterred me from the path once I found it."

Everyone has to discover his or her own indicators for whether they're receiving guidance from the Highest Self or just more chatter from the ego will.

Ego Will Versus Highest Will

Highest will: Attentively relaxed. Allowing the river to flow.
Ego will: Teeth-gritting willpower. Fighting upriver against the current.

Highest Will: Peace and inner stillness even in chaos.
Ego will: Peaceful only when things are going as expected.

Highest Will: Inner sense of rightness. You cannot not do it.
Ego will: Self-doubt and second-guessing. Feelings of uneasiness.

Highest Will: A healthy detachment from others' opinions.
Ego will: Insistent need for assurance and approval.

Highest Will: Quick energy renewal even when task is hard.
Ego will: Tasks all feel uphill and exhausting.

Highest will: A Zen-like absorption in whatever one is doing.
Ego will: A hurry-up-and-get-it-over-with-and-on-to-the-next-project mentality.

Highest Will: A strong sense of purposefulness.
Ego will: Pointlessness.

Highest Will: Support through dreams, intuition, guidance.
Ego will: Reliance only on rational processes.

Highest Will: Rightness is often felt as a sober, quiet yes.
Ego will: Trusts the momentary rush of excitement.

Highest Will: Synchronicities of all kinds increase.
Ego will: Manipulations and personal control increase.

This is, of course, only the beginning of a comparison between personality and Highest Will. What would you add?

Even when we know something is the right choice for us, it doesn't mean there aren't other options the personality might prefer.

"Thy Will *is* my will" is a mantra that suggests to the psyche a much-desired union rather than a battle in which someone (namely, the personality self) has to lose. A slight rewording of concepts can harmonize rather than polarize.

First of all, perspective is imperative. Complete surrendering of the ego will to Divine Will is a very advanced stage of consciousness. In sacred stories that lay out the Way for us, the complete surrender of the ego will to Divine Will is taught as the fourth initiation, the passage into full mastership, and is symbolized by death of the ego. The cross is an ancient symbol for the descent of spirit into matter and the place where the ego is fully sacrificed. In Egypt candidates for initiation were placed in sarcophaguses for three days, where they "died" to their former selves. In addition, medicine men and women have to experience shamanic death in order to become a full servant to their people.

We are told in the legends of Jesus that in Gethsemane, where the disciples he brought with him kept falling asleep, he sweated blood and said, "Can this cup pass?" We are warned that in our Gethsemanes—and we have many of them as we spiral our way toward mastership—all of our well-developed inner disciples (intelligence, discrimination, strength, etc.) often go to sleep at the point when the decision must be reached to surrender any sense of separateness from Godness. And we will probably feel alone, sweat blood, and not want to do it. Nevertheless, at some point we surrender. Then comes the peace and the power to do whatever is asked of us in full consciousness.

These are the turnings on the path that we need to discuss when we are together as disciples. *Of course* the ego is going to fight for its life. It is afraid of dying; it clings to separation, often holds to negativity, feels that it doesn't deserve to be an instrument, bubbles up impulses of shame and blame like so many pollutants from the unconscious. If we wouldn't pretend that surrender is such an easy part of the journey, then we could really help each other through these passages, and the birthing process from death to new life wouldn't be so lonely.

The very word *surrender* can throw us into agonies of ambivalence. A primal urge in us longs for the freedom we intuitively know we will have with surrender. But other aspects of consciousness get testy and rebellious and fill us with dread. What does He/She want of us, anyway? The answer to "What does God/Goddess want?" is *everything*. By giving everything, we will get everything. The irony of our fear of surrendering to God's Will is that God's Will for us is bliss, joy, happiness, and fulfillment.

In a letter, a friend responded to a change I had observed in her eyes the last time we had met. "What you see in my eyes is the silence that comes when one has made a decision after all the clamor, arguing, and jabbering. It is the silence of love; it is the silence that knows. It is the stillness of the voice of God that so moves my soul that I am speechless with the beauty of it."

The Net of Connection

Disciples become aware that they are part of a planetary and inter-dimensional collaborative. Now that we live in cyberspace and are increasingly aware of unseen realities all around us, we're rapidly stretching the boundaries of what just yesterday we considered possible. We're learning to accept realities that we cannot see.

It is interesting that we use the term *net* to describe our high-tech communications. *Net* has been used for hundreds of years in Buddhist and Hindu sacred writings to describe the connecting lines of energy in the universe, as well as the webs that are formed through thoughts and intentions.

Just as the lines of attachment between people are unaffected by time and space, so are belief systems and thought forms. They are like threads weaving patterns within the total net. They crisscross in the morphogenetic field that joins us all, and they resist or en-train with each other, creating compatible or dissonant patterns.

We all live within this webbing of belief systems that forms an invisible and powerful force field. As we Will to break up the old patterns and form new ones, we put ourselves on the proverbial cutting edge in human consciousness.

A person surrendered to the Highest Will becomes a trans-former through which the larger Plan is brought onto the earth plane. Such people are living revelations of truth, the Way, and life. The clarity of their intention cuts like a laser through the mass of lies and confusions.

Masters and avatars are often working the net hundreds or even thousands of years ahead of their times. When we follow their lead, we may or may not see the flowers that grow from the seeds we planted. Usually we see enough results to keep on keeping on. It really doesn't matter if we see the results; no energy is ever lost. And if it takes a hundred years or a thousand for a vision to blossom, we'll still all be around in one form or another.

Exercise: Journey Back to the Light

Note: I suggest that you read completely through this exercise first before beginning it. If you tend to go into altered states that leave you disoriented in any way, then I advise you not to do this kind of exercise.

You might prefer to do this with a partner or a group or to make a tape for yourself. You will want to pause at the points indicated by a series of dots. We will be using a series of time images that coordinate with your breathing. These guided images will gradually take you back to the womb and beyond, and into the Light. Then we will return through the stages of your life to your present age.

As with all journeys into self, it begins with deep relaxation. So use whatever techniques you prefer to release tensions in your mind, body, and emotions. Most of us have monkey mind, so gently unhook from its chatter by focusing on your breath.

Begin by watching yourself inhaling to a count of eight, holding to a count of eight, exhaling to a count of eight, and then pausing for a count of eight. Do this several times, gently and easily. If you start to hyperventilate, then breathe normally for a while. Any time your mind wants to stray, gently say, "No, not that, but this," returning your attention back to your breath.

As you begin, make a contract with yourself to remain aware and conscious of being in your body during this entire experience. The point is expansion, not escape. If at any time you feel you are losing touch with physical reality, deliberately stop, breathe, and return to alertness.

Let's take a journey back in time. On the next outbreath you are going to see yourself easily moving back in time to five years ago. Don't try to remember anything. Rather, allow it to drift into your awareness. An image or a feeling will appear, possibly with emotional content. Don't try to change it; just notice it, all the while breathing normally. Whatever you remember and feel, always be aware of your breathing. . . . Now let that image go, seeing it disappear like smoke into the air.

On the next few breaths you will find you have turned back in time to your early twenties. . . . Accept without judgment any feeling, image, or memory that shows up. If you are now in your twenties or younger, then just accept a current image, whatever your mind sends you. Don't argue with the image; note it. . . . Now release that image and breathe normally.

On the next inbreath remember being a young adolescent, just entering your teens. . . . Accept the image, memory, or feeling. . . . And release.

Before going any further back in time, mentally direct your breath throughout your body, reminding yourself to stay aware of the body.

Now your breath and mind present you an image, memory, or feeling of being a young child ready to enter school. . . . Accept it just as it presents itself. . . . Release and breathe.

Now we are going to use the breath to gradually move back to the womb. Imagine yourself as a toddler. . . . Release and breathe normally. . . . Now imagine yourself as a baby in someone's arms. . . . Breathe easily, be aware of your body. . . . Release the image and breathe. . . . Feel yourself becoming an infant.

Now you find yourself unborn, inside the womb, filling it. . . . As you breathe easily and naturally, you are aware of becoming smaller and smaller, yet smaller, until you are but a dot of awareness. . . . In that tiny speck you know you are still you. . . . Remember to breathe.

On the next breath you find yourself back beyond the

womb, beyond the body, a free being moving quickly toward the Light. The light is irresistible, pure, welcoming, totally safe. It is home. You feel yourself bathed in this Light and then absorbed by it. . . . Allow yourself to fully feel the peace. . . . Breathe in the Light. . . . Feel it breathe you. . . . You are one with the Light. . . .

As you rest in the peace of this unity, you become aware that in that wholeness there is a creative pulse. That pulse is you. . . . Like a heartbeat, the pulse beats the rhythm of I Am. . . . You are one with the Light, and you are the creative pulse of I Am. . . .

Give yourself time to experience both your sense of oneness with the Light and your awareness of I Am. . . . I Am one with the eternal, flowing sea of Light. . . . I Am a conscious current within that sea. . . . I Am. . . . I Am. . . . I Am. . . . I Am aware of myself. . . . I Am aware of the sea moving through me. . . .

As you rest in this awareness, you gradually become aware of a pull toward the Earth. Staying fully aware of the steady rhythm of I Am, in this moment you remember why you wanted to be in incarnation. . . . Perhaps your inner eye looks at planet Earth to quicken the memory. . . . There is purpose in incarnation. That purpose moves into your memory. . . . You remember now why you wanted to be in this life experience. . . . Tell yourself that you will bring that remembrance with you into full consciousness. . . . I Am. . . . I Am. . . . I Am. . . .

You recall why you sought physical expression in this body. . . . You remember why you chose these parents to give you physical form and early imprinting. . . . You even know why you wanted the experience of your culture. . . . Don't try to figure anything out or debate with the information. Just allow your deepest memory to guide you. . . . You remember the intention for this life.

The I Am is a steady beat. As you feel yourself drawn into the body, feel its beat: I Am. . . . I Am. . . . I Am. . . . The beat takes shape in an explosion of life in your mother's womb, you at the center, holding at that moment of physical creation the full spiritual intent of your journey. . . . I Am. . . . I Am. . . . I Am. . . .

Use the next few breaths to bring yourself to full term as an infant. . . . Feel the physical grow around the self that is your eternal self. . . . I Am, I Am, I Am. . . . Release . . . and see or feel yourself as an unborn infant. . . .

The breath now brings you into awareness of being out of the womb, born into the physical world. . . . the eternal I Am continuing its beat. . . . I Am. . . . I Am.

Gradually images, memories, or feelings pass before you as you experience yourself as a baby. . . . Now you are becoming a toddler. . . . Now you are a young child. . . . I Am. . . . I Am. . . . I Am. . . . You are going to school, learning the ways of your world, yet always inside beats the cosmic heartbeat and the intention of your life. . . . Now you are a teenager. . . . You have become a young adult. . . . No matter what was happening on the outside, inside beats the steady affirmation I Am, I Am, I Am. . . .

Gradually, using your breath with awareness, allow images, memories, or feelings of yourself ten years ago to drift into your mind without judgment or manipulation. . . . I Am. . . . Then bring yourself to five years ago. . . . I Am. . . . Bring yourself to your present point in time.

Be aware that intention resounding through the I Am is as steady and strong as it was when you were conscious of your oneness with the Light. . . . Affirm that you are always one with the Light. . . . I Am one with the Light. . . . Affirm that your Will has chosen your individual purpose and you will remember it. . . . I Am. . . . I Am. . . . I Am. . . .

Open your eyes with a prayer of gratitude for the remembrance of your Will and the great privilege of being alive to fulfill it.

If you do this exercise several times, you will begin to have more insight into the reasons certain people and experiences have been drawn into your life. While you don't want to stop the process and analyze why a particular image appeared at the time, note it in your journal and use it as seed for further investigation. There's always a reason the subconscious kicks up a particular memory. It is like being given a jewel. You don't want to toss it aside.

Willing or Willful?

The shadows of the divided will lie at the heart of the whole human dilemma. The battle between the will to separation and the Will to Godness is symbolized in myths around the world, from Armageddon to Luke Skywalker's battling the dark side in the film *Star Wars*. It is important to remember that in the battle Luke finally recognizes that both impulses are within himself.

The piercing light of the sun, symbol for the Highest Will, lights up the landscape of the psyche, while it also defines its deepest shadows. The dark, hidden places that the Light can abruptly expose need to be attended to with patience, compassion, and tolerance. Humor helps. And so does honesty and persistence.

It takes a persistent Will to birth a vision from the soul's realm into the physical world. The next challenge is to use the Will to parent the newborn to maturity, keeping the vision alive and flowing. Otherwise it stops growing and freezes into a rigid form, and alas, too often the form itself is worshiped.

When that happens, the new idea now becomes the "truth," having replaced the "truth" before it, even as it built upon it. Of course, it is inevitable that another piece of the truth will be revealed, resisted, and finally accepted. The history of science and religion is filled with stories of great thinkers first punished and later deified. Our own biographies probably are as well.

What Is the Price of Surrender to Thy Will?

There once was a man who spent years climbing the mountain of enlightenment. As he approached the top he shouted his most burning question: "What must I do to gain enlightenment?" Out of the clouds a voice boomed, "Practice celibacy, poverty, obedience." The man thought for a while and then shouted again, "Is there someone else up there I can talk to?"

Which one of us has not backed off the edge of surrender? Who has not said, "I just can't" (or "I won't")? Haven't we all at some point said no to inner guidance because of fear—fear of losing a relationship, a job, money, position? And how often have we refused an assignment because our lower will insisted on holding on to the status quo?

Before there is resolution between the Highest Will and the personality will, ambivalence can be intense, creating a spiritual paralysis in which we feel split in our loyalty, wanting to serve and at the same time resenting the demands, often not feeling ready or worthy to serve.

Sharon is an extremely talented counselor and teacher. She wrote to me of her struggle to accept her abilities. "I was still resistant to the idea of being anything more than the small me. I was hard core. It was push-pull for years and years. I longed to reach God. It was almost a physical thing. Yet part of me kept saying, 'No, no. You can't do that. Don't you dare! You know what will happen.' *The problem with reaching God was that along the way I would become responsible for using my gifts.*"

Fear of failing or succeeding can be lurking in our shadows. Aaron, a businessman and disciple, said the decision to act on his

Highest Will often created high tension in him, reminding him of the Chinese character for *crisis*, which means both opportunity and danger. "It's pretty scary to know your mission. When I am in touch with it, I have a sense of relief. But I also feel driven. I also feel fear. Suppose I blow it? On a pool table the pockets are spaced every couple of feet apart. On my mental pool table, one pocket is danger, and about two inches away is a pocket called opportunity. So if I am trying to put the ball into opportunity and I miss it, it goes into danger."

Haven't we all periodically felt like kicking over the traces in full rebellion, telling ourselves, "I'm sick of all this. I don't want to examine my motives anymore. I just want to have a good time"? Where and when did we get the idea spirituality was boring, demanding, and no fun? Did religions teach us that? Did you ever wonder why you weren't taught joy above all?

Wouldn't it have been wonderful to run eagerly to our cathedrals and temples, our chapels, mosques, and synagogues? What if we had to strap ourselves into our seats because the very air crackled with possibilities? What if the objective was to give us keys to unlock ecstasy and ways to celebrate Spirit while in the body? What if we were told from the beginning that our Will was one with God/Goddess?

Alas, we were more likely to have been given a list of shoulds. Sometimes we fear that in surrendering to the Highest Will within, we will get another list of shoulds—we should be doing this, we should be doing that. The sad irony of this is that our Highest Will fulfills our deepest intentions; it doesn't crush them.

Make a note to really listen for your use of the word *should*. Yellow caution lights need to go off every time you hear it or use it. It's a warning word that says, "Look out. You've just shifted authority outside of yourself."

❧ Journaling Seeds

1. What did you dream about doing when you were young? What if that was God/Goddess dreaming you?

2. What did you want before you were taught you *should* want something else? What if that earlier desire is what God/Goddess wanted for you?

3. What really brings you rushes of enthusiasm? What if that is God/Goddess inspiring you?

It's in these inner explorations that one often finds the seeds of intention, not in following the didactic posturing of the shoulds. The word *enthusiasm* itself means to be filled with God. How sad when anyone's enthusiasm in self-expression is robbed and replaced with a set of rules. Ultimately it robs all of us, for people living from their enthusiasm bring gifts from their souls to the world.

Agnes repressed her longing to paint until her mid-seventies because of the "should syndrome" in her family, which saw art as "a waste of a good woman's time." Later in life her spirit awakened, and so did her longing to paint. Being courageous, she faced her fears, and at the age of seventy-five she took a course on creativity, which pushed her into confrontation with her own shadows, but she persisted in facing her fears. Today, at eighty-six, she takes classes in watercolor, oil, acrylic, and mixed media. People hang her paintings in their homes and offices. This past spring she won honorable mention in a very prestigious art show.

No Way to Fake It

The Higher Will leaves nothing uncooked. Anything I am doing that is not congruent with my highest intention will be brought to my attention. For example, if I am espousing tolerance and practicing gossip, then I'm energetically negating my intention. Once I practice what I preach, then the words and actions will carry authenticity and authority.

If in our subconscious we have an unrequited ego desire for anything, it continues to set up lures to attract those things. The rush of excitement over getting those desires fulfilled quickly passes, and more is required to feed the desires. Yet the satisfaction of fulfilling one's deepest intention does not pass even in the face of discouragement and disappointments.

The universe will always remind us when the lower will is still running the show. The story is told that in the spiritual community built around G. I. Gurdjieff there was an old man who drove everyone crazy. He was hard to get along with, quarrelsome, messy—the works. After he left, Gurdjieff paid him a stipend to return to the community. The people were upset and questioned Gurdjieff. He told them the man was like yeast. They had come to his community so he would teach them about patience and tolerance and all those good things, and they were being given a chance to learn them through the old man.

Sometimes the process of bringing the demands of the ego under our management feels like training a precocious child who is stamping her feet in a tantrum. Even if the child is potentially a master, she still has to learn to read and clean up her room. When we see that something is off the mark (the definition, by the way, of sin), we must be patient and loving with ourselves as we first acknowledge it, seek to understand it, accept the grace of the universe, perhaps have a great catharsis, and then move back in line with higher intention. With the really resistant, stubborn stuff, "the ante goes up," as one disciple put it, and we often have to repeat the whole process again and again until we are free.

This is true for everyone, and we torture ourselves unnecessarily if we think we're the only ones doing it wrong. It is important for any disciple to remember that we don't even attempt to face the hardest material until we have built up some spiritual muscle first. We have to have a substantial amount of faith, endurance, love, and discrimination before we can take on the false gods we've created on planet Earth.

Remember, it was after he had been committed to his quest for a very long time that Buddha sat under the bodhi tree and faced the major temptations. And it was only after the Baptism, comparable to the second initiation in the mystery teachings, that Jesus met his tempter in the desert.

If we accept and love our humanness, we are more likely to discover our divinity. That we humans have made such a lot of messes here with our free wills, personally and collectively, is also a testimony to our potential to make paradises.

Exercise: Vow Release
from Past Lives

The purpose of this exercise is to unhook ourselves from commitments we made in other lives with our wills. In the subconscious there is no time and space. Wherever and whenever we've used our will to declare vows of poverty, chastity, or allegiance to a system or person, if those vows have not been released, we could unconsciously be motivated by them. I have worked with many people who discovered that even after intense therapies, they were having difficulty staying focused on their intention for this lifetime because they were still holding on to uncomfortable feelings they couldn't release around sex, money, or individuals. Of course, there could be many reasons for this, but certainly an unreleased vow from the past could be a significant contributing force. So this exercise is offered as part of general housecleaning with the Will.

As with all the exercises, I advise you to read the directions carefully and decide if this is an experience that feels appropriate and helpful to you.

Anytime you are going to consciously work beyond the physical, you want to declare that your intentions are for the highest good. Memories can show up in dreamlike images and archetypes. And fears from another time can produce emotional responses that feel as fresh as today's experience. Often we're leaving logic behind and relying on intuition. So you want to enter these kinds of experiences with clarity, affirming that you are seeking the truth and truth only.

1. First light a candle to remind yourself of the One Light in which you live and are protected.

2. Select a prayer that has meaning for you, one that aligns you with your own Spirit. I personally use the Lord's Prayer and a prayer that affirms my intention: "I surround and fill this experience with the Light. I seek truth and truth only as I accept guidance and information that is for my highest Good. I am open to receive insight, and I am grateful."

3. Because we take an inner-child consciousness along on every experience, we need to honor its needs. Sometimes the younger parts of ourselves grow frightened when we start challenging the familiar. They are comforted by the presence of angels or other holy beings. So you might want to invoke such beings to be present. You might say, "I invite the presence of [Kuan Yin, Mary, Jesus, Buddha, Raphael, or perhaps a known teacher in Spirit] to bless this experience."

4. Next image yourself standing in a circle of purple flame. Purple is the color of transformation, and fire burns at every level, including the frequencies in which memories are held.

5. Then you release the vow with the following declaration: "I affirm and claim my divine right to decree what I will hold in my consciousness and my energy field. Through the power of the indwelling Spirit, I decree that all past vows of poverty taken anytime, anyplace, under any circumstances, during any incarnation be at this moment released from my consciousness. I release all individuals, systems, beliefs, allegiances, and emotions surrounding the vow back to the Light.

"I bless this energy as I return it to the Source. I forgive all pain and people around the circumstances of the vow. All limits and misperceptions that have held the vow in place are now dissolved. Into that vacuum pour clarity, creativity, and abundance. I vow to accept the grace of the indwelling Spirit.

"Thank you, Mother-Father-God."

6. Repeat the vow three times in the beginning, and as often as you feel it necessary thereafter.

7. This vow release affirmation can be used to release vows of celibacy as well as vows of obedience to an individual, country, religion, or organization.

One word of caution: Should you choose to write an adaptation of this for yourself, please study the principles very carefully. It is especially important that you fill the vacuum you create during the release with positive intention. Remember, energy is not sentimental, and the laws of energy say that a vacuum will be filled. That's the principle behind negative projections returning "seven times seven." You don't want careless contents to fill that vacuum. Filling the vacuum with Light is always safe, as is the vow to accept grace, which you might want to use as an affirmation for several weeks before, during, and after you perform this exercise.

❧ Twelve Considerations on Will

1. The Highest Will is to the Divine as the sunbeam is to the sun.

2. The Will is a Divine birthright freely given to everyone.

3. The unconditional gift of the Will brings choice and consequences.

4. The longing for "Thy Will" is the longing to be oneself.

5. The Highest Wills of all are connected and can be contacted.

6. The Will sets up an energy matrix, drawing supply to itself.

7. The Highest Will perceives pain and failure as opportunities.

8. The Highest Will knows life is abundant; the ego fears lack.

9. "My will is Thy Will" affirms the union of heaven and earth.

10. Nonresistance to challenges frees the Will to learn and grow.

11. Intention focuses the Will. Patience brings it to fruition.

12. I Am is the mantra of the Will, free to live its truth.

Prayer

Thy will and mine be One.
I give thanks for this perfect day of completion.
Miracle shall follow miracle and
Wonders shall never cease.

—Florence Scovel Shinn

Affirmation

Thy Will and mine be One.
I remember.
This day I Will to _____.
[choose your focus for the day]

Quote

The will is not an effort; it is purpose, choice and decision. In other words, it is a power that directs, initiates and orients.

—Psychologist Robert Assagioli

Faith: Cornerstone of the Cathedral

❧

> *When you surrender to the air, you can ride it.*
> —Toni Morrison, *Song of Solomon*

Imagine I've just offered you a job. You don't know what it is, where it is, what you have to do, or what you will be paid. And did I mention that you have to trust me implicitly, regardless of external circumstances? Interested? Actually you're going to love it. Ultimately it's the only job worth having.

It is the contract your soul asks of you, nothing less, nothing more. At some point, usually after we've tried everything else, we find ourselves face-to-face with the Divine, which says: "I want all of you. Sign here."

It seems to me that with such steep requirements, we should discuss very soberly what it takes to make such an awesome commitment. It starts with forging a faith that is hard as a diamond, is far more valuable, and probably took us about as long to develop as it took the carbon to crystallize deep in the dirt and under intense pressure.

Actually we live daily with a faith in the knowledge and skills of others. In spite of all the detours and malfunctions we see around us, we essentially trust that the everyday world works. Even with our fears and self-doubts, most of us have a basic hope, if not optimism, that drives us toward the future, seeking solutions and believing in possibilities.

When we get too weary or jaded, we renew our hope through our children, with their eager yearning and indefatigable self-confidence. They enter three-dimensional reality still shimmering with light, their awareness of a larger reality not yet dimmed. When that awareness is protected and encouraged, they speak with the ease of someone on a first-name basis with the Divine, like the little girl who announced she was drawing a picture of God. Told that no one knew what God looked like, she replied, "Well, they will when I finish drawing this."

A Child's Faith

All children arrive with unique missions for themselves and us. While they certainly have to be educated, shouldn't we be asking them, "What are you here to do, and how can we help you be who you were meant to be?" Many times the first attack on our faith in ourselves and our purpose takes place in our childhood, when other people's general attitude is more like, "Here's what we think you should believe and be; now follow it."

To become as a little child, as Holy Scriptures around the world advise, we need to return to that original state of pure awareness and claim the kind of faith we see in this child from an ancient Hindu story.

> *A young boy, frightened of the woods he had to walk through on his way to school, was told by his mother to ask Krishna to accompany him to school. He did, and sure enough, Krishna appeared, and the boy felt secure.*
>
> *On the schoolmaster's birthday all the children were expected to bring gifts. The little boy had none, but his mother advised him to ask Krishna to provide a gift. In faith he asked, and lo and behold,*

Krishna materialized a beautiful jug of milk, which the boy proudly placed at his teacher's feet. When the teacher poured the milk from the jug, it immediately filled up again. It happened over and over. Of course, the teacher wanted to know where the boy had gotten such an amazing jug.

"Krishna gave it to me. He walks me to school every day."

The teacher was very skeptical. "Show me this Krishna who walks with you and performs such magic."

So the teacher and the other students went to the woods with the boy, who began to call upon Krishna. Silence. No Krishna. Again and again he called, louder and louder. Again, nothing. There were a lot of jokes by the other students, and the boy was profoundly embarrassed. In tears he begged, "Krishna, please show yourself. They think I am a liar."

There was a moment of silence, and then he heard Krishna speak softly to him. "I cannot come because they do not have your simple faith. When they do, I will come."

"If you build it, they will come" became a familiar expression after the release of the movie *Field of Dreams*. Guided to build a ball field in his fertile Iowa cornfield, but having no idea why, the hero faced ridicule and even the loss of his farm, but he did as asked anyway—*before he had the evidence*. Faith often asks us to act on our dreams and deepest intuitions without benefit of material evidence. Acting only on what we can see is more like calculated risk than faith.

How are you preparing a place for your dream? For example, if you feel guided to be a healer but have no idea where to start, put something in motion that acknowledges the inner guidance: take a class, gather books on the subject, talk with healers, think, meditate, question, pray about it. Anything you do begins the process of giving material life to your dream and starts drawing to you what you will need. As in the movie, for a while you might feel more like you're in a mystery than a manifestation. But one clue after another brings clarity. Meantime, you are forging faith in yourself and your guidance.

Journaling Seeds

1. What were your dreams for yourself as a child? As a teenager? A young adult? In the present time?

2. From what persons or circumstances did you learn to doubt? To be cynical?

3. Are you building in faith now or waiting for evidence?

4. Do you trust your own guidance? How do you recognize that your faith is in operation?

Disciples often have to heal another layer of childhood wounds as they grow into accepting their missions, even if they have already done some of that work. Many of them came into this life with highly developed sensitivities that they were going to need. Yet as children it sometimes meant that they saw more than most people. That's both the good news and the bad. They saw or felt their parents' hypocrisies, their darker emotions, and their frustration and pain, sometimes taking those feelings on themselves. Many felt a deep loneliness, for they were not seen for who they are.

It may seem unnecessarily harsh that a child is thrust into such serious issues as standing alone, sorting out responsibility, and dealing with heightened awareness. In faith, we remember that birth is not an accident, and the soul is not a child. It knows what lies ahead, and it begins its training in the womb. There can be deep levels of grief that have to be transformed as one shifts expectations away from family to Spirit, from external blaming to internal claiming.

It is not enough to have read the books and to be facile with the concepts. Sometimes being bright and educated just gives us more ways to push our vulnerabilities down under. Fortunately, there are excellent books and workshops available to support this work. (See bibliography.)

Faith Recognizes the Light Within

Like travelers on a twisting road, we often have no idea what's around the bend. But we only have to have faith in the next step. We take one baby step and then another, and then suddenly a vista appears and we see the Way more clearly. Through faith in those tiny steps—and sometimes with huge leaps—we gradually re-member. And in that remembrance we discover the power to move mountains.

An old-fashioned word such as *faith* doesn't always ride so crisply along the Internet. It can seem out of fashion, like a me-dieval religious icon. But in all disciplines it is taught that one can-not walk the Way without it. It may be called *strade* in Balinese Hinduism and *pistis* in Gnosticism, but in all cosmologies, from the most primitive to the most complex, faith is always named as a major foundation piece for living a Spirit-directed life.

In the Christian legend the point is made through allegory. In this story Jesus once asked the disciples, "Who do people say the Son of Man is?"

And they replied, "Some say he is John the Baptist, some Eli-jah, and others Jeremiah or one of the prophets."

"But you, who do you say I am?"

Then Simon Peter spoke up. "You are the Christ. The Son of the living God."

And Jesus said, "On this rock I will build my Church. And the gates of the underworld can never hold out against it. I will give you the keys of the kingdom of heaven. Whatever you bind on earth shall be considered bound in heaven; whatever you loose on earth shall be considered loosed in heaven."

Intuition, not logic, recognizes the presence of the Light within. Without faith, everything is vulnerable to the superficial, to outer appearances.

Trust the Wind Under Your Wings

Faith will bring to you all the knowledge and skills you need to ascend the mountain. Once you are there, it shows you the view. And then it says, "Jump."

We may spend years—or lifetimes—on top of the mountain, observing, speculating, enjoying . . . and hesitating. Ego control is tenacious. Yet at some point the inner prompting says: "Do you love the truth enough to jump off this mountain and have faith in the unknown?"

If you do, the wind *will* hold you. It will carry you on great unseen currents into unimagined landscapes in the Spirit. It will connect you to a larger plan in ways your ego could not create even under the best conditions. The wind sweeps across continents and oceans, through times and cultures, depositing seeds wherever the soil is ready. Trusting the unseen wind, the breath of God, we become a seed, or as the twelfth-century abbess and mystic Hildegard of Bingen put it, we become "a feather on the breath of God."

Faith draws from universal supply an endless stream of people, energy, and talents to fulfill intention. When we live by personal manipulation, "who you know" is one of the ground rules in our coping manual. But living by faith is a lot about who and what you don't yet know. As all souls are connected at the spiritual level, that's where the intention of evolution is laid out and work assignments are given. We are participants in an unfolding Plan on earth. We get glimpses of it, but the larger blueprint is as yet beyond our understanding. Evolution—personal, spiritual, physical—is the working energy of that unfolding plan.

Ultimately we all work for the same boss, the Source of all resources. Whatever we need—catalysts, contacts, money, training, everything—is drawn into our patterns at precisely the right time. When we understand that meetings that seem casual and accidental are really part of a larger Plan, we are more likely to be fully present with whoever or whatever crosses our path.

When we say yes to Spirit, we don't really know what we might be asked to do in the future. Our soul knows our deepest intention and will set in motion the attraction that brings all the preparation we need. And this can also mean disappointments at an ego level. Wherever we have a weakness that could compromise our intention, it will rise to the surface asking that we address it. We could run to the ends of the earth to escape a situation and discover that it has arrived with us. "Seek and you shall find" is a working principle of magnetism that attracts to us people and circumstances based on the contents we are holding, consciously or unconsciously, in our psyches. The trick is to know what we're seeking.

Faith in Your Place in the Plan

Some of what we're asked to do is transpersonal. It is not easy to challenge ideas so entrenched in history that they have become basic assumptions about reality. Bigotries—about race, religion, ethnicity, gender, or sexual orientation—are passed down like family jewels. To continue working toward liberating those prejudices in the face of entrenched opposition, knowing the negative attitude might not topple in this lifetime, takes an uncompromised faith, one that is practiced day in and day out.

As it has been wisely asked, which blow finally cracks open the stone—the tenth, the fiftieth, your last one, or mine? What if you are the pivotal person whose thoughts will make the difference?

"You are entitled to the work, but not to the fruits," says Krishna to Arjuna in the Bhagavad Gita. This concept is very different from the prevailing what's-in-it-for-me philosophy. There is actually incredible freedom in not demanding to see results. It's liberating to know that your only job is the one in front of you.

We live and create in many dimensions simultaneously. It is not necessary to choose between our finite and infinite selves. Our finite self might say: "I have eighty-five years to do my thing; here are the possibilities and restrictions." If the thinking stops there, then few outside of saints would be encouraged to dream and then reach beyond their limitations.

Yet many of our greatest accomplishments in all areas of endeavor have been seeded by people who didn't receive rewards in their lifetimes. That Moses led his people to the promised land but wasn't permitted to enter may be a story designed to describe a dynamic of the journey as well as a piece of Jewish history. Dr. Martin Luther King Jr. was one who demonstrated that principle in our time. Every generation since World War II has been touched by the simple faith of Anne Frank, who in the midst of unspeakable horror, even facing her own death, chose to affirm the good.

Among all people, we find those who were willing to be planters, not harvesters. We now enjoy the fruits of seeds planted and fertilized by the courage and often the humiliation, even the blood, of those who have courageously challenged existing thought patterns—peacemakers, prophets, pacifists, abolitionists, suffragettes, scientists attacking superstition, and artists in every medium intent on breaking the rules, insisting the world look at itself with new eyes.

Such people are a fascinating study in integrated faith. They seem prepared to say, as did poet Dawna Markova, "I choose to risk my significance: to live so that which came to me as seed goes to the next as blossom, and that which came to me as blossom, goes on as fruit." What has come to you as seed or blossom from your ancestry, your nation, and your history that asks you now to nurture it to fullness?

Many who live by faith report feeling they have had no choice.

But of course they had a choice; we always do. Many of the things we dread also stalked a lot of them: they were discouraged, ridiculed, outlawed, denied, imprisoned, shunned, assassinated— on and on the list goes. Yet no matter what was done to them, they held to their faith in what they had to bring to the world.

The phrase "no matter what" is the key. Is there anything more liberating than the inner freedom that allows one to say, as did the Plains Indians of America before a battle, "It's a good day to die"? When we can stop, turn around, and say to our very worst fears, "I'm going to do what I'm guided to do no matter what," then we truly taste the delicious freedom faith can bring.

Once we state our intentions in faith, it's up to the universe to work out the details. I have a friend who responds when she is questioned about how she is going to do something, "I don't know, that's God's business; I just work here."

Faith Finds a House

In the spirit of a belief that we sometimes teach a principle best by personal testimony, I'm going to share a chapter from my own journey. It is a tale about learning more about faith through a very basic physical need—housing.

My house drama has four scenes. The first starts when I was still living in the house my former husband and I had shared. During that time I saw clairvoyantly a small and charming contemporary house set in the woods overlooking a lake. Since I liked that kind of house, I thought the vision might be a fantasy.

Months later I was house hunting with a realtor. I requested that we drive to a nearby lake, even though she insisted there was nothing for sale in that area. But there was the house of my vision. The FOR SALE sign had been put up two hours before, and it was within the right price range. Within days I signed the contract. It became my healing sanctuary, and I loved it.

Scene two in this drama began with inner guidance. I had been very content in that house for four years when I began to get clear, intuitive direction to cut back on the volume of my work and to move to the mountains. That would, of course, translate into less income, so it raised a fear that was to prove part of the testing in faith that followed. The inner promptings were more specific than usual, naming a place called High Meadows. I pored over the maps of North Carolina. There was no High Meadows. I then tried to convince myself that it was a symbol guiding me to go to the high, clear places within myself. Deep within, I was sure I was to literally head for the hills.

Intuiting what might lie ahead, I tried to cut a deal. "Okay, I'll move, but here are the conditions: I'll go *only* to Asheville or Boone, *only* where I will have a support system," blah, blah, blah. Spirit never stops our resistance. We can waste all the time we like. So I spent weeks looking for houses in those cities. The right one would not show up no matter what I did. Frustrated, I began to doubt the guidance. And I still kept seeking it.

Part of my frustration was being caught in an attempt to have it both ways. I wanted to have faith in my guidance, and I wanted to have it my way. I intuited that a lesson in obedience to my deepest guidance was about to be served up—not to mention a dosage of nonattachment to the house I was in. But sanctuaries are not necessarily permanent dwellings. During transitional periods we often attract a healing person or setting to us, even a rebound love affair. In my case, it had been a house.

Finally I gave up running around all over western North Carolina; mainly I gave up setting out conditions. And that giving up opened the door to the next part of the drama. I was telling someone who knew nothing about my vision that I was frustrated with trying to find a house in the mountains. She shook her head and said, "Gosh, I wish I could help, but I don't even know anyone that lives in the mountains other than a couple at High Meadows."

"What did you say?" I screamed.

To this day she has no idea why she said High Meadows. It is a neighborhood in Roaring Gap; it is not a town. However, had she said Roaring Gap, I would have paid no attention. So off I went to explore this neighborhood. Naturally, it was in a part of the state where I knew no one—forget a support system. As I drove into it, my eyebrows rose. It was a golf and tennis community filled with beautiful, expensive houses.

"Uh, excuse me, Spirit, but I do believe you have made a mistake this time. I can't cut back on my work *and* move into a country club setting," I said to myself. We learned that most of the houses were leased for short terms, were expensive, and were furnished. I had several rooms of furniture that had to go somewhere.

Yet as I drove around I would occasionally hear the word *divorce* in my mind. I dismissed it, as I did High Meadows by the end of that aggravating day. How had I misunderstood so completely my guidance from Spirit, and what was I thinking of to run around all over the place on a few skimpy clues?

The next day I received a call from someone I'd met at High Meadows. She reported that after I left, she'd remembered one house she knew about. A couple was divorcing; it was a relatively small unfurnished vacation house, and it was empty now. She said she couldn't reach the owner, who lived out of state.

Of course, he answered immediately when I called. As we discussed the house, I began to be nervous. This was probably going to be at least $1,500 a month, and there was no way I could handle that with a reduced income *and* a mortgage payment back in town. In my muddling worry I suddenly heard him say: "Well, I never rented a house to anyone before. I think I'll have to have $325 a month."

And so I moved to High Meadows, just as Spirit had said. What followed was twenty-two months of some of the most intense spiritual training I've ever had before or since. There were times when my faith was diced up and eaten by my shadow. And there were periods of spiritual soaring that sustain me to this day. There were visions I'm still working to fully understand, and long days of flat meditations and irksome confrontations with myself. I remained through two long winters of snow and ice, and often family and friends couldn't make it in for visits. Sometimes I felt very alone, as only thirteen people remained on the whole mountain in those short days and long nights during the winter.

My house on the lake didn't sell for a year. My rational brain would have insisted that it was impossible to cut back income, pay a mortgage, and rent a house. And yet it happened, often with me shrieking right up to the edge, certain I would fall into the abyss. But I never did. The message was quite clear: If I was going to live by faith, that had to include money.

It was during this period that I first saw the words "barefoot on holy ground" printed in front of my inner eyes, and I knew I would write a book by that title. I also knew that the first book I would write during the next two years was not it.

While I rejoiced in the natural beauty and had grown to appreciate the additional training I was receiving, I eventually became eager to get off that mountain. I wasn't clear about when or where to move. As long as I was not too far from an airport or major highway, I was free to go where I desired or was guided. My work requires travel (which I love), and my heart wanted to have a home base near family and friends.

Then the third scene in the house drama began. I decided to move to my hometown and spend a conservative amount of money for rent until I was sure where I wanted to buy a house. Another round of frustration followed as I looked at houses and apartments in the area. It seemed impossible to find anything in my price range big, clean, or safe enough.

So once again I gave up. Assuming it just wasn't time to move back to the city, I planned to go back to the mountains. But I made a date to have lunch with a friend before I left. On the way to meet her I suddenly realized that my mind was wandering and that I was on the wrong road.

Grumbling that I was going to get myself entangled in one-way streets, I decided to cut through a neighborhood I didn't know and see if I could thread my way back to the right road. I found myself slowing down as I drove through a quiet, well-kept neighborhood, one in which there were rarely any rental homes available.

There was no sign in the yard of the house and absolutely no indications that it was empty, but it felt as though it was. A neighbor was standing in the yard next door. I rolled down the window and asked, "Does anyone live here?"

"No," he answered, "the people who were leasing the house moved yesterday." Who knows why he chose to tell me the house had been rented. He did know who owned it, and he told me how to find him. It also turned out that this neighbor actually lived several houses away and just happened to be where I met him at that precise moment.

I hurried over to the owner. Predictably, he was puzzled. How did I know the house was even there, let alone just emptied? "My car found the house," I said. He laughed. Naturally he thought I was joking. As he talked I began to worry about the rent. Then the owner asked for exactly the amount of money I had decided I could spend.

However, there was a hitch. He wanted a large deposit, also the first and last months' rent. While I knew that was fair, it was not realistic for me. It was going to take several thousand dollars to get moved off the mountain, and if I spent a couple more on getting into this house, I wouldn't be able to buy a house for a long time. So I told him I'd think about it.

That afternoon, as I was explaining all this to my mother, she looked away for a moment and then broke into a smile. "That's Mr. Jones. Your father and I were in a dance club with him and

Mrs. Jones thirty years ago." So she and I hopped into the car and went for a reunion with the owner of the house. They laughed and reminisced for an hour or so. And I ended up making a deal to move into his house with no deposit and no first and final months' rent. It made my move possible.

One final scene in the housing-cum-faith drama: After a couple of years I knew it was time to buy my own home again. There were new elements to be considered. Both my mother and I were increasingly aware that she was getting older. And even though she was active and healthy, we needed to consider what her future needs might be. My father was dead, and I'm an only child. The time was right for us to live together.

We had quite a list of requirements. I wanted a three-bedroom house for myself because kids and friends come often. I also needed office space that would accommodate a counseling room, writing area, space for a secretary, storage, and so on. Mother wanted her own complete apartment. Moreover, it had to be on one level, because she was dealing with serious knee problems.

We both love gardens, so we wanted a good-sized yard. And we wanted convenience to shopping. The final thing on her list was to be within fifteen minutes of her sister if possible.

Our realtor called and reported that the first day she took out the listing book, it opened to a house that met every single criteria. And if we had any doubts, it was all of three minutes to my mother's sister's house.

Friends have simply shaken their heads in amazement. Here was a fifty-year-old house that looked as though it had been built for our exact needs. And finding it was just the beginning of the synchronicity. How to get it was the next hurdle. When you are self-employed, you have to go through many more financial hoops than you do when you're employed by a company.

The first miracle was that the owner was eager to sell. He had a huge bill due, and a big house on his hands that could be a white elephant. So he had the house on the market at $4,000 under its appraisal. I offered him $10,000 less than that, assuming I would have to negotiate. He took it.

There was one more final little test of faith to go through. Just days before closing, I learned that I was going to have to pay $10,000 more than expected. The night I got this news a close friend called. When I told her this, she didn't miss a beat: "Well, I'll lend it to you today." She is not a woman of wealth; she, too, is self-employed. I hesitated, but she insisted. Finally I accepted and repaid her with interest within a year. I could never repay her for the value of her faith in me.

My mother and I have been in this house twelve years now, and we both love it and appreciate it, eccentricities and all.

My house metaphor taught me many things about faith:

- Spirit is present in everything. Whenever my life is divided into parts, it is me, not Spirit, that has moved into duality.
- Once again, there are no accidents. There are plenty of *appearances* and *interpretations* that appear as accidents.
- All of us are used by Spirit to serve each other in ways that seem as casual as a remark tossed over a backyard fence.
- We perceive things as good or bad, safe or risky, because of our inner pictures and expectations. Faith leads us to bigger pictures and teaches us to trust the unexpected.
- Faith demands total, not partial, commitment—just as one can't be a little bit pregnant.
- If we have faith in our guidance and follow it, we are plugged into the universal supply line. Everything that we need will be drawn to us in ways we could not imagine or manipulate.
- When our faith is being strengthened, tested, or refined, we often cannot see beyond the next step, the next decision, or the next move. Gradually we learn to trust the unknown, the untested, and the larger plan that is at work in all our lives.

What do I feel I led to do?

Exercise: No Matter What

As disciples, we are often assigned to bring new ideas into the world regardless of appearances and resistance. We commit to doing it, no matter what. This is an exercise in everyday faith, learning more about where the edge of your faith is, and trusting your guidance as it pushes the edge into the unknown.

1. Think of some specific project that you have been inner-directed to do. Maybe you have been concerned about a dangerous corner that has no stoplight, the need for a child care program at work, the beautification of your city. Write an affirmation of your intention to follow your guidance no matter what happens to oppose it: "I am going to follow my guidance to _____, *no matter what.*"

2. While step one seems easy enough in a moment of enthusiasm, usually obstacles show up soon. Pay close attention. The outer resistance will be obvious. Watch your own inner resistance as it presents itself: "I don't have the time," "I knew he [she, they, the company] wouldn't go along," "Well, I tried; it didn't work." Don't judge, but be honest. The most subtle resistance emerges from self-doubt: "Why would they listen to me?" "Maybe I just made this up." *Lack of faith in inner guidance is perpetuated by relying too quickly on outer appearances.*

Notice all of it. Breathe with it, inhaling renewing energy from the universe, exhaling stress and hesitation. Do you still feel guided toward this project? If so, repeat your affirmation: "I am going to follow my guidance to _____, *no matter what.*"

3. Notice and affirm that you are attracting support. This may show up as other people or helpful information obtained through magazine articles, books, and TV shows. Your intuition, dream life, or meditations might be giving you new angles on the next step. Express gratitude for everything.

4. Next comes the hardest part for the ego: releasing investments in results. The project may or may not come to full fruition under your auspices or even in your lifetime. Nevertheless, it will flower in its right time because you planted the seed in your time. An affirmation you can use is "I release this project to the Mother-Father-God, knowing it will manifest in its right form and right timing." At first, releasing the ego's need to have concrete results immediately can feel uncomfortable. But as we keep affirming faith in our guidance, an incredible freedom is born. We learn we don't have to control everything, just follow our guidance at the moment.

5. Part of the training in faith is to commit yourself to supporting positive thought forms and a peaceful, harmonious world for all people. Disciples go beyond wishful thinking. They take responsibility for what they add to our collective life. For example: "I am going to follow my guidance to create understanding between races in my thoughts, my words, and my actions, *no matter what.*"

Just as in committing in faith to a specific project, you will want to notice how many opportunities you are given to plant a seed of understanding and how often you are challenged. Be honest but not harsh with yourself as your own racism (or ageism, sexism, or other prejudice) pops up. That's the way it works. Commit in faith to anything, and the first project is yourself.

Faith in Shadow

Faith creates a climate in which miracles seem to happen. The tribal *sangoma*, the hands-on healer, and the TV evangelist are all relying on an environment of faith in miracles. And they happen. Miracles are the everyday business of the universe.

When the healing doesn't work, the job doesn't come through, the child isn't rescued, then we question and doubt. Why? Our inability to answer that question tears at the heart of faith. Didn't we believe hard enough?

It is misleading and guilt-producing to assume that when things work, we have somehow appeased the gods, who have now "rewarded" us. This deep-seated belief has been with us since we faced our first earthquake or puzzled powerlessly over the mystery of illness and death. Those fears are still floating free in the collective unconscious, ready to activate similar fears we may be harboring. If good health, wealth, and all other good things mean we did something right, what does it mean when we have challenges? Does it mean we did it wrong?

We know that belief is a powerful force. We base our whole lives on our beliefs about ourselves and others. We go to war over beliefs. People can feel less pain and even improve their physical problems with a treatment they believe in, even if it's scientifically unproven.

Beliefs translate into pictures and thoughts instantaneously, and then into chemical changes in the body. Think of a lemon, and your glands work. Remember an embarrassing moment, and you flush. Inner pictures of success or failure produce very different responses.

I remember the death passage of two kind elderly people who had lived and served their whole lives in a strict sin-laden belief system. Their beliefs affected their deaths, both of them refusing to let go of their bodies, enduring great psychic pain all through their passage, one being sure he had not done enough for Jesus and would be judged, the other becoming panicked because she was sure there were demons on the other side.

Ask yourself: "What kind of inner images of my relationship to the Divine am I holding?"

Clearing Out Ancient Beliefs

In the movie *The Witches of Eastwick*, the devil persecuted each of the women who were rebelling against him by tormenting them with fantasies custom-designed around their fears. All our fears are very unique, and many of them don't surface until we rebel against "the devil," that is, lies.

Our fears can be buried deep. Once I worked with a very successful man who longed to use his considerable power to help others but was irrationally terrified that he would do harm. This crisis in his faith had led him to counseling. The time had arrived for him to release fears he had buried from past lives in which he had done harm. He had unconsciously repressed this fear until he acquired enough spiritual muscle to face it again.

The fear was well protected in his psyche. I saw it wrapped in heavy cloth, tied up in ropes, stored in a box, put in a heavy chest closed with multiple locks, carried down spiral steps to a dark basement, buried in a deep grave, covered with dirt and boards, and hidden behind a secret door that had been booby-trapped.

It was supposedly a fail-safe prison for his fear, designed to hold his psyche in chains. Yet there is no place in heaven or hell that the Light of truth cannot go, and nothing that it can't transform. It moves like smoke, even into locked boxes. And it will lift anything, no matter how filled with shame, to the Light.

And so it did with him. He achieved this first of all through the courage to face the problem and the humility to ask for help. He used several tools. He responded well to the wisdom teachings, so we used spiritual knowledge that helped him reframe his past, seeing it as experience and not essential character. He began to see that power was a good thing when used by Spirit, potentially abusive when used by his ego. He became more compassionate and forgiving of himself and others who had misused power. He finally opened the feared, buried box. It held a scepter—the symbol of power.

A past life memory recall helped me free a fear that would have limited my faith in feeling safe in this work. I was barely into the work when I was invited to lecture about it, and I experienced a terror that was nonsensical. I was not afraid of public speaking, I believed fully in the subject matter, and I had learned a great deal that I was eager to share. But there was no mistaking the fear I felt. I prayed for insight, and it took a year for the fear to climb up out of consciousness; even then it came in flashes of insights.

I saw myself as a young Christian woman being led into an arena and then burned at the stake for being part of this heretical religion. I reexperienced everything but the pain. As soon as the smoke started I was out of the body and heard a loving voice gently say, "Now, was that something to be afraid of? All you did was just die." And I got the message. It was just an experience. Life is never destroyed, only experienced in different manifestations and dimensions.

I did a releasing ritual, forgiving everyone involved, and the fear was gone. It was as though it had never existed. The next day I was ready to talk to anyone who would listen.

As there is no time and space in the subconscious, a past life is right now until attachment to it is released. One of the spiritual powers we have is the ability to alter energy regardless of when and where it originated. Anybody or any event can be released. Release translates into freedom.

It is not important to recall past lives. Indeed, it's not even necessary to get entangled in speculations about how it all works. If we look noncritically but honestly at the circumstances around us, if we listen to our bodies and pay attention to our feelings, these things will report accurately what our karma is, collectively and singularly. Unconscious memory may be keeping resentment, self-blame, shame, lack of forgiveness, and so forth in place. Self-responsibility interrupts the pattern, and the inner Light that lives in and through all of us provides all that we need to clean it up—right now.

Disillusionment, Doubt, and Despair

Disillusionment, doubt, and despair—now there's a terrible trio. Or are they more miracles in disguise?

Faith teaches us that there are powerful dynamics at work in any process. Doubt doesn't trust the process and can become very cynical, even doubting the existence of the Divine.

Dismantling our illusions—disillusionment—is one of the goals of spiritual training. The goal isn't really to "find God." The biggest illusion is that we've lost God/Goddess. We can't lose our essential self, which is inseparable from the Beloved, but we can dream ourselves into an illusion of separation. Yet as soon as we long to remember who we are, our illusions are cut away as if by a sharp sword.

❧ Journaling Seeds

1. Review the major disappointments of your life. What did you want and not get? What was the gift in not getting it?

2. What disillusionments have you experienced with people and with beliefs and ideas that you held? What is still "hot" and has emotional charge for you?

3. When did you doubt that God/Goddess was present? In your personal life? In wars, natural disasters, and other large-scale events?

It's great to say, "I have faith that everything will turn out all right." Still, we have to be careful how much we think outcomes must match inner images of how we want things to be, or we'll be disappointed. As is so often the case, duality is the danger, tempting us to say that "turning out all right" equals good and happy, its opposite being bad and miserable. How many times have we heard someone say that a disease, bankruptcy, or job loss was the best thing that ever happened to them?

Many years ago I went through a health crisis that taught me a lasting lesson in faith. I was in the hospital with acute, undiagnosed pain that had gone on for weeks. Although I later understood what was in process, at the time I had no idea if this would go on and on and perhaps even result in death. When your doctors can't find what's wrong, it can challenge your faith in medicine and your own invincibility. Pain grabs your attention, brings you into the moment, and reminds you that the body cannot be left out of the whole process of spiritual evolution.

During this crisis I affirmed one statement over and over in my mind: "There is only God." It ran like internal background music as I talked to others, as I was going through tests, as I came up from deep sleep. I felt that if I submitted to a belief in duality, even acknowledged that there was any other power, I would go over some edge of fear. That constant affirmation sustained me during the crisis. In a few weeks my health returned, in spite of no medical diagnosis. The faith I learned in that experience has supported me through the years.

Despair brings a major crisis in faith. Agonizing to the personality, it seems to penetrate to the very soul. In despair the ego completely bottoms out in helplessness; it cannot fix things anymore. It feels abandoned even by Spirit. "My God, my God, why has thou forsaken me" is a universal cry from a cross. But crosses lead to surrender, and eventually to resurrected life.

In the meantime, and in more detached moments, it is good to remind ourselves and others who may be caught in despair that it is that very sense of helplessness that often allows grace to enter our lives. Psychologist Carl Jung once observed that when we run out of all other possibilities, the universe has to move.

Despair is highly complex and personal, even as it is part of the whole human experience. Its treatment cannot be summarized in a few paragraphs. There are a multitude of things that might help, from food to friends, massages to music. Essentially one deals with despair on the grounds of a belief system and level of awareness.

When one is not in despair, it's wise to build practices that can sustain us if we have a crisis in faith. We might not have strong emotional attachments to doing them, but like a dependable boat, they will carry us through the storm. It's helpful to have one prayer that is really powerful and use it on the hour every hour, minute by minute if necessary. *Japa,* the repetition of a divine name, is also a great support during these times because the name embodies the strength of that being.

Whatever we use, the most important thing is to remember that despair is an experience, not an identity.

Owning Our Ambivalence

Even when we basically have faith in a new possibility, we can get caught up in exhausting ambivalence. We don't want to judge our contradictory impulses. Certainly we've been conditioned for centuries to have them. And we do need to take responsibility for them, because they are not harmless.

We are incredibly powerful beings who channel energy from the universe into whatever we create. The size of the container makes no difference. The universe is totally loving, and its laws are not sentimental. If I am ambivalent, my manifestation will be ambivalent. Every nook and cranny of any idea is filled the way water fills the shape of a pitcher.

Whatever we had faith in yesterday is manifesting today. It will pass, as all things do, so it's wise not to be too overreactive as old beliefs run themselves off. Remember that the physical plane is the last place energy expresses itself. By the time an idea arrives in the physical, it has already had a busy life in the mind and emotions and been shaped and energized by beliefs.

Blind Faith Can't See

Blind faith keeps us outside our own Holy of Holies, for it dooms us to be a follower of the experiences of others. Enlightened ones who have become the Way carry us until we catch on. They provide patterns for us, showing us what peace, love, or stillness looks and feels like. Eventually we merge with those patterns. The purpose is to teach us how to develop our own wings, not to fly on the backs of others.

The Buddha told his disciples not to believe anything he said to them until they tested it in their own lives. Jesus was quoted as saying, "Take up your cross [*your* incarnation and challenges] and follow me [into the Christ consciousness]."

Transcendent beings are not going to magically fix our world without our having to learn our lessons. Expecting to just "go with the flow" is great as long as the flow can get through. A full flow can't get through logjams. Faith does not mean sitting idly on the logs expecting "them" to clear things up. In that case, the only thing that goes with the flow is dead fish.

We can teach techniques to each other, create enhancing rituals and settings, give testimony to our own experiences, reflect for each other, hold the Light, and sometimes heal and catalyze each other. We can even lead another into a brief state of ecstasy. What we cannot do is provide lasting, intimate experience of fusion with the sacred for another.

Any system that demands unquestioning, blind faith probably needs to have its motives questioned. When we have decided to follow a particular way, as we examined in the chapter on knowledge, we do have to submit to prescribed disciplines in order to learn that way. That is a dynamic altogether different from unexamined blind faith, which can lead to exclusivity.

We are like beautiful birds meant to fly freely to the heavens. When we blindly give away our faith, we can become entangled in nets on the ground. Even an aviary is a prison, no matter how comforting it is to have the food delivered.

Exercise: From Fear to Faith

Where we don't trust ourselves, Spirit or the universe shows us an edge in our consciousness. Stretch the edge, and grace will pour in. This is an exercise about deliberately experiencing that stretch.

1. Choose a fear that you are willing to bring into consciousness. Confront yourself with: "I have faith in everything except . . ."

2. Prepare sacred space. Candles, incense, music, chanting, prayer beads, or beloved images all help reinforce intention.

3. Slow down your breathing. Really feel the breath of life circulating. Breathe deep into the abdomen and gently exhale through your mouth. Do this several times.

4. Say a favorite prayer.

5. Invite a Holy Presence to join you. Our inner acolytes are always with us and feel secure with spiritual elders present.

6. Now invite your fear into this sacred and secure setting. Do you know its name? Does it show itself as an image?

Does it have a color? A symbol? A sound? No matter what feelings it invokes, just breathe and stay present.

7. Ask the fear for its history. Don't reject anything. Don't try to evaluate. You may feel that you are making all of it up. That's a natural reaction. You can sort it all out later.

8. Ask the fear if it has a message for you. Listen, don't judge.

9. As you meet the fear, note any sensations or reactions in your body. Later you can do healing bodywork, such as massage, but for now just note where you store your fear.

10. When you feel the information slowing down, move your attention and your breathing to your heart, your center of love. Breathe love into the fear. Feel compassion for it. This part of you has felt separated from God/Goddess and has suffered.

11. Place your hands where the body has held the fear. Talk to the cells: "I love you and I thank you. Now it is time to release fear." Breathe compassion into these cells.

12. Next you must decide "Am I ready to let this fear go? What will be different in my life if I don't carry this fear? What might I give up in my life if I give up this fear?" If you don't feel ready to release the fear, then bless it, knowing you will do so another day. Gradually bring your attention to an alert consciousness and be grateful for whatever part of this fear you have addressed.

13. If you are ready to release the fear, you will have to affirm faith in what you cannot see yet. The following two affirmations will support your intention. The first affirmation is to forgive yourself and all people involved in the fear: "I forgive and release all people, experiences, perceptions, and memories that have held this fear in place, no matter when or how they occurred." The second is to declare faith where there had been fear. For example, if your fear is about lack, you might affirm faith in abundance; if your fear is about abandonment, affirm that the eternal presence is ever with you: "I affirm my faith in . . ."

14. Ask the Holy Being who has been present to bless your affirmations and support release of the fear.

15. You can visually support the release by creating the image of placing the fear in a ring of violet flame. Purple is the color of transmutation, and fire burns at all levels.

16. The last and most important step in this ritual is gratitude, which will release the power within the cells: "I am grateful for the grace that transforms this fear."

17. Breathe with awareness into your body and bring your attention to your physical surroundings.

18. Daily follow-through: Now comes practice, daily seeing yourself free from the fear. Give thanks. Catch yourself when habit would pull you back into it, but always be gentle. Be firm in your intention, but not critical. You may want to do the exercise several times.

Declare something a touchstone, perhaps a small rock or a piece of jewelry. Every time you touch it, affirm your new freedom. Image what that freedom is going to look like as you live it. Make it as real as possible. Write an affirmation that declares the new freedom, and use it like a mantra for at least six weeks. Your consciousness can knock down the block in an instant. Your job is then to reeducate every cell, and that is what creative visualization and affirmation will support.

✿ Twelve Considerations on Faith

1. Faith invites us to dare, to dream, to let go and fly.

2. Faith accepts life cycles that create, sustain, and destroy.

3. Faith lays down the burden of being in control of everything.

4. Faith calls forth the Light from the darkness of self and others.

5. Faith is the declaration of belief in essence, not appearances.

6. Faith *knows*. Hope, a worthy relative, is merely optimistic.

7. Faith requires trust in inner guidance and powers not seen.

8. Faith accepts timing, affirming the unfolding universe.

9. Faith accepts all people and circumstances met on the path.

10. Faith plants seeds without asking for the harvest.

11. Faith trusts the necessity for purification, even when it is painful.

12. Faith will dive into the deepest oceans to gather the pearls.

Prayer

Beloved Creator, here is my heart, fill it with love.
Here is my mind, fill it with truth.
Here is my body, fill it with renewal.
Here is my spirit, fill it with faith.

Affirmation

I walk in faith, knowing that everything that enters my path offers opportunities for growth, clarity, and service.

Quotes

*We never know how high we are till we are called to rise
And then if we are true to plan our statures touch the skies.*

—Emily Dickinson

First you jump off the cliff and you build your wings on the way down.

—Ray Bradbury

Power: Focus for the Flow

✿

The temple bell stops
But the sound keeps coming out of the flowers.
—Bashō

To be alive is to be powerful. Every time we think, feel, or act, we exert power and influence the world.

The very word *power* sends out warning signals, and with good reason. We are acutely aware of the misuse of power on earth. And as we are all carrying karmic memories—personal, ancestral, and collective—most of us are probably wary of ourselves as well as others on this subject.

We've all experienced complex power struggles between men and women, parents and children, siblings, coworkers, neighbors, clans, nations, races, and religions. We bear the scars from jealousy and competition, revenge, resentment, and entitlement—a few of the more familiar spoils of power battles. It's little wonder that power is so negatively charged for us.

I have a colleague who says people would rather be God's instrument of wisdom or love than the instrument of power. The idea of *deliberately* stepping into a powerful role, taking a stand, or speaking a truth can bring up deep ambivalence and a lot of questions.

What is the difference between earth power and spiritual power? Does power come from above or is it created here? Or is it, once again, both? These are not easy questions for anyone, but disciples must address them, for power is both resource and temptation, and avoiding either will compromise intention.

Power in the World

Master teachers around the world concur with the warning Meher Baba gave his students that the higher stages of consciousness bring greater power. One of his devotees quotes Baba as saying, "The object is to get through that one without using the power for anything except the good of others; then you are home free."

The question of whether one shouldn't or wouldn't misuse a position of power is rhetorical until one has the actual opportunity. Then comes choice: "I will use this to glorify myself," or "I'll walk away," or "I'll accept this power and use it to serve the world."

As we look around our world today, sometimes it still seems as if we are in the grip of negative power. We also see old models of reality that are still dominant during this time of transition.

I am reminded of a large, green-leafed oak tree that mysteriously fell in my yard. On the outside it had seemed to be conducting tree business as usual. When it suddenly fell, one could see the decay that had weakened it from within. No one had known it was dying. When it no longer had the inner strength to hold its position, a moderately high wind toppled it over. We have systems that are like that tree, dying from within as a result of decay. And in time they will topple.

Already many conscious people are moving into positions of authority that will facilitate the new growth. The assistant is now becoming the director; the editor is becoming the publisher; the manager moves into the presidency. Visionaries are sitting on city councils and boards of directors, writing books, hanging new images in galleries, making films, going online, giving interviews. They are in ad agencies and teaching kindergarten.

Of equal importance, they are at work in local neighborhoods helping to resolve social problems and redefine the meaning of community and responsibility. They are giving life to new visions, one situation after another, carefully and thoroughly. And they are doing it worldwide. To bring wholeness into a wounded world takes many skills and resources, but all of them require a power that is both gentle and persistent.

No matter what role we're playing, all of us can refuse to give away our power. Choosing the ideas we will energize, we can use our power in every area of life, from speaking out to quietly modeling a new way of relating, one that builds bridges between people instead of perpetuating age-old power struggles.

Young people are questioning the use of power in the systems they will soon have to operate. Many have incarnated to bring dreams of a new vision into actualization, and they need confirmation and support of their instincts and passions.

This is a challenge for their parents and mentors. Of course we want our children to do well, but what does that mean? Money? Status? How-to manuals for surviving in a divided world through self-interest are not going to help them. (When did mere self-interest ever make any of *us* happy, anyway?)

The most practical guidebooks will tell the truth. Page one: The earth is not a resource to be conquered and used by the winners; it is a sacred trust. We are all in this together. You, dear child, are an integral part of that whole, here by intention to contribute your talents, thoughts, and energy. Thanks for coming. How can we support your soul purpose?

Evelyn is a CEO who challenged some young people to think carefully about the power they were soon to have. Asked to speak to students at an Ivy League university, she asked them to look at the concept of "right livelihood" (contribution to the whole without harm to any). "Who will benefit from your educations?" she asked. "Yourselves and your children, certainly. How about the neighbors' children? What color children? American children? The world's children? Where would you draw the line with your assets, your votes, your influence?"

Now her "day job" is to be a CEO. Imagine the seeds she may have planted, watered, or fertilized that day, not to mention the ones she nurtures in the daily rough-and-tumble of business simply by being awake and aware of the opportunities to use power to influence positively.

❈ Journaling Seeds

1. When do you feel powerful? Powerless?

2. What kind of power attracts you? Repels you?

3. What are symbols of power to you?

4. How was power used in your family?

5. How has power been acted out in intimate relationships?

Power as Energy

We live in an endless supply of energy that moves around, through, and between every molecule in the universe. It will fill any size container we bring to it—tiny thimbles, cups, leaking buckets, or pipelines. Consciousness is our vessel, and it collects this powerful energy to use at will. The energy itself is neither good nor bad; it simply is. It is desire that creates matrices of energy in the eternal flow and draws energy to itself.

Power is energy coalesced around intention and then focused with the mind and action. There's not much one can't accomplish in our familiar three dimensions—for good or bad—if one persists in holding the thought and intention long enough.

Imagine that universal energy flows into you as naturally as a waterfall into a riverbed. The water flows freely wherever the riverbed is clear, and it nurtures everything it touches as it journeys to the sea. Yet without definite direction it can be dissipated: it can flood and destroy if it's out of control, or stagnate if it's caught in pools.

Our personal work is to remove the obstructions while we define and maintain the riverbed. The power from the waterfall flows naturally and is never withheld. We can't create that power, but we have the capability to use it creatively or to pollute it. We have the awesome, sometimes frightening privilege of choosing what to do with it, and then facing the consequences of our choices.

The more we purify ourselves, the more energy we can handle and direct without becoming overwhelmed or losing control. This is especially important for disciples who usually open themselves to large amounts of energy to empower their work. To be careless about preparing oneself is risky—a little like running a nuclear power plant and hoping it doesn't have any leaks. The energy will empower *whatever* is in its path. Thus big angels, if blind to their shadows, can have big devils.

Power for Healing

There are dozens of excellent systems for channeling this ceaseless flow into healing. From the most basic techniques of laying on of hands to ones that require advanced training, all recognize that it is *natural* for humans to channel energy through their bodies into the world. Effectiveness depends on the clarity of the consciousness through which it comes.

When a person is in Divine alignment, she or he generates the most incredible power. A highly attuned person often doesn't have to do or say anything—only be present. The power and light simply pour out of them. People want to connect with their aura or touch the hem of their garment. Miracles seem to follow such a person around.

As we clear ourselves of dissonance and distortion, we channel purer and purer energy, and then we become purer because we love enough to offer ourselves as channels for healing. The wounded become healers, and then the healers help the wounded. It's a good system, yes?

"Release for constructive purposes the power you already have, and more will come," said Paramahansa Yogananda, echoing the teachings of the Christ: "To him that has, much will be given." We just have to be willing channels.

The Power of Prayer

Prayer is a powerful and mysterious force. Through it we are reconnected, reminded, and renewed. In prayer we can be fervently active or quietly receptive, pouring out our hearts to the Beloved or quietly listening for Its voice.

Ideally we can "pray without ceasing," meaning we maintain a moment-by-moment awareness of the sacred, regardless of what we are doing. Then our lives truly are prayers. In religious communities of several traditions as much emphasis is placed on maintaining as much prayerful awareness while eating, walking, or tending the garden as on praying in a sanctuary.

Still, most of us need to slow down the mind and breath and reactivate our remembrance of who we are and why we are here. In remembering, the background becomes the foreground, and the act of deliberately remembering (praying) gathers diffuse knowing into concentrated power and directs it like a laser.

Prayer looks beyond what is already manifested on the physical plane. Einstein once remarked that a problem cannot be resolved at the level on which it occurred. Prayer creates receptivity to solutions and possibilities beyond the ego's perception.

Many scientific experiments in prayer support what spiritual practitioners also know: that space and time provide no limits once you leave physical consciousness. You can touch anyone, anywhere, anytime with prayer. Tests have even put the target for prayers inside a Faraday cage lined with lead, which blocks all known electromagnetic energy, and the prayers still get through and affect the target.

We pray, close or far, and it works. Then, remembering that we are working toward resolving the hold of dualism, we also heed the Russian proverb "Pray to God and row for shore."

Our prayers are inseparable from our understanding of our relationship with the Divine. In ancient Hawaii, for example, a kahuna (medicine person) could not attain that position in the community unless she or he could manifest change through prayer. Their prayers took days to prepare: designing the prayer, examining all possible consequences, clearing the mind, and then building energy with the breath to support the prayer.

When Christians first came to Hawaii, the natives initially thought these white people must be very powerful because they prayed and prayed. But when there were no results the Hawaiians could see, they concluded that Christians didn't know how to pray. The white conquerors saw the Hawaiians' religion as heathen. So in order to protect their knowledge of effective prayer, the kahunas buried the information so deep in the language that it was not decoded until this century.

There are as many ways to pray as there are beliefs, from painting sacred markings on the body and singing in praise or lamentation to dancing in sacred circles. Ultimately it is the intention that shapes the prayer. Whenever I am conscious of the sacred, whether I'm baking bread, painting a landscape, or listening to a lonely person, that is my prayer.

The following are ways of praying that are universally recognized as effective. All of them express gratitude.

• *Invocation* prays to one who embodies the sacred for intervention and blessing. As we already live in the minds of Bodhisattvas, saints, masters, and all other ascended beings, through invocation we are calling our attention to their constant presence. Examples: "St. Michael, I pray that my daughter be in your protection throughout her trip"; "Beloved Kuan Yin, compassionate Bodhisattva, we pray that you relieve the suffering of the refugees." Upon finishing an invocation, affirm: "I am grateful."

• *Evocation* is the prayer that calls forth the Light in oneself or another. When the Light that is inherent in all life is released, the highest intentions can be fulfilled. Conscious people often activate the sacred potential in those around them because they recognize and thus evoke the Light that is in all life. Examples: "I am a being of Light, son [daughter] of the Mother-Father-God"; "Karen is a being of Light, daughter of the Mother-Father-God." Upon finishing an evocation, affirm: "I am grateful."

• *Japa,* a Sanskrit term for the chanting of the name of a Holy Being, is a universal practice, as it is recognized in all religions that there is enormous power in the name of an enlightened being. In repeating the name over and over, one seeks alignment with the energy of the Being. Examples: (specific) "Jesus," "Tara," "Babaji"; (archetypal) "Holy Mother," "Divine Father." Upon finishing a round of *japa,* affirm: "I am grateful."

• *Mantras* are prayers that repeat a sacred sound, chant, phrase, or affirmation. Mantras reprogram negatives by the steady reinforcement of positives. A truth we aspire to (pray for) is repeated until we become it. Examples: *"Om mani padme hum"* (Hindu), the jewel in the crown of the lotus; *"La illaha el Allah hu"*

(Moslem), there is only one God. Upon finishing a round of mantras, affirm: "I am grateful."

• *Prayer beads* are used to focus attention, to affirm, or to reinforce *japa* or a mantra. While rosaries and *mala* beads are traditional, making prayer beads for oneself is very powerful, especially if a prayer is said repeatedly while the beads are strung. It is further empowered by choosing stones for the energy they carry, for example, using amethysts to support the breaking of addictions or lapis lazuli to support intuitive insight. Examples: "Blessings upon all life on earth"; "My body is balanced and healthy." Upon finishing a prayer using beads, affirm: "I am grateful."

• *Nondirected prayer* simply prays for the Highest Good for oneself, another, or a situation. It does not specify what that should be. This form of prayer holds a belief in the innate intelligence that is present in all life and therefore energizes the Highest Good. Examples: "May that which is for the Highest Good of all concerned surround and fill this situation"; "Everything in Donald's life is in Divine order." After a nondirected prayer, affirm: "I am grateful."

• *Visualization* is an ancient method of directed prayer that is now used to support everything from cancer therapy to better golf scores. Effectiveness is linked to the depth of conviction and the ability to hold an unwavering, clear thought. Muddled, vague, or changing images produce ambiguous results. Visualization works on the principle that energy will gather around powerful thought forms, which then serve as a blueprint for the physical plane. Examples: while holding an image of our earth as healthy and balanced, "I see Light energizing all life on the earth"; holding an image of a child laughing and running through a meadow, "Kristie's healing is now in process." Upon finishing a session of visualization, affirm: "I am grateful."

Ultimately, maybe the child who simply prayed the alphabet had it right. She said that God already knew what she wanted anyway, so she just repeated the letters.

When Prayers Don't Seem to Work

None of us fully understands why some prayers seem to be answered while others seem to remain unanswered. We don't know all the dynamics at work in any situation. We are like those who are sewing a dream quilt but are assigned to one corner, blind to the total pattern.

There are volumes written in testimony to the power of prayer as well as treatises of despair when the gods seem to turn a deaf ear. In some of the death camps of the Holocaust, people held trials and found God guilty of breaking the Covenant. Others deepened their faith in the fires of that hell.

In his confrontational book *Shadows of Auschwitz*, Christian writer Harry James Cargas says that Jews have asked and continue to ask, "Where was God at Auschwitz?" One can also ask, "Where was the Divine during the Inquisition? During the invasion of Tibet? Where was It during the slave trade and the women's holocaust and all the terrors around the world through time? Indeed, where is the Divine in Kosovo? Africa? Northern Ireland?" Can we ever find an answer to such a question?

Cargas writes, "Many of us have been taught to judge relevance by asking: what is this in the light of eternity? For a time let us put it this way: what is this in the light of the flames of Auschwitz *when humanity ratified hell*" [my italics].

That's it, isn't it? We are given the choice. We pray to a loving universe that answers us with unbounded power, and we choose what to ratify with that power. *We* are the answer to each other's prayers. Until we ratify our oneness, many of us will continue to be sacrificed on behalf of all of us.

As disciples, we wonder with poet Lawrence Ferlinghetti, in this excerpt from his poem "A Buddha in the Woodpile":

If there had been only
one Buddhist in the woodpile
in Waco Texas
to teach us how to sit still
one saffron Buddhist in the back rooms
just one Tibetan lama
just one Taoist
just one Zen
just one Thomas Merton Trappist
just one saint in the wilderness
of Waco USA
If there had been only one
calm little Gandhi
in a white sheet or suit
one not-so-silent partner
who at the last moment shouted Wait

As prayer becomes a staple in their daily diet, disciples do learn to surrender the need to dictate terms to the Divine. Certainly the cry "Just make it all go away" is a natural prayer born of urgency, confusion, fear, and resistance.

Yet there are countless reasons why things are as they are. People are evolving, learning to master limitations, make sacrifices, conquer fears, learn compassion. Karmic issues can get settled because unrelenting circumstances demand attention, and once again we have the opportunity to confront and master an old inner enemy. Many birth new awarenesses through the pain. How many of us can honestly say, "I learned my greatest lessons while I was rich and healthy and emotionally balanced"?

Even another's death is tragic only in perception. People can leave the body at any age as soon as they have accomplished what they came to do. Naturally we grieve the loss, and we might feel abandoned as well as reminded of our own vulnerability.

Still, no prayer uttered for anyone is ever lost. Our prayers might enable her or him to die peacefully rather than get physically well, therein supporting a healing far more important than the physical body. It might be used to release a blockage trapped in memory, bringing about a healing crisis so that the issue can be resolved. Nevertheless, seen or unseen, the prayer *is* answered.

When prayers don't seem to relieve another's suffering, I refuse to numb myself with platitudes. Rather, I pray to understand; sometimes that only leads to a peaceful silence of acceptance. Sometimes an insight comes that so stretches my mind, asking why becomes a pointless question.

I had a vision once of tears being shed in prayer for the human condition. The tears were then collected and offered to the Divine, who blessed the tears and returned them in the form of living water to soothe the very conditions that caused the tears.

Another time I saw in a meditation our prayers for peace disappear like drops of water into a desert. And before I could be discouraged in the face of such prophecy, the prayers met and fused with similar prayers, like molecules bonding. These then attracted similar prayers from another and then another and another, until together we created an oasis in the desert

The Power of Words

Jesus' disciple John wrote, "In the beginning was the Word," the sound that permeates the universe and from which all life is created. The Word is the great breath of the Divine, the *hu* of Eckankar and Sufism, the *om* of Hinduism, the powerful force that shapes energy.

Most of us have been taught very little about the power of words. Once we are attuned to hearing what is being said over and over, we start to really hear how we strengthen the bars of our own prison by the incredible lies about reality that we regularly repeat. In many ways our words are our prayers, because they are our decrees.

Sufis tell us our words should pass through three gates before we speak them: Are these words true, are they necessary, and are they kind?

There is a commanding power in the voice of one who speaks from the integration of soul and ego. The story of Jesus bringing Lazarus back from the dead illustrates this point. Upon arriving at the home of his friend Lazarus for a visit, Jesus learned that he had been buried for several days. Jesus entered Lazarus' tomb and called him back to life. When the universal Christ consciousness is alive in us, it calls forth that which appears to be dead in ourselves and others. "Come forth," it commands. "Come out of the sleep of death. Wake up." It doesn't qualify or justify. The legend doesn't teach "If this is a good time for you, Lazarus, perhaps you would like to wake up." No, it's "Wake up!"

Blessings Are Empowered Words

To bless is to empower. I am not using the term *blessing* as a synonym for *approval*. Rather, I mean it as a decree that calls forth the good inherent in people and situations. Blessings bestow grace upon all things they name. No matter who or what is troubling us, we always have the power to bless it.

Bless the house you live in, and it is filled with grace. Bless the food you eat, the computer you work on, the car you drive, the clothes you wear, the medicine you take, and everyone you meet. All of it responds, right down to the smallest atom.

I learned to use a computer while I was writing my first book. I often became so frustrated that I was all but sure a personal enemy lived in that machine. I finally realized that I was complicating "our" cooperation with my resistant attitude and began to think of it with appreciation. Lo and behold, it changed.

Yes, I know, I also learned more about its technical nature. It's probably not a bad metaphor for understanding why a little more insight into the way people (and things) function changes our relationship to them. In any case, my new computer, Angelique, and I are good buddies. Her complexity is one more way God/ Goddess has of keeping me humble. Fortunately she—and the Divine—are very patient.

To Bless Self and Others

1. Sitting straight, take several long, slow breaths that go deep into the lower abdomen. Watch yourself breathe.
2. With the next few breaths, on the inhale perceive yourself breathing in and accepting the grace of the universe and then consciously directing its Light, power, and love through all of your body's organs and systems one at a time: "I bless my respiratory system," "I bless my eyes," and so on.
3. Be aware of the grace moving through all your subtle bodies, blessing your feelings and your thoughts. Even hostile emotions that you want to release are given up more gently with the blessing of your benevolent Self: "I bless my feelings," "I bless my thoughts."
4. Now you are going to be an instrument of blessing for others. On the inhale take in the power of light and universal love. On the exhale focus the flow of this power out of yourself into the world, starting with your home, family, neighborhood, city, state, country, and world.

Be aware that you have practiced a power that is your birthright: the ability to be a conscious instrument of blessing. And you didn't have to manipulate, control, earn, deserve, or master complicated skills. You just had to breathe and bless. Trusting in the authority of words, remind yourself every day: "What I curse I bind to me. What am I cursing? What I bless, I release. What am I blessing?"

The Power of Humility

Once a rabbi threw himself on his knees before the Ark of the Covenant, which held the sacred scrolls of the Torah in the synagogue. "Oh, Lord," he cried, "I'm not worthy, I'm not worthy."

The cantor followed his lead, also throwing himself on his knees before the Ark with a loud cry: "Oh, I'm not worthy, I'm not worthy."

This whole scene was observed by the janitor, who ran down the aisle of the sanctuary crying with great passion, "I'm not worthy, I'm not worthy."

At which the rabbi turned to the cantor and said, "Just look who thinks he is not worthy."

Disciples claim the power, and that claim is never arrogant. The word *arrogant* originates from Latin and means "to claim for oneself." An awakened disciple no longer has such an illusion of ownership. Such a person knows very well where the power originates—in Spirit.

To accept power from the universe requires humility, not perfection. Most of us struggle with readiness, and few of us feel ready or worthy. Our sense of unworthiness is born, bred, and nourished in the personality, not in the soul. Our souls are made in the image of God. How could we not be worthy?

To "let go and let God," we have to give up our insistence on limitations. This calls for true humility and not the caricature of humility that grows out of low self-esteem. Humility is the courage to say nothing more than "Here I am, use me."

When we are in that state of surrender, the power of Spirit moves through us effortlessly. Through imagined guilt, shame, blame, and fear, we can slam shut our inner doors as firmly as a guard in a maximum-security prison. Whenever I am aware that I'm putting limits on the power because I'm not feeling adequate, I take my attention from myself to the need at hand. What is the gift that God would bring to this person or situation at this moment? This shifts the focus away from self-judging, which cuts off the flow of power. Then I ask to be used for the Highest Good. The next step is to consciously breathe through the heart center to activate unconditional love.

I have recommended this approach to many people who are beginning to give lectures and are facing stage fright, for example. Whether we are presenting to members of a board, the PTA meeting, or an auditorium full of people, the principles are the same. An audience is not a reality in itself. They are just people, one plus one plus one. They are not the jurors and judges of our fantasies. In any situation, even before an "audience" of one, when attention moves from "How am I doing?" to "How can I bring a gift to these people or this person?" the flow shifts to an outward direction and is then very powerful.

The way to prepare ourselves for any assignment is to relate to every person and situation in front of us as if they were the most important business of the universe. Humility gives up the hierarchical classifications.

True humility allows us to be empty enough to be filled. It does not bow and scrape before human conceits. However, it does bow to the sacred in all life. It carries a dignity that pomposity cannot imitate.

I have been blessed to be in the presence of that kind of true dignity, and it is extremely powerful. Ten years after I was taken under the wing of the healer who had led me through the early stages of my work, he walked into a class I was teaching at a conference and for two hours took notes like a schoolboy.

Walking with him after class, I expressed my amazement. He stopped, made me look in his eyes, and said, "No, the time has come for me to sit at your feet." What an incredible teaching example of humility. By his modeling, he continued to teach me, reminded me that good teachers know that their students become the teachers.

Exercise: Watching Your Words

One way to increase awareness of the power of words is to set aside one single day dedicated to watching your words honestly, without either censoring or judging yourself.

- Notice how we carelessly reinforce negatives about ourselves or others: "I'm really afraid of . . . ," "I'm too shy [or fat, or uneducated]," "She can't . . . ," "He shouldn't . . ."
- Notice how we reinforce negatives about changing systems with variations of "You can't fight city hall" or "It's the way it's always been. It will never change."
- Look at the words that express your "duty demons" and exaggerated obligations, words that deny present-moment pleasures: "I should be . . . ," "I ought to . . ."
- Observe words that are withheld in order to punish others: "He wants me to say 'I forgive you,' but let him stew awhile."
- Observe words that are withheld because of fear of the judgments of others: "What will *they* say if I disagree or draw a boundary?"
- Also observe when words are withheld out of wisdom, noting to yourself that is what you are doing: "There is extreme bias here, so I'll not speak."
- Notice how family and cultural myths are reinforced by constantly being retold: "The women in our family have always been matriarchs," "My country [or religion or political group] right or wrong." Then there is the all-purpose "It's just human nature."
- Pay attention to the way we polarize with words: "Men are like that," "Politicians can't be trusted." Note the subtle divisive energy that can gather around words such as *feminist, third world,* or *minority.*

Reeducating the Words

The next step in word awareness is to take increasing responsibility for the words you choose to speak, moment by moment, asking yourself:

- Do you really want to say this? Do you understand what your motive is?
- How can you restate a necessary discipline or disagreement in a nonthreatening way?
- How can you give yourself noncritical, positive words that will benefit your search for self-improvement? Can you rephrase your self-observations so they are not loaded with either self-denial or self-criticism?
- Before you "blow," can you take a few deep breaths and declare an intention to state your case without cruelty or carelessness?
- Before gossiping, can you stop and ask yourself if you really want to participate in this? If you do, why? What's the reward?
- Are you giving away your power to affect the whole by using words that are pessimistic about the planet? Can you find a vocabulary that warns, implores, and points out but is not filled with "ain't it awful" and powerlessness?

Power in the Gray Zones

We are drawn like magnets to anything that holds a lot of energy: places, people with money, position, or celebrity. This is true also of what we perceive as spiritual power. People with earthly power carry such an aura of glamour, it can be hard to see the real person. Sometimes just the names, such as Kennedy or Rockefeller, elicit strong emotional reactions.

Periodically the archetype of one who chose to betray the trust of power materializes in front of us. We can then see once again what happens when power goes awry. Few of us will forget the images of Waco, Texas, the jungles of Guyana, the subways in Japan that were poisoned by sarin gas on orders of a cult's guru, or the mass suicide in Los Angeles of the followers of a messianic cult leader.

Power has also long been recognized as an aphrodisiac. The guru, teacher, priest, therapist, or doctor who misuses his or her power through sexual involvement with students is a cliché. Perhaps these abusers of power started with good intentions. But they haven't cleaned up their shadows.

We are reminded again that there is a direct path to the Source but no shortcuts. As power is neither good nor bad, it is always our choice of how to use it that determines its effect. And we choose in every moment.

Fifteen Minutes of Temptation

Fame, that elusive siren that calls the ego, can be used well by Spirit for its purposes. Shirley MacLaine once said that she thought she had become famous in order to have a podium for transmitting spiritual messages. Many other famous people are positioned for their ability to positively influence others, certainly not for personal glory. Yet many famous people have to walk the edge of the abyss. Take oneself too seriously from an ego level, and it's into the pit. Fame is not an easy choice for a soul to make, contrary to the opinion of those who lust after it.

One doesn't have to be internationally known in order to deal with the power of fame. Local celebrity or prominence in any field can do it. Long before any of us can raise the dead, we can raise a lot of money, applause, or influence. Those opportunities for service often bring visibility, sometimes admiration. Whether one's fame is worldwide or just means that one has the most recognized name in the village, the temptation to misuse power can be the same.

Alan was a humanitarian who became very admired for his good work in his local community. When I asked him how he handled all the visibility, he said, "I treat it as an ongoing seduction." I liked his expression because admiration is not a one-time challenge. It can be addictive and persistent.

One of the better truisms I've heard on fame came from an experienced workshop teacher. She and I tried to comfort a third, inexperienced teacher who was upset because she had had very little attendance at her inaugural lecture. The older woman said to her, "I learned a long time ago that if there are too many hosannas at the beginning of the week, there's going to be a crucifixion before the week is out."

A well-known writer in Europe sent me a letter concerning her feelings about the pedestals people put her on: "Dangerous power to me is the unconscious power that other people give you, but I try my best not to be trapped. To remain in touch with your limits and your shadows and with the complexity of your paradoxes is an excellent antidote to a power complex."

Pedestals are questionable perches for anyone. As one teacher wisely said, "I don't want anyone putting me on any pedestals. If they do, they'll have their eyes right on my clay feet!"

Not only are all of us human, but we carry out our assignments in an imperfect world amidst challenging circumstances. Disciples have to weed out their own desires to sit on a pedestal as well as remaining nonreactive to those who would put them on one—or pull them down from one.

Ultimately, the ideal is to respond neither to praise nor blame. As it was put rather bluntly by one disciple, "If I say to you, 'Oh, you are so wonderful,' and you buy it, tomorrow if I say, 'You stink,' then you have to buy that, too."

The point is made more poetically in a story about Lalla, the fourteenth-century Indian mystic. Not surprisingly, she was sometimes ridiculed. One day she tied two cloths of equal lengths to her shoulders and made a knot in one cloth when she was respected, in the other when she was disrespected. At the end of the day she had the cloths weighed; they were the same.

"Fame," Lalla said, "is water carried in a basket."

Everyone Is a Chosen One

Considering ourselves to be a "chosen one" is another variation on the fame trap. The ego is shameless; it will usurp anything for itself, including a sense of spiritual mission. Any unresolved need to be Mommy and Daddy's favorite child can be turned into imagining we are God/Goddess's favorites. We are *all* here on assignments, and we're all favorite children in the same family. Some know it; some don't. When one is really awake, it's clear that those who are still unaware are merely asleep, not inferior.

Many years ago I attended a lecture by a very famous healer who has now left the body. It was a recital of her accomplishments. I was beginning to get impatient when the man next to me, himself a well-known healer, laughed quietly and said, "That whole generation of healers caught it from all sides. Scientists and doctors both ridiculed them. The church folks thought they were working for the devil. Everyone else was skeptical. If they didn't have enormous egos, they would have collapsed under the criticism."

I immediately shifted my perception into an even deeper respect for the role she and other pioneers from her time had played. I felt compassion for her need to prove herself to a younger audience who, thanks to the efforts of her generation, had a more inviting ground for their work.

This was also a good object lesson in not confusing the message with the messenger. We are all expressing our place in the larger plan according to our understanding and capabilities, and we are tempered by the times in which we live.

We need to be tolerant with each other as we learn to handle all the variations of power we might encounter in fulfilling our missions. We may need to counsel each other occasionally on excesses, but we can do that with humor, patience, and gentle suggestion, and always with compassion for our humanness.

❧ Journaling Seeds

1. How do you know the difference between fulfilling a mission and being a "chosen one"?

2. What do you consider to be "enough"—enough money, popularity, accomplishments, and so forth?

3. How do you feel about money and service?

4. What kind of people do you put on or off pedestals? Have you examined why you do either?

Money: Mindful or Just Mine?

Once there was a sannyasi *who was sitting under a tree outside of town when a robber demanded that he give him the diamond he'd heard that the man had. The mendicant monk said, "Do you mean this stone I found a few days ago? Here, you may have it."*

The robber grabbed the diamond, ran away, and returned the next day, having spent a very disturbing night with himself. He pleaded with the sannyasi *to give him the wealth that made it possible for him to give up the diamond so easily.*

We might make other choices if we were in that setting, but what could be more powerful than having that degree of freedom from attachment? Is there any power on earth that most of us have more ambivalence around than money?

Throughout history humanity has used anything it valued as

currency, from feathers and beads to stones, shells, and animal teeth. Sometimes they've doubled as amulets, and always they were symbols of our values. Sometimes they've been no more subtle than the entrance to a house in Pompeii that pictured a man weighing his penis on a scale in which the weights were gold coins.

The uneasy history of money and spirit puts many disciples on guard. What position are we to take about money? It's clear that money is powerful in the material world; it's muddier in the life of the spirit. As with all aspects of our discipleship, layers of attitudes often have to be peeled away to discover the real questions: "Am I being punished by not having it? Blessed if I do? Do I feel guilty or uncomfortable either way?"

Vows of poverty are often required from those who pursue their spirituality in the religious life. Meantime, the rest of us are busy acquiring, spending, and protecting the currency that we rarely see in anything but symbolic form. Or, on the other side of the coin, we are dealing with it reluctantly, fearful it will somehow pollute our spiritual quest.

We have inherited a long history of strong traditions that separate money and spirituality. Perhaps we need to question why we are so dualistic about money. Why do we think the Divine is in everything *but* money? What are we afraid of? Is there any self-deception in assuming that we are somehow more spiritual if we don't handle money? Why is teaching spiritual principles more "spiritual" than lovingly teaching first grade, farming, or writing songs?

Possibly many disciples today have been trained in earlier lifetimes in monasteries and convents, ashrams, mystery schools, and temples where vows of poverty were required. Those memories can still be influencing us. (Note: At the close of the chapter on the will there is an exercise for releasing vows of poverty taken in any lifetime.)

The minting of money goes back thousands of years to the Sumerian city-states. The word *money* comes from the first mints in the temples of Juno Moneta in Rome. Only priests were allowed to make coins, because they said that the gods imprinted their power into the metal. Then the priests began selling favors and penances. Selling forgiveness and prayers of intervention with the gods has surely begotten some of the darkest progenies of the mating of money and religion.

Is that our great fear—are we afraid of the temptations?

Money as False Identity

There is, of course, nothing inherently good or bad in money. Like anything else, it can be used in service or be self-serving. Money is a great testing: How does one use it and not get caught by it?

Wealth can offer incredible opportunities for spiritual growth through the wise stewardship of resources. Untold good is done in the world through the generosity of those who share their material abundance.

Having a lot of money never protects anyone from personal challenges, even as we must admit, as Plato once said, that "the rich have such condolences." There is always the risk that wealth can insulate us and perpetuate an illusion of entitlement, safety, and permanence, creating distance from unpleasantness, stroking the ego, and dulling our longing for spiritual clarity.

Any of us can get caught in those traps no matter how much we have or don't have. As wealth is always a relative thing—in some cultures it depends on how many cows or goats we have—all of us have to examine the use of the resources that pass through our lives. It's the consciousness, not the amount, we must monitor.

Even learning how to give it away consciously is a question

disciples will face. The Hebrew Talmud teaches three levels of charity. The highest way to give is to give work so that people can earn for themselves. The second highest way is giving anonymously, and the third is to give and expect admiration and acknowledgment in return.

A business consultant told me that the man who started the Hard Rock Cafe sold it for $140 million, went to India, and built and staffed a high-tech hospital complex for $70 million. His guru told him to go out and create another chain of jazzy restaurants, make another couple of hundred million dollars, and give half of that to a charitable cause.

The movie *Brother Sun, Sister Moon* is about St. Francis of Assisi, who left his prosperous family to live in voluntary poverty and follow a life of spiritual service. As the story unfolds, St. Francis has an audience with the Pope. There is a poignant moment in the film when the Pope kisses St. Francis' feet, blesses him, and then slowly backs off to resume his own role, which is burdened with ceremony and riches. It is a sad commentary, with no words needed. St. Francis is clearly freer than the Pope—one could even say richer—and yet the Pope has his own role to play in the human drama. Perhaps he even tolerates the riches in order to play his part.

In sacred stories around the world there are wealthy disciples as well as those who are poor by choice. The Hebrew Job was identified as the richest man in the East. Vimalakirti was an extremely wealthy disciple of the Buddha. Layman Pany was a wealthy and well-known Zen master who sank all his possessions so that others wouldn't be attached to them.

It's the degree of detachment and nonidentification with the money that matters, whether there is a lot of money or a little. The trap is not money per se. The trap is money as identity, and it's a hard one to escape once we are caught in it.

There was a master who had many wealthy students as well as

poor ones. She told them it was hard for a rich person to become enlightened but possible "when the money has the effect on the heart that the bamboo's shadow has on the courtyard,"—that is, it does not disturb a single bit of dust.

When Is There Enough?

The actual monetary figure that represents "enough" varies, and few of us actually believe we've arrived at it. It is an evaluation we must make ourselves—society will not help. The media and the Joneses will surely remind us that there is never enough.

Occasionally one hears of a single individual who has resisted societal pressure and found "enough." In 1994 it was reported that Oseola McCarty, then an eighty-seven-year-old African-American woman from Mississippi who had never made much money in her life, had been saving since she was eleven years old and had given $150,000 to a university for scholarships.

A doctor told me that he and his wife decided to make their lifestyle more congruent with their values, starting with redefining what is enough: "I used to think it had to be $150,000; now maybe $30,000 is enough." He said he was learning that only some of his abundance comes in the form of money; sometimes it arrives in a meal or a gift. "So I love the issue of money now. It takes me to a new edge in my exploration, another place to be open and aware."

In their influential book *Your Money or Your Life*, Joe Dominguez and Vicki Robin suggest viewing money as an exchange for our life energy. We give up a great deal of life energy to own a car or a house. When I give up so much life energy that I am no longer enjoying my life, then perhaps my possessions cost too much, and no amount of money can compensate for that.

Conscious Consuming

Mindfulness with money has many faces, including buying and investing. Susan inherited a large sum of money and has worked closely with a financial advisor, who helps her avoid investing in exploitative companies. She acknowledges that the profits are lower with the companies that don't exploit, and she feels this constitutes right action with her money. Cruelties and exploitation can be tidied up by the time they reach annual reports. If we invest in companies that do exploit, then we're part of the problem.

As our old paradigm continues to shift, we are seeing more and more companies proving the truism echoed in both the Quaker tradition and Buddhism, that one can "do well by doing good." These companies are providing new models for what is possible— and being profitable in the process. Generally they are incorporating practices that support ecological, gender, community, and racial balance. The more we support these companies and their products, the stronger the challenge will be to businesses that only value the bottom line, perceiving people and the environment as expendable to avoid reduced profits.

Whether it's personal or business, it takes a great deal of caring and attention to put your money where your mouth is. To earn, spend, and invest money unconsciously is easy in our culture. We do not have as many models for money mindfulness and companies that not only tithe and recycle but know when to say "enough" and refuse to buy from producers who exploit people, land, and other species.

Whenever I feel impatience with having to be so deliberate, I ask myself: "If I am not conscious with *all* of the resources I have in my present circumstances, why do I think the universe should give me responsibility for more?"

Exercise: *Abundant* and *Detached*

- Spend an afternoon observing and contemplating the abundance, generosity, and renewal of nature. What can this teach about your nature?

- Pay your bills consciously. Light a candle, express gratitude. Bless each bill you can pay—and those you can't. Include the phrase "thank you" on check endorsements.

- Consider time and talent as well as money when you tithe. Where would you like to put at least 10 percent of each?

- Give more than 10 percent—and don't tell anyone.

- Place an empty bowl or cup on an altar or desk, reminding yourself that your needs will be filled.

- Don't give in to dualistic thinking. Instead affirm: "God/Goddess is present in all of my resources."

- Give away something you really love as an exercise in nonattachment.

- Make random acts of kindness a daily habit.

- Every night offer all your resources to Spirit: "I give thanks to the Source of all my blessings, and I offer them to be used for the Highest Good."

- Every night release your anxieties about temporary lack by placing them on an altar and affirming the truth behind appearances: "I affirm that everything in my life is guided by my Highest Self, and for this remembrance I give thanks."

❧ Twelve Considerations on Power

1. Power is in the present moment, here and now.

2. Vision is concretized through persistent harnessing of power.

3. True power does no harm to self, other people, or other species.

4. Managing power well is part of spiritual craftsmanship.

5. Money, position, fame, and talent are resources, not identities.

6. Spiritual power seeks to uplift others, not to be put above them.

7. Both body and psyche have to be strong to handle power.

8. Power is in choosing to act, not react.

9. Powerful world service begins with full responsibility for self.

10. Spirit power serves, then detaches from results.

11. Words are decrees. Bless and release; curse and bind.

12. The chalice emptied into the world is endlessly refilled.

Affirmation

I am a child of the universe and accept the privileges and responsibilities of being an instrument through which the Plan is manifested on earth. May my words, thoughts, intentions, and actions be empowered by the Divine for the good of all creation.

Prayer

Peace up to heaven
Heaven down to earth
Earth under heaven,
Strength in every one.

—Traditional Gaelic blessing

Quote

When you, as a disciple, try to live harmlessly—in thought and word and deed—and when nothing is held back materially, emotionally or from the angle of time, when physical strength is so given and the gift of all resources is accompanied with happiness, then the disciple will have all that is needed to carry on his work and the same is true of all working groups of servers.

—The Tibetan teacher Djwhal Khul, in Alice Bailey's *Discipleship in the New Age*

FULFILLING THE WAY

Creating: Dancing with the Beloved

Transforming: Renewing the Promise

Enduring: Going the Distance

Serving: Returning the Gift

(9) Creating: Dancing with the Beloved

❧

Do the thing you fear and the death of fear is certain.
—Ralph Waldo Emerson

I have a large abstract painting in my home done by a Light-filled German artist. When people come upon it unexpectedly, their hands invariably go to their hearts. There is not a single visual clue in the swirling mass of color that this painting is about the love that is at the heart of creation. Yet that was the artist's intention, which is clearly communicated. People get it.

All of us are leaving a trail of our intentions everywhere we go and in everything we do. And we are unconsciously reading the trails left by others. Psychically sensitive individuals can track a person's life and activities, even whereabouts, through clothes and personal items. Our auras register resonance or dissonance in response to the energy that is flowing, or trapped, inside homes, businesses, and public places.

Years ago a repairman came to my house and commented on my living room, noting that it reminded him of another customer's living room. I laughed to myself, because what he had no way of knowing was that the woman of whom he was speaking and I were in a healing/meditation group together. Our living rooms don't remotely resemble each other in furniture, color, or design. Actually what he was picking up on was a similar energy; he simply didn't know how to name it.

Pilgrimages are made to the grave sites of enlightened or saintly beings in all faiths because the vibration of the person is still strong, even in death. At Hindu religious celebrations people will wait in line to simply touch the place where a holy being has sat or even walked. I have watched people prayerfully touch the chair where Mother Meera had sat to give *darshan* (blessing). These are variations of touching the hem of Jesus' garment. The glow of a holy person permeates everything that he or she touches, and the imprint of the vibration remains.

Although I had studied his work, the first time I actually saw Michelangelo's sculpture, I was unprepared for the energetic impact that reached across four hundred years and through cool marble to speak to my heart. One particular statue, a pietà made for his own tomb, has three figures he sculpted and one done by a student. The student's work is well executed, but I found it to have a fairly lifeless beauty, while the dominant Michelangelo figure of an old man moved me to tears.

As we are all made in the image of God/Goddess, it is our birthright, privilege, and responsibility to create, together and alone. There is no way to avoid creating as long as we are alive. To think, feel, speak, or act is to create. We are either reenergizing existing realities or starting new patterns in the ether. When we don't deliberately choose what we will energize, we surrender our creative powers to the status quo or, worse yet, to the forces of ignorance.

Creators, Not Creations

Conscious creations are like glowing rings of light that continue on and on, empowering everything they touch. Meanwhile, the conscious creator has probably moved on to create anew. Therein lies the great key: Create precisely with knowledge, intention, and excellence, then release your creation completely.

Every act of creation is important *and* all things pass. These two insights are twin pillars of a disciple's understanding of creation. There is a unique pleasure in creating with excellence simply for the joy of the process, without regard for permanence. Good chefs know this, as do good hosts and anyone else living in the moment.

In a beautiful book entitled *Painted Prayers: Women's Art in Village India*, author Stephen P. Huyler describes and illustrates the exquisite drawings village women paint at the entrances to their houses and under the trees in the morning, seeking the Goddess' protection. In a few hours these beautiful drawings are smudged, yet no one has any regrets or hesitation about repeating the drawings the next day. "It is the moment of creation, the intent of the heart that is important. Art, like life, is considered territory."

It's wonderfully freeing to realize that while we must be responsible for anything we have created, we are not our creations—not the fame or the shame, not the money or the poverty, not the good or bad marriage, not the good or bad health. If we mistakenly think we *are* the creation, then we risk becoming either defensive or egotistical. We have created situations to reflect our understanding, set up scenarios to complete karma and train talents for the dharma, the flow of life.

That shift from creation to creator is a big one. It is the shift in the disciple's awareness from ego identification with the finite phenomenal world—from which all things pass—into an identity as an infinite being whose birthright is to create, release, and create again. The more clearly we know our eternal cosmic identity, the more skillfully we can play the parts we create in the passing drama.

Manifestation Is Spiritual Technology

This story was told by the great Chinese sage Chuang Tzu. In ancient China there was a master carver of horses who created beautiful things by first stilling his mind and thinking of nothing for three days. Then came three days of giving up all concern for personal benefit. After five days praise or blame meant nothing. After seven days he didn't even feel his hands belonged to him. Then he could see the horse in the grain. He brought his own nature into harmony with the wood, began carving, and the horse would emerge.

The Hebrew word *Jehovah* means "I am imagination and manifestation"—not one or the other, but both, a vision that materially expresses.

All sacred teachings say that we could manifest anything if we truly believed it. The materializations of a Sai Baba or a shaman and the miracles of healing are all possible because of unwavering belief. The fact that we can maintain our personal and collective problems so long is testimony to the power of our belief.

We even create a new body all the time. Scientists tell us that every cell in our body recycles. In less than a year we replace about 90 percent of the cells in our bodies. We are constantly in the process of making a new liver, a new stomach lining, new skin, even a new skeleton.

As Deepak Chopra says, "The reality is that your physical body is not a frozen anatomical structure, but literally a river of intelligence and information and energy that is constantly renewing itself every second of your existence."

"Empty" space—out there or inside our bodies—is alive with all possibilities. Subatomic particles are moving around in the cells of our bodies at high speed. Imagine them less as tiny little physical things and more like movements of energy that carry information. Energy moves through, around, and between the tiniest units

of matter. If we move our consciousness into that space and imprint new images, then we create anew.

There was a little boy who was progressed into the twenty-third
century through hypnosis by a psychotherapist. In this progressed
state he was twelve years old. While he was in that time frame
he was asked what he would do if he broke his leg. And the boy
said, "What do you mean?" They repeated the question. The boy
responded, "Why would I want to do that? I don't have any intention to hurt myself."

I like this story because I believe we *will* be teaching the principles of manifestation as a science in the twenty-first century, and
there *will* come a time in which our children will fully understand
the creative power of their minds. We don't want to teach them
just to rearrange the symptoms of a troubled world, which was
created from yesterday's limited thinking. We must teach them to
look inside and tap that boundless sea of universal energy out of
which come all things—butterflies and star systems, skeletons and
new worlds.

Working with the Laws of Manifestation

• Clarity of intention at every level establishes a matrix of
energy to which resonant energy is attracted. It begins to call to
itself all that is needed to fulfill the intention. From countless
possibilities, the people that must be met, the doors that must be
opened, and the timing that must be precise are all created in a
perfectly choreographed dance, one that the ego could not possibly manipulate.

• Before committing to a deliberate creation, ask yourself,
"How does this serve my larger intention or mission?"

• Thoughts are real, and they will manifest if consistently held.
The laws of creation are not sentimental. Observe that war is bad

and think peace. Observe unpaid bills *and* think prosperity. It takes attention to observe *and* not energize what you see.

• Evaluate all the ramifications and implications of what you want to create. Can you live with the consequences? Can you handle the new challenges? Invariably surprises present themselves as the equation changes. Is that okay?

• Allow for a lapse of time between vision and manifestation, the shift from the yin of receiving a vision to the yang of actualizing it. Create from your deepest creative desires, release, relax, and wait for it to manifest in perfect timing.

• Begin acting as though you were already living the manifestation of the dream. What would the new creation feel like, look like, smell like? How real can you make it?

• Express gratitude. Remember that gratitude releases the power.

• Pray in faith; work with tenacity.

• Don't get immobilized by dualistic thinking: "Do I wait for the universe or do I create myself?" The universe will open the way. You must choose how to travel it.

• Enjoy and don't get attached. Everything matters; everything passes.

Atom and Eve

Two forces are always at work in creativity: the masculine, yang, kinetic force and the feminine, yin, magnetic force. Yin-ness stretches and receives. Yang-ness shapes and focuses. We need both aspects to be developed within ourselves. If not, our need for balance will compel us to seek it in others.

When we are whole, all energies are in a homeostatic state, perfectly balanced. The tiniest movement contains a polarity, yin and yang, within that wholeness. The nature of these two creative forces has been recognized and symbolized in every aspect of existence, from the most cosmic and philosophical to the most concrete. Even foods, metals, and body organs have been designated yin or yang.

I read of a study in which the researchers took thousands of photographs of two people engaged in a conversation. The results revealed a fascinating portrait of our need to seek balance. Every time one made even a microscopic shift, the other would unconsciously make a complementary adjustment. A hand moved to the chin. The other readjusted a hand on the arm. One moved forward almost imperceptibly; the other relaxed ever so slightly. Without being consciously aware of it, both were dancing perfectly.

Birds landing on a fence will maneuver around until they find the right balance between each other. We do the same thing at parties. As soon as someone joins a conversational grouping, everyone readjusts their energy, not only for personal comfort and space, but unconsciously to reestablish group balance.

We are energized by the dynamic tension that occurs when these two poles are held in the same space successfully, especially between lovers. We also recognize the right balance of that creative tension when we say cars or clothing or any well-designed object is "sexy"—meaning filled with a concentration of this creative energy. Absorbed in a Zen moment of throwing a pot or executing a perfect golf swing, we experience that creative tension in balance.

Couples who exist in that state are, as colleagues of mine teach, "dancing with dolphins," performing a magical duet in which no one is leading and no one has control over what is going to occur in the water. This happens when men and women are not relating to each other as sexual or success objects.

Without the God there is no Goddess
And without the Goddess there is no God.
How sweet is their love.
The entire universe is too small to contain them.
Yet they live happily in the tiniest particle.
The life of one is the life of the other.
And not even a blade of grass can grow without the both of them.
                                                    —Bhagavad Gita

Kundalini Energy

All traditions speak of the "fire" or the "baptism by fire" that burns away impurities. The term *kundalini* (the name of an ancient earth Goddess) has become the accepted term to represent this transformative process. T. S. Eliot described that process in *Four Quartets* as being "redeemed from fire by fire."

Spiritual science teaches that after the life force energy has been used to build the subtle and physical bodies, a reservoir of the dynamic energy coils at the base of the spine. It is frequently likened to a snake that rises along the spine when the time is right for further growth. Usually we are not even aware of it, although it provides a steady enlivening and occasionally sends a frisson up the spine.

The snake, with its ability to shed its skin, is never far from our spiritual symbology. In Swami Muktananda's book *Kundalini*, he reports that Hebrew esoteric teachings suggest that the serpent's name in the Garden of Eden was Kundalini. The swami goes on to state, "The mission of the serpent is to initiate the evolutionary process in Adam and Eve."

The caduceus of the ancient Greeks, the symbol of healing for the ancients as well as for modern medicine, portrays the intertwining, spiraling snakes of the risen masculine and feminine sexual energy. Cobras on the headbands of initiates in ancient Egypt signified wisdom and enlightenment. The mastery of St.

George over the dragon in order to use its fire is echoed in Mayan temple sculpture. The counterparts on the earth are the terrestrial ley lines that the Gnostics called serpent trails and the Chinese called dragon paths. Certain sects in India require the kissing of a cobra's head during initiatory rites. Snakes have been worshiped in cults in Egypt and Greece. Handling poisonous snakes is proof to certain extreme fundamentalist Christian sects that they are filled with the Holy Ghost of reborn life.

Spiritual science teaches that all our physical and subtle bodies are energized by creative sexual energy through a network of thousands of directional lines of energy called *nadis*, the most important being in the center of the spinal column, a central channel known as *shushumna*.

In the return to wholeness we gradually raise the creative energy through two forces, the yin and the yang—in Sanskrit, the *ida* and *pingalla*. These two energies climb up the spine in a double helix, winding around the *shushumna*. The one on the right, the *pingalla*, is fiery, solar, and masculine. Its destination is the pineal gland. The one on the left, the *ida*, is cool, lunar, and feminine, and it's headed for the pituitary. Their union in the head is symbolized as a mystical marriage.

In its ascension, kundalini energizes anything in its path. It is a mysterious, intelligent force that transforms at a cellular level and in the process destroys what is no longer needed. Because it is a purifying force, it brings to the surface unresolved karmic issues. Clearly this is a good and necessary thing; nevertheless, it isn't always a comfortable process.

Many traditions teach the science of deliberately raising the kundalini energy through preparing, stimulating, and activating nerve and brain centers and carefully bringing the energy through the chakras. Unfortunately, in the West we didn't inherit those precise trainings.

Wherever the kundalini process is unrecognized, the ground is fertile for ignorance, superstition, and dismissal. In that case all the usual professionals one might look to for support during a kundalini arousal are as uninformed as everyone else. Individuals experiencing the dramatic extremes of kundalini can be doubted, accused of fantasizing or of being possessed, or declared mentally, spiritually, or physically sick.

Fortunately, we in the West are becoming more proficient in decoding the mystical language and knowledge that the Eastern traditions have refined through centuries of observations and the teachings of unbroken lineages. Several groups who are interested in bringing the medical, psychological, and spiritual together are synthesizing knowledge from around the world on this universal force. One such organization, Spiritual Emergence Network, offers people referrals to conscious bodyworkers, doctors, counselors, and ministers both in America and Europe. They also train professionals to distinguish between spiritual emergence and distressed psychological states.

While spiritual emergence is an ancient dynamic, it is a young science in the West. It is providing a major step in honoring our wholeness, for it acknowledges the validity of spiritual experiences in the body and emotions as well as the soul. One hopes that its development will take away both the language of psychosis, which has haunted humans since the age of reason began, and the language of superstition and fear that has sometimes plagued spiritual mystical experiences.

However, I do have to laugh when I think of the challenges that lie ahead in bridging this ancient science into our modern perceptions. Imagine the response of any doctor or scientist you know if you described kundalini thusly: "And Shakti, seeking the embrace of her lover Shiva, spirals up my spine." Need I say more? Still, if physicists can speak of particles using words such as *wanders* and *lovely*, then there's hope.

Kundalini Arousal

Kundalini arousals can be triggered by many things. Certainly devotion, longing, and consistent spiritual practices invite it. It can also occur spontaneously during trauma or even in childbirth. One researcher, Dr. Russell Parks, even suggests that the highly charged electromagnetic fields generated by TVs, computers, microwaves, and other devices are accelerating such arousals.

The planetary shift we are experiencing is stimulating a lot of spontaneous kundalini activity. While it would be ideal to have an enlightened teacher to monitor an arousal, as yet that's not possible for most people. So don't be discouraged—or frightened—if you don't have a teacher physically present. When I was in the most tumultuous part of a kundalini passage, I experienced pretty much the same steps and progress as those who were being led through it by a physical teacher. Certainly I was aware of inner spiritual guidance, which we all always have. We must never forget that masters and teachers are always at work on the inner planes: they don't have to be in this dimension in order to dispense their blessings or guidance.

With or without a physical teacher, it is essential that serious disciples educate themselves on this important subject. (See the bibliography.)

Some Symptoms of Kundalini Arousal

The clues that one's kundalini energy has begun to rise are very individualistic, and therefore it is hard to diagnose. Yet there are similarities in the process that show up regardless of religious or cultural background.

If you are experiencing several of the following symptoms, you might be in a kundalini arousal. It is, however, extremely important that you use a lot of common sense—and that includes eliminating other possibilities. As you can see, many of the symptoms would be the same for certain emotional, mental, or physical illnesses. So we must be intelligent in our evaluation. Seek out information and people who are informed.

Body
- Sensations of burning or intense heat, concentrating on particular organs
- Extremes of cold
- Electrical charges
- Crawling, itching, or tingling sensations
- Uncontrolled muscle spasms
- Spontaneous yoga postures
- Pain with no apparent cause
- Old injury sites aggravated
- Extreme fatigue or high energy
- Perceptual distortions
- Changes in eyesight
- Acute insomnia
- Inner sounds, roaring or whistling
- Inner pressure in head
- Hidden disharmonies and malfunctions in the body brought to conscious awareness

Emotional
- Accelerated confrontation with feared issues and old unresolved material
- Emotional swings from despair and depression to pure ecstasy, joy
- Outbursts of laughter or tears
- Alternating feelings of both powerlessness and great power
- The sense, fear, or images of death and dying
- Confusion and mindless fear

- Heightened sense of all emotions in self and others
- Feelings of both aloneness and unity

Mental
- Heightened perceptions, both physical and ESP
- Visions and prophecies
- Thoughts racing or slowing down
- Irrational thoughts
- Momentary dissociative thought patterns
- Temporary memory losses
- Intensified dream life
- Long periods of daydreaming
- Blank periods or spontaneous trance states (increased right-brain activity)

Spiritual
- Feelings of Oneness with life
- The sense of completion with major karmic issues
- Increased detachment
- Awareness of spiritual guidance
- Strong sense of true identity, the I Am of Self
- Bursts of creative expressions, awe, and sometimes ecstasy and great clarity
- Whole-body orgasms that flood the body with bliss
- Contact with other dimensions
- Abilities to heal and/or channel information
- Sudden bursts of light within and/or keen awareness of the Light in all life
- Near-death experiences
- The sense of encounters with holy beings

Staying Poised During a
Kundalini Arousal

If you are experiencing a kundalini arousal, remember that it is nature's way of bringing you home to your truest self. It will ultimately bring you heightened sensitivity and creativity; it will clear away attachments, clarify your mind, and open your heart.

After struggling out of its chrysalis, the butterfly Self will emerge. In the meantime, here are some suggestions to consider:

- Most important is to trust your process; trust your body.
- Honor the experience.
- Use common sense.
- Investigate other possible explanations.
- Give yourself time, patience, and support.
- Listen to *your* body's dietary needs. There are no strict rules. Sometimes the body needs a heavier diet than usual; other times it needs a lighter diet or a fast.
- Reconnect with Mother Earth, the land, the water, and so on.
- Breathe more deeply and evenly, and get more fresh air.
- Explore the use of complementary healing modalities such as acupuncture, homeopathy, chiropractic, and massage.
- Reduce disturbing sounds in your environment. Consciously select music for both listening and moving.
- Give yourself rest periods of peaceful silence.
- Pray and meditate as usual. If the intensity at times feels too great, simplify both the prayers and the meditations.
- Express gratitude; it supports all processes.
- Try not to resist even the hard parts. Practice surrender.
- Journal your experiences and don't edit your feelings.
- Accept reframed perceptions. Reality might be redefined.
- Acknowledge psychic openings. Don't overreact; just notice them.

- Find a body discipline that bridges body and spirit, such as yoga, tai chi, or chi gong.
- Create rituals of release. Don't hold on to images and memories that might emerge. Bless and release them.
- Garden. Earth work balances and grounds.
- Avoid drugs (except those prescribed by your doctor), including alcohol.
- Ask others for what you need: understanding, space, or whatever.
- Avoid critical, nonsupportive people if possible.
- Drink lots of water.
- Take retreats to a supportive environment where there are people that understand the process, such as a retreat center, convent or monastery, or healing spa.
- If you have a teacher, great. If you do not, utilize excellent sources for help available in books and tapes.
- Stay informed, not alarmed.

Gopi Krishna brought messages to the West on kundalini. He did not have a teacher or follow a strict system, nor did he have a formal education. What he did have was a great devotion to the Divine. After seventeen years of meditation and mental exercises, he experienced a full flowering of the kundalini, and after twelve challenging years he was transformed. He wrote many books, some of which are classics in the field of kundalini research, as well as hundreds of poems and prophecies. He wrote, "I live in a charming and melodious world, pulsating with life and intelligence. It is as if a radiant living Presence encompasses everything that exists both within and outside of me. This illuminated state of mind, in the course of time, will become the natural state of every man and woman on Earth."

Exercise:
Fountain of Light

Here's a very simple but effective technique for becoming acutely aware of your ability to move energy from one place to another. It can also revitalize your own energy when you're tired or stressed. Image a fountain of liquid light that originates at the base of your spine. On the inhale, breathe the flow up your spine through the top of the head. On the exhale, release it into your whole auric field of energy. Then repeat. Notice any places along the route where the flow hesitates or feels blocked. Gently bathe that area. Breathe with awareness through every part of the spine, through each chakra. Do this until you feel an even flow.

Sexual Energy:
Oil in the Lamp

Sexual energy is creative energy, which is raw life force. It's the animating, vital force that moves in immeasurable abundance throughout the universe. We are as fascinated and as puzzled by it now as when we first met the serpent in the garden. And we still long to regain the paradise that was lost when the masculine and feminine were split.

The ideal of wholeness has been portrayed throughout the world in enduring symbols, among them the Egyptian ankh, the Taoist circle of light and dark, Solomon's seal of interlacing triangles, the Indian peace pipe of stem and bowl, the last card in the tarot deck, the World, in which the polarities are united.

In alchemical texts, the wise one places the tree of life in a washing trough that is then filled with the elixir of life, which is heated by the dragon's fire, the sexual energy, that makes the tree bloom. Even the Greek hermaphrodite—equal parts of Hermes and Aphrodite—attempts to unite opposites.

Tibetan Buddhism and certain Hindu cults graphically depict the path to wholeness in sexual terms, in some cases using the lingam (male organ) and the yoni (female organ) as objects in worship. Tantric yoga teaches the bridging of the physical and the spiritual through mastery of sexual energy.

In the great temple complex of Khajuraho in central India, there is a field of sculptures that symbolically describes the plight of the divided self. At the base of the statues are figures that are trying every sexual position possible to make a union happen. As the sculptures rise along the temple walls, so does the success of the mating, until the top figures show a balanced masculine-feminine embrace, the Beloved found in wholeness.

Judas betrayed Jesus to the Roman solders with a kiss, a symbol of affection. He was the one of the twelve who wanted the kingdom immediately: he wanted instant gratification. Astrologically, Judas is Scorpio energy, the creative power that can be used to transform or destroy. Symbolically it is said to fly like an eagle or crawl like a scorpion.

Was there a Mary Magdalene? Probably, but she also became the archetypal abused feminine energy corrupted into sexual exploitation and transformed by the presence and love of the inner Light. The allegory that began in the garden with the fall from wholeness finds resolution in this story of redeemed sexual energy returned to the awakened consciousness.

Were there really ever a Demeter and Persephone in Greece? Maybe not, yet their story, which formed the basis for the lesser Eleusinian mysteries, so perfectly describes aspects of feminine (soul) transformation that centuries later we still tell that story of the separation, search, and reunion of mother and daughter.

We are at the edge of emergence from more than twenty-five hundred years of repression of the Divine feminine. During these dark ages the Mother's materiality, Her very earth, Her sexuality and abundant fertility have been seen as dangerous threats to the spirit longing to return to the Father. She gives life, and She takes it. She strips us of our illusions and then cradles us in Her healing arms, and we are birthed anew by Her. She is moist and fertile and sexual. And in the old model, hopefully now dying, She was there to be conquered.

One cannot understand sexual energy without understanding the feminine aspects of the Divine. She is the creative energy of the Holy Ghost, the Shakti of Hinduism, the Shekhinah of Judaism, the Holy Glow.

✿ Journaling Seeds

1. Review your history with the feminine aspect of the Divine. Who, if any, were your feminine spiritual role models?

2. How much were you taught about the Sacred Mother? What messages about Her were unspoken but firmly communicated?

3. Do your practices include the Mother?

4. Do you use the term *Goddess*? Why?

Vital Energy, Vital Choices

There comes a moment on the path when the powerful force of sexual energy demands full attention. Mystics throughout time have reported extreme swings in their sexual energies as they stretch and grow. The testing might come with boredom and fatigue ("I just can't play these sexual games anymore"), with disinterest ("What's wrong with me? I've lost all interest in sex"), or with just the opposite ("I'm tormented by sexual fantasies. The more I wake up, the more I want to have sex").

The first step is always to take a personal inventory of beliefs, not only of the dominant inherited attitudes of our families, but also of the popular sexual climate in which we came of age and began an active (or not) sexual life.

Sexual energy, the creative life force, can be used at the spiritual, mental, emotional, or physical levels, all of which exist on one continuum. This energy starts with the highest frequencies of the spiritual self, where wavelengths are the shortest, and descends into the density of the physical, where wavelengths are longer.

The ancient teachings say that when sexual energy is used for the highest aspirations, it destroys anything harmful to the body, revitalizes the cells, and brings youthful energy to the body. Taoist medicine has a treatise that teaches the use of sexual energy to heal various diseases and organs of the body.

A master or great teacher might elect to use the vital energy for purposes other than physical gratification. He or she might choose to give that energy to students, chelas, and disciples, thus from a spiritual dimension empowering their journeys. Often students are dramatically energized in the presence of such a being because this person carries so much of this vital energy, what is called Shakti in Sanskrit.

Second, sexual energy can be collected and used at the mental level to shape and fuel ideas. One could say that an inductive thinker and a deductive thinker working together on a project are having a kind of sexual experience.

Third, sexual energy can be used to feed the emotional body. Desire can be stirred into arousal when it is focused at this level. Fantasies, anticipations, excitements, all the stuff of romance can become quite addictive. The risk is that loving gets confused with getting high on the longing itself.

Last, the creative energy can be brought into the physical to create a baby, and/or it can be released in orgasm, which floods the nervous system with momentary awareness of unity. One can imprint the orgasm into full awareness by remembering during the afterglow that peace is truly one's natural state. Enlightened states are often likened to whole-body orgasms.

Primitive consciousness simply seeks only physical release of the sexual energy. There are endless partners for that; almost anyone will do. The next step is a refinement of the emotional body, which requires more than physical satisfaction from just anyone. There's a need for family, a sense of place and belonging, of being loved. As we develop, the need for partners with compatible interests and ideas grows. The more we are spiritually awake, the more we feel the need for a partner who also shares spiritual longing and purpose.

Soul mates are couples who have vibrational harmony in several (if not all) of the frequencies up and down the continuum. Our romantic myths encourage physical and emotional mating, yet often treat the mental and spiritual as luxuries, nice to have but not necessities.

As our longing for reunion with the Divine becomes a driving motivation, our primary desire for marriage with the inner Beloved develops. Even if we might prefer to have a physical partnership, we are no longer searching outside ourselves for a missing part, for someone else to make us whole. We are already complete. The ideal sexual relationship at this point is a whole self self-consciously pairing with another whole self for enrichment and support, not completion.

We do establish ties with sexual partners. Feelings and thoughts can travel through those ties just as they would through telephone wires. Physical separation doesn't destroy those bonds, since they exist in the subtle dimensions. This means we can continue to be affected by the feelings and thoughts projected through the cord by a former lover until that tie is dissolved.

I recommend that clients and students who are choosing to clear up karmic and energetic ties make a list of everyone they have ever had sex with and then create a ritual of blessing and release. The ritual needs to include forgiveness of any misleading or harmful intentions. Remember that your mind can travel unlimited by time and space, so you can release all past life connections.

I once had a very intelligent client who was formerly a call girl. She wanted to release her past, but she simply couldn't remember all the men she had been with. She solved this problem by visualizing an auditorium filled with all the men she had had sex with for money. She told them that she totally forgave each of them, released them, and asked their forgiveness.

Celibacy or Intimacy?

Many disciplines teach that sexual energy can be gathered and directed. Michelangelo allegedly warned his students that what you give sexually at night cannot be put on the canvas the next day. Coaches encourage athletes to avoid physical sex before major competitions. During times of intense creativity geniuses in every field have chosen to abstain.

Celibacy is encouraged and even required in some spiritual training. The stated purpose of imposed celibacy is to capture sexual energy and refocus it for service, worship, and personal transformation. However, like the circus lion that seems tamed, sometimes our instinctual drive breaks through the controls. Perhaps the lion is more likely to lie down willingly with the lamb when it has evolved into peacefulness rather than because it was chained in proximity. Celibacy that serves the soul occurs in its own natural time, like ripe fruit that falls effortlessly from the tree.

We might psychologically build a case against celibacy, knowing the inner suffering of repression and the outer results of projections. We could point to its abuses and traps. Nevertheless, it is offered as a valuable option and is encouraged during certain passages of our lives.

Jane and Rob made an unusual choice for an American married couple. Previously sexually active, they decided they wanted to take vows of celibacy. They both have Ph.D.s, run a consciousness community, teach all over the world, and have a full, rich life. Many people couldn't deal with the fact that a healthy couple in midlife would make such a choice.

Jane commented, "Many individuals were enraged at me because it's such a deep model that a woman must service the masculine."

Rob added: "To others I was always the victim and she was always the persecutor. I had to remember that I had a choice. I asked people why they were not allowing us to embrace something as a couple and learn from it without judging our choices as a codependent, dysfunctional, pathological problem."

Why *is* celibacy so often dictated and/or embraced? And why do others insist the lessons on the path are more quickly learned through intimate relationships? For example, the Dalai Lama, himself a celibate, once suggested that following a spiritual way in relationships was actually often the most effective way to learn these lessons.

For many disciples, the path of human intimacy is a powerful form of spiritual practice, providing a daily classroom for loving compassion. They learn to enjoy sex without demanding that their partners fulfill their longing for bliss with the Divine.

Intimate relationships hold up a mirror to our rejected parts of self. They shine a light on our growing edges. One way of looking at it is that it is easier for the celibate to back off that edge because she or he is not presented with these challenges on the material plane day after day through an intimate relationship.

On the other hand, the attentive celibate has no choice but to work the edge inside of self because there is no one on which to project unclaimed parts of self.

Obviously, devotees of one approach or the other can argue convincingly, and perhaps wisdom's way is to acknowledge that each route eventually takes us where we're going, and no doubt we've tried them all in our journey through time. A whole range of consciousness lies between sex by choice and sex by compulsion.

It's not possible to eliminate sexual energy. The question is what is best for you now. It may not be what is best for you during another period in this life. Many people choose celibacy during a transition period and later enter into an intimate relationship. Others follow a way often recommended in Hinduism and Buddhism, the way of the householder: After the family is raised, the couple chooses to spend the second half of their lives concentrating on the spirit.

The wisdom of the ages has not decreed that sexual energy should be repressed, least of all that it is evil. Quite the contrary. The wisdoms acknowledge and respect sexual potency first for the creation of new life, then for the preservation of life, and finally as the source of regeneration.

Exercise:
Releasing Former Sexual Partners

1. Start by setting the intention to commit to unflinching honesty as you explore what can be learned from your experience with the person.

2. See the person in front of you and, regardless of the drama, look with wise eyes. This *is* a son or daughter of the Divine.

3. Breathe consciously into relaxation and centeredness.

4. Image both the person and yourself standing in your own fields of light.

5. Say this prayer of release: "I bless my experience with you. I forgive you and myself for any hurts inflicted at any level. I decree that all ties between us from this lifetime or any other be at this moment dissolved and returned to the Source. Thank you Mother-Father-God."

6. If you discover that the tie persists, there are two other actions that will reinforce the release. Imagine a sword of light in your hands that draws a circle around you, cutting away ties that are not for your highest good. You can also ask your angel to support this action. If you request help from St. Michael, for example, he comes with a sword. You are not calling upon an entity but rather a vibration in the cosmos with which you can align, like praying to the sun and receiving a sunbeam. Another action is to see yourself standing in one circle of purple flame and the other person in another circle. Fire burns at every level, and purple is the color of transmutation. Then repeat the prayer of release (step 5) to complete the ritual.

My Shadow or Yours?
Probably Ours!

Corrupted sexual energy is all around us—rape, child molestation, addictions, pornography, prostitution. Enraged or thwarted sexual energy lurks behind a high percentage of murders, and it lies at the core of black magic. When sexual energy is corrupted, it does inestimable harm, not only in the obvious ways, but also in the psychological distortions of shame and blame, self-disgust, and profound confusion.

While we may not have been involved in extreme misuses of sexual energy, probably all of us have had sexual fantasies and experiences about which we are not clear. How could it be otherwise? We have been consistently imprinted with double-edged sexual messages since birth—"Go for it" and "Don't." No matter how much we have tried to curb it by rules, each day pure sexual energy spills out of its puritanical containers and reflects back to us both our fascination and our fear of its power through all forms of media, in pop culture, and even in politics.

During times of intense change, sexual energy sizzles. Our current obsession with outer sexual expression might not even be all that it appears. Some of it is possibly an acting out of the overload of energy that is racing along human nervous systems, as well as an attempt to deal with the karma being pushed to the surface.

As soon as we say yes to our Godself, all of our unexamined sexual ambivalence, exiled into the dark corners of consciousness, begins to stir and make itself known. That stirring is often experienced first in the second chakra and interpreted as sexual in the genital sense of the word. That energy can be brought up to any other chakra through the breath combined with imaging. Confronting our sexual programming is part of the journey into self-awareness, and it is essential at this point that the disciple not reject these feelings, no matter what surfaces. Denial is what drives feelings deeper into the shadows.

The more spiritually clear we become, the more sexual energy is present. It's recognized as charisma. Whether or not it is empowering or dangerous depends on the consciousness that uses it. Disciples often have a lot of charisma, and it attracts. When the flame is bright, people are drawn to it for warmth from the cold or for light in the dark. We did not create the flame; still, we are responsible for managing it.

One spiritual teacher explained it this way: "When you are teaching truth, there is an effervescence that comes out of you, a sparkle. I see it coming out of me as waves; these waves of energy connect. People are used to equating that light in an intimate sexual way. I give hugs, but I stay lovingly detached."

Projections and Transference

While teachers, therapists, and doctors who get involved with students and patients are the ones we hear the most about, anyone who has awakened his or her spirit often experiences heightened sexual energy. Even after we have examined our programming and attitudes, we still have to decide how to walk with others who project their unfulfilled sexual needs and fantasies in a dynamic known as transference. We usually think of transference as occurring in the psychotherapeutic process, but it can happen in any situation where one person is seen by another as the answer to one's prayers.

Handling projections requires absolute clarity with self and with the other, no matter how complicated the equation. Within clarity we can then make choices. Disciples report that there is a reduction in the number of sexual projections directed to them as they became clearer themselves and more responsible about their own shadow material around sexuality. As one business executive explained, "I really feel that I am not putting out that seductive vibe anymore. The energy is there, but there is no need to run that dance."

Rita, a lecturer, said that she had been so unsure about handling all the sexual attention that she attracts in her work that she chose to be celibate for seven years as a discipline. "For the first time in my life I was able to have friendships with men that I felt were really valid friendships. I quit seeing men as some kind of sexual object. Today when I travel and I realize that the sexual thing is happening, I take the initiative and make clear to people that I am married and that I value my relationship."

Samuel is a Rolfer who deals with sexual projection directly. "I think it's a serious mistake not to acknowledge it. You need to be honest about it. I might tell a woman that I'm glad she finds me attractive, and I love her very much, too, but I choose not to act that out because of my commitments. I find then that I don't have to do anything with the energy. It just moves to an appropriate place on its own."

After self-honesty and self-responsibility for one's sexual energy, what can a disciple do about sexual projections?

Don't deny, don't energize, and don't shame. Be unrelentingly self-honest; observe; draw clear boundaries; comment if appropriate. And choose what you want to do with the energy. As Sheila, a psychotherapist, once told me, "You have to sacrifice that intimacy in order to take on the more important intimacy with self."

One effective way to redirect sexual energy that is coming

toward you is to start breathing through your heart center and send that breath of love to the other person and stay steady with it. While you cannot do anything about another's choice, it will generally be hard for someone to maintain a tango solo. I did this practice with someone who I later overheard tell another, "I never knew quite what happened. I had one idea, but before I knew it, she had turned me into a friend." Redirecting sexual energy works, and it works without rejection.

Exercise: Raising Sexual Energy

There are many times when we choose not to express sexual feelings on the physical level: death or sickness, the absence of a partner, a transition in consciousness. One doesn't have to be stuck with physical frustration.

I received the following exercise while meditating upon questioning the conscious raising of sexual energy. I later learned it is an ancient technique, variations of which are taught in Tibetan Buddhism and certain yoga practices. This technique proves very quickly that sexual energy is just that—energy—and can be consciously moved.

1. The first step is to decide on a specific image of something you want to create. Don't be abstract. It might be a new garden, a painting, a project of any kind. Create a clear image that you can drop into your mind's eye like a slide when it is called for.

2. Increase your awareness of the breath, breathing with full abdominal breaths and inhalations that exhale from the abdomen up through the lungs.

3. Focus attention on the reproductive organs, appreciating them and becoming very conscious of the miraculous role they play in your life.

4. Begin to experience sexual stimulation in the second chakra. You may choose to practice this technique through memory of a highly sexual and pleasant experience in the physical. As the stimulation persists, don't try to control or alter the natural reactions of the body: expansion, tingling, warmth, moisture.

5. Inhale, and with your breath scoop up energy from the second chakra, store it in the solar plexus (third chakra), and exhale. Then inhale, scoop energy up from the solar plexus to the heart center (fourth chakra), store it, and exhale. Inhale and scoop the energy from the heart center to the throat center (fifth chakra), store it, and exhale.

6. Now get your image ready. Inhale, scoop the energy from the throat to the forehead center (sixth chakra), put your image in front of your mind, and exhale into that image.

7. Repeat this process a total of three times. On the last time be sure you have scooped all the remaining energy from the second chakra and brought it to your image.

8. Now check out your body. Is it more even? Not stimulated any longer? Look at your slide. What happened to it? Typically it will have become more complete, brighter, clearer.

Ambivalence: The Rebel Within

Wherever there is ambivalence, creating is weakened or delayed. As one client wrote me, "I am a little bit afraid to begin. The material is ready but not yet my mind."

Ascended beings are probably the only souls who have no personal agendas left, therefore no ambivalence. In the meantime, most of us need to be very attentive about where our houses are divided. Often when we can't seem to corral the necessary energy to birth our desires, there's real ambivalence in the subconscious. There's a good chance "somebody" in there has not gotten with the program.

Back to the basics: Know thyself. Blessing, not rejecting, of the rebel is required. Healing can't happen in a climate of rejection in either the inner or outer world. There are reasons why rebel elements are in the psyche. Sometimes they were originally developed as healthy defenses against intolerable pressures, as with a child who builds a fortress against constant criticism.

Working through the fears that guard an inner fortress and sorting out the internalized voices of others takes persistent, loving patience. Yet the rewards of such effort are beyond estimation. Enemies become allies. The inner critic can be coaxed through acceptance and tender patience into becoming an agent of discrimination. Hesitation can be converted to healthy caution, becoming a support, not an inhibitor, of intention. If the protectors of the fortress are dismissed, denied, or despised, they don't go away; they just go down into the shadow, where they sabotage our true creativity.

Perfectionism Versus Excellence

In the mountaintop experiences we glimpse the potential for a better world. That's the good news. The crash can come when we attempt to manifest a vision into a plane of reality still thick with violent thought forms and resistances. To help bring forth the vision, we must be dedicated to excellence. To insist that our vision be implemented perfectly, right now, in an imperfect world is to be caught in unhealthy perfectionism, a particularly nasty little virus that consumes our creativity.

There is a difference between creating with excellence and getting caught in perfectionism. What would you add to these lists?

- Perfectionism negates satisfaction or fulfillment.
- Perfectionism is self-critical and by extension critical of others.
- Perfectionism has no joy in it.
- Perfectionism does not relish the fortuitous mistake.
- Perfectionism doesn't like unplanned surprises.
- Perfectionism is self-denying, sabotaging.
- Perfectionism is an imagined state of completeness: "*Then* I'll be good enough."

On the other hand:

- Excellence fuels deep fulfillment through creative contribution.
- Excellence thrives on the process itself, delighting in the doing.
- Excellence learns from mistakes and then releases all blame.
- Excellence offers one's best to the Divine and to the world.
- Excellence doesn't depend on outer affirmation, but appreciates it.
- Excellence is self-affirming, life-giving.
- Excellence focuses intention, creates, and then releases.
- Excellence reflects respect for all undertakings, large or small: "*Now,* here I am, as I am; use me."

Inner Blocks to Creativity

Before we leave this chapter to look at other aspects of discipleship, I suggest you do inner research to discover if any of the following are potential blocks to your creativity. Remember this is about self-knowledge, not self-judgment.

- The shoulds and oughts
- A dominating inner "duty demon"
- Low self-esteem, feelings of unworthiness
- Worry about the opinions of others

- The assumption that experts know best
- Competition and comparisons that breed jealousy and envy
- Old family myths: "She was creative; I was the practical one"
- Fear of ridicule, rejection, disapproval, exposure
- Fear of loss of dignity, relationship, control, job
- Fear of change: What must die so you can birth anew?
- Tyranny of intellect: rational dismissal of creative ideas
- Negative self-talk
- Fragmenting, not choosing areas for concentration
- Unexamined assumptions about reality
- Unexamined cultural myths
- Devaluing of intuitive self
- Perfectionism
- Talking about it rather than doing it
- Reluctance to risk the unknown
- Reluctance to be a beginner needing help and information
- Not naming what you want to create
- Lack of clear intention
- Devaluing and minimizing creative needs

✖ Journaling Seeds

1. Where is your house divided in your creative purpose?

2. Do you value yourself "as is" or by comparison, by personal best or by winning?

3. How do you deal with constructive criticism?

4. What will you risk? What is the worst that could happen? What is the best?

5. Are you willing to support this intention with all your resources? Are you willing to commit to the discipline required?

Ceaseless and unconditional creative energy is paradoxically the most personal and impersonal of powers. It will fuel whatever we immediately desire, and that includes our addictions, our blocks, and even lies that we think are harmless or that we start to believe ourselves.

Once we are awake, the lag time between choices and consequences is reduced. Perhaps we simply become more quickly aware of how thoughts, words, desires, and intentions are manifested in the material world. It is also a necessary part of the training in responsibility for what we put in the world—instant karma, we sometimes say. It also allows us to see where we are blocked.

In *The Artist's Way* Julia Cameron says, "Remember that it is far harder and more painful to be a blocked artist than it is to do the work." (Read *artist* as an artist of life: parenting, business, teaching, whatever and wherever one's creative expression is.)

✖ Twelve Considerations on Creativity

1. Create with care; all things matter. Let go gently; all things pass.

2. Creating is inevitable. Is it conscious? That's the question.

3. Clarity of intention is a requirement for powerful creation.

4. Sexual energy is the golden vitality of the universe.

5. The universe will fill whatever size container is open.

6. Inhale the grace; exhale your gift. One breath, indivisible.

7. Forever lovers, yin and yang expand/contract, give/receive.

8. Perhaps "they" were wrong. In the silence, listen. It is good.

9. When "How am I doing?" becomes "This is a gift," energy shifts.

10. Embrace your fears, and they will become your allies.

11. Life is movement, not a museum. Delight in risks and shifts.

12. Create with awareness of the effect unto seven generations.

Prayer
With beauty before me, I walk.
With beauty behind me, I walk.
With beauty below me, I walk.
With beauty above me, I walk.
With beauty all around me, I walk.
—Traditional Navajo prayer from the Beauty Way

Affirmation
I create intentionally with my thoughts, my passion, my words, and my actions.

Quotes
If you live too much by intellect, your brain responds to creative urges by going to the marketplace to haggle price. The lover says there are a thousand different doorways, many creative outlets. When we talk about creative living, we are essentially talking about the courage to love life.
—Julia Cameron, *The Artist's Way*

All the hemispheres in existence
Lie beside an equator
In your heart.

Greet Yourself
In your thousand other forms
As you mount the hidden tide and travel
Back home.

All the hemispheres in heaven
Are sitting around a fire
Chatting

While stitching themselves together
Into the Great Circle inside of
You.

    —Hafiz, twelfth century, from *The Subject Tonight Is Love*,
    Daniel Ladinsky

Transforming: Renewing the Promise

❧

Although the wind
blows terribly here,
the moonlight also leaks
between the roof planks of this ruined house.

—Izu Shikibut, tenth-eleventh centuries

Transforming is the act of consciously altering the rate of energy of anything, whether it's a single cell or a society. Love, will, power—all aspects of discipleship reinforce and enhance each other in the transformational process.

We're always shaping and reshaping energy with our minds, desires, and actions. Either we're *deliberately* working the raw material of our classrooms or we're *unconsciously* energizing patterns that repeat like a kaleidoscope, rearranging the same pieces of colored glass in amusing combinations.

Transformation takes place after the highs of the first spiritual rushes and insights and before we integrate them. For most of us, it takes a lot of discipline to deal with old challenges in a new, aware way, to retrain old habits and corral rebel parts of self.

Tibetan Buddhism teaches that there are several ways to transmute a challenge on the earth plane, and we need skillful means to discern which way is appropriate and harmless. One way is to accept the challenge as a karmic necessity. We can also allow a problem to fully manifest and appoint an inner observer to watch it unfold and learn from it. The third way is to lift the challenge to a higher perspective, generate a lot of energy, and then infuse it with the higher awareness. This requires a lot of concentrated skill and consistency.

For example, if I have been treated unfairly by someone and I wished to use this latter method, I would go beyond who is right and wrong to see my oneness with the person; holding to the truth behind the appearance, I could change the energy pattern.

Through the centuries we've marked our moments of transformation with rituals, catechisms, magical elixirs, amulets, and magic wands. We have mystic stones to kiss, lanterns to rub, talismans to protect us, icons to revere, and chants to intone. We visit sacred sites and power points, retell our sacred stories in fairy tales and legends, and drink from healing waters as well as baptize and cleanse ourselves in them.

We also seek to discover, name, and organize stages of transformation. The ten (or seven or twelve) most effective ways to conduct business, sports, your sex life, your mental health, or your spiritual life call to us from book, video, and magazine covers and invite us to seminars on every subject imaginable. Perhaps in a world of information overload we sometimes simply want sound bites and bumper stickers. Yet the drive to gather, understand, and focus is also part of our spiritual being's seeking to shape a reality in our familiar three dimensions.

History teaches us that there *are* rhythms in transformation, patterns that can be seen, understood, and made usable and teachable to others. If a twelve-step program or a seven-step model provides encouragement, helps remove illusions, and takes us deeper into understanding ourselves, then it is a useful tool. As a teacher, I have observed seven distinct stages through which we pass during changes, and those seven became the scaffolding for my first book, *Where Two Worlds Touch*. These are Beginning Form, Challenge, Resistance, Awakening, Commitment, Purification, and Surrender.

Psychologist Dr. Russ Parks developed a plan to help his clients move from perceiving themselves as victims to being self-empowered as they deal with problems. He says the first perceptual shift is to see the situation at hand as a problem. The next shift is to see the problem as a challenge. The third shift in perception is to view the problem as a test, and finally to see it as a message from the person's soul that says, "What is it I need to learn?"

No matter how disciples are seeing our problems at the moment, we must be patient and persistent and never dismiss the choices we've made thus far. We take many detours that appear to be delays and avoidance before getting on our spiritual superhighway. Along all the byways, important soul work is being done. Karmic contracts are being fulfilled, unfinished business completed, desires run off, skills gathered, spiritual muscle built. How long it takes to heal wounds, rectify wrongs, and dispel lies depends on countless individual factors.

We are always on our path even when it seems we are lost. "Nowhere" is often the venue for a spiritual crisis which can, like a health crisis, precipitate deep healing. "Nowhere" is sometimes where we have to go before we get exhausted with running from ourselves.

Moments and Meetings
That Transform

Turning points are frequently setups for transformation: "moments that divide time," novelist Ann Rivers Siddon calls them. They become reference points for a lifetime.

Sometimes the turning comes as a devastating quick cut, as in the death of someone close. It can come on the heels of disappointment or despair. Our life's direction can even turn on meetings with someone whom we might never see again. When we are ready, someone always comes to open the door.

A musician friend told me of a casual meeting that changed his life. He had been a spiritually aware child, but when he went to college he wanted to experiment, so he told his spirit that he would reconnect when he was twenty-nine. Mysteriously, at exactly twenty-nine he sat beside a woman on a bus reading a book on mind science.

"That was my connection," he said. "I read the book over her shoulder. She told me about mind science. It was as if all the molecules of the universe started tingling at a new pitch. I started going to the Mind Science Institute. As I listened to them doing mind treatments, I thought, 'This just lifts the parameters off potential.' "

Mark is an actor who attended a lecture by Ram Dass purely because he had gotten a role as a cardinal and was "seeking a way into the part." Or so he thought. Spirit always finds a setup when we're ready for energy to shift.

In his personal life Mark was emotionally worried about his ambivalence toward the impending arrival of a baby. In his lecture Ram Dass said what Mark called the magic words: "You don't achieve freedom despite your incarnation; you achieve it *through* your incarnation."

"What I heard was that I had to embrace the baby. I told my wife how much I loved her and the baby. From that day on it has been marvelous in spite of the ups and downs."

I like this story because it is a reminder that we never know who is listening. We are instruments for each other whether we know it or not. I doubt that Ram Dass had any idea he had catalyzed change that day. He was simply speaking his truth.

Loss into Gain

Turning points often involve loss, and loss offers unique opportunities to transform. In an article in *New Age Journal* called "The Bald Truth," Geneen Roth, speaking of losing her hair to chemotherapy, quotes a Zen teacher who helped her: "Essence is the part that cannot be weighed or measured. . . . When everything you thought disappears, there is still something that remains. A beingness, an isness, a presence, and it is that something, and the recognition of it, that brings peace, strength, fulfillment, and happiness."

In an article in *Directions* magazine (May 1992) metaphysical minister Loy Moncrief describes her choice to transform the devastating loss of a child to sudden infant death syndrome into a renewal of life. "I went out and dug a large vegetable garden and set out to nurture life in the face of death. I planted flowers everywhere. I gathered large groups of houseplants. I started keeping goldfish. I put out feed for the birds and squirrels. I looked for opportunities to nurture life in all forms." She was determined not to blame, but to accept and transform. Part of her ritual of release was to visualize holding her baby in uplifted arms and offering it to the Creator.

Another disciple, Patricia, also found the loss of a child to be her greatest opportunity for learning to transform. She said: "I had always had a fear of abandonment. I had this wonderful son who was the light of my life, my only child. He was twenty-one, and he drowned. He was the most important and wonderful thing I had ever done with my life. So being stripped of my identity was hard, but now I am finding out who I really am. I used to run away from emotional pain. Now I realize that it's like catching flu. It feels bad, but it's going to go."

Illness can also be the entry point into transformation. Overcoming illness and the threat of death is part of the archetype of the wounded healer. The healer grows in compassion and insight, and by overcoming the illness, he or she brings to others the authority of true knowing.

One therapist who ministered to the dying told me, "I've had to let go of myself into the abyss. I know that the therapeutic work I've done there is surgery on the ego. The more I can let go, the better I can help other people to let go."

We've all been blessed by people who have experienced devastating losses and convert their pain into educational and fundraising efforts in the hope of preventing the same problem from happening to others. We've seen this in everything from people dedicated to getting drunk drivers off the road or finding stolen children to starting support groups for various diseases. Such people model for us the transformational promise inherent in the most devastating tragedies. No less influential are those who quietly choose to model for their families and neighbors the capacity to turn loss into gain.

❧ Journaling Seeds

1. What experience has seemed most unfair in your life? How has your understanding of this experience evolved over time?

2. Have you experienced great loss? How have you dealt with grief or anger? How has it changed you?

3. Have you found gifts in the loss?

4. Who or what have you not forgiven?

Keys to Transforming

Transforming is the day-by-day reshaping and redefining of our challenges into stepping-stones for our journey. Here are seven essential tools for the process. Remember, the basics always include intention, attention, practice, integration, and gratitude.

1. *Transforming any situation begins with accepting it.* We don't have to like it; we just have to accept that it exists. We can say no, draw clear boundaries, even take legal action if necessary—all while accepting what is. As long as there is resistance, there can't be transformation.

Acceptance doesn't waste energy in denying outer circumstances that can't be changed. We can always choose our way of relating to those circumstances, and that will affect everything, including the amount of stress we manifest in the body.

We don't lose power in acceptance. We *gain* it. Acceptance is not passive. One can be quite active within acceptance. We think more clearly, and that allows us to perceive more quickly, assimilate the gifts in a situation, and complete the karmic lessons. We then build the spiritual and psychological muscle to cope and endure and eventually transform.

Evelyn was a top executive in a large corporation when she suddenly lost her job. After much pain, she rediscovered her soul and her path of self-discovery.

"I discovered that I didn't know who I was. I realized suddenly that I had no idea of how to get through my day if I wasn't working. I knew what you ate if you had a business lunch, but I didn't know what you ate if you are just a human being."

She decided to accept the situation, and then she started to learn. "By being fired, I got the money to spend the time to investigate spirituality, which was a miracle. Plus I found out that many of the people who worked for me that I had thought were just being nice to me because I was their boss were actually my friends, which was a big shock to me."

2. *Giving up the victim mind-set leads to transformation.* From a limited perspective, many things are clearly not fair. If we hold reality up to a fairness test of one lifetime in the physical dimension, it would obviously flunk. Those who cannot or will not go beyond the outer evidence in search of a greater truth can get stuck in the mire of victimhood for a long, long time. In such a pit, the original crime is continually reenacted.

Clearly, there is a difference between being a situational victim (of a robbery, for example, which in itself is certainly frightening) and being the victim of long-term abuse or extreme violence. Post-traumatic stress syndrome is a very real condition that is best treated by a therapist or doctor. I am certainly not taking such extreme situations lightly, but ultimately even the extremes are experiences and not identities. All wounds can eventually be healed.

Our longing to let go of and reshape any negative experience will attract to us the tools we need to get out of any pit. Refusal to let go feeds bitterness, resentment, and endless stress. It separates us from the very practices that would bring us new insights and closure. *And* it doesn't make the lesson go away. The soul is not really sentimental, and it is not going to back off a hard lesson any more than we would let our children pout or storm their way out of learning to read or getting a vaccination.

When we realize that our incarnation is a classroom—however painful the lessons taught there may be—then we can find the resources to help us let go of victim consciousness and its seduction into endless helplessness. There can be many reasons for a painful classroom. Some are highly personal, as disciples scrape away at heavily encrusted soul material; some are very transpersonal, as disciples commit to service. We are all also participating in the gradual transformation of national, gender, racial, and species patterns. We must also remind ourselves that we are sharing a planet with millions who also have free wills to create.

Blame and self-pity can easily become a habit, a way of positioning ourselves in relationship to everything that happens. "I'm not who I want to be because of my job/my ex-wife/my lack of money" and so on. The irony is that even if all the restrictions were magically removed, unless we learn the lesson, our psyche will re-create circumstances that might not look exactly the same, but will put us toe to toe with the same issues.

The way out of victimhood is very convoluted if we believe there is an outside power withholding blessings and passing out curses. The universe gives us the grace to come home by choice, not as punished children. The last-ditch effort of the inner victim is to blame the gods who live anywhere but inside.

In order to heal the darkest feelings, including rage and grief, we have to embrace them as the first step in transforming them. That takes courage since it can be very frightening to move into previously disallowed feelings. Doing so frees us, and models to others a road out of hell that leads to heaven.

Helena, a psychologist and spiritual teacher speaking of her recovery from childhood abuse, put it this way: "Of course we need to talk about what happened, but there has to come a time when we take off the banner that says 'I am an abused child.' Underneath it is the banner 'I am a child of God.' "

3. *Being present in the moment transforms the illusion that any part of life is ordinary.* Living in the moment is a learned skill that takes infinite patience and attention. Left unattended, our minds quickly become bored, reactive, and undisciplined. Being undisciplined with one's attention is like giving power to passing currents that may or may not be going in your direction.

In the eternal now, we are no longer battling ghost images of the past and rehearsing an imagined future. If we stay fully present long enough, we will retire our illusions of separateness and realize that we're already where we are going. Focus becomes less on what's wrong and more on what is, less on life after death and more on life right now.

One classical way of training mindfulness is to eat with total attention. Dr. Jon Kabat-Zinn, author of *Full Catastrophe Living* and meditation teacher, has his students take five full minutes to eat one raisin. Slow, deliberate attention is paid in this kind of practice to every subtle cue of appearance, texture, smell, and taste. Awareness of every aspect of eating—or walking, or dressing, or anything—can heighten our awareness of how we experience all aspects of life.

In *Touching Peace: Practicing the Art of Mindful Living,* Nobel Laureate and Buddhist teacher Thich Nhat Hanh says, "The miracle is not to walk on water. The miracle is to walk on the green earth in the present moment, to appreciate the peace and beauty available now. . . . It is not a matter of faith, but of practice."

Andrew was a dancer when he met the teacher who challenged all his previous training that things had to be done just right. She said to him, "It is not a matter of having taste; it is having the capacity to taste what is present, to behold. Behold!"

4. *Transforming requires prioritizing, disciplining our attention, and making time for spiritual practice.* Prioritizing our time also includes finding time to be alone—"intentional solitude," as writer Clarissa Pinkola Estés calls it. Many rise early to ensure an hour of their own. Others take periodic silent retreats and vision quests. A Brazilian teacher/healer I know takes four hours every day in solitude, even when he is traveling. Recently a colleague told me he had cut back on his teaching schedule because he realized he did not have time to do the very practices that he taught others.

One way to keep one's priorities clear is to make a habit of regular evaluation. Some disciples start the day with "What do I want to do?" and end it with "And what did I do?"

Kathy is a businesswoman and minister who says that whenever she questions her priorities she asks herself two questions: "Would I do this if no one in the world knew about it? And would I do this if everyone in the world knew about it?"

If we wait to do a practice until we feel like it, most of us would rarely do it. Certainly intuitive feelings guide our original choice. And that choice has to be renewed over and over with practice. As my friend said about an aunt who had to be told the same thing repeatedly, "She doesn't stay told." Neither do we at the early stages; otherwise we'd all be ascended masters by now.

Discipline evaluates our use of time, energy, resources. It doesn't limit possibilities; rather, it allows us to set temporary boundaries in order to integrate and focus. Discipline ultimately frees our joy. Unless we focus on our talents and desires, they can easily get lost in procrastination, fragmentation, and the sheer dailiness of life.

Discipline is remembering what you want. It's not about following the demands and rules of others. Even if we're following directions in order to master a step-by-step practice, we're doing it because it's what we want for ourselves.

Transformation in this dimension requires physical grounding and discipline in the body. As we explored in the chapter on the body, spiritual awareness is not about escape from the body; it's about waking up while in it.

Most of us are not going to push the physical envelope as far as monks in the Himalayas, who are trained to sit in snow and learn to generate warmth, until they can use their minds to dry wet sheets wrapped around their bodies. The fact that it can be done challenges our assumptions about the limits of the body-mind.

When we are no longer distracted from our truth by disgruntled employees, the evening news, or the broken washing machine, we might not need so many conscious disciplines. In the meantime, the disciplines can help.

5. *In meditation we return to the ground of our being, where all things are transformed and made new.* The benefits of meditation range from reducing body stress to increasing mental concentration, helping everything from your immune system to your tennis game. Its greatest gift is remembrance. In stillness we gradually identify the elaborate wardrobe of identities we've worn like costume changes in a stage play, and we touch the Self that is playing all those roles.

Getting the mind quiet is the step that precedes expanding it. People all over the world have discovered that this is best done by giving the mind something else to do: Watch the breath, focus on a single idea, chant a mantra, repeat a sound. Each of these requires practice.

Many people assume they must be meditating wrong because they experience everything from an uncomfortable body to a restless mind that quickly gets bored and wants to rerun its continuous loop of addictions and fascinations. These reactions are the norm, not the exception. With practice we pass through the cloud cover formed by the ceaseless chatter of the ego mind and enter the expanded silence of the universe, returning home, realizing while still in the body that we never really left.

The meditative state may be our natural state. The Earth's natural vibrational frequency, called the Schumann resonance, is approximately eight cycles per second (based on the speed of electromagnetic radiation divided by the circumference of the Earth). In a relaxed state we also vibrate at approximately 7.8 to 8 cycles per second. Our brain-wave activity in the alpha state, deep meditation, is in this range.

It's best to give yourself permission to explore until you find a meditation practice that suits your needs. And even then, don't put unreal expectations on yourself. There are many excellent books on meditation. I particularly recommend Ram Dass's *Journey into Awakening* because it clearly and honestly addresses most of the questions about meditation.

6. *Dialoguing within Self, with the "other," and with the world creates bridges that transform the world.* Communion and dialogue are more than mere communication. They are the synthesis of deep listening and sharing of the essential Self in which lost parts of Self can be heard again; other species can be heard; the angels and cocreators and guides in other dimensions can be heard.

Dialogue sets the possibility for deeper meaning and insight to occur by staying in the moment and suspending assumptions. That is part of deep listening.

Where there is deep respect, we can dialogue with the life force in any form and receive information. Healers know this. Gardeners know it, as do children before they are taught otherwise. Artists know it when there is no separation between the instrument and the music, the paint and the painter.

The rules for communion with another life-form are quite simple: (1) respect, (2) harmlessness, (3) awareness of the force field that connects all life, (4) expectant relaxation that neither makes demands nor asks for behavior that is incongruent with its nature. We wouldn't ask a fish to live on land or an angel to materialize as proof for an ego.

Dialogue with elusive parts of self is an extremely useful technique for insight. For example, to say "I doubt many spiritual teachings" might create inner conflicts, as we may immediately argue with all the aspects of self that don't doubt. However, if you can say to yourself on paper, "I want to dialogue with the part of me that doubts," then it's easier to listen and understand. It's a great way to address shadow material.

Many times I have seen in readings that people have a particular aspect of self that holds the critical key to their edge of growth, but because of fear or denial, it gets so tangled up with their personality that it holds them hostage.

One woman I worked with had an inner housekeeper who kept around her waist a ring of keys to every door in the house. She was very critical and judgmental, and reluctant to open the doors to the basement. But she was only doing her job as she understood it. The recommendation in the reading was to dialogue with the housekeeper self. There were good reasons she had been given the keys in the first place, and if she was listened to, those dynamics could be understood and she could gradually be made part of the *accepted* inner world. In time, with love and patience, her critical nature could be refined into discrimination.

A musician I know employs a method of dialogue with his "celestial disciple" that breaks through rational thinking by allowing his Highest Self to write as fast as possible. "Put your pencil on paper and go with the first word that comes through. It's like improvisational piano, where you plunk down one chord and see what is the next chord."

7. *Rituals are transforming moments in which the sacred is experienced.* From christenings that welcome us into this world to funerals that send us to the next, we mark our passages and turning points with rituals. One minister calls them "spiritual revitalizations." They tell us we are in a significant moment in time and space. The symbols alert the subconscious to pay attention: "This is important; it must be acknowledged."

Rituals can make the transcendent immediate and alive. They provide links between the visible and nonvisible worlds, actually grounding the spiritual. Yet like all practices, if they are performed by habit and not from the heart, they become rote exercises, meaningless and suffocating to the living spirit.

We can support ritual by creating sacred space. Sacred space is a state of mind and intention, limited only by imagination. I've seen powerful sacred space created by groups in gyms, in private homes, in institutional classrooms, in groves of trees, and by streams and waterfalls.

In ancient traditions, a place of vision that centered ritual was called the *omphalos*, a beehive-shaped sculpture representing the navel of the world. Symbols for the *omphalos* are found all over the world in sanctuaries such as Delphi in Greece. You can consecrate your own center of the world, a sacred place that symbolizes the connection between heaven and earth.

Through the years I have created many ceremonies, and I find people eager for new ones that offer completion as well as celebration. For example, the forty-year-old woman whose first blood was never noted is at last, through ritual, welcomed into her womanhood; a soldier finally ends the war through a ritual of release; and an elder enters the crone stage of her life wearing a crown instead of an apology.

"Do this in remembrance of me" is the mandate for the Christian Eucharist. It is also a remembering of who we are and the reason we are here. And it is celebrated universally, which strengthens its significance.

Bread is a symbol of the cycling life force in the physical; wine symbolizes the outpouring of Spirit, the sacrifice through which all life is sustained. The Persians gave bread and wine to the sun god Mithra. And the ancient Sumerians gave cakes and drink to the Queen of Heaven. Jews still bless and offer unleavened bread and wine to God at the Passover Seder. And cultures around the world have used blood in their ceremonies. In Christian practice, taking bread and wine helps celebrants remember the cosmic Christ that is ever present.

Writer Dorothy Spruill Redford created a modern healing ritual while in the search for her own roots. She orchestrated an event that brought over two thousand descendants of the slaves who worked and lived at Somerset Place back to the antebellum plantation in Washington County, North Carolina. Many who attended the event were white descendants of the slave owners.

In her book *Somerset Homecoming* she tells stories of the slaves who built the plantation over two hundred years ago and of the lives of their descendants. She writes of a Jewish newspaperman whose family had been victims of the Holocaust. He couldn't believe the degree of joy he saw on the day of gathering. He had expected only sorrow.

"Slavery was horrible, and it was about death. But at Somerset it was also about life. We died here, but we also gave birth here.

And we grew beyond this place." The ritual gathering celebrated the growth and closed the circle.

A Transformational Ritual Across Time

The transformation of energy is not confined to the here and now. Through forgiveness, we can transform distortions from the ancient past as well as complete unfinished business from this life. Neither death, distance, nor earth time is an obstacle.

John's father had been dead for sixteen years when John finally faced and transformed his grief. "Unfortunately, during much of our time together Dad diligently tried to 'save' me from evil," John said. "I labored to prove that I was whole. Dad's death ended the unresolved debate, and with heavy resignation I buried him. I was forty-one and tired from all those years of arguing my innocence."

Years later John's therapist suggested that his unidentified grief could be about his father. He soon found himself going back into the grief to resolve it. He used visualization and writing as a process tool. In his mind he returned to the time of his father's death, held him, bathed him, honored him, and then wrote a eulogy. He lived it for more than a day, starting at about three in the morning, when he wrote the eulogy. "I read it, cried, rewrote it, read it, and cried." This is an excerpt from his eulogy:

I bury your body, Dad. I grieve your passage for my earthly loss. In spirit I stand here by your grave. I ponder our bodies, sculpted of this enigmatic clay. Isn't it strange: you gave me life and now give me death? I never felt my death before. I was to have been immortal. You created death for me. I feel you in me now. You are the Father I chose, after all. There is a reverence and goodness about you I never knew so well before. Now, full of gratitude and joy I claim this gift of you in me. If we were blessed to pass this way again, we would share a hard-earned bond of unity, honoring the nature of our eternal communion. Could this be memory of past and future mingled? It is any wonder that I love you so.

At the end of his ritual John felt his father had been spiritually exhumed, even resurrected, and now his fathering was complete.

What in your past needs to be completed? Who needs to be forgiven?

Exercise:
Twenty-One-Day Prayer Prescription

You can prove the transformative power of prayer to yourself by taking one clear intention and following this prescription for twenty-one days. You'll only need a few minutes to do the whole day's requirement, but you will need to offer it your full attention.

1. The prescription starts with a prayer upon waking.

2. Immediately follow your prayer by stating the intention you have chosen for the twenty-one-day prayer prescription.

3. Offer your intention and affirmation three times during the day.

4. At bedtime offer the prayer upon retiring.

As you prepare for bed, review the day—without judgment. Old critics might appear. Calmly review incidents that either reinforced or blocked the expression of your intention. That might include telephone calls, books, memories, conversations, or anything else. Journaling about the confirmations or challenges relevant to your prayer can provide insights.

Just before you say your final evening prayer, release on an altar of Light all of the people, events, and attitudes of the day.

As you go through the twenty-one days, you may find that first day's enthusiasm diminishes as the old pattern kicks up resistance. Notice it; don't deny it. Choose not to engage or energize. *Don't reject; don't react.* Breathe out the resistance as though it were a breath you no longer need. Let it dissolve harmlessly back into nothingness.

PRAYER UPON RISING
I give thanks for this day.
I give thanks for my life on Earth.
I give thanks for the privilege of serving.

STATEMENT OF INTENTION
I will to . . .
   Examples:
I will to finish my degree with ease and excellence.
I will to improve my relationship with my boss.
I will to release my fear of public speaking.

AFFIRMATION
I empty myself that I may be filled.
I release opinions so I may be taught.
I accept the revelations of my soul with gratitude.

PRAYER UPON RETIRING
I surrender my Intention to Mother-Father-God.
I seek guidance as I sleep.
I empty that I may be filled.
I am Grateful.

Exercise:
A Quartet of Daily Transformers

1. Choice is your birthright. Claim it. Say to yourself: "*This* moment I choose to love. *This* moment I choose my conscious behavior."

2. Spend five minutes of concentrated time writing, "I am grateful for . . ." List first the personal (children, my home), which then becomes the transpersonal (the beauty of the world, the opportunity to serve, etc.).

3. Use two sets of prayer beads, one to affirm, one to let go.

4. Write private codes to yourself that reflect your intention, such as "Remember" or "Love [your initials]." Place them in your wallet, on your mirror, on your desk, and so on.

Through the
Valley of the Shadow of Death

The bristlecone pine is six thousand years old. In times of stress it gathers its main force into a single line with bark around it and allows the rest to die.

Death and birth are an inseparable duo in the dance of transformation. Everything in the universe surrenders its life that something else might live. Death in one form becomes birth in another. Water becomes mist and cloud; smoke and ash are born of burning wood; the plant is sacrificed to the animal; the flower becomes the seed; youth is surrendered to maturity.

I once had a vision in which a white wolf and a white hawk brought dead wild things to a chapel in the woods, where the creatures were brought back to life. Blood turned into tears and tears into anointing waters. I was reminded yet again of our spiritual capacity to call forth life from the appearance of death.

All over the world the death-to-life cycles in consciousness are told in legends and rituals. Disciples have met their lonely confrontation with ego death in caves and tombs, sarcophaguses, the underworld, even the belly of a whale. They then return reborn to the world carrying a message of resurrection.

Dying to the past doesn't come easily. The ego identifies and clings to its creations, most of all the physical body. One of the classical ways of training the psyche to accept the impermanence of all things is to contemplate one's own dying and decomposing. Accepting the reality of physical death, one is more likely to accept the little deaths along the way. Then physical experience is more fully savored moment by moment, since there is no need to freeze it into immortality out of fear—for there will be another body when needed, even perhaps, as Benjamin Franklin once said, "a newer and better edition."

The late astronomer and writer Carl Sagan kept a postcard of the *Titanic* on his shaving mirror. On it was a message one William John Rogers had sent friends in Wales. It said, "Dear friend. Just a line to show that I am alive and kicking and going grand. It's a treat. Yours, WJR." It was posted the day before the ship went down with Rogers on board. Sagan kept it to remind himself that "going grand" was at best temporary.

To seriously meditate on one's death may seem macabre to the average Westerner, but it isn't. What we brush aside because we fear it is not harmless. Fear constricts energy. It enthrones itself like a tyrant in the subconscious, sometimes obsessing on youth, denying, distorting, and missing the riches of all cycles of life. Fear undermines the living of life at full stretch.

Until we accept our own mortality, we can spend a lot of our time and vital energy avoiding that reality or postponing living. As one friend described his father: "He spent his whole life preparing to enjoy his life."

That we really do choose our way of relating to death was sharply underlined for me during one particular week in Europe in which I was called to the bedside of three dying people. The first was a spiritually aware eighty-six-year-old woman. We talked freely about death, laughing, crying, and speculating about how it would be on the other side. She was my teacher that day; I was honored to be invited into this intimate passage.

Later that week I sat in a back bedroom of a small cottage in the Jura Mountains of Switzerland with a twenty-one-year-old dying of myasthenia gravis. We didn't speak each other's language, but we communicated more through the universality of his experience than through the translator. He was weary and knew his life would soon be over. He wanted understanding. We talked soberly, but not sadly, about death. I left humbled by his courage, renewed in my own. He, too, was a teacher to me.

And finally, at the week's end I met with a forty-two-year-old woman dying of cancer. I immediately realized she was in denial, refusing to talk about death or even the meaning of her life. She wanted me to tell her she would live. I wanted to help her, but I had to take my cues from her. Following my inner guidance, I made her a tape of breathing in rhythm with ocean waves. I never mentioned dying, but I talked a lot about waves ebbing back into the sea. I was told she used it until the day she died. She, too, was my teacher, for I saw the high price of resistance.

I wish she could have known the peace of Elaine, a professional weaver, who told me a few weeks before her death, "If things don't turn out for this life, I'll just weave rainbows." I'll bet that's just what she's doing.

Transiting is the Hardest Part

In alchemy the four stages of transformation begin with the *negredo*, the mystery of the dark unknown. In that model it is taught that a person gradually first sees the lightness of all things, then the

goldenness of life, and finally *pavanis* is called into consciousness—
the peacock's tail, the oneness in which all things exist. Alchemy
teaches that the work of transformation begins with dissolving
back into the *prima materia*, basic matter. At that point our carefully constructed views of the self and the world experience die.

The death of the familiar often plunges us temporarily into a
dark stew of confusion. The terrain is uncharted. We've broken
with old patterns but new ones haven't emerged, and the ego
struggles to find order. During such times of spiritual crisis, we
can feel pulled apart in a spiritual purgatory of indecision.

We need to be honest and kind with each other about the
uncomfortable, in-between stages of transformation. We tend to
feel vulnerable during transitions, sometimes experiencing free-
floating anxiety, restlessness, or inexplicable tears, sometimes having strong body reactions such as diarrhea or sleeplessness. If we
don't know that all these symptoms are the possible, even probable
fallout of giving up old patterns, we can easily think we're doing
something wrong. Letting go is a total experience that will be
acted out in mind, body, and spirit. When things are frozen, there
isn't much pain; it's when they defrost that the pain begins.

One disciple told me that up until his transformation, his career
had been ego-controlled and his spiritual life mental. "It had
taken me about as far as my head could take me. For me the way
now was through emotions and intuition. My balance came
through that experience of dying where I had to give up all control. I didn't know what the next step would be, and I didn't have
any friends or support, but I surrendered to it and got to the point
of saying, 'I don't care what it is, God, I'll do it.' "

We know that fake holiness is a big trap along the way. We
don't want to get caught in death passages with imaginary rules of
sainthood. As one experienced disciple put it, "It's more important to be authentic than it is to be neat and clean and maintain an
image." *Of course* the death of any myth we hold about ourselves
causes momentary grief. But it also means we have chosen to give

up more limitations, and the joy and freedom that come will make any death a willing gift.

Yet during the process we can hesitate. This moment in the process is perfectly stated in the last lines of poet Denise Levertov's poem "Salvator Mundi: Via Crucis" as she wrote of Gethsemane: "Sublime acceptance, to be absolute, had to have welled / up from those depths where purpose drifted for mortal moments."

To Sacrifice Is to Make Holy

The word *sacrifice* bothers us. It seems heavy with ecclesiastical foreboding. Often spiritual seekers will argue with it, dismiss it, even get defensive about it. We might know the long-term benefits, but the short-term can look pretty scary, as it involves, as the Taoists say, letting go "of the ten thousand things" even as we respect them.

Sacrifice characterizes the entire story of transformation. Becoming conscious is a continual process of giving up, letting go of myths, attitudes, habits, prejudices, old karmas, resentments, self-images, securities, insecurities, and all illusory identities. In order to have a truth, I must give up the lie; to expand my consciousness, I have to give up my limits.

If we feel we are being forced to let go of anything because it's a rule, resentment drops deep into the subconscious. Eventually we scream at God/Goddess, "After all I've given up for you!" The trap is false martyrdom.

When the letting go is a loving choice from deep within Self, it becomes a loving offering to God. *To sacrifice means to make holy.* All of our experiences, no matter how bizarre or distorted, can be made holy. The Divine absorbs all of our offerings—every hurt, mistake, hatred, regret, and self-loathing, every sadness over the roads not taken as well as the ones that were—and they are transformed as they are offered.

Sometimes the temptations and those things we are asked to

sacrifice are not in the darker side of our nature but grow out of talents and strengths. For example, one might sacrifice much-loved privacy in order to obey inner guidance to accept a public role. Unconditional love says yes, not "yes . . . if."

More, the Divine wants what we love best. The Hebrew legend of Abraham's obedience to God's command to offer his beloved only son, Isaac, as a sacrifice dramatizes a turning point in the life of a disciple. We may not ever have to lose what we love the most, but we may have to be willing to sacrifice it to the highest calling.

Don was a Catholic priest who was guided to leave the priesthood. "My biggest temptation was to sell my integrity and my truth for a lifetime of security and fame within the church. I walked away after nine years in the seminary and twenty-three years as a priest. I did so with no severance pay and no pension. It was one of the best moves that I ever made. Pain impelled me to choose; courage sustained me along the way."

> *The disciple learns by daily increment. The Way is found by daily loss. Loss upon loss until, oh, the Way.*
>
> —Tao Te Ching

Where Are the Hooks?

Most of us are not going to follow a path of total outer renunciation, which is, of course, an old and honored way that eliminates the consuming distractions of materialism. Like every other path, it offers temptations for self-deception. One could actually "give up" everything and still be deeply attached.

The degree of inner attachment determines how free we are. To "sell all that I have" means to give up attachment to ideas, opinions, false securities, and identities. Then I am teachable.

I recall hearing Ram Dass tell the story of his sexual attraction to someone on the very first day of his return to America from

India after he had been proudly celibate for quite a while. The desire had been repressed, but it was not gone.

Natalie Goldberg, author of *Writing Down the Bones*, shared a similar experience in *Tricycle* magazine (winter 1993) in which she spoke of feeling she had made a lot of progress in her Buddhist practices. But when she met a famous Buddhist teacher, she admitted, she wanted him to know of her accomplishments!

If you have any questions about what she is saying, just try going to the next seminar or party and keeping your accomplishments, titles, education, and economic status to yourself. Without judgment, notice the clues to your ego identity that you work into a conversation, and notice reactions to them from others. Stella says she is "ignored and treated like a little old lady" until people become aware she is a well-known teacher's mother, then she suddenly becomes the "queen mother."

Ask yourself two questions: "Do I know who I am regardless of what I am doing? Do I know who I am whether I am winning or losing?" Lakers coach Phil Jackson writes in *Sacred Hoops*, "Losing is a lens through which you can see yourself more clearly and experience in the blood and the bones the transient nature of life."

Now ask yourself:

- Do you know who you are in either poverty or wealth?
- Are you using the things in your life, or are the things in your life using you?
- Do you feel entitled to them?
- Where do you stop your generosity?
- Beyond the basics of food and warmth, what luxuries have now become essential to your happiness?

I saw a documentary in which social workers in rural India reported that the rise in the number of abused women paralleled the increase in the number of televisions in the village. It was their professional opinion that the television was creating desire for more things than the dowries of the women could provide, and the frustration was leading to increased violence.

Certainly that seems extreme to our culture, but is it really? What is the cost of our feeding the insatiable appetite of materialism? Whenever I pose the question of materialism and the spiritual quest in workshops, it invariably stirs strong feelings that range from rationalizations to ambivalence and guilty feelings over having—or not having—abundance.

The flip side of desire is revulsion. Whatever we intensely repel is as revealing about our shadow attachments as what we hold, maybe even more inhibiting, because it can be so easily denied.

"I want, I want, I want" is the mantra of materialism and a setup for frustration when things don't appear or, ironically, often when they do and we have to face the fact that they were not what we wanted after all. Imagine the confusion in the subconscious when we have conflicting desire messages. "I want to be free and detached" and "I want more and more things."

I loved the cartoon in which the Dalai Lama opened an empty box for a birthday present and exclaimed, "Oh, just what I wanted—nothing."

Doubts and Disillusionment

Dear Dorothy. I don't like it here. I went home. It's all an illusion.
Love, Toto. P.S. I took the shoes.

—Seen on a T-shirt

When projections or expectations backfire or don't materialize, we suffer and say, "I was *so* disillusioned," as if the universe had let us down. If indeed we mean what we say about getting conscious, why aren't we saying with delight, "Yes—another illusion has been shot down"?

The point is vividly made in many practices. In some Zen training a statue of the Buddha is broken in front of a devotee being initiated into the order. The monk or nun must seek Buddha mind, not just adore the mind of the Buddha.

Young students in the Hopi tribe grow up enchanted with the masked kachina figures that magically appear during ceremony. During an initiation rite in the sacred kiva, they see that the "magical" kachina figures are not supernatural, but are actually fellow tribe members. No doubt this is a disorienting, disenchanting moment, but it is a necessary dismantling of illusion if they are to mature in real spiritual power.

Similar ceremonies take place among peoples in Africa. The Ndembu ceremoniously destroy before the young initiatory candidates a figure they had previously thought was sacred. Even the first disciples of Jesus, witnessing the physical death of their master, had to experience the shattering of any illusions that an immediate earthly kingdom would manifest.

Such moments are extremely important turning points for disciples. One either becomes disillusioned to the point of despair and gives up, or one begins to mature in the spiritual quest, seeking deeper understanding and connection with the Divine instead of being satisfied to be indulged, deceived, or placated. At such a juncture, many seekers have declared they no longer believe in a Divine Power when they discover It is not made in their own image.

One Buddhist meditation teacher observed, "Doubt is probably the most insidious mind state there is. One is frequently tempted to go for the worldly security. Yet I was miserable before. And you have to keep reminding yourself of that. Your society, even your most intimate friends don't always reflect back to you that you are doing the right thing. What you're giving up is stuff that was the source of all your suffering."

Another disciple remarked, "Doubts are a period of broadening my perspective. When I start doubting something, I know I'm going to be changing my perspective, reevaluating my belief. Doubting is just the rational mind adjusting to what you are doing, and where you are going."

Dark Nights and Wildernesses

Smooth seas do not make skillful sailors. —African proverb

The inevitable dark nights of the soul and wilderness experiences are periods of testing that take us to the heart of our beliefs, desires, and intentions. Tentative, conditional faith can be ripped apart in a dark night like trees uprooted during a storm.

Novelist Morris West said it well in *Shoes of the Fisherman*: "One has to abandon altogether the search for security and reach out to the risk of living with both arms. One has to embrace the world like a lover. One has to accept pain as a condition of existence. One has to court doubt and darkness as the cost of knowing."

In dark nights of the soul, we can temporarily lose awareness of connection to the Divine. Meditations go dry; emotions feel flat; prayers feel empty; our efforts seem pointless. One can endure anything if one feels connected, and doubt everything without it. During dark nights of the soul, the very spiritual supports we have relied upon seem to disappear, and many times peers can be at a loss to help. We can feel abandoned, left doubting ourselves and the gods.

These are testing periods for the soul, times when, as Ram Dass said, "you have lost the flavor of life but have not yet gained the fullness of divinity."

One disciple summed up her perceptions during a dark passage with this: "I tried to pray to God, but it was like praying to the very person who had caused my misfortune."

One of the profound lessons of the dark is that over time it becomes one of our greatest teachers. We learn to accept its awesome grace as one would receive the teachings of a beloved master whose discipline is hard, but whose wisdom will lead us through the darkness of our own illusions, which is the real threat.

Many experience deep aloneness during the excursions through their dark nights. Before we live in the awareness of Oneness, we must accept our inescapable aloneness: being born alone, dying alone, experiencing true consciousness alone. We simply don't grow conscious by committee.

We never really are alone. We are always supported in the visible and invisible worlds, but those who are themselves awake do not indulge in misguided rescues to steal away our chance to wake up. And those who don't understand our longings can be like the crabs who pull each other back into the boiling pot if one tries to climb out.

One disciple wrote: "Some days there is this space all around me as big as the deserts in New Mexico and no one comes by, and no one calls my name, and it is achingly beautiful, and high and so solitary. In that aloneness is another illusion, but in my small humanness, it is a mystery of aloneness."

We face our temptations alone, and they come wrapped in custom packages. They often show up during dark, lonely passages. Along with the obvious tugs to give allegiance to fame, money, and power, one of the most insidious seductions is just to give up the quest.

Fear, rebellion, and anger can appear suddenly: "Get off my back," "What did I do wrong, now or in another life?" "I just want to live a normal life." The depth of that latter urge was explored by Nikos Kazantzakis in the novel *The Last Temptation of Christ*, in which the final temptation of Jesus was to get down off the cross, marry Mary Magdelene, and lead a normal life.

Disciples report that their temptations range from feelings of unworthiness to wanting to be like everyone around them. They note the temptation to hide in the distractions of work, food, sex, entertainment, and, as one said, "my to-do and should lists." And, of course, there is our old friend procrastination.

The Temptations

Try making up your own temptation list. I did, and I promise it will be very revealing. Just ask yourself: "What twelve things could seduce me off my path (and perhaps do on occasion)?"

The shadows in the transformational process at first seem formidable. Within them the fires burn hot and unrelenting. Yet it is from the combustion of such heated elements exploding in the soul that the diamond self is formed.

We must embrace the shadows as we do the light, one experience at a time. Perhaps it is not your soul's intention to descend deeply into the fires in this lifetime. Maybe you've already done it; maybe you will at some future time. Still, as disciples, we need to understand these passages and be compassionate with ourselves and each other. You or I may be the only reminder of grace that comforts someone who is feeling lost in a wilderness.

Angela said that she constantly reminds herself in dark times that it is "*through* the valley of death, not *to* the valley of death. It isn't the end of movement, it is continuous. *Through* is my key word."

❧ Twelve Considerations on Transforming

1. Work your edge until all that brought you to it is released.

2. Break out of prison. Forgive everyone, everything.

3. Even the loveliest vessel is useful only because of its empty space.

4. Spirit transforms old or fresh mistakes with equal ease.

5. Disciplines actualize intentions; they teach us how to fly.

6. Resistance to discipline keeps one on the ground indefinitely.

7. Sacrifice is a universal law. Withholding is self-destructive.

8. We return to oneness by solitary choice, not by committee.

9. Angels and allies lift our wings even though we are afraid of free fall.

10. Change quickens when authority shifts from outer rule to inner rule.

11. The numinous becomes ordinary through patient practice.

12. Find the center of the storm. Out of chaos comes new order. (Chaos theory)

Prayer

I enter the quiet of sacred sanctuary. I surrender all of my pain, even my need to know why. I accept the promise that in time I will understand. In this moment I open myself to the tender ministering of the angels. I rest in the remembrance that all suffering will pass. Only love is eternal. I give thanks for that sustaining love, which at this moment is transforming my understanding and restoring peace.

Affirmation

I give my [fear, anxiety . . . name whatever it is] to the Mother-Father-God, knowing that it is being transformed into a great good that will bring peace, insight, and love.

Quote

Seek and never cease seeking until you find, and when you find, you will be troubled. After you have been troubled, you'll come to marvel and then you'll reign over all.

—Jesus, in the Gospel of Thomas

Enduring: Going the Distance

❧

> *After ecstasy, the laundry.*
> —Zen saying

As people awaken spiritually and stretch, the first question they usually ask is, "Now, what did I intend to do in this life?" As remembrance comes, it brings a high quite unlike any other. Peace, relief, anticipation, and passion all flood our awareness.

Then comes the commitment. Yes, I will teach those children; yes, I will write, paint, go to Bongo Bongo, run for city council, whatever. When the personality says yes to the soul, giant gears inside the psyche begin moving into place.

Goethe once wrote, "Until one is committed, there is hesitancy, the chance to draw back. . . . The moment one definitely commits oneself, then Providence moves too. All sorts of things occur to help one that would never otherwise have occurred. . . . Whatever you do or dream you can do, begin it. Boldness has genius, power, and magic in it. Begin it now."

Once we make the commitment, two dynamics show up. First, synchronicity increases, bringing into place everything that we need to manifest intention. Second, it becomes clear that the intention is going to require an unqualified dedication of all resources in order to come to fruition. Committed intentionality requires endurance. We take responsibility for choices, educate talent, and refine skills. And we wait, sometimes years, for the universe to put all the right pieces in the right place at the right time.

Because we are all connected, the larger plan unfolds by bringing all the elements we need together at the right moment, in right timing, through synchronicity. When synchronicity is working its magic, it seems that the universe will do it all for us. What it really does is bring the opportunity, open the door, create the meeting, move into place whatever we need. We begin to realize that we've gone to work for a very large outfit that runs the universe. We're not in charge anymore . . . and we're more responsible than ever. Persistent effort is now going to be required.

One of the many balancing acts disciples learn is waiting patiently for assignments and then working steadily to fulfill them. Since I have worked independent of any organization for twenty years, I have gotten lots of opportunities to practice this balance. I have not had a physical employer to tell me to go here or there, do this or that. It's also true that I haven't had anyone to write me a paycheck every month. The universe is my "employer," God/Goddess my "boss." Gradually I learned to trust my intuitive guidance to help me find a way to pay my bills as well as direct my work. I have never solicited business as such, yet I have traveled and taught around the world.

My experience, which is common among countless disciples, underlines the point that we don't have to manipulate the world when we are doing what we came to do. Our soul is connected to everyone else's, so collaborations from the soul level take over. The universe has contacts we don't know exist!

For example, years ago I received a query out of the blue from a group in Iceland. They had heard a tape I had done in Germany. I knew very little about Iceland at that time, but I politely thanked them and sent them a list of workshops. They wrote back saying that they had decided they couldn't risk it financially.

The next week I went to Switzerland to teach, and sitting in my class was a man from Iceland who had nothing to do with the group who made the original invitation. The population of Iceland is small, and it was highly unlikely that someone from there would show up in a classroom in Zurich, Switzerland. But he did. After the workshop he called Iceland and made a recommendation. I returned home to find an invitation from the original group. I went, fell in love with the people and the country, and have returned to teach several times since.

Those who have made a commitment to live their truth can report similar synchronistic incidences that set up the venue and contacts for their work. They arrive in our ordinary lives like exotic gifts from the universe. And we need to share those magical moments with each other as encouragement and reminders.

Staying Committed During the Silences

Equally important, we should share with each other the times when we have to simply endure, with little or no outer evidence that the universe is paying attention. Many of us can probably report projects we felt led to develop for which we felt no tangible sense of cosmic support, sometimes even leaving us with scalding self-doubt. Which one of us would hesitate with an angel talking in our ear? To hold to one's truth through long silences tests the true strength of one's commitment.

Spirit will ask nothing of us that we are not prepared to do, and it will stretch us beyond anything we thought possible.

Sometimes the very intensity of an awakening can be enough to carry us through a lifetime of commitment in spite of human doubts, worldly rejections, and periods of fumbling in the dark. A true epiphany can do this, for in such rare moments it seems God/Goddess writes in the very air in front of us.

We see this with those who have had near-death experiences.

No matter how much ridicule or dismissal their revelations encounter ("It's probably just brain chemistry" skeptics say) people
who have consciously visited other levels of life and returned to
this one usually can't be budged in their knowing. They know
that they know. Knowing prepares us to endure; mere theorizing
has no muscle for endurance.

Not all of us experience dramatic epiphanies that announce the
Divine presence in no uncertain terms, and I doubt if any of us
do all of the time. Often it's more like the sun gradually burning
away the fog of illusion, perhaps now and then bursting forth in a
brilliance that lights up the inner landscape. Any amount of truth
is a light through the dark, and once it is received, we must follow
its lead no matter where it takes us.

Whether we are struck blind by the light on our road or just read
the road maps well, disciples are dedicated to being instruments
through which truth can speak and function in the world. And that
is going to call for a lot of endurance, because the world doesn't always welcome the gift.

I'm in, No Matter What

Endurance is a sober word. I was tempted to find other euphe-
misms; "hanging in there" and even "going the distance" don't
sound quite so weighty. Spiritual language abounds with words
such as *beloved, joy, flowing*—all those wonderful feel-good terms
that the heart responds to with warmth and longing. And then
comes *endurance*. Clunk. What is *this* going to look like?

While survival is the first order of business, it isn't enough for
developing endurance. There are a lot of bitter survivors.

Endurance builds spiritual stamina. It helps to tell ourselves, "I
will persist even if I can't afford it, don't have the time, or am
overloaded, too tired, bored, or restless. I will do it when I'm inspired, or when the whole thing gets tiresome. I'll stay with it
even if 'they' resist it. I'm committed, and I won't look back,

regardless of circumstances or convenience or how long it takes—a month, a year, a lifetime."

Spiritual endurance functions with an elegant simplicity. It is quite different from stubbornness, which can be rigid and subject to cracking with a few blows. Rather, endurance bends and molds to circumstances as it steadily pursues the goal, patiently, quietly, boldly.

Endurance is the sustaining force for all the other inner aspects of discipleship. Love goes the distance because it can endure anything. Faith stays strong in spite of appearances because of endurance. Power and will require enduring strength to accomplish intention. Endurance pushes knowledge to its edges, matures discernment, grounds intuition.

Endurance can dig its feet in for the long and often tedious business of shaping eureka experiences into concrete, visible realities. It sustains us through endless hours of research in a lab, writing a book, getting a law changed, working the edge in any capacity.

If we wait for evidence *before* we make a long-term commitment, we won't last long. It would be as futile as making a vow to lose weight and then looking in the mirror the first day to see if it worked. "No? Well, I guess I was wrong."

Journaling Seeds

1. What kind of things can tempt you to give up on your path?
2. What are your strengths and weaknesses in personal discipline?
3. For what are you willing to endure almost anything regardless of the cost in time, money, relationships, and so on?
4. How do you sustain your commitment during the silences?

The Patience to Seed Change

Waking up brings with it moments of clarity and sometimes infuses us with the passion of the zealot. It's usually a bit of a shock to face the reality that a lot of the world can't see what now appears obvious to you: "I want everyone to see this wondrous thing I have discovered." But old forms don't die easily. They don't really even like to be disturbed. Holy scriptures from around the world echo the words of Jesus: "The light came into the darkness, and the darkness liked it not."

Your Light is going to expose lies, no matter how lovingly you offer it. "Get real," our spiritual guides might say. "The world is not going to give up its favorite lies easily." The words of those who are already walking the path of discipleship are frequently serious but ultimately encouraging, for they remind us that simply because the world doesn't immediately accept all of our visions, it does not mean we are doing our place in the dharma wrong. In fact, it can be evidence that we are doing it right.

> *The student told the master that she wished*
> *to become a teacher of the truth.*
> *"Well, then, are you ready to be starved,*
> *dismissed, made fun of until you're forty-five or so?"*
> *The startled student wanted to know what*
> *wondrous thing would happen then.*
> *"You will be used to it," said the master.*

It can take generations of committed disciples bringing light into darkness to change old models of reality, because old forms are held in place by habit and assumptions about reality that are passed along from generation to generation as living truths. If we give in to the ego's demand for concrete results on transforming large issues, we get very, very discouraged and can feel about as brave and effective in the world as a baby kitten mewing protest into a jungle.

There is an incredible freedom in giving up the need to see results. I find that the degree to which I surrender my need for proof is a measure of my willingness to be unconditional in my dedication. As long as we are working strictly under the mandates of the ego we confine our perspectives to the time frames of *kronos*, the human sense of time that demands results here and now. Surrendered to our highest intention, we move into the service of *kiros*, Divine timing, and those days and nights look a bit different. I learned years ago not to get too excited when Spirit said, "Soon," which might mean in the next decade or so, or even in this lifetime.

Discipline Is Freeing

We've looked at the importance of discipline from different perspectives. Now let's consider how necessary it is in order to go the distance on our path.

In the early years of the consciousness movement we didn't hear a lot about discipline. "Go with the flow" was the dominant philosophy. Being nonresistant to the flow of events is good advice. And it's very misleading when it suggests you don't have to use discipline to bring about change in yourself or the outer world. That is like suggesting you could raze an old house, clear the property, then build a good strong house with no blueprint, effort, or skills. No matter how high we fly in our visions and dreams, we have to "nail the landing," as they say in gymnastics. And that takes practice.

As ruthless as it sounds when one first contemplates it, there comes a time when we must seriously consider the biblical metaphor in Matthew 5:30: "If your hand offends you, cut it off." After we have recognized, analyzed, and embraced those habits that have been getting in the way of our commitment, then the next step is to give them up. It's great if they just dissolve effortlessly. If not, then loving self-discipline will say, "Enough, just do it." Just watch your mouth. Just meditate. Just clean up the diet . . . whatever. Just do it!

The Disciplines

We might have to deal with resistance to the word *discipline* because of the negative associations it has for us, notably in terms of parents and educational and religious institutions who attempted to mold us in their image. But personal discipline is liberating. It allows us to prioritize in the midst of overwhelming choice.

The object of discipline is to become free, not rigid, rule-ridden, or a perfectionist. We aren't really free until we have developed a certain amount of personal discipline. When we take up a new art form or a sport, we feel awkward and ill at ease with the form itself and its equipment. Yet with patience and discipline comes the flow; *then* we can break the rules and experiment. If our attitudes and mouth are out of control, there is no freedom; we are simply at their mercy. First we have to endure the discomfort of bringing all of our "equipment" under our conscious management.

The ease with which enlightened people move in the world is the result of their taking in hand all parts of themselves, and that includes both talents and shadows. I recall hearing a lecture given by a well-known Jungian therapist and being impressed with the exacting precision of his words. They were sparse and to the point, cutting like clean diamond points. I asked him later if he just naturally spoke that way. He said no, that in reality he had spent a great deal of time learning to master that style of public speaking.

The ballet dancers who make their art look so easy do so because of the tedious daily attention to every part of the dance. The same is true with the potter, the banker, and the schoolteacher. If we pay attention to all the parts of our dance, sooner or

later the moves will reside in our cells. And then it will be graceful as it enters the world around us. Gracefulness in life and in
the dance comes from integrating inspiration and discipline.

Once we say yes to our deepest intention, we can find ourselves
having to say no to a lot of other appeals. As Beverly, a disciple/
artist, stated very pragmatically, "If I'm going to be here doing
this, then it means that I can't be there doing that. It requires discipline because I am aware of so many possibilities that have attraction for me."

Hal, a disciple and social work leader, agrees that we have to
say no, even to ourselves, in order to do what we came to do. "I
have a healing role within an organization. But to do that well,
I have to set aside a great many personal things I want to do, the
way I want people to see me, and the way I want to spend my
time. It's not hard, but it requires a type of growing up and a type
of discipline. And there is a child inside me who wants to go off
and play and not do these things. *Obedience* is a good word to use
because I often want to rebel against that. I have to say no to all
that because I have to be in the moment."

Endurance Ignores the Odds

We face challenges that call for extraordinary endurance because the risk of despair is so great. It is naive to say otherwise.
Major illness, financial pressures, the care of elderly parents or
handicapped children: This can be the stuff of our initiation into
endurance.

I have a friend who was born with cerebral palsy. She is bright,
independent, and funny, and she has had to endure living in a difficult body all of her life. I admire her, not because she was born
cosmically conscious and has no problem with her limitations, but
precisely because she does have problems with them and consistently works to bring them into consciousness.

Anne is a disciple and filmmaker who set out ten years ago to make a second documentary, her first having been a small but critically acknowledged film shot in the mid-1980s about the famines in Africa. The new film is about the wisdom of various indigenous peoples around the world.

The years it has taken to do this film are a recital of everything that could go wrong, from broken financial promises to betrayals, from prohibitive regulations within countries to arguing factions within tribes.

In the face of near bankruptcy, she had and lost a full-time job while she developed, fought for, and shot footage around the world. She has been disappointed, enraged, totally discouraged, physically exhausted. And she is creating an important film that will have a great impact on untold numbers of people.

Asked why she hasn't given up, she commented, "I never had a choice. I couldn't *not* do it, in spite of what others said." I have talked with her often during her bouts of discouragement, and even when her heart and at times her health and finances were broken. I've seen how she continues to rely on the spiritual intention of the film to get her through. Even though, of course, we always have a choice, committed people frequently speak of being driven to persist in spite of the worst discouragement.

People who are models of the power of endurance exist in every field of human endeavor, although most of them are unknown to us by name. Think of the freedom fighters in every country in the world, often tortured and imprisoned, who have sustained beliefs in human goodness in spite of their personal suffering. Remember the suffragettes who put up with devastating humiliations year after year to bring public attention to the denial of women's human rights.

Publishing history is filled with stories of best-sellers that sold millions of copies after having been repeatedly turned down by publishers—Richard Bach's *Jonathan Livingston Seagull* for one, and the Harry Potter books for another.

Louisa May Alcott, who wrote *Little Women*, was encouraged by her family to be a servant or seamstress. Beethoven was called hopeless. Caruso was told he had no voice; Fred Astaire, no acting ability. Thomas Edison was pronounced stupid, and in words to the same effect, so were the sculptor Rodin, the writer Tolstoy, and Charles Darwin. Even Albert Einstein, who didn't speak until he was four, was described by a teacher as "mentally slow" and was later refused admittance to the Zurich Polytechnic School.

How did these people do what they did? They endured. Walt Disney went bankrupt several times before Disneyland came into being. Abraham Lincoln's life is a checkerboard of as many rejections as acceptances—childhood poverty, heavy debt, lost jobs, lost elections, failures in business, and finally, in 1861, the presidency of the United States during the most trying era of American history. It was Lincoln's well-honed ability to persevere that brought his nation through the Civil War. Winston Churchill also experienced a lifetime of failures before he made history at sixty-two, leading his country through World War II.

Clearly these people managed to do "impossible" things. One of my favorite examples of doing the "impossible" was accomplished by Harriet Tubman, who was born around 1820 and died in 1913. She has been an inspiration and a teacher to me whenever I felt my challenges were too great. She was born a slave, owned by another human; she couldn't read or write and didn't know what existed beyond the boundaries of the plantation. As if this weren't enough, she suffered epileptic seizures.

Yet she was also given visions and inner direction that told her to save her people. Now, this was clearly "impossible." Nevertheless, she managed to escape from the plantation. Chased by men and hounds, she made her way through a wilderness she had never seen, let alone mapped, and found her way to freedom. She then proceeded to rescue hundreds of other slaves via the Underground Railroad, leading them through every sort of danger to freedom, never losing a single one. Then she helped the Union Army, taking them behind the enemy lines in the South, again never losing anyone. When the war was over she turned her attention to being a suffragette, lecturing all over the country, and writing a book about her life.

There are many things to learn from this amazing woman's life. Endurance is surely one of them.

Building Endurance

In the next chapter we're going to examine burnout and look at ways of supporting ourselves while serving, which is inseparable from endurance, as are all other aspects of discipleship.

In the meantime, consider some of these suggestions for enduring over the long haul.

- Take it one day at a time, moment by moment. Ask: "What do I need to do in this moment? What is its gift? What is the task?"

- Don't rehearse a future that may never happen, or review a past that keeps happening in your mind. Release them all.

- Remind yourself that life is a process, not an event. Remember: process, not product; privilege, not pressure.

- Patience with others begins with patience with self. Be tender with yourself.

- The longest journey begins with one step . . . and then another . . . and another.

- Accept interruptions, delays, detours, and the unexpected. Maybe the universe has something wonderful in mind that you didn't plan.

- Notice but don't energize obstructions. On the best days see them as challenges: "Can I make even *this* conscious?" On the worst days, just keep on affirming the truth behind appearances.

- Let go of disappointments that things didn't progress as

hoped or planned. Unreleased disappointments can get stockpiled.

- Take care of *all* of yourself. Care for your younger self with playtime; your physical self with good food, exercise, body-work; your emotional self with activities and people that nurture; your mental self by giving it a break (go to the movies, read a novel, talk to a child or an elder, etc.).

- Create balance in your life. Commitments that require endurance are frequently demanding. What puts your life in perspective and centers you? What fills you up?

Exercise: Lifelines

Create a beautiful scrapbook filled with your favorite quotes, poems, images, affirmations, prayers, mantras, scriptures, stories. If you do this as a spiritual practice when you are feeling clear, then it will be there to remind you of the underlying truths when you hit those periods of fatigue, discouragement, or confusion.

You can also create a second, small book that travels easily in a purse, backpack, or piece of luggage that contains the real pearls that sustain you through any challenge or temptation.

The Shadow Side of Endurance

Even such a sterling quality as endurance can move you into the dark side of the moon.

The ego attends all our workshops, reads our books, and will shamelessly take all of your resources for its own purposes. I sometimes think the ego personality likes the spiritual vocabulary best of all. It offers so many "acceptable" places to hide.

✖ Journaling Seeds

1. How do you recognize within yourself the difference between passionate commitment, obsession, and fanaticism?

2. Do you know when you are simply being stubborn? How does that differ from dedication?

3. What is the difference between martyrdom and endurance?

4. Can you see things as they are and still hold the vision of what they can be?

5. Most important, *why are you enduring? For what purpose?* ✓

If the answer to the question of why you are enduring comes back as "Because I have to; because my heart and my intuition tell me this is right for me no matter what the outer world says," then you are probably using your power to endure consciously.

If shoulds and oughts pop into your mind, be careful. If the answer comes intellectually framed, filled with quotes from other people and systems of thought, beautiful though they may be, watch out. That goal might not be yours. And if it's not, it isn't likely to sustain you over the long stretch.

Without honest self-examination, any of us can become like the proverbial mule with blinders on, stubborn and inflexible, dutifully plowing the row in front of us, having no idea why. Religion by rote is an example of that. If our goals are unexamined, we can end up like the man who said, "I don't know where I'm going, but I'm making great time!"

Hurry Up and Wait

The first substantial lesson we get in endurance is often to be patient and wait. "Wait upon the Lord," we're told. His and Her timetables rarely looks like ours! Often all we can see is the next baby step in front of us. The big picture is out of focus.

Having a vision and shouting it to the world is brave, of course. But offering the world viable applications of the vision takes world-class endurance. Impatience, on the other hand, is a world-class saboteur.

I've been in this consciousness movement long enough to watch enthusiasms come and go. And I have watched disenchantment set in. Where is the new golden world we've talked about for decades? Doubts and disillusionments fall like autumn leaves. We truly are separating the girls from the women and the men from the boys when it comes to holding visions steady during these intense times of planetary purification.

Probably no one finds spiritual waiting easy, but in Western culture waiting of any kind produces anxiety and great fear of failure. We start this hurry-up programming in the cradle. It's a disease that is communicable. Sometimes it seems that if you haven't written your first book, gotten your MBA, or amassed your first fortune by thirty years of age, you are falling behind. Achievement has been made into a god, and its mantra is hurry-hurry, hurry-hurry.

In the 1960s and early '70s, the baby boomers, who were challenging lifestyles built strictly on outer achievement, had their own mantras: "Drop out," "turn on," and "tune in." Many did drop out for a while, woke up spiritually, did their psychological work, and then reentered the world with their sleeves rolled up, ready to dedicate themselves to changing systems.

For many it took a decade or two of training to position themselves with the authority it takes to make changes on the material level. Now these boomers and the generation following them are moving into key spots in corporations, hospitals, publishing firms, dot-com companies, and other places of influence. They have endured the training, discipline, and backlashes. Often they've had to wait for systems to provide the tiniest opening and for other collaborating disciples to arrive.

Some philosophies encourage appreciation of a body of work that spans a lifetime, rather than evaluating success or failure too quickly. Marilyn is a brilliant and talented artist who paints on silk. She particularly admired the extraordinary beauty of hand-painted kimonos from Japan. So when a famous Japanese silk artist was showing in a museum in Manhattan, she attended his opening, which exhibited exquisite kimonos that he had created and which would sell for thousands of dollars each.

In meeting him, she expressed her admiration and blurted out, "I think you will be a living national treasure." (A living treasure is a Japanese tribute in which masters of certain crafts are held in such esteem, they are named national treasures.) The man smiled at her and said, "Perhaps in time. I'm quite young yet." He was in his mid-fifties at the time.

Stop, I'm Getting Off

If hurry-up is the sickness, what is the solution? As usual, it is self-responsibility and choice.

All of us occasionally feel the stop-the-world-I-want-to-get-off desire. Some do say, "Enough!" and choose the way of complete departure from the mainstream, entering cloisters and monasteries. Others go half and half, choosing to live in communities of like-minded people.

Another choice is to simplify to the point that survival doesn't take all of our strength. More and more people are opting for "voluntary simplicity," deliberately choosing a lifestyle that is less consuming and less cluttered. Laura is a brilliant woman who had been a serious disciple for many years and was also well on her way to a successful career in the scientific community. She feared that in the environment of hurry-up-and-achieve she was going to miss her own life. When she faced a crossroads in her life, she chose to leave her job and go into a monastery for a year.

Meditating for hours every day, with no way to escape from the busy mind's creations, and living a simple life took no small amount of endurance. Yet this practice rearranged her priorities. Over the next few years she alternated trips to the monastery with living in the city, gradually making her way back to the mainstream, carefully picking and choosing what she served. At this writing she is teaching in a monastery. She knows she has a contribution to make in the world. And wherever her life takes her, she will go the distance with her inner direction because she has the courage to challenge the false gods that will rob us of all our strength and service if we allow them.

Marsha Sinetar writes of people with similar motivations. In *Ordinary People as Monks and Mystics* she reports her research with people making the choice for what she calls "social and self-transcendence." Responding to their inner call, these people took a new look at where they were spending their time, devotion, and energy, all of which is the working energy of endurance. Through self-transcendence these people are seeking the mystical life within daily awareness.

I was very interested in her comments because they reflected what I have seen in my own practice. Increasingly, people who are working in all walks of life are seeking mystical experiences, and they don't want to leave the world behind. They are discovering how to be in the world but not of it. These individuals are the prototypes for a world to come. You are no doubt one if you are reading this book. Ask yourself what it means to you to be in the world but not of it.

When we're no longer the captives of a frenzied life lived according to someone else's deadlines, we can better experience and enjoy our own process. The process itself becomes our achievement, and excellence becomes a moment-by-moment, project-by-project, person-by-person experience. We'll give our best here and now, and savor the doing.

After All I've Done for You

For most of us, to go the distance will demand sacrifices. And if we make our sacrifices in dedication to a higher intention, no matter what the price, they bring peace and a sense of rightness.

The darker side of sacrifice is false martyrdom. I qualify this with the word *false* because there really is such a thing as giving up one's life for another. There are initiations in which one puts aside all personal concerns to serve the well-being of others.

Yet endurance put in service to false martyrdom is very dark indeed. It often leads to self-righteousness, disappointment, even bitterness. "She'll put up with anything" we hear of such a martyr. In such a case, endurance has been taken over by a neurotic agenda of the lower self.

"What am I putting up with and why?" is a good question for any of us. To endure with love and patience the raising of a severely handicapped child, the care of an elderly parent, or the tedious dismantling of an old system serves everyone's evolution. And while one cannot speak to the karma of another, it is doubtful that putting up with an abusive relationship with another adult, a job you hate, or a lifestyle designed by someone else's values serves anyone.

"I'm Saved; You're Lost; He's Damned"

Endurance is particularly insidious when it is employed to support prejudice of any kind. We know that extreme bias will announce itself outrageously, completely ignoring scholarship and factual inquiry. A conscious disciple is not likely to get caught in that web. Most that I know would really see themselves as beyond the extremists, who are in every persuasion and who declare that they are God's chosen. As one Middle Eastern scholar once said to me, "With the extremists there is no debating who is right or what is right about a point. It's very simple: You're wrong, and they will hear nothing else."

The need to be in an inner, select circle, privy to unique insights into the universe, seems to tempt us at every stage. And as with all aspects of discipleship, it becomes more and more subtle. I have seen almost as much exclusivity in so-called New Age circles as I have seen in fundamentalist religions. To go the distance on our own path, we do need to have a deep conviction that it is the right way for us. Whatever way we choose, it will demand a great deal of tenacity and discipline. We follow a particular path for many reasons, including culture, temperament, and karma. So do others, for their equally valid reasons.

For example, suicide would not be considered a spiritual act for most of us. Yet I once read a group of letters written by Japanese kamikaze pilots from World War II to their parents the night before they flew suicide missions. They are filled with statements of calmness, surety, and nobility. They could endure a deliberate death fully anesthetized by a powerful belief system.

When I was researching African traditions, if I had listened to common Western assumptions, African religions would have been distorted by reports of animal blood and so-called magic spells. Africans must have laughed a lot at white people's inability to comprehend thousands of years of healing arts and spiritual wisdom as superstition.

The challenge of bridging belief systems was well told by Dr. Malidoma Patrice Somé in his book *Of Water and the Spirit*. Dr. Somé returned to his homeland in Burkina Faso when he was twenty years old after having been kidnapped, raised, and educated by Franciscan monks from the time he was four. He announced that he wanted to be initiated into the wisdoms of his people, but the elders hesitated about allowing him to go through initiatory training, feeling he probably couldn't do it since he had been so programmed by the white man's philosophies. Much of the training required a suspension of the Western views of reality. It was very hard, yet his uncompromised intention allowed him to endure.

"My way or no way" is not just an interruption in the flow; it's a dam. The first principle of the universe is that all life is One. We have countless ways of arriving at that realization. The disciple picks one and honors all.

Fear Stops the Flow

Endurance needs a steady source of nourishment to stay vital and energized. When fear cuts off the valve to the universal supply, we can feel weakened in our resolve. Everything begins to feel like an uphill climb because we have to rely strictly on our limited human power. Our strength comes from what we believe is the source of our supply.

Anytime we align ourselves with an idea that challenges the status quo, we can experience inexplicable fears bubbling up from the collective memory pool, or from individual past life records. These fears can weaken our resolve and give us the feeling that our strength is leaking away.

Of course, our fears are so interwoven with our memories from this life or another that they're as unique as our fingerprints. Over the years I have observed two common fears, the fear of using power and the fear of persecution. These are worthy of our examination for two reasons: because they're part of the past we're seeking to purify, and because they can freeze an intention in its tracks and make endurance impossible.

Fear of Using Power

We've all danced again and again through all our many lifetimes to the tunes of *maya*, that mystical lady of illusion. We've all compromised our intentions because of fear, gotten caught in the seductions of money, power, and status. That's how we've learned. Yet hiding in the shadowy corners of memory can be the fear that if we dare to exercise power, we'll repeat the same mistakes. We have to forgive ourselves and recognize that whatever we've done in the past was just experience that taught us what does and doesn't work.

Judgment is a human invention to keep ourselves and each other in line. While the universe will certainly give all of us ample opportunities for learning and balancing, it never judges.

Adam was a dynamic, talented, and bright young man who showed every possibility of succeeding at whatever he chose to do. While in college (predictably, at age twenty-one, during a cycle change), he suddenly became vague and unfocused; he couldn't or wouldn't make a decision. After psychological and physical tests revealed nothing that would indicate such an extreme change, he was sent to me.

What was immediately revealed was that as Adam approached adulthood he found himself confronting a fear he'd been carrying from a past life—the fear of making a mistake and misusing his power. Our work revealed that in a previous life he had used the power of his position and authority to make military decisions that resulted in many deaths, and he had never forgiven himself for this experience.

As we discussed this subject, Adam began to recognize that his lethargy was a cover for the fear that he might hurt someone else if he was in a position of power again. As we worked together, he began to understand that the military decisions were made in the context of another set of values and another culture. I tried to help Adam understand that it was just experience and part of his training in understanding and functioning in three-dimensional reality.

I recommended that Adam take the path of a vision quest. To do this, he would first have to undergo purification rituals in a sweat lodge under the guidance of a medicine man or woman. This had a link with other positive associations in his subconscious and isn't necessarily what I might recommend for someone else. Such recommendations are always highly individualistic. However, sometimes the psyche needs to experience the catharsis of ritualized release.

Adam undertook his quest, and that led him to harness his spiritual power to express this life's intention. He learned through his quest guide to redefine masculine warrior energy and that masculine power did not have to translate into conquest.

I've recommended various martial arts to parents of certain children with similar subconscious memories that have left fear, ambivalence, or confusion in the psyche about power and strength. Tai chi, kung fu, aikido, and other martial arts teach many things, among them balance, self-mastery, and self-confidence. It is important, of course, that these arts be taught by a spiritually conscious person. Like all other practices, they can be usurped to serve the lower ego perspectives as well.

However, a skilled teacher in the martial arts who places emphasis on spiritual, mental, and emotional discipline can help his or her students feel more comfortable with the energy they feel surging through them. They can be less intimidated by power if they have confronted and learned how to channel energy. Until they are comfortable with their own strength and power, they can't endure much of anything, for the fear is too great that they will harm someone.

Equally important is their opportunity to experience, respect, and balance the power of both yang and yin energies. They learn that power in action fulfills the vision, but power in alert receptivity is what receives the vision in the first place.

Fear of Persecution

The fear of being persecuted keeps many potential disciples hiding behind accepted social, political, and religious conventions. Many men and women carry ambivalence about revealing their truth because of violent past life experiences. Torture, exile, and imprisonment are just a few of the ways humans have persecuted each other. As we have all incarnated as both sexes, our repressed fears could have originated in either male or female incarnations.

Many women today carry the rage and terror of the burning times when religion sanctioned systematic torture and death. In the fourteenth through the sixteenth centuries, several million people were put to death as witches. Most of them were ordinary women—wives and mothers, midwives, herbalists, and healers. Being accused was all it took in many cases to be arrested.

I have heard the legacy of these times echoing down through the centuries, depositing traces of the paralyzing fears in our collective consciousness. Many women who are eager to express their wisdom and actualize their dreams in the world discover that they are mysteriously afraid. A woman doesn't even have to have experienced a persecution directly. It is enough to encounter it in the sea that holds all our collective human memories.

It doesn't really take a lot of rattling of the chains to activate these fears today. As we move deeper into the age shifts, the ultra-conservative religions would once again sentence the feminine to a role of submission and powerlessness. Put the woman behind a veil, back in a man's castle, and exile the feminine from the centers of influence. Evolution says, "No way," yet generations of women must still endure the backlash of the transition times in which we live.

Many women have come into this life with the soul intention of helping to restore awareness of the Mother aspect of the Divinity. They embody the message of the Mother not only in their gender, but in the deeper wisdom of the feminine they carry in their karmic patterns. They are building bridges across which their daughters and granddaughters—and their sons and grandsons—will walk. The Mother and the Father live in us all.

As women commit themselves to bringing the awareness of the Mother into the physical, they sometimes snag themselves on inner fears of persecution, memory traces held from other lifetimes in which they, or their brothers and sisters, paid for our collective terror and repression of the divine feminine with their lives.

To deliberately embrace our inner fears takes great courage. A therapist/disciple who has been through her own fires commented, "You eventually develop a fearlessness. The idea that you are not going to be given more than you can deal with becomes more than an idea, but an internal, absolute knowingness. Then you feel as though you can trust the universe."

There is no one who can endure longer than the one who has confronted her worst fears, which then, like the Wicked Witch of the West in *The Wizard of Oz*, melt into nothingness. Once we have faced down our worst fears, what can stop us? As the adage says, there is no one stronger than the person who has nothing to lose.

✖ Twelve Considerations on Enduring

1. Endurance empowers all other aspects of discipleship.

2. Endurance shapes by gentle insistence, not by heavy blows.

3. Endurance makes possible the birth of visions into form.

4. Endurance holds to truths not seen during the dark times.

5. Endurance is unconditional: "I'm in, no matter what."

6. Endurance sees purpose and learning in failure and success.

7. Endurance notices what is and energizes what can be.

8. Endurance accepts discipline in order to achieve excellence.

9. Endurance gracefully sacrifices the lesser for the greater.

10. Endurance combines soul purpose with material muscle.

11. Endurance is patient and perseveres with the process.

12. Endurance has no beginning or end: "I endure because I Am."

Exercise: Empty in Order to Be Filled

This simple meditation practice has no cultural context.

Begin by relaxing with deep breathing. Imagine holes in the tips of your fingers and toes. With each breath imagine that you are draining tensions out. Do this until you feel totally relaxed.

Close the holes. Breathe normally. Relax. Be aware of being empty of tension. Fill yourself up with the Light as you would a pitcher, starting with your feet, using your breath to draw forth the Light. Pause and exhale as needed.

Once filled with the Light, mentally push the Light outside the skin of your body. With every inhalation be aware of your body; see your feet touching the earth. With every exhalation extend the Light in every direction, seeing that there is no limit to how far you can expand: touching the earth, touching the heavens, breathing in and out.

Prayer

Hello, Divine Oneness. We are gathered here within You, this special group of Your beings. We thank You for this day. We thank You for each other. I thank You for me. We dedicate this day to the honor of Oneness. We ask that everything we need be provided for. We ask that everything we do today, say today, or hear today be only to the highest good, in my highest good, in the highest good for all life everywhere throughout the universe. End of message.

—Aboriginal morning greeting

Affirmation

*I can do all things through the
inner Christ, which strengthens me.*

Quotes

When nothing seems to help, go and look at a stonecutter hammering away at his rock perhaps a hundred times without as much as a crack showing in it. Yet at the hundred and first blow it will split. . . . And I know it was not that blow that did it—but all that had gone before.

—Jacob Riis

*The woods are lovely and dark and deep
But I have promises to keep,
And miles to go before I sleep,
And miles to go before I sleep.*

—Robert Frost, from "Stopping by Woods
on a Snowy Evening"

I feel that as long as the earth can make a spring every year, I can. As long as the earth can flower and produce nurturing fruit, I can, because I'm the earth. I won't give up until the earth gives up.

—Alice Walker, in New Dimensions radio interview

There is nothing softer or more yielding than water, and on earth there is nothing stronger. In time it will wear away the hardest rock.

—Lao Tzu

Serving: Returning the Gift

✘

It is in the shelter of each other that the people live. —Irish proverb

Serving is the natural outpouring of compassion from an open and full heart. When I give of myself, I renew my contract with the universe. When I withhold myself, I am no longer in sync with the flow that connects me with the rest of life. I become as a rock in a fast-moving river, destined to be worn down but in the meantime resistant, out of the flow and beaten by the very waters that would carry me to the sea. There can be as much pain in being full and not giving of oneself as there can be in feeling empty. In giving, the disciple empties him- or herself to be filled again and again.

Nature reminds us that everything we have, we owe to life serving life. We would not breathe oxygen were it not for the exhalation of the great forests. We depend on algae that know how to filter excess salt from the sea. From simple protozoa and single-celled organisms the very first basis of our life was built.

We are serving life, laying the foundation for future generations even as we now enjoy the benefits laid down by all who have gone before us. Hubris of the spirit is in some measure the arrogance of thinking that one arrives anywhere by oneself.

Nothing is lost in the universe, and sometimes an act that will change the direction of the world begins with a single seed that falls in fertile soil. We are all potentially carrying a piece of an answer. Perhaps the 1930s movie *It's a Wonderful Life* is a Christmas tradition for many people, less for its cinematic excellence than for its reminder of the importance of a single life.

Because of our limited perspectives, we sometimes imagine that our efforts are insignificant. Nothing could be further from the truth. There is no way to avoid influencing the world. We are cells of consciousness in the living world organism, which is being shaped moment to moment by each of our thoughts, emotions, words, and actions. Since we don't know who will eventually receive even the smallest kindness, we might choose to relate to everyone as if he or she is here to save the world.

Laura Esquivel, author of *Like Water for Chocolate* and *The Law of Love*, shared that she begins each day with a ritual of burning incense, meditating, and asking the universe for permission to write. In an interview she said, "Because all of the work that you are going to do that day will change the universe. Your energy, your work, your movements will change the balance. So you should ask the universe, please let me live to work."

Through the years materials I have offered in a lecture or written in a book have reflected back to me from the most unimaginable places. That has sensitized me into a strong sense of responsibility for what I put into the world. We simply never know whom our words or actions will ultimately influence.

What Dream Is Dreaming You?

Service is the disciple's mission on earth. Intuitively we know that we incarnate for a purpose that is far beyond mere survival or endless self-glorification. People often have distinct feelings of purposefulness in childhood. Even when their adult assignments didn't resemble their childhood fantasies, the baselines are often the same.

Abby grew up with Albert Schweitzer and medical missionaries as her heroes. This disciple found out that medical school wasn't for her, yet her path of service led her into interesting variations of those childhood dreams. "I didn't end up being a medical missionary, but I did end up helping to form a very avant-garde psychiatric hospital and pioneering a holistic approach to the treatment of mental health problems. So I ended up being a missionary in the medical field right in my hometown."

✂ Journaling Seeds

1. As a child, did you ever want to "save the world" or rescue animals? Why?

2. How have youthful dreams influenced the choices you have made as an adult?

3. Who are your current heroes and heroines?

4. Have you ever felt called to do something from your deepest Self? How did you respond?

In his book *The Call* David Spangler tells of the amazement of his own spiritual guide in response to people's questions about their calling. "The call was to discover in the here and now, in all the ramifications and details of his or her individual life, how to be his or her essence, which was love . . . the primal background call, the call to love oneself, to love others and to love that presence and mystery we name the sacred."

To answer the call to love fully is to say, as did Gandhi, "My life is my mission."

Many of us would resonate with a disciple named Megan who

is a business consultant and an intuitive. "I kept asking, 'What is my mission?' expecting a definitive answer such as teaching or counseling or healing. One day I got this message in my meditation: 'Do you want to be used as you see it, or do you want to be used as I see it?' " Megan realized that her mission was simply to serve and that God/Goddess would provide the opportunities.

"I now believe all missions are serving. Being kind, loving, and supportive to a total stranger in the grocery store may have the ripple effect of touching millions of people all over the globe. It's not the size of the job you are called to do that's of value. It's the selfless commitment to do what you're called on to do."

Who, Me? If Not, Who?

We all can feel powerlessness in the face of societal problems that appear overwhelming. Yet if we stay awake, we can attune to that moment when the soul says, "Now," and the ego says, "Okay." We never know when such a moment will arrive.

For Russian artist Maria Yeliseyeva, that moment arrived when she visited an orphanage in Moscow, where opportunities for the children were very limited and offered no programs for building self-worth and creativity. Even though she had young children of her own, she made the commitment to use art as a vehicle for mentoring the children in the orphanage. At the time, there was almost no support. But that soon changed in a totally unpredictable way. On one of his trips to Russia, Dr. Patch Adams went to the orphanage with a group of American doctors who were traveling with him as clowns. They were profoundly touched by the work Maria was doing, and from that connection Maria's Children Foundation was born. Sparked by another doctor, Dr. Jan Adams, support grew in America, and in a few years thousands of dollars were raised.

In 2000 Maria's single seed burst into full bloom in America when the original art of children from the orphanage was displayed and purchased in galleries in Washington, D.C., Minneapolis, New York City, and Seattle.

The moment is rarely as dramatic for us as it was with Alfred Nobel, who gave millions to support the Nobel Peace Prize that he established. He had made his fortune in explosives. When his brother died, the newspaper printed the wrong obituary, so that Alfred Nobel read his own obit while he was still alive. He was apparently horrified and saddened by his identity as a producer of so many destructive inventions, so he set up and funded the various prizes, which subsequently served the whole world.

For one American teacher the moment arrived when she was ironing. She contacted me from the Czech Republic, writing that she had been teaching for years in a school in America, frustrated with many of the circumstances. "Most of us returned each fall saying, 'Only nine more years till I retire—I can do that.' But each day a little life disappeared from our eyes and hearts and was transferred into our retirement accounts to be lived at some future time, nine years from now. One day I heard Vaclav Havel, the president of the Czech Republic, on the radio saying that they needed English teachers in his country. I suddenly said, 'I can do that.' " And she did, and she is a happy, fulfilled person.

Marsha found her mission and moved from helplessness to action through a local environmental cause that involved facing down a large corporation that was creating toxic products. She joined a grassroots boycott and soon was making a speech that was so moving, it was later published in a local paper. "I've learned a lot. I've seen how a small group of four or five deeply committed individuals can cause a ripple to become a wave."

Sharon Tennyson, whose story is told in *Citizen Diplomats*, and who is founder of the Center for Innovative Diplomacy, is an extraordinary woman who insists she was an ordinary wife, mother, and nurse when she felt compelled to go to Russia during the

Cold War era. She was horrified that so many people assumed that nuclear war was inevitable. She wanted to reach out in peace to the average Russian.

Without knowing exactly the purpose of that first trip, other than the need to communicate, and in spite of not knowing the language, she listened to her inner guidance and jumped into the unknown. The universe set up the agenda after that. Since then Sharon has led several dozen groups to Russia to meet, interact with, and build bridges of understanding with shopkeepers, children, dancers, the young and old—ordinary people.

The seeds for her mission to Russia were cooking in Sharon for a long time. As a child of the South, she had been upset at society's treatment of African-Americans. Years later, as a young mother in the suburbs, she organized tutoring programs that helped black children who had been in substandard schools prepare for the academic challenges of integration.

Disciples are frequently given early assignments, so to speak, and if they are faithful to them, other opportunities follow. The universe uses the vessel that has proven it won't break or leak.

Timothy is a disciple, spiritual scholar, and hemophiliac who was consciously aware of the risks when he volunteered to be the first person to be treated with a genetically engineered blood factor. As a result of the success, he was asked to talk at a world conference. "What could be more Aquarian than to be involved in that kind of scientific, medical, transformational research? We will see more and more of those breakthroughs happening in genetic research at the very time that other structures are falling apart."

Most of us are not going to be assigned to the furthermost corners of the earth. And maybe we won't be making major speeches. But whatever our service is, we will be guided to it if we are open and willing.

Teacher, writer, and disciple Ann D'Arien says the first requirement in life is to show up. Sometimes wisdom advises to just say,

"Here I am." As a friend says, "Just keep breathing and be willing." Another starts her day with this simple prayer: "Show me the perfect thing to do this day and do it perfectly through me."

How to Recognize Your Assignment

1. It feels right. The body, spirit, and intuition say yes.
2. Enthusiasm is present. Doing your own thing and doing God/Goddess's thing are increasingly the same.
3. There is a sustaining interest even in the face of hardship.
4. You can't not do it and have inner peace.
5. Money is not the criterion. Typically you think, "I can't believe they pay me to do this," or "I'd do this with no pay."
6. An ability to renew after intense effort or fatigue. Tired doesn't mean burned out.
7. Synchronicities of all kinds occur that provide the right encounters or the necessary training, contacts, funds, or insights.
8. People absorbed in their missions don't watch clocks too closely. There is a Zen presence in their service.
9. The joy is in the doing. One's interest lies in the moment and not necessarily in the results. Immediate gratification becomes less and less a motivation for excellence.
10. There is an absolute gratitude that you can do the work. I recall a poignant moment with a doctor in which tears broke through his normally controlled demeanor when he spoke of the sheer privilege of practicing medicine.
11. Humility is ever present, and you recognize that it is a grace to fulfill a calling. Paramahansa Yogananda often said, "I am not the guru. God is the guru. I am only his servant."
12. One understands the principle of being willing to give before receiving.

There once was a poor beggar in China who held out his rice cup to the emperor, who was passing in parade. He expected it to be filled. Much to his surprise and disappointment, the emperor asked him for a gift.

The beggar took two of the smallest grains of rice he could find in his bowl and gave them to the ruler. That evening he found two nuggets of gold in his bowl exactly the size of the rice grains he had given the emperor.

Volunteering as a Path

The teacher taught that the true reformer was one who was able to see that everything is perfect as it is. Why, then, reform anything?

"Well, there are reformers and reformers," said the teacher. "One type lets action flow through them while they themselves do nothing. These people change the shape and flow of a river. The other reformers generate their own activity, and they are like people trying to make the river wetter."

Thousands upon thousands of us are instruments through which the river is being reshaped. And we're doing it by giving hours every month to local civic, religious, social, and political organizations or by going into disaster zones and depressed areas as the hands and feet of the Mother-Father-God. Untold numbers offer daily service for neighbors, families, and friends. Most expect nothing in return.

As every servant knows, giving of oneself is the most delightfully selfish thing we can do, for the "helper's high" is a deeply fulfilling experience. Service is also recognized around the world as the quintessence of being god/human. There is much truth in this statement: The greater the master, the greater the servant.

In the companion book to a 1996 PBS series called *Visionaries*, Bill Moyers speaks of the recurring theme in every corner of the world when people give of themselves: "While everyone else is scurrying about in their roles as either planners or players in some grand corporate scheme, there is a whole group of people who approach life differently. They get up every day and involve themselves in the details of living. This day, this moment, they simply give and trust that the rest will take care of itself. *They are visionaries, not because they see into the future, but because they see into the moment"* [italics mine].

One such group, the Human Service Alliance, is based in Winston-Salem, North Carolina. This unique organization, which is completely funded by donations, was created over a decade ago. Volunteers have given thousands of hours and come from all over the United States to serve their four major in-house projects: the Center for the Care of the Terminally Ill, the Respite Care Project of Families with Developmentally Disabled Children, the Health and Wellness Project, the Mediation (Dispute Resolution) Project, and a restaurant whose profits go to charity. The organization outlines their concept for effective group service work as follows:

1. Having a clear purpose
2. Avoiding all negative criticism of other members of the group
3. Fostering cooperation
4. Establishing trust
5. Leaving personal agendas at the door
6. Participating in group projects

Since 1987 the Institute of Noetic Sciences in California has been presenting the Temple Award for Creative Altruism. In one of their newsletters they summed up their five very simple observations of creative service:

1. Each of us makes a difference.
2. Individuals and groups can often meet needs that established groups cannot.

3. You don't have to go out of your way to find opportunities to serve.
4. Sometimes the courage to venture into the unknown is important.
5. Caring comes first.

Ganga Stone won a Temple Award for her work in founding God's Love We Deliver, a nonprofit organization that prepares and delivers hundreds of gourmet meals twice a day to homebound people with AIDS. She said, "The decision to serve others is the highest impulse of the human heart and the rewards of such service are beyond measure. If you wish to taste this joy, then just do it. Just take one step. . . . It doesn't really matter what you do; it only matters that you do it."

The Many Faces of Serving

The Hindus describe four ways of giving to the world: We can give food *(ana)*, money *(swarna)*, education *(vidya)*, or wisdom *(jnana)*. A devotee can evolve through the practice of karma yoga, service in the world. No matter how we choose to give, in serving each other we serve the sacred, fulfilling the mandate "If you do it unto the least of them, you do it unto me."

Some view those who serve the world as troublesome. Servers insist on calling our attention to what needs fixing. They point out that the emperor has no clothes. They ask us to acknowledge the elephant in the living room that everyone talks around.

The most effective way any of us serve is to live our lives as consciously as possible. Persons living their truths walk into a room and positively affect everyone and everything in it, literally changing energy from one frequency to another.

My mother radiates a great deal of light. Once when she was having physical therapy following surgery, the therapists said that every time she was in the rehab unit, everybody there got better.

She didn't preach or do anything. She was simply being a healing presence, quietly offering transformational energy for anyone receptive to it.

Our personal intentions are so interwoven with the purposes of evolution, they are inseparable from the good of all life. The daily choices we make are influencing the world. Let's look at three examples of this.

1. *One form of service to the whole is to create balance between polarities.* Divinity is, of course, beyond gender, but in this earth dimension one expression of polarity is gender. On this earth we are not very balanced in terms of yin and yang energy. Not only have we valued yang energy more than yin, but its power has been too often distorted into overspecialization, acquisition, and conquest. We can interpret our disregard, ignorance, or fear of the feminine aspect of the Divine in no small measure by how we treat yin qualities in both males and females as well as how much we protect— or not—the rights of all women everywhere.

Since World War II, in spite of backlashes that are a predictable cycle in growth, there has been a growing awareness and celebration of the Divine feminine in books, tapes, videos, magazines, conferences, and thousands of small groups all over the world. As we express this awareness we will also be celebrating the conscious return of our Mother in the hearts of both men and women.

The ultimate fruits of this movement will be *balance, not more polarization.* Because, of course, the Mother never left; we just didn't see Her. In the meantime we have a lot of work to do to teach all of our children to love and honor their Holy Mother *and* their Holy Father. As we create inclusive language, hymns, sanctuaries, and rituals that honor our wholeness, we will help heal the polarity split in our psyches that is the source of so much suffering on this planet.

A great service is offered to the planet every time any one of us is willing to resolve our own sexism. It may not always be possible or appropriate to resist the sexism around us, but we can consciously avoid energizing it, especially through our choice of words. Language reflects a world of assumptions and beliefs about reality. Words matter. Disciples learn to use them deliberately.

I once debated with an architect who insisted the word *God* embraced the concept of the feminine, even though it was considered to be gendered masculine. When I asked him if his blueprints casually indicated "more or less two inches," he admitted that the only way to get exactly what he wanted was to have a specific blueprint. Words are one of the ways we design the blueprint for what we want to manifest.

2. *Another form of service is to help dissolve the collective shadow.* For example, I know many Germans who are using their energies to help clear the collective Nazi shadows that linger over Germany and threaten to erupt wherever there is hatred. Not all are as extreme as the Carmelite nuns living just outside Dachau who took vows of silence in order to pray for both Jews and Germans. Many participate in events such as the "chain of lights," which peacefully protested against the rise of hatred. Mainly they just live their values, which permeate the very air that everyone breathes.

A few years ago, during a workshop I attended in Germany, I observed the effects of one woman's courage to confront the shadow. A Jewish-American therapist Dr. Judith S. Miller, author of *Direct Connection: Transformation of Consciousness*, taught the workshop and shared her personal process of dealing with the Holocaust. She had become interested in particular archetypes through her clients, explaining that often when they had a positive breakthrough, they experienced variations of Christ imagery, regardless of their religious background, and when they were under emotional and spiritual siege, their dreams frequently contained Nazi symbology, regardless of their nationality.

She arrived for her first visit to Germany in Berlin the weekend the wall came down. Then later that week she visited a concentration camp and was overwhelmed with grief. She confessed to workshop participants that after her experience at the camp, she simply wanted to get away from Germany and Germans.

But her return to the airport routed her through what had been East Germany, and she found herself on a train with East Germans traveling to the West to visit family and friends they hadn't seen for years because of the wall. The whole train was celebrating; people were clutching addresses in their hands, crying and hugging strangers. She felt her kinship with them. That train ride was a profound spiritual journey for her, from the darkness of Auschwitz to the light of human liberty.

She said that she really got it that Nazism was not simply a German thing; it was the dark shadow of all humans—Germans, Jews, and everyone else. The effect on her audience was immediate and profound. Her honesty and vulnerability in sharing this with a German audience seemed to give them freedom to share their grief because she honored the fact that the problem was universal, not just German.

People popped up all over the audience with tears and stories, expressing their desire to clean up the thoughts of shame and blame in their country. It was a powerful, moving, and cathartic experience for everyone present. I have no doubt that the circles of healing set in motion that day are still at work—all because of one disciple's courage to stand before a group and tell her truth.

Repressed energy of any kind will find an outlet, even if it takes generations. We can't see with the naked eye a gene that passes down a physical illness, but we can treat it once we know it's there; neither can we see a psychic gene, but we can discover it and treat it. Just as family phantoms are being increasingly recognized in various therapies, the human family also has its phantoms that must be treated.

As an English therapist remarked to me, "Everything that is not conscious gets passed on. We have the job of either making some kind of sense out of it or passing it on to our children. Guilt is unacknowledged generational shadow that hangs like a millstone around our necks. Guilt is feeling responsible for something that you could not possibly be responsible for."

We all hold vast libraries inside us. It doesn't matter if we don't cognitively know the specific ancestral patterns. No matter how mysterious, the very cells of our bodies hold all the information we need, and we can access it in many ways that complement traditional therapies, including body therapies, visualization journeys, hypnotherapy, imaginary dialogues with ancestors, "talking" with the problem, doing release rituals, and so on.

Start with a clear intention: "I want to know." Write that intention in your journal. Pray for guidance. Then pay attention and remember that the whole universe is connected, so you will draw to yourself answers to all your questions.

Most important, respect the fact that you have chosen at some deep level to challenge and then transform some inherited belief, prejudice, or illusion. Your karma has placed you in the pattern; your spiritual craftsmanship will break the pattern.

3. *Many disciples are called to serve in the marketplace.* It's little wonder that "You can't fight city hall" became a cliché for failed attempts to alter systems. The weight and mass of tradition plus the tangled wires of bureaucracy can be intimidating and just about always frustrating.

Even something that is meant to do good can bog down in habitual ways of approaching problems. Lynn worked at the United Nations and attended an international conference on food and nutrition. Even though there was a major famine at the time in Africa, she said there were dozens of people from all over the world spending days debating and defining the fine lines between level I malnutrition and level II malnutrition.

Fortunately, there are pioneers among us who are restructuring systems so well that they are, as the Buddhists and also the Quakers advise, "doing well while doing good." These new models are like healthy green promises offering alternatives.

One of the most exciting places we are seeing these practical disciples is in business where they are challenging an insatiable, seducing materialism that has consumed without conscience—the environment, other species, the politically and economically weak, and even its own employees and customers. Such disciples are successfully introducing healthy new ideas in spite of downsizing, corporate takeovers, the big swallowing the small, and atmospheres that make the notion of job security an oxymoron. They are confronting the theology of the bottom line. People are brave to become heretics here, for they are questioning some of the most sacrosanct beliefs that drive our culture.

These "heretics" are smart, educated, passionate about new models, and very skilled in succeeding in the old dominant models—which is essential, or else they don't get in the door. As a pragmatic teenager once said to me, "How are you going to change the system unless you are in it?"

In the last decade many visionary business disciples have moved into positions of power. They are now sitting on boards of directors, designing new programs, making budgets, funding exciting new projects, hiring inspired young people, shifting priorities within departments.

These new entrepreneurs, disciples in the marketplace, talk freely of the interconnectedness of all life on the planet, employing spirit in the workplace, and serving humanity as both the process and the product—all while making money for everybody.

The spirit soars when you are satisfying your own basic material needs in such a way that you are also serving the needs of others, honorably and humanely.
—Anita Roddick (CEO of the Body Shop), *Body and Soul*

"Socially and environmentally responsible" is a term that has entered the mainstream as a desirable criterion in everything from making a product to investing money. One way all of us serve the whole is by refusing to buy products that are not with the global program. This means we have to pay close attention and not get hooked emotionally by the spin masters who would exploit our sentiments in their ads but not change their policies.

> *Goodness is not something out there standing still, like a rock, as most business leaders assume. Like invisible electric waves, goodness moves around us, but it has to be actively sought out and created. We have to choose to be a part of it. We have to choose to be good. We can do it only in connection with others. Benevolence is more than making a deal. It's an attitude of being in relation, and a will to do something good. Do well; do good. Do both.*
>
> —Tom Chappell (founder, Tom's of Maine),
> *The Soul of a Business*

Growing with a Group

Sometimes service can feel very lonely. The work itself is often not among people who share your spiritual views, even if they are professional peers. It can be very hard to deflect the false messages we are bombarded with daily. Joining a group of like-minded others who meet regularly is a steady reminder of your own values.

Men can have a hard time finding spiritual support in a society that affirms different values for them. Several successful professional men attended a workshop together recently. When I asked them what happens if they bring up spiritual matters in the locker room, boardroom, or operating room, the answers varied from "There would be embarrassed silence" to "The subject would be changed; somebody would start talking sports or the stock market." They all agreed that in the marketplace, their walk was very lonely. To sustain their own callings, they really need the support of a spiritual community.

Our ideal in the West of the rugged individualist, mobility, and abundance has often created a by-product of loneliness. We can feel quite isolated even in the middle of thousands of people. Occasionally the thin veneer of separateness is ripped away by the traumas of natural or man-made disasters, and then we remember we are family.

Scott Peck wrote in an essay, "The Fallacy of Rugged Individualism," "that as we cannot be all things to ourselves and to others, we need a new ethic of 'soft individualism.'"

"When we deny that we need each other," he suggests, "this denial can be sustained only by pretense. Because we cannot ever be totally adequate, self-sufficient, independent beings, the ideal of rugged individualism encourages us to fake it. It encourages us to hide our weaknesses and failures. It teaches us to be utterly ashamed of our limitations. It drives us to attempt to be superwomen and supermen not only in the eyes of others but also in our own."

The power of the group is reflected in the Hopi saying "One finger can't lift a pebble." The group mind is a powerful tool for service, whether it is expressed in a full-blown intentional community, a group formed to stir a grassroots movement for what one disciple calls "shoulder-to-shoulder projects," or Mastermind groups. (These are typically small groups of people who come together to support the personal goals of its members.) Even a group traveling together with a common intention can serve as a supportive community. I've taken groups of seekers to Bali, Greece, and Scotland who reported that the community they experienced with like-minded people during two weeks of travel supported them in their service long after the trip was over.

I know some extremely busy people who formed a group because they were always hip-deep in assignments and felt that they periodically needed the support of people who shared their ideals in order to remember why they were so busy with their assignments in the first place.

Patrick, a therapist and business consultant, was a member of that group. "We committed to a year's worth of solstices and equinoxes. We create sacred space and ritual, and we play. And it has woven a fabric of community that has been priceless to me. We are all struggling to weave the sacred into the day-to-day that we have to deal with. A lot of conversations in our group are about that process. How do you deal with relationships, right livelihood, right action, right politics?"

A small group meeting with a focused intention can provide a regular oasis in which we are renewed. *Sangha* is the Buddhist term and *satsong* the Hindu for spiritual community. As in a dogon, temple, church, mosque, tribal sacred ground, or synagogue, people gather for support, to share common spiritual goals, to pass on wisdom, and to practice together.

Spiritual community is also being created on the Internet. In cyberspace we can touch with our minds. However, we must be careful, for community requires that we also touch with our hearts, and it is very easy to turn off the computer if we don't like what we see. Yet the possibilities for reinforcing the real etheric net that connects us in spirit are enormous. Imagine the possibilities when hearts and heads are in sync from New York to Sydney to Beijing—all independent of local politics.

John Naisbitt of *Megatrends* fame cites the shift from hierarchy to networks as one of the ten directions that will mold the future. Networking will ride the borderless waves that connect all people, so that no matter how much control appears to be held by governments, corporate monopolies, and the media, people will have freedom and a growing power to link intentions.

Group Work

1. The group pools power, which exponentially increases with the numbers. We can do together what we cannot do alone.
2. Each participant brings a unique contribution, and each is a thread in the karmic tapestry of the group.

3. Nurturing spiritual communities promotes equality in giving and taking.

4. The group becomes a microcosm of the society. Weaknesses and strengths, both of which offer opportunities for growth, will emerge.

5. Groups provide opportunities for learning how to weave personal goals with larger goals.

6. Groups become more luminous as participants pour energies into them. This presence in turn nurtures everyone who participates.

7. The person in the group who is angry, skeptical, or rebellious may be acting out unexpressed attitudes within the group.

Remember the old Hawaiian practice I referred to earlier that when anyone in the family went "off," the whole family would gather to see what was wrong in the family, not just what was wrong with that one person who may just be the carrier of the family problem.

When the whole human family has an outbreak of madness, wouldn't it be wonderful if we asked ourselves what is amiss in our family such that this disharmony has occurred? Of course, that would mean we would have to say *we* have AIDS, *we* are experiencing famine, *we* are on the receiving end of cruelty, *we* are subject to racism. *They* would become just a grammatical convenience and not the definition of the "other."

The Compassion of the Bodhisattva

There's a tiny little verse in the story of Jesus that describes a passage that every disciple of the truth eventually must make. It says, "Jesus wept." The story places him on a hillside overlooking Jerusalem. Seeing all the pain and the ignorance, he just cried. And so do we, sometimes just watching the evening news. After the tears comes the practical work down in the valley.

Remember that the ultimate manifestation of compassion is the Bodhisattva, who has so completely mastered the lessons of the earth plane that he or she need not return, but who stays here as long as any of us is still in the dark and suffering. Archetypically, the Bodhisattva becomes a beloved figure to whom we turn in our darkest moments for support. So it is with Kuan Yin, Goddess of compassion and mercy, a Bodhisattva who is as familiar and beloved in the Far East as Mary is in the West.

Many people who follow a dedicated path of service have taken Bodhisattva vows many, many lives ago and are committed to the goal of serving all of humanity no matter how many more lifetimes it takes. Consciously we may have forgotten that we did so, for the actual declaration of intention is dimmed by gravity, density, karma, and illusions of personality. Yet the soul remembers and quickens in response to the pain of others with a compassion that sees beyond all deeds into the soul.

Perennial wisdom teaches that at the point of knowing Oneness, the disciple can take on shadows from the collective to purify them. Shamans call it "eating shadows." Tibetan Buddhism teaches meditations on breathing in the pain of the world and breathing out compassion, mercy, and love. They teach devotees to offer any merits of their practice to the universe on behalf of all humanity.

My own spiritual guidance has been that we can do this only if we are very clear about the issues ourselves. For example, if I wish to breathe in the pain of those in despair in order to release it, I must be very, very sure I have no attachments left to my own despair. Otherwise my despair would be increased. The authenticity of such a practice requires the marriage of compassion and detachment. Detachment means acceptance without judgment—unlike indifference, which only negates compassion.

Our Western ears are attuned to psychological language that is wisely wary of anything that smacks of rescue or enabling. Practices for cleaning up the collective shadow are not about rescue. They are about transforming the psychic environment for everyone.

Prayer for the World's Suffering

I gather the tears of all sentient beings into a chalice in my heart, and I offer it to the Divine. I am empty, and I wait. The living water fills my vessel to overflowing, and I joyfully pour its renewing life into the world. I breathe in your pain, all my relations, and I breathe out the grace that belongs to us all. For the immeasurable gift of this alchemy, I give thanks.

Exercise:
Meditation with the Bodhisattva White Tara

1. Sitting comfortably, center yourself with relaxed breathing.

2. Visualize the White Tara, a Bodhisattva who serves all of humanity. See Her sitting on a full moon that is held by a flowering lotus. Behind Her is another full moon. On Her forehead is the Sanskrit symbol for the tone *Om*.

3. Invite this image into your heart. There you become one as She totally dissolves into your being. You are filled with the sound *Om*. You are filled with Light. You are filled with the compassion of the Bodhisattva.

4. Visualize rays of light emanating from Her inner presence which is in you. See it radiating in all directions.

5. Send these rays of light to all sentient beings everywhere on this planet and beyond.

Exercise: The Spiritual Think Tank

If you would like to help out with a need you observe but you don't quite know how to begin, try having a spiritual think tank session with yourself or a group.

Step 1. There's only one rule: No idea, no matter how wild, is exempted. Allow the creative mind to percolate uncensored. "What if . . ." is a good stimulus. We cut off access to universal mind or our own imagination with "Yes, but . . ." We abort messages from the Infinite when we trash a new idea with "It won't work because no one has thought of it before" or "because the implementations are not apparent" or "because it's not comfortable."

Step 2. Pick one idea. Shelve the others for now.

Step 3. Think up ways to implement that idea with the same creative freedom as in step one.

Step 4. Now, and not before, list possible obstacles. They can now be treated to a think tank time of their own. Consider them as challenges.

Step 5. Sleep on it; ask for guidance; wait for further inspiration. Don't worry about the end product.

The Saboteurs of Service

*Do not feel totally, personally, irrevocably responsible for everything.
That's my job.*   Love, God/Goddess
                                                        —On a poster

Learning to serve wisely is an essential part of spiritual craftsmanship. It requires intelligent management and balance. Otherwise we can easily get burned out or caught in obsessiveness, perfectionism, and all kinds of messianic traps.

Love awakens compassion, and we can feel completely overwhelmed, even psychically paralyzed, by the cries for help that sound from every quarter of the globe. The "poor"—meaning all those who suffer from any kind of lack—are always with us.

Once our psyches are relatively clear of any illusion of being indispensable, we're still faced with how to manage our service. "Oh, the universe will find someone else to aid them" is probably true, but to a committed disciple this response can seem like a flippant dismissal of real concerns about people and situations we don't have time to help. There is no such thing as time—and we run out of it.

"It will all work out somehow," when applied to racism, sexism, ageism, pollution, and poverty, is a very spiritually naive attitude to take. The Zen master told students who were just waiting for grace that he believed God had already done His share. I think She has, too. The more faith we have in providence, the more we realize we are used as its problem-solving instruments.

Finding Our Balance

As we seek our balance, we might encounter the deep ambivalence voiced by a social worker who admitted, "Part of me wants to help; part of me just wants to run. I am both totally gratified and afraid of being eaten up."

Most of us have both altruistic and selfish motives, an ambivalent inner mixture of yes, no, and maybe. If we wait until we are without doubts, with no mixed feelings and only sterling motives, most of us would never feel ready. Yet the truth is always ready to be told and served.

If we accept aspects of ourselves that are not so developed, magnanimous, or altruistic, then we take them on the journey with us. They're like beloved, injured relatives who can't fully participate at present, but with love and acceptance, in time they will.

Many of the challenges in serving are transpersonal; they just go with the territory. Even when we are psychologically clear, we have to acquire skills. Given the hundred methods we could use, which one will work in this situation? With these people? This problem? How do we lead as visionaries but stay within sight of the people being led? When do we delegate? What is the right use of resources—time, money, energy?

In *The New World Servers*, the Tibetan sage channeled through Alice Bailey said, "Often the mistakes about errors of judgments made by the well-intentioned disciple find their cause in the disciple's failure to recognize when to work and when to refrain, when to gather in his resources and when to direct them outward in manifestation, when to speak and when to remain silent."

Balance starts with self-knowledge. No one can tell another person what is too much or too little. Someone who finds the 10 percent tithing guideline for time, money, and energy quite adequate is not going to understand the person whose passion and joy is service. Arbitrary standards for how long or how intensely one "should" serve before being pronounced neurotic would probably eliminate most of the excellence accomplished in the world.

Disciples who are clear in their purpose repeatedly report they can sustain long periods of concentration and work much longer without exhaustion than those around them. Being tired is not the same thing as being burned out. Being chronically tired may be. As a doctor told me, "I do best for a long time when I am real clear about what I can do and what I can't, what my job is and what my job is not."

Margo, a disciple and a therapist, made a similar observation: "I did the work five years before I decided to *do* the work. When I decided to truly be committed to the work, my stress levels changed, and I had a much greater tolerance because I wasn't trying to run away. I was present to do the work."

Messiahs and Martyrs

Many of the freedoms we enjoy today are the gifts of true martyrs—scholars and statesmen, mystics, scientists, and ordinary people who refused to bow to tyranny and have endured imprisonment, torture, and death. We would insult their memory to suggest that true self-sacrifice is anything less than a glorious example of love.

However, false martyrdom caricatures real sacrifice and is filled with hooks. When true sacrifice has been made on our behalf, we are filled with gratitude, even awe, and a desire to give back. False martyrdom leaves us feeling guilty, angry, and shamed—beholden, as they used to say in the South.

As there can be many challenges to serving—being misunderstood, witch hunts, undeserved criticisms, fatigue, lack of appreciation, resistance, little or no payback, and others—it is fairly easy to feel martyred.

Our society stands in awe of a Mother Teresa and at the same time is suspicious of do-gooders who insist on bringing our attention to the needs of those who are falling through the cracks. Often our culture encourages us to be like the man who whispers to his friend who requested a cigarette just before they both were to be shot, "Don't make trouble."

If you find yourself thinking during a frustrating stretch, "After all I did for *them*," watch out. The martyr virus may be attacking you. The only known cure is self-knowledge. The virus is likely to have roots in a sense of unworthiness. Do I really have to prove myself to God/Goddess? Am I willing to accept grace and love for myself? If I love myself, I will love you, and I probably won't have to martyr myself in order to earn love.

Messiah complexes can be very subtle. Observe children yelling, "Look at me," and we're reminded of the need to be seen and appreciated. The question is, how many of those needs are met and integrated as we mature, and how many sit in the cellars of the subconscious procreating like mushrooms? It's not the ego per se that is the problem. But a *healthy* ego defines success more by personal best than by being better than others.

It is a privilege to be *a* messenger; it is a trap to think one is *the* messenger. The flow is everywhere. Spirit pours living water into all receptive and prepared vessels. There is great wisdom in not confusing the messenger with the message. Certainly the ideal messenger is one who embodies the message and becomes a living model of the message—he or she *is* love, peace, wisdom.

Naturally, we don't all wake up at the same time; we don't all have the same amount of knowledge or clarity in any one lifetime. But we all do have the same amount of God/Goddess within us, whether we know it or not. People admire the Light in others because their own Light resonates with it. They just may not have consciously discovered it yet.

Remember that admiration is not the same thing as adulation. The dynamic that draws soul to soul begins to lose its sweet magic when one person is seen as superior to the other. The spiritual dance is one of equals.

The disciple's task is to remain poised, learn to recognize projections, and not believe their own press. In time, those who excessively adore the disciple have to be weaned from the source of their adoration. That is only possible if the disciple has no need for their dependencies. In the meantime we have to remember who we are, not what is projected onto us.

❧ Journaling Seeds

1. How do you keep your heart open and not get overwhelmed by the needs you see around you?

2. How do you know "when to hold, when to fold"?

3. How do you keep your own energies renewed?

4. How do you balance your needs with those of others?

5. How do you realize when you have, as a friend colorfully says, "quit preachin' and gone to meddlin' "?

Burnout: Up in Smoke

In *The Seven Habits of Highly Effective People* Stephen R. Covey tells the story of a man feverishly sawing down a tree. He is exhausted; he has been at it for five hours. When it is suggested that it would go faster if he sharpened the saw, he answers, "I'm too busy sawing."

No matter how much we love what we do, if we do too much, too long, without balance, we're likely to burn out. There are a lot of excellent materials available on the signals and treatments for burnout, and I recommend studying them. We need to share information about this phenomenon, which stalks servers.

Terms describing burnout have gone mainstream: "workaholics," "fried," "burned to a crisp," "going up in smoke." Burnout is so serious in Japan that they have even named a cause of death produced by overwork, *karoshi*. It can be a built-in hazard in fulfilling one's mission, and that is largely a management issue. And it can be symptomatic of a serious dysfunction that needs to be treated at the casual level before excess takes it completely out of control.

First Warning: Worshiping the Work Ethic

One of the most ingrained attitudes we have is that productivity equals worth. "What do you do?" is probably the question strangers most often ask each other. Few raised in Western culture could possibly escape the work ethic, which is passed on in families and reinforced in institutions.

Women have traditionally been socialized to define their success by how much they give to everyone but themselves. Yet increasingly they're experiencing the same message men are given, which is that you are what you accomplish. Often even our children are pressured to excel both in and out of school.

Nowhere is burnout more likely to be more of an occupational hazard than for people in service professions—social workers, therapists of all kinds, medical personnel, religious professionals (and their families). These professionals carry a high rate of burnout-related dysfunctions such as addictions and stress-induced illnesses.

Diane Fassel's research in *Working Ourselves to Death* confirmed that countless numbers of these professionals said "the explicit message they received in their training was that they had been given a special call by God to serve others. They were ordained to serve. Others' needs should come before their own. To act differently amounts to blasphemy."

Service can turn into a double bind once you are publicly recognized as one who is willing to help. Your heart motivates you from within, while people in need push from without. There can be an assumption that you are accessible at all times.

Others are vulnerable as well. Women who don't work outside the home can be treated as if they are available to volunteer for anything and everything. People often drop in on artists and writers as if they weren't really working since they work at home. Wealthy people can be treated as though they are obligated to offer financial support to everything going on around them. Grown children can assume their parents are there to serve constantly as baby-sitters for the grandchildren. And on and on the list of assumptions goes.

Ram Dass makes a significant point in *How Can I Help?* when he says, "It's not always our efforts that burn us out; it's where the mind is standing in relation to them. *The problem is not the work itself but the degree of our identification with it*" [italics mine].

Warning Signs of Burnout

- *Inability to be in the moment.* One of the first clues is the inability to set projects aside and be present for all of our life, not just its tasks. Relationships begin to suffer because we are chronically preoccupied. Watch out if you are finding yourself regularly problem-solving over dinner, during workouts, or at social gatherings.

- *Too busy to evaluate.* The feeling of always being in debt with time seems to plague the server. The world is accelerating; so are the demands. The virus of busyness has mutated in our culture to the point of virulence. Constantly rushing from one have-to to another leaves little time to heal, renew, and savor.

- *Fantasizing another lifestyle.* Disciples say that sometimes their first clue comes when they begin fantasizing a different way of life. A therapist said she knew she was starting to get fried extra crispy when she fantasized opening a florist shop in a small town. My fantasy is a garden shop.

- *Product, not process, becomes primary.* There may be a feeling of wanting to just "get it over with." End products could include praise, credit, or money. They may be anticipated by-products, but once the actual joy of the doing is gone, burnout is probably hanging around the edges.

- *Too much for too many.* To try to be everything to everybody is a guaranteed setup for burnout. The more one serves, the more the opportunities expand. I read a study that concluded that the one common denominator among successful people was the ability to put first things first.

- *Physical disharmonies.* Bodies rarely lie. Untraceable aches and pains, sudden drops in energy, loss of appetite, stuffing with comfort foods, or interrupted sleep are potential signals. Quick fixes for exhaustion are like filling a colander with water. Believing that you work better under pressure might do for a while, but as a way of living, it's a setup to crash and burn.

- *Emotional disharmonies.* A warning light blinks when we are impatient with what once brought joy. Emotions can swing from boredom to enthusiasm. Not being available to friends and family can mean loving intimacies are being sacrificed to too much work, too much giving, not enough receiving.
- *Mental disharmonies.* Variations of writer's block can happen when the mental body says "enough" and no matter how much you push and cajole, it will not yield another creative thought. Or it offers the same one again and again. Forgetfulness, as in all these symptoms, can have many causes; burnout is one of them.
- *Quality begins to suffer.* Projects and programs, even therapies begin to sound predictable, lacking in energy, tired. One disciple said that for him to teach in burnout was "like a physician trying to do an operation with a bent and dented scalpel. I will harm people, so I just stop."
- *Service becomes servitude.* The enthusiasm and inspiration for serving is dulled, if not completely gone. Slaves are rarely joyful. But they are great candidates for false martyrdom.

Saving Fish from Drowning

Once in meditation I saw an image of a self-destructive person whom I knew flailing away in the ocean. My guidance was to throw a lifeline, and I was warned that if I went into the water myself, it would be neither right nor wrong; there would simply be two of us drowning.

Many times the difference between service that empowers both server and served and service that cripples one or both is hard to detect. Almost all service can appear at times to be codependent, and it is very dangerous to assume that every act of sacrifice is codependent.

Codependency is a real potential trap for the disciple. Fortunately, there's a growing body of material to help us diagnose and treat this pattern. Much of this material is the gift of various addiction recovery programs.

"My philosophy is that God never gives up on us," said Tamara, director of a successful program for alternative sentencing. "Yet when we make decisions we are responsible for them. If we fall flat on our behinds, we have to pick ourselves up. I continue to be there for them, but from a distance, in my head and in my heart. There is such a difference in feeling when you really do let someone be responsible for his own life."

A therapist expressed that philosophy directly to a client who was trying to make her keep him alive when he threatened suicide. "I take no responsibility for your life. But I will argue with you and fight on behalf of your life."

Rescue	Support
Strings attached	Nothing wanted in return
Increase dependency	Encourage independence
Exhausted, depleted	Tired, but quickly renewed
Fixing things	Encouraging, not solving
Holding shoulds	Releasing shoulds
Loss of personal power	Power comes through and out
Fuzzy boundaries	Clearly defined boundaries
Seeing only your own power	Seeing another's power
Invested in results	Service for its own sake
"I'm competent; you're not"	"You are also competent"
Self-righteous	Accepting
"I'm well, but you're sick"	"We both are growing"

What would you add to these lists?

Boundaries That Free Us

Establishing boundaries is an expression of self-love and self-responsibility. Ultimately, it is an expression of true love for the other. How can I honor your space if I don't honor my own? To allow self-abuse in any way is more likely to be a dance of unfinished business than an expression of love.

It can be very difficult to separate out real need from the need for attention, recognizing what's your row to hoe, and what's simply a row that needs hoeing that can just as easily and sometimes more appropriately be done by another.

I remember my amazement when a wise woman, formerly a mother superior, said to me, "You have to learn to be ruthless"—a concept that was at first hard for me to consider because of the connotations of the word. Yet it became the seed for many inner examinations of how to serve fully and maintain boundaries that support sanity and health. And, of course, the person I needed to be ruthless with was myself.

Boundaries for Clean and Clear Service

There are many techniques for setting boundaries. Regardless of the outer steps, they all start with inner choices. If we don't make the inner decision, the outer won't hold under pressure.

- Examine your true motives for serving.
- Be honest about your limits. How many people can you see, how many hours can you contribute, how much energy can you put out before you lose it?
- Don't compare yourself with anybody else—ever. We all have different karmas, intentions, and cycles.
- Maintain clear communications with your intimates. Honest talk and fair negotiation establishes everyone's needs and can reduce fears.

- Prioritize. Then prioritize the priorities. Stick to it. Exceptions happen, but be sure that they are just that and not unconscious sabotage of established boundaries.

- Release those things that are not yours to do, and release people who need skills other than yours. Release projects that don't fit into your scheduling priorities.

- Keep referral lists of other people who provide services comparable to yours or other services. No one can be all things to all people.

- Discipline yourself to release daily interactions. As soon as someone leaves your space, affirm, "I release all energy connected to this person." Visualize both yourself and your coworker, client, or associate within your own individual energy fields to reinforce your awareness of boundaries.

- Use release practices nightly. For example, every night I release on a mental image of an altar of Light those people I have worked with that day—not in a spirit of dismissal, but rather to turn the relationship from my personality over to the Divine.

- Holding the Light for another in thought or prayer may be the most powerful help you can offer. You don't always have to be there to "be there." Mental and spiritual energies travel outside time and space.

- Cleanse your work space regularly with water, sage, sweet grass, incense, salt, Epsom salts, candles. Psychic energy from another can linger in the environment. World servers who ignore energetic cleansing in some way often get sick. You wouldn't consider using dirty sheets or unclean instruments; energy clearing and cleansing is no less important.

Recovering from Burnout

Releasing on a regular basis is extremely important. Ruth was the head nurse on the pediatric floor of a major hospital. She was consistently strong in dealing with all the traumas, suffering, and death she saw. Then one day, over one dying child, she completely snapped and was never able to work again as a nurse. Her grief was cumulative. She had never released any of the children at an energetic level.

We can do many things to counter burnout. We could all learn a lesson (even if we can't follow it fully) from Albert Einstein, who only worked in the mornings in his lab. He often spent his afternoons sailing, and said that the idea for relativity came to him as he was eating an apple.

I keep a quote from Thomas Merton in my office as a wise reminder:

> *To allow one's self to be carried away by a multitude of conflicting concerns, to surrender to too many demands, to commit one's self to too many projects, to want to help everyone in everything is to succumb to violence. Frenzy destroys our inner capacity for peace; it destroys the fruitfulness of our work, because it kills the root of inner wisdom which makes that work fruitful.*

Here are some things you can do to take care of yourself, stay healthy, and treat early symptoms of service burnout:

- Say no.
- Plan regular retreats, including mini ones, within a day or week. Even an hour counts if it is totally for yourself.
- Name your blessings; slowly savor them.
- Discover what my friend calls "good enough" for the ordinary tasks; save your uncompromised positions of excellence for the stuff that matters.

- Laugh.
- Eat lots of things that are good for you.
- Drink lots of water.
- Seek out positive support systems and positive people.
- Play with animals and with children.
- Get your hands in the soil, your feet on the ground.
- Do something totally out of the rut (remember that a rut is a rut, even if it's fur-lined).
- Get rid of stuff; unclutter your life; simplify.
- Do little things that could make your life less stressful.
- Slow down everything. Speed is not the yardstick for excellence.
- Turn off the radio, TV, stereo; listen to the silence; be still. . . . *Now* carefully choose the sounds you want.
- Be aware of your breath.
- Meditate every day.
- Own your own needs and name how you are going to have them met.
- Offer yourself special treats.
- Place your hand on your heart with compassion for yourself.
- Try some new four-letter words, such as *rest* and *play*.
- Ask for what you need.
- Go to the woods, the mountains, the sea; nature will restore you.

Go to the mirror, look in your eyes: You are a child of God/Goddess, and you are never, never alone.

✿ Twelve Considerations on Serving

1. What if the future turned upon your next act? What then?

2. Motion isn't action. Choose carefully.

3. Peak experiences touch the spirit. Serving materializes it.

4. No one feels ready to serve life, but life is ready to use you.

5. Look closely. The one you serve wears the face of the Beloved.

6. Evolution has no elite corps, only those who serve it.

7. Random acts of kindness are a start toward a life of kindness.

8. Don't confuse real need with misplaced desire.

9. Cooperation instead of competition allows everyone to win.

10. Trust the process. Fruit grows naturally from seed.

11. My brother's *keeper*? I *am* my brother and my sister.

12. All of the past served the present that I may serve the future.

Exercise: Personal Mission Statement

Businesses and organizations use mission statements to define and clarify intentions. It takes time, contemplation, and deep inner listening to write a strong personal mission statement, which you can then use as a periodic reference to review your use of time, energy, and talents.

Start with your most philosophical intentions. What do you feel you want to accomplish at all levels? It may seem unwieldy at first, but as you rewrite and evaluate, keep simplifying, paring away the extraneous, affirming the essentials.

An example of a personal mission statement:

My life mission is to manifest my spirit in the physical, mental, and emotional planes with intention, balance, and clarity.

My professional mission is to serve as I am guided, which for now is through counseling, teaching, and writing about the interconnectedness of mind, body, and spirit.

My personal mission is to evolve by giving and receiving love, expressing gratitude, seeking self-knowledge, and accepting personal responsibility for all that I put into the world.

Affirmation
Beloved, I am here. Use me as Your instrument.

Quotes
Knowledge is not enough. Risk your knowledge with action, and then you will know whether it is genuine, pretension, or just information.
—Sri Chitrabandh

A monastery that had once been a vital spiritual center fell on hard times. The monks no longer had any passion, humor, or real delight in the Divine. The old paint on the walls was peeling; weeds were overcoming the garden; the whole place looked forlorn and unloved. So, of course, young people were not at all interested.

The abbot was greatly worried, so he sought the advice of the sage in the hills, who told him immediately what the problem was: "You have the Christ living in your monastery!"

Naturally the abbot was startled. "How is that possible?"

"Well," added the sage, "he is in disguise. That is all I can tell you."

The abbot took this mysterious information back to his staff, who were equally astonished. "Who could that be? Brother Sebastian? Oh, no, he is always late, always forgetting the words to the chants. Still . . . maybe that is his disguise. Do you suppose Brother John, who can't seem to get out of the rain, is using that as his disguise?"

As they reviewed the community, they realized there was no way they were going to recognize the Christ in disguise. So they decided *that just to be sure, they should treat everyone as if he were the Christ. And so they did.*

Soon the whole place changed. The monks walked straighter, became interested again in singing, and served with gusto. They painted the walls and weeded the garden. And miracle upon miracle began to happen.

So, of course, the young people were very attracted. And the monastery once again flourished.

Invoking the Twelve

※

B egin by focusing on the Light that is within your being. Within that Light is the clear perception of the Buddha mind, the radiance of the universal Christ, and the love of the Bodhisattva. Where are you the most aware of the Presence— your head, your heart, your solar plexus? Breathe into that place; feel your sense of personality melt into the larger awareness of Self. Rest in the breath of this Light. Now call forth each of your inner disciples.

1. First I direct this Light into my heart and behind it. I am aware of the fire it ignites. I feel it expanding to fill my chest. Perfect love casts out all fear. There is only love; love is my teacher; love is the energy that sustains my life; love is the energy I give to all life.

I am loved. I am love.
For love I give thanks.

2. I move my awareness of the Light deep into the brain. Here my Will is activated. I claim my divine birthright to choose. I choose the Will to good. I choose the path I will follow. I choose to fulfill my soul's intention. I surrender my limited will to Divine Will, knowing Thy Will is for my highest good.

> *Thy Will and mine are one.*
> *For the Will I give thanks.*

3. The Light begins to energize the pineal gland, awakening remembrances of the unlimited power of the God within, renewing my faith. Faith can move mountains. Whatever I am doing, my faith is strong that the indwelling Light will draw to me all that is needed to fulfill my purposes and needs.

Faith is the foundation of my inner temple.

> *For faith I give thanks.*

4. The awakening powers of the Light move toward the back of my throat. Here lives the logos, the power of the Word. I declare my intention to speak the sacred sounds, to be the Mother-Father-God's verbal power on this planet. I take responsibility for all that I create or energize with this power.

I claim the authority of the inner Light to heal and transform.

> *For power I give thanks.*

5. Bathing my brain in Light, I now energize my reasoning faculties. I appreciate the perennial wisdom and sciences I have inherited. I dedicate my knowledge to service. I aspire to true knowledge, discarding superstition and cultural, religious, racial, and gender bigotry.

I seek truth and truth only.

> *For knowledge I give thanks.*

6. The Light settles between my eyes, causing all the cells there, physical and subtle, to quicken. I perceive with clarity and new insight. I am receptive to the inspiration of dreams and visions. I welcome divine guidance.

I am guided intuitively to right thought and right action.

For Divine revelation I give thanks.

7. The Light moves into my lower abdomen. My ability to discern truth is cellular. I sense it in my body. As I cannot serve two masters, the higher laws and the lower, I choose to give authority to the higher laws. Confusion is no more.

I am led from the unreal to the real, from darkness to Light.

For discernment I give thanks.

8. The Light streams throughout my body. Intelligence exists in every cell. Through my body I ground spiritual intention in the world. May the Higher Plan, directed by the universal Christ, the Buddha, the angels, and the masters, be fulfilled in the physical dimension.

I honor my physical body as a sacred vessel.

For the truths of the body I give thanks.

9. The Light moves through my intestines. I am willing to release old habits, old resentments, all that blocks, limits, and poisons. I let go and give up all that is no longer needed. I forgive all harm from this life or any other, freeing myself and all others. I accept the fires of purification knowing they burn away anything that stands between me and self-realization.

I am free of the past, empty and ready to be filled.

For the alchemy of transforming I give thanks.

10. The Light gently moves throughout my entire reproductive system. I bless this life-generating force and forgive myself completely for any perceived misuse of this power in the past. I am free to choose how I will direct this universal life force, knowing it will energize my thoughts, words, and actions.

I am made in the image of God, therefore a Creator.

For the power of creating I give thanks.

11. Now the Light moves into the middle and lower back. I feel its power supporting me, moving into the muscles, fortifying my resolves, maintaining my equilibrium in chaos, renewing my strength should I falter. I know that I am committed to my path without reservation. However long it takes, whatever the challenge, I will endure.

Here I am, Beloved. I will be steady.

For the strength of enduring I give thanks.

12. Becoming aware of the Light just over my head, I am aware that its radiance guides my path. It is a star of illumination, reminding me of the greater purpose of my incarnation, to serve the earth and all that lives here. Gaia is my physical mother, and it is a joy to offer my time, energy, talent, and intention in service to the Plan unfolding on earth.

I dedicate my life to serving the highest good on this earth.

For the privilege of serving I give thanks.

Now experience the inner strength, the sense of being alive with all of your powers at your command, each cleared and cleansed, each awaiting your command to move into service. Gently pour

Light throughout all of your bodies, starting with the physical, then into the etheric, the emotional ranges, the mental, filling up your entire aura. See your integrated self sending out great pulsating waves of balanced wisdom and compassion. As you claim these powers you send them forth into the world. You are a wave of the universal Light now manifesting in this world. Rest in this knowledge.

Affirmation of the Twelve

❧

I awaken and remember that I am
One with the Mother,
One with the Father,
One with All That Is.

In faith I affirm this truth
as I live in both the mystery and the manifest.

Divine purpose infuses my will and supplies all the power I need
to fulfill my place in the Plan.

Unconditional love for all sentient beings flows through me
into the world.

I know these truths through my feelings and the wisdom of my body,
through the legacy of knowledge preserved and passed on to me
in the perennial wisdoms and through the grace of inner revelation.

I have developed the powers of discernment
that enable me to perceive accurately the real from the unreal.

I am made in the image of the Divine and am therefore creating
realities in my body, my emotions,
my mind, and my spirit,

and I take full responsibility for all that I create.
Through the eternal rhythms and expressions of yin and yang,
I bring balance between heaven and earth, the inner and the outer.

Through the alchemy of truth and love, I am transforming all of the fears,
mistakes, misperceptions, and limitations of the past.

I am enduring all that is necessary to live the highest truths
of my beingness.

For this remembrance
and for the privilege of serving, I give thanks.
So be it.

A Closing Wish

Our paths have crossed, and I am grateful that you invited me to share your journey for a little while. My inspiration has been the disciples who, like yourself, are choosing to give their time and energy to the life of our beloved planet during this new birthing.

May you always remember who you are.

May all your highest intentions flower and seed the future . . . even until seven generations.

And so it goes, the unbroken gift of life to life.

Namaste—blessings.

There is a field beyond right and wrong. I will meet you there.

—Rumi

For information on tapes and workshops:
  Gloria D. Karpinski
  Winston-Salem, N.C.
  E-mail: gkarp12@aol.com
  Web site: www.gloriakarpinski.com

Bibliography

✤

A Course in Miracles. (The scribe/author of this work chose to remain anonymous.) New York: Foundation for Inner Peace, 1975.

Addington, Jack E. *All About Goals and How to Achieve Them.* Marina del Rey, Calif.: DeVorss, 1977.

Almaas, A. H. *Essence: The Diamond Approach to Inner Realization.* York Beach, Maine.: Samuel Weiser, Inc., 1986.

Anand, Margo. *The Art of Sexual Ecstasy.* New York: Tarcher/Putnam, 1989.

Anderson, Sherry R., and Patricia Hopkins. *The Feminine Face of God.* New York: Bantam Books, 1992.

Anodea, Judith. *Wheels of Life.* St. Paul, Minn.: Llewellyn Publications, 1989.

Arguelles, Jose. *The Mayan Factor.* Santa Fe, N. M.: Bear and Co., 1987.

Artress, Lauren. *Walking a Sacred Path: Rediscovering the Labyrinth as a Spiritual Tool.* New York: Riverhead, 1995.

Ash, Mel. *The Zen of Recovery.* New York: Tarcher/Putnam, 1993.

Aurobindo. *Sri Aurobindo, or The Adventure of Consciousness.* New York: HarperCollins, 1974.

Bach, Richard. *The Adventures of a Reluctant Messiah.* New York: Delacorte, 1977.

———*Jonathan Livingston Seagull.* New York: Avon, 1974.

445

Badaracco, Joseph L. Jr., and Richard R. Ellsworth. *Leadership and the Quest for Integrity.* Boston: Harvard Business School Press, 1993.

Bailey, Alice. *Initiation, Human and Solar.* New York: Lucis Trust Publishing, 1980.

———*Serving Humanity.* New York: Lucis Trust Publishing, 1981.

———*The Seventh Ray: Revealer of the New Age.* New York: Lucis Trust Publishing, 1995.

Barks, Coleman, trans. *Lalla: Naked Song.* Athens, Ga.: Maypop Books, 1992.

Barody, Theodore A. Jr., M.D. *Ascension: A Beginner's Manual.* Waynesville, N.C.: Eclectic Press, 1989.

Beattie, Melanie. *Co-Dependent No More.* Center City, Minn.: Hazelden Foundation, 1987.

Becker, Ernest. *Escape from Evil.* New York: The Free Press, 1985.

Bentock, Itzak. *Stalking the Wild Pendulum.* Rochester, N.Y.: Inner Traditions International, 1988.

Berensohn, Paulus. *Finding One's Way with Clay.* New York: Simon and Schuster, 1972.

Berger, Barbara. *Animalia.* Millbrae, Calif.: Celestial Arts, 1982.

Berry, Jason. *Lead Us Not into Temptation.* New York: Doubleday, 1994.

Berry, Thomas. *The Dream of the Earth.* San Francisco: Sierra Club Books, 1988.

Birenbaum, Barbara. *A Birthday Wish.* Clearwater, Fla: Peartree, 1988.

Blake, William. *The Complete Poems.* New York: Viking Penguin, 1978.

Blavatsky, H. P. *Isis Unveiled.* 1877. Reprint. Pasadena, Calif.: Theosophical University Press, 1972.

Blofeld, John. *Bodhisattva of Compassion: The Mystical Tradition of Kuan Yin.* Boston: Shambhala, 1988.

Bloom, Harold. *Omens of Millennium: The Gnosis of Angels, Dreams, and Resurrection.* New York: Putnam, 1996.

Bly, Robert. William Booth, ed. *A Little Book on the Human Shadow.* San Francisco: Harper, 1988.

Bock, Janet. *The Jesus Mystery.* Los Angeles: Aura Books, 1983.

Boles, Martha, and Rochelle Newman. *Universal Patterns.* Bradford, Mass.: Pythagorean Press, 1990.

Boone, J. Vaughn. *De-Rive-W: The Magic Formula.* Charlotte, N.C.: Delight Publishing, 1992.

Borysenko, Joan. *Minding the Body, Mending the Mind.* New York: Bantam Books, 1988.

Bradley, Marion Zimmer. *The Mists of Avalon.* New York: Ballantine, 1984.

Bragdon, Emma. *A Sourcebook for Helping People in Spiritual Emergency.* Los Altos, Calif.: Lightening Up Press, 1988.

Brenan, Gerald. *St. John of the Cross: His Life and Poetry.* Ann Arbor, Mich.: Cambridge University Press, 1973.

Briggs, John, and F. Daniel Peat. *Turbulent Mirror: An Illustrated Guide to Chaos Theory and the Science of Wholeness.* New York: Harper and Row, 1989.

Buber, Martin. *I and Thou.* trans. Walter Kaufman and S. G. Smith. New York: Simon and Schuster, 1971.

Burrows, Ruth. *Guidelines for Mystical Prayer.* Denville, N. J.: Dimension Books, 1978.

Caldes, Marlene F. *Inner Voices.* Corte Madera, Calif.: Prospering Naturally, 1990.

Cameron, Julia. *The Artist's Way: A Spiritual Path to Higher Creativity.* New York: Tarcher/Perigee, 1992.

Campbell, Joseph. *The Inner Reaches of Outer Space.* New York: Harper-Perennial, 1988.

———. *The Masks of God, Creative Mythology.* New York: Penguin, 1968.

Canfield, Jack, and Mark Victor Hansen. *The Aladdin Factor.* New York: Berkeley Books, 1995.

Carey, Ken. *The Starseed Transmissions.* San Francisco: HarperSanFrancisco, 1991.

Cargas, Harry James. *Shadows of Auschwitz: A Christian's Response to the Holocaust.* New York: Crossroads, 1990.

Carlebach, Shlomo. *Shlomo's Stories: Selected Tales.* Northvale, Calif.: Jason Aronson, Inc., 1995.

Carroll, Lee, and Jan Tober. *The Indigo Children.* Carlsbad, Calif.: Hayhouse, 2001.

Carter, Forrest. *The Education of Little Tree.* Albuquerque: University of New Mexico Press, 1986.

————*The Eagle's Gift.* San Diego: Paermer Books, 1981.

————*The Fire from Within.* New York: Pocket Books, 1991.

————*Journey to Ixtlan: The Lessons of Don Juan.* New York: Simon and Schuster, 1991.

————*The Second Ring of Power.* New York: Pocket Books, 1991.

————*A Separate Reality: Further Conversations with Don Juan.* New York: Pocket Books, 1991.

————*Tales of Power.* New York: Pocket Books, 1991.

Castaneda, Carlos. *The Teachings of Don Juan: A Yaqui Way of Knowledge.* Berkeley: University of California Press, 1968.

Cerminara, Gina. *Many Mansions.* New York: William Sloane Associates, Inc., 1950.

Chappell, Tom. *The Soul of a Business.* New York: Bantam, 1994.

Chia, Mantak. *Awaken Healing Energy Through the Tao.* Santa Fe, N.M.: Aurora Press, 1983.

————*Taoist Ways to Transform Stress into Vitality.* Huntington, N.Y.: Healing Tao Books, 1986.

Chopra, Deepak. *Ageless Body, Timeless Mind: A Practical Alternative to Growing Old.* London: Rider, 1993.

Clark, Glenn. *The Man Who Tapped the Secrets of the Universe.* Waynesboro, Va.: University of Science and Philosophy, 1989.

Cohen, Alan. *The Dragon Doesn't Live Here Anymore: Loving Fully, Living Freely.* Farmingdale, N.Y.: Eden Publishing, 1981.

Connelly, Dianne M. *Traditional Acupuncture: The Law of the Five Elements.* Columbia, Md.: The Centre for Traditional Acupuncture, Inc., 1975.

Covey, Stephen R. *The Seven Habits of Highly Effective People.* New York: Simon and Schuster, 1989.

Craven, Margaret. *I Heard the Owl Call My Name.* New York: Dell Publishing, 1980.

Dalai Lama. *The Essential Teachings of His Holiness, the Dalai Lama.* Ed. Marianne Dresser, trans. Zelie Pollon. Berkeley: North Atlantic Books, 1995.

Daniel, Alma, Timothy Wyllie, and Andrew Ramer. *Ask Your Angels.* New York: Ballantine, 1992.

Dass, Ram, and Mirabai Bush. *Compassion in Action: Setting Out on the Path of Service.* New York: Crown Publishers, 1992.

Dass, Ram. *Still Here: Embracing Aging, Changing and Dying.* New York: Riverhead Books, 2000.

Dass, Ram, and Paul Gorman. *How Can I Help? Stories and Reflections on Service.* New York: Alfred A. Knopf, 1985.

Dass, Ram, with Stephen Levine. *Grist for the Mill.* Mill Valley, Calif.: Orenda Publishing/Unity Press, 1977.

Davis, Bruce. *Monastery Without Walls.* Berkeley: Celestial Arts, 1990.

Davis, Mary Ogden. *Metanoia: A Transformational Journey.* Marina del Rey, Calif.: DeVorss, 1984.

Davis, Roy Eugene. *The Hidden Teachings of Jesus Revealed.* Lakemont, Ga.: CSA Press, 1980.

———*Life Surrendered to God: The Science of Kriya Yoga.* Lakemont, Ga.: CSA Press, 1990.

DeCaussade, Jean-Pierre. *Abandonment to Divine Providence.* New York: Doubleday and Co., 1993.

———*Heart of the Enlightened: A Book of Story Meditations.* New York: Doubleday, 1991.

———*One Minute Wisdom.* New York: Doubleday, 1986.

DeMello, Anthony. *Sadhana: A Way to God.* New York: Doubleday and Co., 1984.

———*Song of the Bird.* New York: Doubleday, 1984.

———*Taking Flight.* New York: Image/Doubleday, 1988.

———*Wellsprings.* New York: Doubleday, 1986.

Deymaz, Linda. *Mommy, Please Don't Cry.* Gresham, Ore. Vision House Publishing, 1996.

Dialogue of the Savior. Gnostic Manuscript.

Doczi, Gyorgi. *The Power of Limits.* Boston: Shambhala, 1981.

Dominguez, Joe, and Vicki Robin. *Your Money or Your Life: Transforming Your Relationship with Money and Achieving Financial Independence.* New York: Viking Penguin, 1992.

Douglas-Klotz, Neil. *Prayers of the Cosmos: Meditations on the Aramaic Words of Jesus.* San Francisco: Harper, 1990.

Duff, Kat. *The Alchemy of Illness.* Bell Tower, N.Y.: Crown Publishing, 1994.

Durkheim, Karlfried G. *Hara, the Vital Center of Man.* New York: Routledge, Chapman, and Hall, 1988.

Edinger, Edward F. *Ego and Archetype.* Boston: Shambhala, 1992.

Edwards, Jonathan. *Selected Writings of Jonathan Edwards.* Ed. Harold Simonson. Prospect Heights, Ill.: Waveland Press, 1992.

Eisler, Riane. *The Chalice and the Blade.* San Francisco: HarperSan Francisco, 1988.

Embley, L. Lawrence. *Doing Well While Doing Good: The Marketing Link Between Business and Nonprofit Causes.* Englewood Cliffs, N.J.: Prentice Hall, 1992.

Emerson, Ralph Waldo. *Emerson's Essays.* Reprint. New York: HarperCollins, 1981.

Esquivel, Laura. *The Law of Love.* New York: Crown Publishers, 1996.

Estés, Clarissa Pinkola. *Women Who Run with the Wolves.* New York: Ballantine, 1992.

Evans-Wentz, W. Y., ed., *Tibetan Book of the Dead.* 1927. Reprint. New York: Galaxy Books, 1960.

Farrell, Warren. *The Myth of Male Power.* New York: Berkeley Publishing, 1994.

Fassel, Diane. *Working Ourselves to Death, and the Rewards of Recovery.* San Francisco: HarperCollins, 1993.

Ferlinghetti, Lawrence. *These Are My Rivers: New & Selected Poems.* New York, N.Y.: New Directions, 1994.

Fillmore, Charles. *The Twelve Powers of Man.* Unity Village, Mo.: Unity School, 1985.

Fisichella, Anthony J. *Metaphysics, the Science of Life.* St. Paul, Minn.: Llewellyn Publications, 1984.

Forrest, Jodie. *The Rhymer and the Raven: The Book of Fate.* Chapel Hill, N.C.: Seven Paws Press, 1992.

——— *The Elves' Prophecy: The Book of Being.* Chapel Hill, N.C.: Seven Paws Press, 1996.

Forrest, Steven. *The Night Speaks.* San Diego, Calif.: ACS Publications, 1993.

——— *Sky Mates.* Chapel Hill, N.C.: Seven Paws Press, 1988.

Fortunato, John E. *AIDS: The Spiritual Dilemma.* San Francisco: HarperSanFrancisco, 1987.

——— *The Coming of the Cosmic Christ.* San Francisco: HarperSanFrancisco, 1988.

Fox, Matthew. *Original Blessing: A Primer in Creation Spirituality.* Santa Fe: Bear and Co., 1996.

———*The Reinvention of Work: A New Vision of Livelihood for Our Time.* San Francisco: HarperSanFrancisco, 1995.

Freeman, R. Edward. *Business Ethics.* New York: Oxford University Press, 1992.

Galland, China. *Longing for Darkness: Tara and the Black Madonna.* New York: Penguin, 1991.

Gawain, Shakti. *Living in the Light.* Mill Valley, Calif.: Whatever Publishing, Inc., 1986.

Gilbert, Daniel R. Jr., *The Twilight of Corporate Strategy: A Comparative Ethical Critique.* New York: Oxford University Press, 1992.

Gill, Derek. *Quest: The Life of Elisabeth Kübler-Ross.* New York: Ballantine Books, 1982.

Glaser, Chris. *Coming Home: Reclaiming Your Spirituality.* San Francisco: HarperSanFrancisco, 1990.

Golas, Thaddeus. *The Lazy Man's Guide to Enlightenment.* New York: Bantam Books, 1983.

Goldberg, Natalie. *Writing Down the Bones: Freeing the Writer Within.* Boston: Shambhala, 1998.

Goleman, Daniel. *Emotional Intelligence.* New York: Bantam Books, 1995.

Griffiths, Bede. *Universal Wisdom: A Journey Through the Sacred Wisdom of the World.* San Francisco: Harper, 1994.

Grof, Christina. *The Stormy Search for Self.* Los Angeles: Tarcher, 1990.

Guyon, Jeanne. *Experiencing the Depth of Jesus Christ.* Beaumont, Tex.: Seedsowers, 1996.

Hafiz. (Versions by Daniel Ladinsky) *The Subject Tonight Is Love.* N. Myrtle Beach, S.C.: Pumpkin House Press, 1997.

Haich, Elisabeth. *Initiation.* Redway, Calif.: Seed Center, 1974.

———*Sexual Energy and Yoga.* Santa Fe: Aurora Press, 1983.

Halifax, Joan, Dr. *The Fruitful Darkness: Reconnecting with the Body of the Earth.* San Francisco: HarperSanFrancisco, 1994.

Hall, James. *Sangoma: My Odyssey into the Spirit World of Africa.* New York: Tarcher/Putnam, 1994.

Hall, Manley P. *The Secret Teachings of All Ages: An Encyclopedia Outline of*

Masonic, Hermetic, Quabbalistic and Rosicrucian Symbolical Philosophy. Los Angeles: Philosophical Research Society, Inc., 1978.

————*The Ways of the Lonely Ones.* Los Angeles: Philosophical Research Society, Inc., 1979.

Hample, Stuart, and Eric Marshall, comps. *Children's Letters to God: The New Collection.* New York: Workman Publishing, 1991.

Hanh, Thich Nhat. *The Heart of the Buddha's Teaching.* Berkeley: Parallax Press, 1998.

————*The Miracle of Mindfulness: A Manual on Meditation.* Boston: Beacon Press, 1987.

————*Touching Peace: Practicing the Art of Mindful Living.* Berkeley: Parallax Press, 1992.

————*Zen Keys.* New York: Doubleday, 1974.

Hariton, Anca. *The Butterfly Story.* New York: Dutton Children's Books, 1995.

Hart, Hornell. *Your Share of God: Spiritual Power for Life Fulfillment.* Englewood Cliffs, N.J.: Prentice Hall, 1958.

Harvey, Andrew. *Hidden Journey.* New York: Viking Penguin, 1992.

Haule, John R. *Divine Madness: Archetypes of Romantic Love.* Boston: Shambhala, 1990.

Hendricks, Gay, and Kathlyn Hendricks. *At the Speed of Life: A New Approach to Personal Change Through Body-Centered Therapy.* New York: Bantam, 1993.

Herzog, Roberta, Dr. *Legends of Anelleh.* Scotland Neck, N.C.: Crystal Publications, 1982.

Hillman, James. *The Soul's Code: In Search of Character and Calling.* New York: Random House, 1996.

————*Thought of the Heart and the Soul of the World.* Woodstock, N.Y.: Spring Publications, 1992.

Hodson, Geoffrey. *The Hidden Wisdom in the Holy Bible,* vol. 1. Wheaton, Ill.: Quest-Theosophical Publishing House, 1967.

Hoeller, Stephan A. *Jung and the Lost Gospels.* Wheaton, Ill.: Quest-Theosophical Publishing House, 1993.

Holmes, Ernest. *The Science of Mind.* New York: Tarcher, 1997.

Houston, Jean. *A Mythic Life: Learning to Live our Greater Story.* San Francisco: HarperSanFrancisco, 1996.

————*The Search for the Beloved: Journeys in Mythology and Sacred Psychology.* New York: Tarcher, 1989.

Hugo, Victor. *Les Misérables.* New York: Fawcett, 1987.

Huyler, Stephen P. *Painted Prayers: Women's Art in Village India.* New York: Rizzoli International Publications, 1994.

Ivanova, Barbara. *The Golden Chalice.* San Francisco: H. S. Dakin, 1986.

Jackson, Phil. *Sacred Hoops.* New York: Hyperion, 1995.

Jamison, Kay R. *An Unquiet Mind: A Memoir of Moods and Madness.* New York: Random House, 1997.

Jampolski, Gerald. *Love Is Letting Go of Fear.* Berkeley: Celestial Arts Publishing, 1995.

————*Teach Only Love.* New York: Bantam Books, 1984.

Johnson, Robert. *Femininity Lost and Regained.* New York: Harper Perrenial, 1991

————*He: Understanding Masculine Psychology.* New York: Harper-Collins, 1989.

————*Owning Your Own Shadow.* San Francisco: HarperSanFrancisco, 1993.

————*She: Understanding Feminine Psychology.* New York: Harper-Collins, 1989.

————*We: Understanding the Psychology of Romantic Love.* San Francisco: HarperSanFrancisco, 1985.

Johnston, William. *Christian Zen.* New York: HarperCollins, 1974.

Jung, Carl G. *Memories, Dreams, Reflections.* New York: Random House, 1989.

————*Modern Man in Search of a Soul.* London: Harcourt, 1955.

Kabat-Zinn, Jon. *Full Catastrophe Living: Using the Window of Your Body and Mind to Face Stress, Pain and Illness.* New York: Dell, 1990.

Kabir. *Songs of Kabir.* Trans. Rabindranath Tagore. San Diego: I.B.S. International, 1989.

————*Try to Live to See This!* Trans. Robert Bly. Saint Paul: Ally Press, 1976.

Kamenetz, Rodger. *The Jew in the Lotus.* San Francisco: HarperSanFrancisco, 1994.

Karpinski, Gloria D. *Where Two Worlds Touch: Spiritual Rites of Passage.* New York: Ballantine Books, 1990.

Keating, Thomas. *Open Mind, Open Heart.* Rockport, Mass.: Element, 1991.

Kenyon, Tom. *Brain States*. Naples, Fla.: United States Pub., 1994.

Keyes, Ken. *A Handbook to Higher Consciousness*. Berkeley: Living Love Center, 1975.

Kidd, Sue Monk. *God's Joyful Surprise*. San Francisco: HarperSanFrancisco, 1989.

———*When the Heart Waits: Spiritual Direction for Life's Sacred Questions*. San Francisco: HarperSanFrancisco, 1992.

Kilpatrick, Joseph, and Sanford Danziger, M.D., comps. *Better than Money Can Buy: The New Volunteers*. Winston-Salem, N.C.: Innersearch Publishing, 1996.

King, Serge Kahili. *Urban Shaman*. New York: Simon and Schuster, 1990.

Klein, Jean. *Ease of Being*. Durham, N.C.: The Acorn Press, 1984.

Konner, Melvin. *The Tangled Wing: Biological Constraints on the Human Spirit*. New York: Henry Holt and Co., 1990.

Kornfield, Jack. *A Path with Heart*. New York: Bantam, 1993.

———*A Still Forest Pool*. Wheaton, Ill.: Quest–Theosophical Publishing House, 1985.

Kramer, Joel, and Diana Alstad. *The Guru Papers: Masks of Authoritarian Power*. Berkeley: Frog Limited, 1993.

Krieger, Dolores. *The Therapeutic Touch*. New York: Simon and Schuster, 1979.

———*Therapeutic Touch Inner Workbook*. Santa Fe: Bear and Company, 1996.

Krishna, Gopi. *Higher Consciousness and Kundalini*. Norton Heights, Conn.: The Kundalini Research Foundation Ltd., 1970.

———*Kundalini: The Evolutionary Energy in Man*. Boston: Shambhala, 1997.

Kunz, Dora. *The Personal Aura*. Wheaton, Ill.: Quest-Theosophical Publishing, 1991.

Kushner, Harold. *When Bad Things Happen to Good People*. New York: Avalon Books, 1983.

Kushner, Lawrence. *God Was in This Place and I, I Did Not Know: Finding Self, Spirituality, and Ultimate Meaning*. Woodstock, N.Y.: Jewish Lights Publishing, 1993.

———*Honey from the Rock*. Woodstock, N.Y.: Jewish Lights Publishing, 1990.

LaBerge, Stephen. *Lucid Dreaming: The Power of Being Awake and Aware in Your Dreams.* New York: Ballantine Books, 1986.

Lapierre, Dominique. *Beyond Love.* New York: Warner Books, 1991.

Larkin, David, ed., *Magritte.* New York: Ballantine Books, 1972.

Lawlor, Robert. *Sacred Geometry: Philosophy and Practice.* New York: Thames and Hudson, 1989.

LeGuin, Ursula. *The Wizard of Earth/Sea.* New York: Bantam Books, 1984.

Levertov, Denise. *Candles in Babylon.* New York: New Directions, 1982.

Levi. *The Aquarian Gospel of Jesus the Christ.* 1907. Reprint. Marina del Rey, Calif.: DeVorss, 1972.

Levine, Stephen. *Who Dies? An Investigation of Conscious Living and Conscious Dying.* New York: Anchor Books, 1982.

Lindbergh, Anne Morrow. *Gift from the Sea.* New York: Random House, 1991.

Love, Jeff. *The Quantum Gods: The Origin and Nature of Matter and Consciousness.* New York: Samuel Weiser, 1979.

MacGregor, Geddes. *The Gospels as a Mandala of Wisdom.* Wheaton, Ill.: Quest-Theosophical Publishing House, 1982.

————*He Who Lets Us Be: A New Theology of Love.* New York: Paragon House Pub., 1987.

Martin, Joel, and Patricia Romanowski. *Our Children Forever: George Anderson's Messages from Children on the Other Side.* New York: Berkley Publishing, 1994.

Matthiessen, Peter. *The Snow Leopard.* New York: Viking Penguin, 1987.

McLaughlin, Corinne, and Gordon Davidson. *Spiritual Politics: Changing the World from the Inside Out.* New York: Ballantine, 1994.

Meade, Margaret. *Blackberry Winter: My Earlier Years* Gloucester, Mass.: Peter Smith, 1989.

Miller, Alice. *Drama of the Gifted Child.* 3rd ed. New York: Basic Books, 1997.

————*For Your Own Good.* New York: Farrar, Straus and Giroux, 1990.

Miller, Judith, Dr. *Direct Connection: Transformation of Consciousness.* Danbury, Conn.: Rutledge Books, 2000.

Millman, Dan. *The Way of the Peaceful Warrior.* Tiburon, Calif.: H. J. Kramer, 1984.

Mindell, Arnold. *Working on Yourself Alone.* New York: Viking Penguin, 1990.

Mitchell, Stephen. *The Gospel According to Jesus.* New York: Harper-Collins, 1991.

Mitchell, Stephen, ed. *The Enlightened Heart: An Anthology of Sacred Poetry.* New York: HarperCollins, 1993.

Moore, Thomas. *Care of the Soul.* New York: HarperCollins, 1992.

————*Soul Mates: Honoring the Mysteries of Love and Relationships.* Hingham, Mass.: Wheeler Pub., 1994.

Morrison, Toni. *Beloved.* New York: Alfred A. Knopf, 1987.

Mosher, Bill. *Visionaries.* Maryknoll, N.Y.: Orbis Books, 1995.

Moss, Richard, M.D. *The Second Miracle.* Berkeley: Celestial Arts, 1996.

Muktananda, Swami. *Kundalini: The Secret of Life.* South Fallsburg, N.Y.: SYDA Foundation, 1979.

Nair, Keshavan. *Beyond Winning: A Handbook for the Leadership Revolution.* Phoenix Ariz.: Paradox, 1988.

————*A Higher Standard of Leadership: Lessons from the Life of Gandhi.* San Francisco: Berrett-Koehler, 1994.

Nearing, Helen K. *Light on Aging and Dying.* Gardiner, N.Y.: Tilbury House, 1995.

Needleman, Jacob. *Money and the Meaning of Life.* New York: Doubleday and Co., 1994.

Noble, Vicki. *Shakti Woman: Feeling Our Fire, Healing Our World* San Francisco, Calif.: HarperSanFrancisco, 1991.

Nolan, Albert. *Jesus Before Christianity.* Maryknoll, Calif.: Orbis Books, 1992.

North, Carol S. *Welcome, Silence: My Triumph over Schizophrenia.* New York: Avon Books, 1989.

Notovitch, Nicolas. *The Unknown Life of Jesus Christ.* Joshua Tree, Calif.: Tree of Life Publications, 1996.

Nouwen, Henri. *The Wounded Healer: Ministry in Contemporary Society.* New York: Doubleday and Co., 1979.

Oliver, Mary. *New and Selected Poems.* Boston: Beacon Press, 1993.

Oyle, Irving, M.D. *The New American Medicine Show.* Santa Cruz, Calif.: Unity Press, 1979.

Papastavro, Telliss. *Gnosis and the Law.* Tucson, Ariz.: Group Avatar, 1972.

Parrish-Harra, Carol E. *The Aquarian Rosary: Reviving the Art of Mantra Yoga.* Tahlequah, Okla.: Sparrow Hawk Press, 1988.

————*Messengers of Hope.* Black Mountain, N.C.: New Age Press, 1983.

Paulus, Trina. *Hope for the Flowers.* Mahwah, New Jersey: Paulist, 1972.

Rama, Swami, et al. *Meditation in Christianity.* Honesdale, Penn.: The Himalayan International Institute of Yoga Science and Philosophy of the USA, 1989.

Rama, Swami, Rudolph Ballentine, and Alan Hymes. *The Science of Breath.* Honesdale, Penn.: Himalayan Publishers, 1979.

Ramacharaka, Yogi. *Raja Yoga or Mental Development.* Chicago: Yoga Publication Society, 1934.

Redford, Dorothy Spruill. *Somerset Homecoming.* New York: Doubleday, 1988.

Reilly, Patricia Lynn. *A God Who Looks Like Me: Discovering a Woman-Affirming Spirituality.* New York: Ballantine, 1996.

Richards, M. C. *Centering.* 1964. Reprint. Hanover, N.H.: Wesleyan University Press, 1989.

Rilke, Rainer Maria. *Letters to a Young Poet.* trans. M. D. Herter Norton. New York: W. W. Norton and Co., 1934.

Roberts, Jane. *Seth Speaks: The Eternal Validity of the Soul.* New York: Bantam, 1972.

Roddick, Anita. *Body and Soul: Profits with Principles.* New York: Crown Publishing, 1994.

Rogers, Carl. *Freedom to Learn.* Englewood Cliffs, N.J.: Prentice Hall, 1994.

————*On Becoming a Person: A Therapist's View of Psychotherapy.* Boston: Houghton Mifflin Co., 1995.

————*A Way of Being.* Boston: Houghton Mifflin Co., 1995.

Rumi, Jalaluddin. *The Mathnawi of Jalaluddin Rumi.* Ed. T. K. Nicholson, Oakville, Conn.: David Brown Book Co., 1926–1992.

Safire, William. *The First Dissident: The Book of John in Today's Politics.* New York: Random House, 1992.

Saint-Exupéry, Antoine de. *The Little Prince.* San Diego: Harcourt Brace and World, Inc., 1943.

Sanford, John. *C. J. Jung and the Problem of Evil.* Boston: Sigo Press, 1991.

————*Healing and Wholeness.* Mahwah, N.J.: Paulist Press, 1977.

Sannella, Lee. *The Kundalini Experience: Psychosis or Transcendence?* Lower Lake, Calif.: Integral Publishing, 1987.

Sardello, Robert. *Love and the Soul: Creating a Future for Earth.* New York: HarperCollins, 1996.

Sarton, May. *Collected Poems: 1930–1993.* New York: W. W. Norton & Co., 1993.

Schacter, Jacob J. and Jeffrey S. *A Modern Heretic and Traditional Community.* New York: Columbia University Press, 1996.

Schaef, Ann Wilson. *Escape from Intimacy.* San Francisco: HarperSan-Francisco, 1990.

————*Meditations for Women Who Do Too Much.* San Francisco: Harper-SanFrancisco, 1990.

Schwartz, Stephen R. *The Compassionate Presence: Meeting and Greeting a Love That Will Not End.* Piermont, N.Y.: Riverrun Press, 1988.

Scott, Cyrill. *The Initiate.* York Beach, Maine: Samuel Weiser, 1979.

————*The Initiate in the Dark Cycle.* York Beach, Maine: Samuel Weiser, 1991.

————*The Initiate in the New World.* York Beach, Maine: Samuel Weiser, 1991.

Seale, Alan. *On Becoming a 21st Century Mystic.* New York: Skytop Publishing, 1997.

Sewell, Marilyn, ed. *Cries of the Spirit: A Celebration of Women's Spirituality.* Boston: Beacon Press, 1991.

Sheehy, Gail. *The Silent Passage.* New York: Pocket Books, 1995.

Shinn, Florence S. *The Game of Life and How to Play It.* New York: Simon & Schuster, 1986.

————*The Power of the Spoken Word.* Marina del Rey, Calif.: DeVorss, 1978.

————*The Secret Door to Success.* Reprint. Marina del Rey, Calif.: De-Vorss, 1978.

————*Your Word Is Your Wand.* Reprint. Marina del Rey, Calif.: DeVorss, 1978.

Siegel, Bernie S. *Love, Medicine and Miracles: Peace, Love and Healing.* New York: Harper and Row, 1989.

Sinetar, Marsha. *Developing a Twenty-First-Century Mind.* New York: Villard, 1991.

———*Ordinary People as Monks and Mystics.* New York: Paulis Press, 1986.

Sloss, Radha R. *Lives in the Shadow with J. Krishnamurti.* Reading, Penn.: Addison Wesley Publishing Company, 1993.

Smith, Betty. *A Tree Grows in Brooklyn.* Cutchogue, N.Y.: Buccaneer Books, 1981.

Smith, Elliot. *Social Psychology.* New York: Worth Publications, 1994.

Smith, Huston. *The Religions of Man.* New York: Harper and Row, 1986.

Somé, Malidoma Patrice. *Of Water and the Spirit.* New York: Tarcher/Putnam, 1994.

Spangler, David. *The Call.* New York: Riverhead Books, 1996.

———*Everyday Miracles: The Inner Art of Manifestation.* New York: Bantam Books, 1996.

———*The Laws of Manifestation.* Marina Del Rey, Calif.: DeVorss, 1978.

———*Reflections on the Christ.* Forres, Scotland: Findhorn Foundation, 1977.

Spilsbury, Ariel. *The Mayan Oracle.* Santa Fe: Bear and Co., 1992.

Spong, John S. *This Hebrew Lord.* San Francisco: HarperSanFrancisco, 1993.

Squire, Larry, Dr. *Memory and the Brain.* New York: Oxford University Press, 1987.

St. John of the Cross. *The Dark Night of the Soul.* trans. E. Alison Peers. Garden City, N.Y.: Doubleday and Co., 1959.

Steindl-Rast, David. *A Listening Heart: The Art of Contemplative Living.* New York: Crossroad Publishing, 1983.

Steiner, Rudolf. *The Reappearance of Christ in the Etheric.* Spring Valley, N.Y.: Anthroposophic Press, 1983.

———*The Riddle of Humanity.* London: Rudolf Steiner Press, 1916.

Stone, Barbara. *Cancer as Initiation: Surviving the Fire.* Chicago: Open Court, 1994.

Stone, Joshua David. *The Complete Ascension Manual.* Sedona, Arizona: Light Technology Publishing, 1994.

Sugrue, Thomas. *There Is a River.* Reprint. Virginia Beach, Va.: A.R.E. Press, 1989.

Suzuki, D. T. *Zen Mind, Beginner's Mind.* New York: Weatherhill, 1970.

Talbot, Michael. *The Holographic Universe.* New York: HarperCollins, 1992.

Tao Te Ching. Trans. Gia-Fu Feng and Jane English. New York: Vintage, 1972.

Tebecis, A. K. *Mahikari.* Tokyo: L. H. Yoko Shuppan, 1990.

Thunder, Mary Elizabeth. *Thunder's Grace.* Barrytown, N.Y.: Station Hill Press, 1995.

Thurman, Robert A. F. *Essential Tibetan Buddhism.* San Francisco: HarperSanFrancisco, 1996.

Tillich, Paul. *The Courage to Be.* 1952. Reprint. New Haven, Conn.: Yale University Press, 1964.

Toms, Justine Willis. *True Work: The Sacred Dimension of Earning a Living.* New York: Bell Tower, 1998.

Tweedie, Irina. *Chasm of Fire.* Rockport: Element Books, 1993.

———*Daughter of Fire.* Inverness, Calif.: Golden Sufi Center, 1996.

Urantia Book. Chicago: Urantia Foundation, 1955.

Van Buitenen, J. A. *Mahabarata.* Chicago: University of Chicago Press, 1978.

Van Dyke, Henry. *The Other Wise Man.* New Orleans: Paraclete Press, 1984.

Walker, Alice. *The Same River Twice.* New York: Scribner, 1996.

Walker, Barbara G. *The Crone: Woman of Age, Wisdom and Power.* San Francisco: HarperSanFrancisco, 1988.

Warner, Gale, and Michael Shuman. *Citizen Diplomats.* New York: Continuum, 1987.

Watson, Lyall. *Beyond Supernature.* New York: Bantam, 1988.

———*The Romeo Error.* New York: Doubleday, 1974.

Way, Robert, trans. *Cloud of Unknowing.* Trabuco Canyon, Calif.: Source Books, 1994.

Weiss, Brian L. *Many Lives, Many Masters.* New York: Simon and Schuster, 1988.

West, Morris. *The Shoes of the Fisherman.* London: Mandarin, 1994.

Wheatly, Margaret J. *Leadership and the New Science.* San Francisco: Berrett-Koehler Publishers, 1993.

White, David. *The Bhagavad Gita: A New Translation with Commentary.* New York: Peter Lang Publishing, 1989.

White Eagle. *The Path of the Soul.* Hampshire, England: The White Eagle Publishing Trust, 1959.

Whitman, Walt. *Leaves of Grass.* New York: Eakins Press Foundation, 1966.

Whitmyer, Claude, ed. *In the Company of Others: Making Community in the Modern World.* New York: Putnam Publishing, 1993.

Whyte, David. *Fire in the Earth.* Langley, Wash.: ManyRivers Press, 1992.

Wiesel, Elie. *Evil and Exile.* Notre Dame, Ind.: University of Notre Dame Press, 1990.

Wilbur, Ken, ed. *The Holographic Paradigm and Other Paradoxes.* New York: Random House, 1982.

———*Sex, Ecology, Spirituality: The Spirit of Evolution.* Boston: Shambhala, 1995.

———*Grace and Grit.* Boston: Shambhala, 1992.

———*A Brief History of Everything.* Boston: Shambhala, 1996.

Williams, Jay G. *Yeshua/Buddha.* Wheaton, Ill.: Quest-Theosophical Publishing House, 1978.

Wilson, Colin. *Beyond the Occult.* New York: Carroll and Graf Publishers, 1989.

———*Mysteries.* New York: Putnam, 1980.

———*The Occult.* New York: Random House, 1973.

Wink, Walter. *Engaging the Powers: Discernment and Resistance in a World of Domination.* Minneapolis: Augsberg Fortress Publishers, 1992.

Wipf, Jane L. *Blankets: A Grief Journey.* Fargo, N.D.: Spiritseeker Publishing, 1993.

Wolf, Fred Allen. *Eagle's Quest.* New York: Simon and Schuster, 1992.

———*Parallel Universes.* New York: Touchstone Books, 1988.

Woodman, Marion. *Addiction to Perfection.* Sarasota: Bookworld Distribution, 1995.

———*The Pregnant Virgin.* Sarasota: Bookworld Distribution, 1995.

Woodman, Marion, and Elinor Dickson. *Dancing in the Flames: The Dark Goddess in the Transformation of Consciousness.* East Lansing, Mich.: Shambhala Publications, 1996.

Wright, Lawrence. *Saints and Sinners.* New York: Random House, 1994.

Yogananda, Paramahansa. *Autobiography of a Yogi.* 1946. Los Angeles: Self-Realization Fellowship, 1971.

————*Whispers from Eternity.* Reprint. Dallas: Amrita Foundation, 1978.

Young, Arthur M. *The Geometry of Meaning.* Lake Oswego, Ore: Robert Briggs Assoc., 1984.

————*The Reflexive Universe: Evolution of Consciousness.* Reprint. Lake Oswego, Ore: Robert Briggs Assoc., 1985.

Zemke, LeRoy E. *Thoughts for Transformation.* St. Petersburg, Fla.: Emberlight Publishers, 1996.

Zukav, Gary. *The Seat of the Soul.* New York: Simon and Schuster, 1990.

————*Soul Stories.* New York: Simon and Schuster, 2000.

Zweig, Connie, and Jeremiah Abrams, eds. *Meeting the Shadow: The Hidden Power of the Dark Side of Human Nature.* New York: Tarcher/Perigee, 1991.

Index

discernment (*cont.*)
  judgment and, 144
  lessons in, 149–53
  perspective and, 139–40
  possibilities and, 140–41
  prayers on, 154
  psychic abilities and, 147–48
  questioning and, 131–34
  quotes on, 155
  refinement and, 137–38
  teachers and, 144–46
  twelve considerations on, 153–54
  visualization and, 148–49
disciples
  change and, 27
  characteristics of, 66
  consciousness and, 64
  defined, 4–6
  fear and, 126
  in religions, 24
  sacred stories and, 17
  tasks of, 38
Discipleship Forums, 66–67
discipline, 376–78
disillusionment, 263, 364–65
Divine Mother, 43
Djwhal Khul, 106
Dominguez, Joe, 297
doubt, 263, 364–65
doubting Thomas syndrome, 91
dreams, 113–14
duality, 38–57
  balancing, 21
  body and soul, 156
  ego and the Divine, 39
  fear and, 56
  love and, 211
  mind and, 87
  money and, 294

  paradox in, 45–47
  power and, 51–52
  rebel parts of self and, 47–48
  results of, 24
  sacred and profane, 42–45
  shadow self and, 53–57
  talents and, 49–51
Duff, Kat, 179

earth, 28, 157
ego, 39, 52, 69, 195, 219, 225–27, 237
Egyptian Book of the Dead, 217
Einstein, Albert, 139, 277–78
Eliot, T. S., 312
emotional intelligence, 84–85
Emotional Intelligence (Goleman), 84
emotions, 160–64
empathy, 210–12
endurance, 370–96
  affirmations on, 395
  building, 381–82
  challenges and, 378–81
  committment and, 372–73
  discipline and, 376–78
  exercises on, 382, 394–95
  fear and, 389–93
  invoking, 438
  journaling on, 374, 383
  patience and, 375–76, 383–87
  prayers on, 395
  prejudices and, 387–89
  quotes on, 395–96
  sacrifice and, 387
  shadows of, 382–93
  twelve considerations on, 393–94
energy
  See also sexual energy
  body systems of, 166–69

number 12 and, 62–63
patience and, 375
power and, 284
sacred stories and, 19
Schueman channeling and, 106
surrender and, 177
sword symbol and, 34
Way and, the, 16
will and, 221, 227, 238
journaling
  on the body, 160
  on creating, 335
  on discernment, 138–39
  on endurance, 374, 383
  on faith, 246, 263
  on knowledge, 88, 93, 97
  on love, 196
  on power, 275, 293
  on revelations, 109, 111, 122
  on service, 399, 422–23, 422–23
  on symbols, 109
  on transformation, 344
  on will, 222, 236
Journey into Awakening (Ram Dass),
  350
judgment, 144, 195, 390
Jung, Carl, 48–49, 105, 265

Kabat-Zinn, Jon, 347
Kali, 34
Kali Yuga, 27, 171
Kazantzakis, Nikos, 367
King, Martin Luther, Jr., 5, 250
knowing. *See* revelations
knowledge, 73–100
  See also revelations
  affirmations on, 100
  "I don't know" and, 91–92
  invoking, 436

memory and, 85–89, 157–60, 207
mind and, 83–85
power and, 95–97
prayers on, 99
quotes on, 100
shadows, 90, 92, 93–95
spiritual sciences and, 74–78,
  80–83, 96, 97, 313
twelve considerations on, 97–98
Kramer, Joel, 131
Krishna, 22, 217, 249
Krishnamurti, 45
Kuan Yin, 194, 198
kundalini, 312–19
Kundalini (Swami Muktananda), 312

Lapierre, Dominique, 219
Last Temptation of Christ, The
  (Kazantzakis), 367
Law of Love, The (Esquival), 398
Leonardo da Vinci, 107
Levertov, Denise, 361
Life Begins at Ninety, 141
Like Water for Chocolate (Esquival), 398
Little Book of the Human Shadow, The
  (Bly), 42
Little Prince, The (Saint-Exupéry), 109
Lives in the Shadow with J. Krishnamurti
  (Sloss), 45
love, 189–214
  See also unconditional love
  affirmations on, 212
  agape, 190–93, 203–4, 211
  challenges of, 204–7
  compassion and, 196–98
  counterfeits and, 204–7
  empathy and, 210–12
  exercises on, 203–4, 213
  fear and, 191, 208–10, 208–10

religion(s) (*cont.*)
    spiritual craftsmanship and, 65
    spiritual sciences and, 74, 76
    symbol of swords in, 34
resistance vs. acceptance, 224–25
revelations, 101–29
    affirmations on, 129
    channeling and, 105–7
    dreams and, 113–14
    exercises on, 127–28
    fantasies and, 123–25
    fear and, 125–26
    gifts of the spirit and, 125
    intuition and, 114–17
    invoking, 437
    knowing and, 103–5
    prayers on, 128
    quotes on, 129
    reverance for life and, 117–19
    secretive about, 109–10
    shadows and, 120–26
    symbols and, 107–9
    twelve considerations on, 128
    visions and, 111–13
rituals, 136, 352–54
Robin, Vicki, 297
Rodegast, Pat, 107
Roth, Geneen, 343
Ruelle, David, 32
Rumi, Jalal ad-Din ar-, 12

Sacred Hoops (Jackson), 224, 363
sacred stories, 17–21, 25, 62–63, 226, 296
sacrifice, 222, 361–62, 387
Saint-Exupéry, Antoine de, 109
"Salvator Mundi: Via Crucis" (Levertov), 361
sangha, 414

satsong, 414
Schueman, Helen, 106
sciences, spiritual. *See* spiritual sciences
Search for Signs of Intelligent Life in the Universe, The, 84
service, 397–434
    affirmations on, 433
    balance and, 419–20
    boundaries and, 428–29
    burnout and, 423–26, 430–31
    codependency and, 426–27
    compassion and, 415–17
    exercises on, 417–18, 432–33
    forms of, 406–12
    with groups, 412–15
    invoking, 438
    journaling on, 399
    love as, 193–94
    martyrs and, 421–22
    messiahs and, 421–22
    mission and, 398–406, 432–33
    quotes on, 433–34
    twelve considerations on, 431–32
    volunteering and, 404–6
    work ethic and, 423–24
Seven Habits of Highly Effective People, The (Covey), 423
sexual energy, 320–32
    celibacy and, 325–27
    exercises on, 331–32
    nadis and, 313
    projections and, 329–31
    shadows and, 328–29
    transference and, 329–31
sexuality, 44, 48
shadow(s)
    balancing light and, 54–57
    body, 174–83